POLITICAL CATHOLICISM
IN EUROPE, 1918–1965

POLITICAL CATHOLICISM IN EUROPE, 1918–1965

Edited by

Tom Buchanan and Martin Conway

Clarendon Press · Oxford
1996

Oxford University Press, Walton Street, Oxford OX2 6DP

Oxford New York

Athens Auckland Bangkok Bombay
Calcutta Cape Town Dar es Salaam Delhi
Florence Hong Kong Istanbul Karachi
Kuala Lumpur Madras Madrid Melbourne
Mexico City Nairobi Paris Singapore
Taipei Tokyo Toronto
and associated companies in
Berlin Ibadan

Oxford is a trade mark of Oxford University Press

Published in the United States
by Oxford University Press Inc. New York

British Library Cataloguing in Publication Data
Data available

Library of Congress Cataloging in Publication Data
Political Catholicism in Europe, 1918–1965 / edited by
Tom Buchanan and Martin Conway.
p. cm.
Includes bibliographical references and index.
1. Catholic Church—Europe—History—20th century.
2. Christianity and politics—Catholic Church—History—20th
century. 3. Europe—Politics and government—1918–   4. Europe—
Politics and government—1945–   5. Europe—Church
history—20th century. I. Buchanan, Tom, 1960–   .
II. Conway, Martin, 1960–   .
BX1490.P65   1996
324'.088'22—dc20   95-25450
ISBN 0–19–820319–5

1 3 5 7 9 10 8 6 4 2

Typeset by Alliance Phototypesetters
Printed in Great Britain
on acid-free paper by
Biddles Ltd., Guildford & King's Lynn

Acknowledgements

Most of the chapters in this volume were initially presented as seminar papers in Oxford and we are grateful to the History Faculty of the University of Oxford for financial assistance with the organization of the seminars. Subsequently, a number of the contributors met at the University of Sheffield, and we are also grateful to this institution for its hospitality. Throughout the preparation of the book, we have benefited greatly from the encouragement of Dr Tony Morris of Oxford University Press. Three anonymous readers also provided valuable suggestions at a formative stage. We would also like to thank Mr Brian Hitch and Ms Wendy Jack for their kind assistance at various stages in the preparation of the manuscript. We are also grateful to the History Faculty of the University of Oxford for a grant towards the cost of the final editing of this volume and are particularly indebted to Mark Potter for his work in proof reading and indexing the manuscript. Above all, however, the editors wish to express their heartfelt thanks to the contributors for their work and for the commitment which they have displayed to the project.

T. B.
M. C.

Contents

Notes on Contributors

TOM BUCHANAN is University Lecturer in Modern History and Politics at the University of Oxford's Department for Continuing Education, and a Fellow of Kellogg College, Oxford. He is the author of *The Spanish Civil War and the British Labour Movement* (1991).

MARTIN CONWAY is Fellow and Tutor in Modern History at Balliol College, Oxford. His *Collaboration in Belgium: Léon Degrelle and the Rexist Movement* (1993) has also been published in French and Dutch translation.

TOM GALLAGHER is Reader in Peace Studies at Bradford University. He is the author of *Romania After Ceaucescu: Nationalism Defines Democracy* (1995) and of *Portugal: A Twentieth Century Interpretation* (1983).

DERMOT KEOGH is Jean Monnet Professor of European Politics at University College, Cork. His publications include *The Vatican, the Bishops and Irish politics, 1919–1939*, (1986) and *Ireland and Europe, 1919–1948* (1988).

KARL-EGON LÖNNE is Professor of Contemporary History and Historiography at the Heinrich-Heine University, Düsseldorf. He is the author of the monographs *Benedetto Croce als Kritiker seiner Zeit* (1966), *Faschismus als Herausforderung* (1981), and *Politischer Katholizismus im 19. und 20. Jahrhundert* (1986). On these and other topics he has also published numerous articles in German and Italian periodicals and collections.

PAUL LUYKX was until 1994 Senior Lecturer in Contemporary History at the Katholieke Universiteit, Nijmegen, The Netherlands. He has published a variety of books and articles, especially on the history of Catholicism and on the historiography and theory of contemporary history.

JAMES F. MCMILLAN is Professor of European History at the University of Strathclyde. He is the author of *Housewife or Harlot: The Place of Women in French Society* (1981), *Napoleon III* (1992), and *Twentieth Century France* (1992), as well as of many articles on modern French history.

FINÍN O'DRISCOLL' was awarded an MA from University College Cork for his thesis on the Irish Social Catholic Movement, 1919–1939. He is currently studying at Wolfson College, Cambridge for a PhD on G. K. Chesterton, Hilaire Belloc, and the Distributist Movement.

JOHN POLLARD is Professor of History at Anglia Polytechnic University (Cambridge). He is the author of *The Vatican and Italian Fascism, 1929–1932* (1985) and of a number of essays on political Catholicism in Italy. He is co-editor with Peter Kent of *Papal Diplomacy in the Modern Age* (1994).

MARY VINCENT is Lecturer in History at the University of Sheffield. Her book on Catholicism in the Second Spanish Republic is to be published by Oxford Historical Monographs.

Introduction*

MARTIN CONWAY

This book explores an unduly neglected dimension of the history of twentieth-century Europe. Catholic political parties and movements have been among the most successful in Europe during the twentieth century, flourishing in a wide variety of national and political contexts. And yet, compared with the considerable—indeed, some might argue, excessive—attention which historians have lavished on Fascist, Liberal, Socialist, or Communist parties, few historians have chosen to pay attention to the phenomenon of political Catholicism. While there has been a steady interest in particular aspects of the subject such as Church–State relations or the development of individual Christian Democrat parties, there remains a marked lack of scholarly work on the political articulation of Catholicism in Europe.

Even the briefest résumé, however, reveals the important role played by movements and parties either wholly or partially Catholic in inspiration in twentieth-century Europe. Catholic parties first emerged during the last decades of the nineteenth century but it was in the years after the First World War that they became a prominent feature of European life. The Partito Popolare Italiano was of central importance in the Italian political crisis after the First World War while the Centre Party played much the same role in Germany during the latter years of the Weimar Republic. In the 1930s the dictatorships of Salazar in Portugal, Dollfuss in Austria, and Franco in Spain had an undoubted Catholic inspiration. Movements of Catholic resistance (and collaboration) flourished in Axis-occupied Europe during the Second World War, and Christian Democrat political parties enjoyed both electoral success and almost uninterrupted political power in Germany, Italy, and the Low Countries from the 1940s onwards. Indeed, all European countries with significant Catholic populations experienced in one form or another the influence of Catholic political ideas. In states such as Germany or Italy this took the form of important and durable Catholic political parties, but, as a number of the chapters in this volume seek to demonstrate, the absence of equivalent parties in states such as Ireland, Portugal, and Great Britain did not prevent the existence of a tradition of political Catholicism which in more indirect ways also influenced the histories of these countries. Political Catholicism has, thus, without doubt formed a major element of the historical landscape of twentieth-century Europe.

* I would like to thank my co-editor Tom Buchanan for his help in preparing this introduction. We are also grateful to Jim McMillan, John Pollard, and Mary Vincent for their comments and helpful advice.

1. Parameters and Definitions

The term 'political Catholicism' demands some definition. As used in this volume, it is intended to describe political movements (broadly defined to encompass both political parties and a wide range of socio-economic organizations, as well as groups of intellectuals and others) which claimed a significant, though not necessarily exclusively, Catholic inspiration for their actions. As such, the scope of this volume is both wider and more restrictive than other possible definitions. On the one hand, it does not merely comprise those Catholic movements which were created by, or could claim some sort of authorization from, the Papacy or from national hierarchies. Political Catholicism was never merely a product of the Church authorities and many Catholic political movements were at pains to stress their autonomy from the Church. On the other hand, it does not seek to include all Catholics who engaged in political action. The simple fact that individuals were Catholic in their religious faith does not of course in itself imply that their faith influenced their political beliefs and actions. The Catholic character of the movements discussed in this book arises therefore less from the fact that they were composed of individuals who could be categorized as Catholic believers, than from the Catholic goals and values of the movements. Political Catholicism does not mean Catholics who were active in politics but political action which was Catholic in inspiration.

The chronological and geographical scope of this volume also requires explanation. All terminal dates in history are arbitrary and the decision to concentrate on the period from the First World War to the 1960s in no sense implies that this era of political Catholicism can be considered in isolation from those which preceded and followed it. Nevertheless, these dates have been chosen because they encompass, however imperfectly, an era when a particular form of organization and mentality characterized Catholic politics. Much of political Catholicism during the inter-war years was derived from Catholic political and intellectual developments of the later nineteenth century and this is reflected in the attention which a number of the contributors to this volume pay to the pre-1914 era. Nevertheless, it was only after the First World War that political Catholicism reached its full fruition in most countries of Europe, as the vestiges of nineteenth-century Catholic hostility towards the political process gave way to efforts to articulate a distinctly Catholic form of politics. The justification of the 1960s as the conclusion to this volume is perhaps more self-evident. Though the impact of the Second World War should not be minimized, Catholic political action in the 1940s and 1950s remained to a surprising degree rooted in the mentalities and forms of organization of the pre-war years. The 1960s, however, marked a decisive caesura in Catholic politics. The specific impact within Catholicism of the profound changes introduced by the Second Vatican Council was reinforced by the wider social and political transformations which took place in Europe during that decade. Catholic religious practice fell markedly in much of Europe and new forms of Catholic-inspired political action emerged which rejected the hitherto dominant assumption that the Catholic faithful were a community united by particular beliefs and interests.

The geographical scope of the volume is intended to include all the major Catholic states of Western Europe. As the chapter devoted to Great Britain demonstrates, Catholic political action was also of significance in a number of European states in which Catholics formed only a relatively small minority. The book does not, however, consider all those countries in which Catholic political movements developed.[1] In particular, those countries of Central and Eastern Europe which passed under Communist control after the Second World War are absent from the volume. The emergence of Catholic political movements in these states during the inter-war years mirrored in many respects developments elsewhere in Europe but their post-1945 history clearly diverged substantially from both the democracies of Western Europe and the dictatorships of the Iberian peninsula.

The parameters of the volume are also defined by historiographical considerations. Monographs on particular instances of Catholic political action published in recent years have done much to demonstrate the importance of the phenomenon as well as to highlight the scope for further research.[2] Nevertheless, the overall impression remains one of relative neglect. In particular, it is striking that the emergence—especially in France—of the so-called 'new religious history' which has done so much to revivify the study of religion in nineteenth- and twentieth-century Europe[3] has not yet led to a renewal of interest in the political manifestations of the Catholic faith. At present, the only general accounts of political Catholicism in modern Europe are those of J. M. Mayeur in French and K.-E. Lönne in German respectively.[4] The most recent analysis in English is that provided by J. H. Whyte. His *Catholics in Western Democracies: A Study in Political Behaviour* analyses Catholic political development in Western Europe and compares it with the history of

---

[1] In particular, it has unfortunately proved necessary to omit Austria and Switzerland. *Re* Austria, see A. Diamant, *Austrian Catholics and the First Republic* (Princeton, 1960); L. Gellott, 'Defending Catholic interests in the Christian State: The Role of Catholic Action in Austria 1933–1938', *Catholic Historical Review*, 74 (1988), 571–89; E. Weinzierl, 'Austria: Church, State, Politics and Ideology 1919–1938', in R. J. Wolff and J. K. Hoensch (eds.), *Catholics, the State and the European Radical Right 1919–1945* (Boulder, Colo., 1987), 5–30. *Re* Switzerland, see U. Altermatt, *Der Weg der Schweizer Katholiken ins Ghetto* (Zurich, 1972); id., *Katholizismus und Moderne: Zur Sozial- und Mentalitätsgeschichte der Schweizer Katholiken im 19. und 20. Jahrhundert* (Zurich, 1989); E. L. Evans, 'Catholic Political Movements in Germany, Switzerland and the Netherlands: Notes for a Comparative Approach', *Central European History*, 17 (1984), 91–119; R. Ruffieux, *Le Mouvement chrétien-social en Suisse romande 1891–1949* (Fribourg, 1969).

[2] See, notably, F. Lannon, *Privilege, Persecution and Prophecy: The Catholic Church in Spain 1875–1975* (Oxford, 1987); J. Pollard, *The Vatican and Italian Fascism 1929–1932* (Cambridge, 1985); M. Winock, *Histoire politique de la revue 'Esprit' 1930–1950* (Paris, 1975); J. Hellman, *Emmanuel Mounier and the New Catholic Left* (Toronto, 1981); J. Gergely, *A politikai katolicizmus Magyarországon (1890–1950)* (Budapest, 1977).

[3] e.g. G. Cholvy and Y.-M. Hilaire, *Histoire religieuse de la France contemporaine*, 3 vols. (Toulouse, 1985–8). See also the highly comprehensive survey J.-M. Mayeur (ed.), *Histoire du Christianisme*, xii (n.p., 1990) and R. Aubert, *The Church in a Secularised Society* (London, 1978). The most authoritative synthesis of the 20th-cent. development of the Catholic religion is provided by H. Jedin, K. Repgen, and J. Dolan (eds.), *History of the Church*, x. *The Church in the Modern Era* (London, 1981).

[4] J.-M. Mayeur, *Des partis catholiques à la démocratie chrétienne* (Paris, 1980); K.-E. Lönne, *Politischer Katholizismus im 19. und 20. Jahrhundert* (Frankfurt a. M., 1986). On the 19th cent., see also P. Misner, *Social Catholicism in Europe: From the Onset of Industrialization to the First World War* (London, 1991).

Catholic political action in North America and Australasia.[5] His central conclusion—namely that political Catholicism in Europe has been characterized by a
concern with the defence of the Church and the faithful against alien non-Catholic
influences (a so-called 'closed Catholicism')—has considerable validity though the
book focuses only on a select number of West European democracies.

Probably the most influential analysis of political Catholicism in English remains
Michael Fogarty's *Christian Democracy in Europe 1820–1953*. Written at the high tide
of Christian Democrat electoral success in the 1950s, the book provides a valuable
analysis of the post-war emergence of Christian democracy, even if from the perspective of the present day it appears much influenced by the character of its times.
Fogarty's concern is to trace the emergence of a distinctive Christian democrat political tradition from its origins in the nineteenth century to its political maturity in
post-1945 Europe. This preoccupation with the undisturbed and self-contained
trajectory of Christian democracy requires Fogarty to be highly selective in his consideration of European Catholic movements. The book is essentially concerned with
a central band of Catholic territories stretching from the Low Countries through
western Germany and Switzerland to northern Italy, and it pays less attention to the
rather different history of Catholic political movements in the Iberian peninsula and
central Europe. Similarly, Fogarty chooses to focus on the pre-1914 era and the years
after the Second World War while passing over in silence the anti-democratic
Catholic movements which flourished in Europe during the 1930s.[6]

The relative neglect of the phenomenon of political Catholicism has several origins. Historians tend to share the assumptions of their environments and, especially
among British and North American historians of twentieth-century Europe, there
has often been an unstated belief that Catholic political movements were no more
than the dwindling manifestations of a Catholic religion which itself was destined to
disappear with the gradual development of a secular society. More generally, however, the dominant interpretation of European history since the First World War has
portrayed Europe as a battlefield between conflicting secular ideologies of left and
right, each of which offered an alternative model of political, social, and economic
organization. Catholic movements, both by virtue of their religious inspiration and
their reluctance to identify with the conventional categories of left and right, fit
uncomfortably into this schema. Consequently they have tended to be subsumed
somewhat awkwardly into secular political categories. Hence, the willingness of
many Catholic movements in the inter-war years to side with the anti-democratic
right gave rise to the often misleading concept of 'clerico-fascism'; while, conversely,
the emergence of substantial Catholic political parties which worked within the
democratic structures of post-war Western Europe has encouraged historians to
regard all Catholic political movements after 1945 as manifestations of 'Christian
democracy'.

This reluctance to consider movements of political Catholicism in their own terms

---

[5] J. H. Whyte, *Catholics in Western Democracies: A Study in Political Behaviour* (Dublin, 1981).
[6] M. Fogarty, *Christian Democracy in Europe 1820–1953* (London, 1957). See also pp. 10–11.

has had a number of consequences. Most obviously, it has served to marginalize the significance of Catholicism as a political force in the history of twentieth-century Europe. By drawing attention away from the remarkable number of Catholic political movements which emerged in Europe from the First World War to the 1960s, it has inhibited an appreciation of the political ideals espoused by many European Catholics. Despite a number of valuable general accounts of Catholic politics, there remain many aspects of the subject which await scholarly examination. In addition, however, the neglect of Catholic political movements has warped historical under-standing of the role of Catholicism in twentieth-century Europe. It has been cus-tomary to consider 'Catholicism' and 'politics' as essentially separate realms which only came into contact as an accidental consequence of conflicts between the rival jurisdictions of Church and State. This interpretation, which owes much to the lib-eral definition of religion as an essentially private matter of conscience, is at odds with the stance adopted not only by the Catholic Church but by many of the Catholic laity who made no distinction between their religious beliefs and their actions in the public sphere. Catholicism, for them, was not a private matter of conscience but a faith which determined both their private morality and their public actions. How close a connection Catholics made between their religious faith and their political choices depended on a wide variety of factors but, as the success of many Catholic political movements demonstrated, for large numbers of Catholics in twentieth-century Europe religion could not be divorced from politics. Far from being an arti-ficial oxymoron, political Catholicism was therefore a logical reality.

The evidence of the vitality of Catholicism both as a religious and a political force within twentieth-century Europe is substantial. Though levels of religious practice declined steadily in almost all areas of Europe during the nineteenth century, the first half of the twentieth century saw a modest renaissance in Catholic fortunes. In some areas, notably in Spain and Portugal, urbanization and industrialization caused this downward trend to continue, but elsewhere the numbers of those participating in the Catholic religion appear to have stabilized or even increased modestly.[7] More important than such quantitative trends, however, was the transformation which took place in attitudes among the Catholic faithful. Though a number of recent works have rightly undermined the image of the nineteenth century as one of remorseless secularization,[8] it was in the first decades of the twentieth century that the Catholic faith fully recovered a mood of self-confident optimism. Encouraged by a wide range of political, social, and cultural changes which weakened the structures of nineteenth-century liberalism while simultaneously providing a new impetus to religious faith, Catholics practised their religion with a new assertiveness and energy. Participation in pilgrimages, parades, and political campaigns as well as the rapid

---

[7] e.g. Y.-M. Hilaire, *Matériaux pour l'histoire religieuse du peuple français XIXe–XXe siècles*, ii (Paris, 1987), 9–10; J. Wolffe, *God and Greater Britain* (London, 1994), 68–74.

[8] J. Sperber, *Popular Catholicism in Nineteenth-Century Germany* (Princeton, 1984), 279–82 and 292–4; R. Gibson, *A Social History of French Catholicism 1789–1914* (London, 1989); D. Blackbourn, *Marpingen: Apparitions of the Virgin Mary in Bismarckian Germany* (Oxford, 1993).

expansion in the membership of Catholic associations, all bore witness to the new-found eagerness of the laity to commit themselves publicly to their faith and to place the values of Catholicism at the centre of their lives.[9]

Catholicism was, thus, for much of the twentieth century emphatically not a reli-gion in decline and the chapters in this volume are intended to serve as a corrective to the marginalization of political Catholicism in the historical literature of twentieth-century Europe. They do not make any pretence to being definitive either in their coverage or in their interpretations. Much research remains to be carried out on political Catholicism before such judgements can prove possible and the contribu-tors have been encouraged to write interpretative essays rather than providing com-prehensive accounts of their subject. This explains in part the diversity evident in the approach adopted by the contributors. While some have adopted a largely chrono-logical format, others have treated the subject in a more thematic manner. Diversity is also evident in the interpretations provided by the contributors. Though all the authors share a belief in the importance of analysing political Catholicism, the de-lineation and explanations of this phenomenon provided in the individual chapters differ in a number of important respects. This diversity will, it is hoped, act as a stimulus to further research and debate.

Despite these differences of interpretation, this volume is based on the twin prem-isses that a distinctive Catholic political tradition has been evident in many—if not all—of the countries of Europe during the twentieth century; and that sufficient similarities existed between these manifestations of political Catholicism for it to be possible to consider it as a European phenomenon. Neither of these premisses is in-controvertible. Much of the historical literature of twentieth-century Catholicism has assumed that there existed a number of divergent definitions of Catholic political engagement which at their most extreme gave rise, for example, to those Catholics who supported the Mussolini regime in Italy and those Catholic radicals favourable to a Catholic–Communist alliance in France during the 1940s. Such an interpreta-tion does not necessarily minimize the importance of Catholic politics but it does imply that political Catholicism was no more than the sum of its competing parts. Similarly open to question is the assumption that political Catholicism transcended to a greater or lesser degree national boundaries. Though the Catholic faith has con-sciously sought to present itself as a universal Church, the nature of Catholicism has clearly been moulded by socio-economic, political, and ideological factors internal to individual countries which have given rise to distinctive national Catholic mental-ities. Here again, such an interpretation, while not denying the existence of Catholic politics, would suggest that the points of convergence between Catholic political movements in different European nation-states were, at best, of secondary import-ance and, at worst, no more than an illusion. These issues are addressed in this intro-duction as well as in the chapters which follow.

---

[9] E. Fouilloux, 'Courants de pensée, piété, apostolat: Le Catholicisme' in Mayeur (ed.), *Histoire du Christianisme*, xii. 117–21.

2. Factors of Unity and Division

The nation-states of twentieth-century Europe provided very different circumstances for the development of movements of political Catholicism. It was inevitable therefore that Catholic political movements should have reflected the particular national environments in which they emerged. These national influences were both historical and contemporary in nature. The structures, mentality, and character of Catholicism differed markedly in individual states of Europe as a consequence of a rich heritage of historical factors. The Catholicism of, for example, twentieth-century Germany differed therefore from that of France, not only as a consequence of differences in the size and socio-economic composition of the Catholic population but also because of the influence of particular historical events on the character of the Catholic faith. These differences remained evident in the nature of the Catholic political movements in the two societies. In France, for example, a deep-rooted antipathy to the Republic as the historical legacy of the anticlerical Revolution of 1789 continued to exert a powerful influence on Catholic political choices up to and beyond the Second World War. In Germany, on the other hand, it was the minority status of the Catholic community within the Prussian-led German state of the nineteenth century which remained the principal influence on Catholic politics. Protestant Prussia, and more especially the Hohenzollern dynasty, was seen as the historical opponent of German Catholicism and led Catholics to favour a federal political structure protective of Catholic interests.[10]

In addition, contemporary political circumstances also exerted considerable influence on Catholic political movements. In states such as Belgium, the Netherlands, or Italy after the Second World War where the balance of electoral politics enabled the Catholics to exercise sustained political power, there was an evident incentive both for Catholics to unite behind a single political party and to identify with the parliamentary political system.[11] On the other hand, in non-democratic states such forms of political organization were not possible and the nature of political Catholicism depended to a large extent on whether the regime was sympathetic to Catholic ideals and ambitions. Thus, for example, in Nazi Germany or, to a lesser extent, the Mussolini dictatorship of the latter 1930s, Catholics were forced into a stance of *de facto* opposition—if not resistance—to regimes which opposed Catholic political ideals and sought to minimize Catholic influence in society.[12] Catholic attitudes towards the Austrian dictatorship of Dollfuss and Schuschnigg during the 1930s and the long-standing Franco and Salazar regimes in Spain and Portugal were different again. All three regimes owed their origins at least in part to the support of Catholics and all accorded the Catholic Church a privileged role within both State and society. The consequence was to draw many Catholics into alliance with the regimes, even if with the passage of time the identity between Catholic interests and those of the regime came to diverge.[13]

[10] See pp. 35–6 and 156–7.   [11] See pp. 192 and 245–6.
[12] See pp. 82–5 and 170–6.   [13] See pp. 24, 118–22, and 139–45.

The extent to which national 'peculiarities' determined the form adopted by political Catholicism within different nation-states was, however, accompanied by substantial similarities in the nature and the ideals espoused by Catholic movements in different European countries. The existence of this distinctively Catholic political tradition in the era from the First World War to the 1960s can be defined in both negative and positive terms. Negatively, almost all forms of political Catholicism—be they the advocates of authoritarian political reforms in the 1930s or the Christian Democrat parties of the post-1945 era—defined themselves against other socialist, liberal, and right-wing political traditions. Alliances—of convenience or of principle—with such non-Catholic groupings were of course possible (and frequently concluded) but there remained an implicit or explicit awareness that these other movements possessed different intellectual and social principles from those of Catholicism. In positive terms, it was this awareness of a distinctive corpus of Catholic social and political ideas which gave coherence to the different manifestations of political Catholicism.

This Catholic political tradition did of course change over time. While in the troubled circumstances of the 1930s, many Catholics rallied to visions of an authoritarian political system and corporatist social order, in the post-1945 years it was a cautious acceptance of a democratic system and of a neo-capitalist social market economy which characterized much of Catholic politics. Nevertheless, these changes—as well as the diverse and often divergent forms in which they were expressed—should not be allowed to disguise the existence of a common core of beliefs. A commitment to the defence of the Catholic religion was of course one such rallying-point but so too was the vision of a communitarian (but not socialist) social order in which the disruptive influences of liberal individualism and of untrammelled capitalism would be offset by new social institutions which would reinforce the bonds of community. Greatly encouraged by the role enthusiastically assumed by the Papacy as the intellectual guardian of a unitary Catholic truth, such ideas run as a common—if twisted—thread through the Catholic politics during the fifty years after the First World War.

These ideological bonds were nevertheless rarely, if ever, sufficient to offset the manifold sources of division which bedevilled attempts at political unity within Catholic ranks. Common adherence to the religious faith and to the social and political ideas of Catholicism were precarious and generally insufficient bases upon which to build Catholic political unity. In countries such as France, despite the transient success of General de Castelnau's Fédération Nationale Catholique after the First World War or of the Mouvement Républicain Populaire after the Second World War, no Catholic political movement ever emerged which could claim to be the dominant political expression of the French Catholic community.[14] Moreover, even in countries such as Germany, Italy, or the Low Countries where powerful Catholic parties enjoyed a quasi-monopoly over Catholic electoral loyalties both before and after the Second World War, these parties were often little more than coalitions of different

---

[14] See p. 35.

Catholic social and political organizations, whose common loyalty to the party went hand in hand with a desire to reinforce their own position at the expense of other elements within the party.[15]

Internal division was always inherent to the Catholic politics of Europe. The sources of division ran deep. If papal teachings dismissed class conflict as one of the many heresies of Marxist socialism, it rarely proved possible to insulate the Catholic community from the impact of such tensions. Despite the decline in religious practice among much of the industrial working class of Europe during the nineteenth century and the rise in support for Socialist parties, there remained a strong Catholic working-class tradition. Especially, in regions such as the Ruhr, the Basque country, and certain industrial regions of France and Belgium, Catholic workers formed a large and self-confident force.[16] With the broader democratization of society, such workers were increasingly reluctant to follow passively the guidance of predominantly bourgeois Catholic political leaders. Catholic trade-unionism grew rapidly after the First World War and in Germany, France, and Belgium gave rise to increasingly powerful Catholic trade-union confederations which demanded a reorientation of Catholic political priorities towards a concern for the working class. Such working-class Catholic activism was mirrored by the emergence of Catholic organizations similarly determined to protect the interests of the peasantry and of the bourgeoisie. Already in the 1890s, peasant associations were a prominent feature of rural Catholic politics, while the economic crisis of the inter-war years gave rise to manifold Catholic movements of middle-class defence. To mediate between these divergent and increasingly assertive interest groups was therefore imperative for any Catholic political movement which sought to pose as the representative of Catholic opinion.[17]

Nor were tensions of social class the only such source of division. Differences of region, of generation, and of intellectual outlook and temperament between the advocates of an intransigent Catholicism uncompromisingly hostile to the evils of the modern era and those more inclined to find some form of accommodation with the reality of a pluralist, industrial, and urban society were always close to the surface and remain evident in present-day Catholicism. These manifold sources of division provided the fault-lines within political Catholicism, and it was along these lines that Catholic political unity tended to splinter in times of crisis. Thus, in Italy after the First World War, it was predominantly the Christian democrat groups which remained loyal to the Partito Popolare Italiano led by Don Sturzo while much of the

[15] See pp. 162–7 and 190.

[16] H. McLeod, *Religion and the People of Western Europe 1789–1970* (Oxford, 1981), 126–7.

[17] See pp. 51, 163–5, and 196–7; W. L. Patch, *Christian Trade Unions in the Weimar Republic 1918–1933: The Failure of 'Corporate Pluralism'* (New Haven, 1985); I. Farr, 'Populism in the Countryside: The Peasant Leagues in Bavaria in the 1890s', in R. J. Evans (ed.), *Society and Politics in Wilhelmine Germany* (London, 1978), 136–59; R. G. Moeller, *German Peasants and Agrarian Politics 1914–1924: The Rhineland and Westphalia* (Chapel Hill, NC, 1986); C. Strikwerda, 'Corporatism and the Lower Middle Class: Interwar Belgium', in R. Koshar (ed.), *Splintered Classes: Politics and the Lower Middle Class in Interwar Europe* (New York, 1990), 210–39.

Catholic middle class chose to ally itself with Mussolini against the liberal parliamentary system.[18] A broadly similar pattern of events arose with regard to Catholic attitudes towards the Vichy regime in wartime France[19] while in the 1960s it was these various sources of division which finally destroyed any sense of Catholic political unity in much of Europe. In the light of such tensions, many historians have therefore chosen to dissect political Catholicism in terms of a number of distinct and largely self-contained Catholic political traditions. Hybrid terms such as 'Christian democracy', 'clerico-fascism', 'liberal Catholicism' and 'ultramontane Catholicism' have become commonplace in analyses of Catholic politics. Yet, as historians have long been aware, such summary descriptions often suggest a clarity which is misleading.[20] The struggle to define the contours of different Catholic political traditions[21] simplifies the complex links which existed between various groups and individuals, and attempts to isolate a particular Catholic tradition from the wider political context must inevitably appear somewhat arbitrary.

These difficulties have been particularly evident in the approach adopted to the phenomenon of 'Christian democracy'. The dominant historiographical analysis of twentieth-century political Catholicism has tended to prioritize the existence of a distinct Christian democrat political tradition which first emerged in the nineteenth century and gradually grew in strength until it emerged as a dominant force in the democratic Catholic politics of much of Western Europe after the Second World War. There are several reasons for the emphasis placed on this interpretation. In part, it reflects the ascendancy among historians of Catholicism of a progressive Catholic intelligentsia, sympathetic to the goals of Christian democracy and eager to acknowledge the achievements of those historical figures who shared their ideals.[22] Coupled on occasion by a reluctance to acknowledge the significance of other forms of Catholic politics, this historical tradition inevitably tends towards a teleological interpretation of political Catholicism, in which pre-Second World War Catholic political movements are perceived largely in terms of how they laid the basis for the democratic Catholic politics of the future. As the chapters in this collection make clear, there is much that is of value in such an interpretation. It is indeed true, as James McMillan makes clear in his chapter on France,[23] that the dominant phenomenon in the history of political Catholicism in much of Western Europe has been the gradual abandonment of a natural identification with the politics of the conservative right and the emergence of a Catholic political tradition of the centre-left. Yet the danger inherent in the application of hindsight is that it highlights only a particular 'canon' of significant Catholic movements and individuals at the expense, for example, of those many Catholic movements of the inter-war years which opposed any identification with the values and structures of liberal democracy.[24]

---

[18] See pp. 80–1.   [19] See pp. 55–8.

[20] J.-M. Mayeur, 'Catholicisme intransigeant, catholicisme social, démocratie chrétienne', *Annales Economies, Sociétés, Civilisations*, 27 (1972), 483–99.

[21] See the attempts at definition in A. M. Pazos (ed.), *Un siglo de catolicismo social en Europa 1891–1991* (Pamplona, 1993).   [22] e.g. Fogarty, *Christian Democracy in Europe 1820–1953*.

[23] See p. 34.   [24] See pp. 24–5.

Moreover, such an interpretation can also lead to the anachronistic belief that those who described themselves as 'Christian democrats' in the circumstances of the 1890s or the 1920s shared the political ambitions of those who described themselves as such in the post-1945 years. This belief in an essentially unchanging Christian democrat political tradition provides a somewhat flawed account of the historical reality. As a number of historical studies in recent years have made clear, the use of the term 'Christian democrat' in the 1890s and the early years of the twentieth century encompassed a wide range of Catholic beliefs, many of which were opposed to a liberal democratic political system. Often influenced by the paternalist notions of the late nineteenth century with its nostalgic vision of a pre-industrial society of natural hierarchies, such 'Christian democrats' were precursors of post-1945 Christian democrats in name only.[25]

The undoubted existence of different subsidiary trends within political Catholicism should not therefore be allowed to disguise the countervailing forces which worked in favour of political unity among Catholics. Not only did Catholic political movements possess a distinct identity derived from allegiance to a common Catholic intellectual heritage, but this unity was fostered by other more tangible realities. The influence of the Church itself, so anxious in the Netherlands after the First World War or in Italy after the Second World War to guarantee the political unity of all Catholics,[26] was one such factor in favour of cohesion but so also was the milieu in which many Catholics lived. Confessional differences, be they between Catholics and Protestants or between Catholics and non-believers, were part of the daily fabric of the social experience of many European Catholics during much of the twentieth century. Especially in states such as the Netherlands, Switzerland, or Germany where Catholics formed a minority grouping, the sense of Catholic distinctiveness was reinforced by an imposing array of educational, cultural, and social confessional institutions which provided an all-embracing environment for the Catholic faithful. Finally, political unity on a national level was also encouraged by the need to defend the particular interests of the Catholic population and its religion. Though the great heyday of anticlericalism was, at least outside Spain and Portugal, long since past, the defence of the Church and of its affiliated schools, youth associations, and other institutions provided a range of political issues which especially during election campaigns served as a rallying-point for the Catholic faithful. Similarly, the experience of Fascist rule in Italy and Nazism in Germany, as well as of foreign occupation elsewhere in Europe during the Second World War, provided further occasions for Catholics to unite to defend the institutions of the Catholic faith.

---

[25] The adoption of the term 'democrat' by such groups in francophone and southern Europe (in German-speaking Europe, the term *Volk* was more usual) was intended only to indicate their popular orientation. It did not imply support for a democratic model of politics. See E. Poulat, 'Pour une nouvelle compréhension de la démocratie chrétienne', *Revue d'Histoire Ecclésiastique*, 70 (1975), 5–38; Mayeur 'Catholicisme intransigeant', 483–99; P. Nord, 'Three Views of Christian Democracy in Fin de Siècle France', *Journal of Contemporary History*, 19 (1984), 713–27; Misner, *Social Catholicism in Europe*, 194–7 and 222–3.

[26] See pp. 86–7 and 228–9.

Political Catholicism was, thus, in most countries during this period a delicate balance between centrifugal and centripetal forces. In the 1960s, the pendulum swung decisively in favour of the centrifugal forces, breaking asunder any sense of unity and inaugurating a new era in terms of Catholic political engagement. But the eventual collapse of the forms of political Catholicism which characterized the era considered in this volume should not lead one to assume that their existence was in some sense artificial. On the contrary, the remarkable dedication with which millions of European Catholics joined, supported with their labours and financial donations, or simply voted for political movements which were inspired by Catholic ideals reflected a reality which historians underestimate at their peril. Movements of political Catholicism which transcended divisions of region, ethnicity, generation, or social class in the name of a shared commitment to the values of Catholicism were always to some extent seeking to act in defiance of the gravity of historical reality but it is nevertheless the electoral and political success of these movements rather than the many inevitable instances of their failure which remains their most prominent feature.

3. The Papacy

Throughout the period considered in this volume, the direct and indirect power exerted by the Papacy constituted the most significant single influence on the character of Catholic political action. It is easy to exaggerate the centrality of the Papacy to European Catholicism. Both a long-standing anticlerical tradition inherited from the nineteenth century, as well as the aggrandizing pretensions of the Popes themselves, have tended to attribute to the Papacy an importance—as a force for good or evil—which clearly exceeded the real extent of its power.[27] Nevertheless, the era under consideration in this volume did undoubtedly witness what Étienne Fouilloux has aptly described as 'l'apogée de la romanité au sein du catholicisme'.[28] From the First Vatican Council of 1869–70 onwards, the Papacy under the leadership of a series of like-minded and determined Popes used every means at its disposal to assert its central role in the defence, propagation, and definition of the Catholic religion. Their ambitions always exceeded their achievements; yet the reality of the increase in the power and prestige of the Papacy was incontrovertible. In part, this change reflected the new methods of communication. Photography enabled the physical image of the Pope to be widely diffused among the faithful. The railways which annually brought thousands of pilgrims to Rome to pay homage to the Popes and Vatican Radio (established by Marconi in 1931) which enabled the Popes to speak directly to the faithful throughout Europe provided the means for the Papacy to acquire an unprecedented tangible presence in the lives of Catholics. But it was also a revolution in the structures of the Catholic faith. The Papacy became the administrative, ideological, and emotional focus of Catholicism, the guardian of orthodoxy and the agent of change.[29]

---

[27] S. Stehlin, *Weimar and the Vatican 1919–1933* (Princeton, 1983), vii.

[28] Fouilloux 'Courants de pensée', 116.

[29] Ibid., 122–8; M. Agostino, *Le Pape Pie XI et l'opinion publique (1922–1939)* (Rome, 1991), 11–70;

Despite certain modest differences in emphasis, the Popes were united in the purpose to which they intended to dedicate their power. During the pontificates of Pius IX (1846–78), Leo XIII (1878–1903), Pius X (1903–14), Benedict XV (1914–22), and more especially those of Pius XI (1922–39) and Pius XII (1939–58), the Papacy became the absolute monarchy of the Catholic faith. Profoundly suspicious of the social, economic, and political trends of the modern era, the Popes—assisted by the powerful Vatican bureaucracy, the Curia—defiantly sought to assert the distinctiveness of the Catholic religion. Amidst a world in crisis, the Church and above all the Papacy should, they believed, serve as a supernatural fortress. Their consistent purpose was to remodel the internal structures of the Catholic Church in order to create a strict hierarchy from the supreme authorities in Rome, through the national ecclesiastical hierarchies and the priesthood to the laity. Metaphors derived from the secular worlds of the military or civilian bureaucracy permeated papal declarations, and unquestioning obedience was demanded from their followers. The autonomies long enjoyed by national ecclesiastical hierarchies were steadily eroded; papal responsibility for all key appointments was asserted; and new centralized forms of doctrinal training were introduced in seminaries.[30] Above all, the Papacy sought to propagate a distinctively Roman form of religious piety. The cults of the Sacred Heart of Jesus, of the Christ King, of the Pope, and, above all, of the Virgin Mary were prominent features of twentieth-century Catholicism which, though they clearly derived much of their strength from the manner in which they responded to the aspirations of the faithful, were to a significant extent shaped by papal initiatives and encouragement.[31]

The increase in the organizational and religious importance of the Papacy was matched by the remarkable energy which the Popes devoted to declarations not only on matters of doctrine but on a wide range of social, political, and cultural issues. No fewer than 185 papal encyclicals were issued between 1878 and 1958[32] as well as innumerable messages, radio broadcasts, and speeches to a vast array of different audiences. This vast range of papal pronouncements has come to be regarded—especially by sympathetic Catholic commentators—as constituting a coherent and unitary corpus of Catholic doctrine. This was certainly the wish of the Popes who intended that their teachings should provide comprehensive guidance for the faithful on all matters from Communism to tourism.[33] In reality, however, this impression of unity was to some extent spurious. Significant differences both of emphasis and content existed between many papal declarations, while others were often deliberately couched in such general terms that their meaning was open to a variety of different interpretations.

Fogarty, *Christian Democracy in Europe*, 246; A. Hastings, 'Catholic History from Vatican I to John Paul II', in id. (ed.), *Modern Catholicism: Vatican II and After* (London, 1991), 1.

[30] Agostino *Pie XI*, 3, 24, 28–31, 49, 111–14; Fouilloux, 'Courants de pensée', 159–64.

[31] Fouilloux, 'Courants de pensée', 189–206.

[32] M. J. Schuck, *That They Be One: The Social Teaching of the Papal Encyclicals 1740–1989* (Washington, 1991), 45.

[33] Agostino, *Pie XI*, 77–8; J.-B. D'Onorio, 'Eccesacerdos Magnus', in J. Chelini and J.-B. D'Onorio (eds.) *Pie XII et la Cité: la Pensée et l'action politique de Pie XII* (Aix, 1988), 36.

The unity of the papal pronouncements therefore arose not so much from their specific instructions as from their consistent preoccupation with a number of central concerns.[34] Foremost among these was an insistence that Catholicism alone offered a solution to the problems of the modern world. As Pius XI unambiguously declared: 'The first and principal cause of every form of disturbance and rebellion is the revolt of man against God.' Consequently, the goal of the Papacy was, in the words of Pius XI again, 'the re-establishment of the Kingdom of Christ by peace in Christ'.[35] This universal project derived much of its tone of confident certainty from its reliance on neo-Thomist Catholic philosophy which, since the promulgation of the encyclical *Aeterni Patris* of 1879, had come to form the basis of theological orthodoxy for the modern Papacy. The writings of Thomas Aquinas provided the Popes with an architectural vision of a world created and sustained by God's divine purpose. The sins of men had led them into error and had brought disorder into this rationally ordained universe and it was only through a return to the teachings of the universal Church—as made known through papal declarations—that a just world could be re-created.[36]

This 'ultramontane fundamentalism', as it has been termed,[37] not only justified the pre-eminent position of the Papacy within Catholicism but also encouraged the Popes to give expression to their vision of an alternative social and political order. Central to this papal message was a commitment to a social order of communities in which the anomie and self-interest of liberal individualism as well as the statist collectivism of socialism and fascism would give way to a new spirit of personal fulfil-ment and mutual assistance. Major political reforms formed an essential element of this somewhat nostalgic vision. Though the Papacy occasionally expressed its com-mitment to a 'real democracy' (notably in Pius XII's Christmas Message of Decem-ber 1944),[38] there was little doubt that the Papal political ideal was far removed from the individualist and secular principles of a liberal parliamentary system. At the same time, the Papacy repeatedly expressed its opposition to Italian Fascist and German Nazi glorification of the State. Quite apart from the threat which such doctrines posed to the autonomy of the Church, the Papacy rejected these 'totalitarian' ideas as subordinating the will of the individual to the false secular deities of nation and race.[39] Instead, the political structure envisaged by the Papacy was one in which a strong central authority was combined with the maximum possible devolution of power. As Pius XI's enthusiasm for the dictatorial regimes of Salazar in Portugal and Dollfuss in Austria during the 1930s illustrated, a strong central power was regarded as essential to maintain social and political order but it was to be accompanied by the application of the principle of subsidiarity, by which responsibility for many

---

[34] Schuck, *That They Be One*, x and 173–80.   [35] Ibid., 55 and 70–2.

[36] Ibid., 67–9; Fogarty, *Christian Democracy in Europe*, 433; O. Köhler, 'Teaching and Theology', in H. Jedin and J. Dolan (eds.), *History of the Church*, ix. *The Church in the Industrial Age* (London, 1981), 307–18.

[37] C. Weber, 'Ultramontanismus als katholischer Fundamentalismus', in W. Loth (ed.), *Deutsche Katholizismus im Umbruch zur Moderne* (Stuttgart, 1991), 20–45.

[38] D'Onorio, 'Eccesacerdos Magnus', 55.   [39] Ibid., 45–6; Agostino, *Pie XI*, 104–6.

socio-economic issues should be devolved from the central state to the 'natural' communities of region, profession, and family.[40]

The social doctrines of the Popes were similarly concerned to avoid the twin evils of statist centralization and anarchic individualism. As articulated in perhaps the most influential single encyclical of modern times, *Rerum Novarum* issued by Leo XIII in 1891, and reiterated both in Pius XI's encyclical *Quadragesimo Anno* of 1931 as well as numerous other public statements, the Papacy expressed its firm opposition to the ethos and structures of the capitalist economy.[41] The notion of a hidden hand which worked to ensure the common good held no appeal for the Popes who saw in the free-market system—and more especially in its apparently remorseless tendency towards monopoly—only the selfish desire of individuals to satisfy their own material ambitions at the expense of others. It was above all the industrial workers who were the victims of unrestrained economic growth and from the 1890s onwards papal declarations repeatedly denounced the material sufferings and social marginalization of the proletariat. Papal solicitude did not, however, imply support for a socialist reorganization of society. Socialism and communism were rejected by the Papacy not merely because of their atheistic and materialist ideology but because their collectivist notions of economic organization threatened both family life and the right to private property which papal teachings deemed to be essential to a just society. Caught between capitalism and collectivism, the Papacy tried to articulate a 'third way' which would control the abuses of capitalist competition while retaining personal ownership of property. Its most tangible expression was the enthusiasm expressed by Pius XI in *Quadragesimo Anno* for a corporatist reorganization of society in which networks of socio-economic corporations would bring together employers and employees to resolve conflicts of interest as well as ensuring the ascendancy of social justice.[42] In this rather utopian manner, the individual competition and class conflict of the modern world would, so papal statements proclaimed, be replaced by an organic community in which all of the elements of society worked together for the common good.

The elaboration and diffusion of these general statements of social and political principle formed only one part of papal involvement in European politics. Though the Papacy consciously sought to present itself as a primarily spiritual institution, its position at the head of the manifold branches of the Catholic Church as well as its quasi-sovereign status as the ruler of the Vatican State obliged the Papacy to engage with the world as it was. Encyclical statements of principle therefore always went hand in hand with diplomatic and political initiatives intended to ensure protection for the Catholic Church in an often hostile world. During both world wars, the

---

[40] W. Weber, 'Society and State as a Problem for the Church', in Jedin, Repgen, and Dolan (eds.), *History of the Church*, x. 238–9; J.-M. Pontier, 'Pie XII et la démocratie', in Chelini and D'Onorio (eds.), *Pie XII et la Cité*, 265–91.

[41] P. Furlong and D. Curtis (eds.), *The Church faces the Modern World: Rerum Novarum and its Impact* (Scunthorpe, 1994).

[42] Agostino, *Pie XI*, 94–102; M. J. Schuck, *That They Be One*, 63–5 and 81–6; J. D. Holmes, *The Papacy in the Modern World* (London, 1981), 79–80.

Papacy remained rigorously neutral, condemning the belligerence of the participants and calling on them to renounce war in favour of a compromise peace.[43] This was
an often unpopular stance which, especially in the aftermath of the Second World
War, led to accusations that the Papacy could have acted more effectively to protect
the victims of Nazism,[44] but it also undoubtedly enhanced its position as an institution which stood above the conflicts of nations. In times of peace, the Papacy was also
at pains to stress its neutrality in political conflicts and proved willing to reach agreements with regimes of different political characters. Especially during the pontificates of Pius XI and Pius XII, the Papacy energetically set about concluding treaties,
termed concordats, with a large number of European states. No fewer than forty such
concordats were concluded during the inter-war years, including, most notably,
those with Poland in 1925, Mussolini's Italy in 1929 (the so-called Lateran Treaties
which settled the long-standing dispute between the Vatican and the Italian state),
Nazi Germany and Austria in 1933, and eventually Spain in 1953.[45] The purpose of
the Papacy in reaching these quasi-diplomatic formal agreements was both defensive
and offensive. Its primary aim was to ensure that there could be no return to the anticlerical policies which had been pursued by a number of European regimes in the
latter nineteenth century. Especially in the uncertain atmosphere in Europe in the
years after the First World War, the Papacy feared a new wave of attacks on the Catholic faith. Thus, by concluding these treaties, the Church sought to provide legal
protection for the Church and its manifold affiliated social, educational, cultural, and
economic institutions, as well as resolving long-standing points of grievance over
matters such as payment of clerical salaries and ownership of Church property.[46]

At the same time, however, the concordats also reinforced the power of the Papacy
within the Catholic Church. By concluding agreements directly with national
governments, the Vatican served to tie the national ecclesiastical hierarchies more
closely to the Papacy. The treaties reinforced the status of the Church as an international institution centred on Rome and the Papacy was always careful to ensure
that the agreements enabled it to make the principal ecclesiastical appointments
within the national churches. In this respect, therefore, the concordats formed an
integral element of the Papacy's consistent aim of imposing its own priorities and
leadership on the Catholic Church. The concordats concluded with Fascist Italy and
Nazi Germany were, for example, notable for their lack of attention to the protection

[43] J.-M. Mayeur, 'Les Églises et les relations internationales: L'Église catholique', in id. (ed.), *Histoire
du Christianisme*, xii. 305–34; O. Chadwick, *Britain and the Vatican during the Second World War*
(Cambridge, 1986), 57–78; A. Rhodes, *The Vatican in the Age of the Dictators 1922–1945* (London, 1973),
235–82.
[44] S. Friedländer, *Pius XII and the Third Reich: A Documentation* (London, 1966); L. Papeleux, *Les
Silences de Pie XII* (Brussels, 1980), 261–9; J. Conway, 'The Vatican, Germany and the Holocaust', in
P. Kent and J. Pollard (eds.), *Papal Diplomacy in the Modern Age* (Westport, Conn., 1994), 105–18.
[45] J. Pollard, *The Vatican and Italian Fascism*, 4–5; Stehlin, *Weimar and the Vatican*, 52; id., 'The
Emergence of a New Vatican Diplomacy during the Great War and its Aftermath 1914–1929', in Kent and
Pollard (eds.), *Papal Diplomacy in the Modern Age*, 75–87.
[46] Stehlin, *Weimar and the Vatican*, 368–70; G. May, 'The Holy See's Policy of Concordats from 1918
to 1974', in Jedin, Repgen, and Dolan (eds.), *History of the Church*, x. 177–83.

of the political freedoms of the Catholics of Italy and Germany. Instead, it was the interests of the Church and more especially those of the Papacy which they sought to protect.[47] The superficial political neutrality represented by the concordat policy was therefore largely illusory. Though the concordats were in part no more than an overdue settlement of relations between Church and State, they also served the Papacy's quest for a more centralized and authoritarian Catholic Church able to act largely independently of state interference. Those states willing to accord the Church such a status were rewarded with expressions of papal sympathy while those, such as the Spanish Republic of the 1930s or, in their latter years, both Fascist Italy and Nazi Germany, which refused to accord the Catholic Church any special rights were strenuously denounced.

It was during the pontificate of Pius XII from 1939 to 1958 that the autocratic power of the Papacy reached its fullest expression. An aloof, austere figure who had spent his entire adult life in the service of the Vatican bureaucracy, Pius consciously sought to reinforce the hold which the Papacy exercised over all aspects of the life of the Church. Ecclesiastical power was further centralized in Rome and a long series of papal messages provided guidance for the Catholic faithful on religious, social, and cultural matters. Despite initiating some significant liturgical reforms, Pius XII's vision was essentially that of an unchanging—even immobile—Church which, as his most influential encyclical *Humani Generis* of 1950 declared, rejected innovations in the teachings and structures of the Church. Dissidents who contravened the theological and political orthodoxies of the Papacy were expelled from positions of influence while strenuous energies were devoted to encouraging those forms of piety favoured by the Papacy. This was most evident in the further impetus given to devotion to the Virgin Mary. Marian shrines such as Fátima in Portugal and Lourdes in France were the objects of particular Papal solicitude and the bull *Munificentissimus Dei* issued in 1950 gave to the Marian cult a new status by declaring the doctrine of the assumption of the Virgin Mary into heaven.[48]

In the last years of the pontificate of Pius XII, it became increasingly evident that the attempt to freeze Catholicism in a particular mould was encountering resistance from elements of both the clergy and the laity, notably in France, Germany, and the Low Countries. Nevertheless, few would have predicted the speed and the scale of the ecclesiastical and doctrinal changes which occurred after the death of Pius XII in 1958. By summoning the Second Vatican Council (the first general assembly of the Church since the First Vatican Council of 1869–1870), the new pope, John XXIII, made himself the catalyst of a series of radical reforms which in their collective impact on the Church, the Papacy, and the Catholic faith have been described as the most important event in the history of Catholicism since the Council of Trent which

---

[47] Mayeur, 'Les Églises et les relations internationales', 301–5; Rhodes, *The Vatican in the Age of the Dictators*, 147–8.

[48] M. J. Walsh, 'Pius XII', in Hastings (ed.), *Modern Catholicism*, 20–6; Chelini and D'Onorio (eds.), *Pie XII et la Cité*; H. Graef, *Mary: A History of Doctrine and Devotion* (London, 1965), ii. 146–50; N. Perry and L. Echeverria, *Under the Heel of Mary* (London, 1988), 242–3.

launched the Catholic Counter-Reformation of the sixteenth century.[49] The wider
political impact of the Second Vatican Council which opened in October 1962 and,
after the death of John XXIII in June 1963 and the subsequent election of Paul VI,
finally concluded in December 1965 is considered both later in this introduction
and in the subsequent chapters. Its impact upon the Papacy as an institution was,
however, considerable. The new constitution of the Church, *Lumen Gentium*, proclaimed in 1964, substantially dismantled the authoritarian internal structure of
the Church. Though the Papacy remained the central headquarters of the Church,
the Pope exercised his power not as an absolute monarch but as the head of the collective council of bishops. The symbolism and pomp of monarchical hierarchy was
replaced by a novel emphasis on collegiality, a change symbolized by the adoption of
the phrase 'people of God' to describe the manner in which all elements of the
Church—bishops, clergy, and laity—were active participants in the life of the Catholic faith.[50]

Similarly revolutionary was the change which the Second Vatican Council
brought about in the attitude of the Church towards the modern world. The siege
mentality of the early twentieth century which had oscillated between the defence of
the faithful against alien modern influences and an offensive spirit of Catholic reconquest, was dispensed with in favour of what the declaration *Gaudiam et Spes*
issued in the final session of the Council in December 1965 portrayed as an active
engagement with contemporary society. No longer did the Church claim to possess
a monopoly over truth and, just as the Papacy began a policy of *rapprochement* with
the Protestant and Orthodox churches, so the Catholic clergy and laity were encouraged to engage in dialogue with their fellow non-Catholic citizens.[51]

Not all the reforms initiated by the Second Vatican Council have been carried
through and, especially during the pontificate of John Paul II, there has been a determined attempt to return to a more authoritarian structure for the Church by which
the Papacy has sought to recover its role as the guardian of Catholic orthodoxy.[52]
Nevertheless, the central reforms initiated by the Council have remained in place and
have had an incontrovertible impact on European political Catholicism. By abandoning any attempt to direct the political engagement of the Catholic faithful, the
Council did much to encourage—even if it did not entirely cause—the new disparate
forms of Catholic political engagement which emerged in much of Europe during
the 1960s.[53]

---

[49] H. Jedin, 'The Second Vatican Council', in Jedin, Repgen, and Dolan (eds.), *History of the Church*,
x. 146. See also O. Chadwick, *The Christian Church in the Cold War* (London, 1992), 115–27.

[50] Jedin, 'Second Vatican Council', 133–4; A. Flannery (ed.), *Vatican Council II: The Conciliar and
Post-Conciliar Documents* (Dublin, 1992), 350–426.

[51] Jedin, 'Second Vatican Council', 144–5; Flannery, *Vatican Council II*, 903–1001.

[52] A. Hastings, 'Catholic History' in id. (ed.), *Modern Catholicism*, 8–9. The encyclical *Veritas Splendor*
issued in 1993 represents the most categorical attempt by John Paul II to return to a vision of the Papacy
and of the Church based on the model of Pius XII. See J. Wilkins (ed.), *Understanding Veritas Splendor*
(London, 1994).

[53] See pp. 32–3.

4. The Evolution of Political Catholicism 1918–1965

The rapid emergence of Catholicism as a political force in much of Europe in the years following the First World War was the culmination of trends evident during the previous half-century as well as the product of the manifold changes wrought by the war itself. The 'politicization of Catholicism'[54] which took place in many European countries in the late nineteenth century had been partly imposed on Catholics by the actions of others. The state-directed policies of discrimination against Catholics in the Netherlands, Switzerland, and Bismarckian Germany during the so-called *Kultürkampf* of the 1870s as well as anticlerical campaigns by liberal political groups in France, Italy, and Spain had in effect obliged many Catholics to become conscious of their collective identity.[55] But the gradual emergence of a sense of community among Catholic populations also owed much to changes taking place within the Catholic faith. Encouraged by the Papacy and by national ecclesiastical hierarchies, this was nevertheless primarily a force 'from below'.[56] Increasing levels of education and urbanization fostered a new, more modern, religious identity, in which religious belief gradually came to stand alone as something distinct from expressions of communal identity and the observance of rites of passage. It would be wrong to exaggerate the extent and pace of the transformation which had taken place; nevertheless, the Catholics of Europe in 1914 were on the whole much more inclined than had been their forefathers to think of their Catholic identity as a conscious personal choice. Ritual and tradition was gradually giving way to a new Catholicism which was more individualist and, as it encouraged Catholics to think of themselves as a distinct community bound together by shared beliefs, also more collective.[57]

This Catholic identity spilled over from the religious sphere into other areas of social, cultural, and—ultimately—political life. The late nineteenth century witnessed a remarkable boom in the membership of Catholic associations throughout Europe. Women's groups, youth and educational movements, co-operatives, peasant leagues, sporting associations, workers' guilds, and trade unions; all participated in the rapid development of what particularly in Germany, Switzerland, and the Low Countries came to take on the character of a Catholic subculture isolated from the wider society.[58] This 'closed' model of Catholicism has long attracted the attention of sociologists and political scientists who have seen in it a process of 'ghettoization' or

---

54 Lönne, *Politischer Katholizismus im 19. und 20. Jahrhundert*, 10–11.

55 See pp. 35–6, 70, 156–7, and 219–20, Blackbourn, *Marpingen*, 106–112; Altermatt, *Der Weg der Schweizer Katholiken ins Ghetto*; Lannon, *Privilege, Persecution and Prophecy*, 136–8.

56 See pp. 225–6.

57 Gibson, *Social History of French Catholicism*, 258–9; F. Lebrun (ed.), *Histoire des catholiques en France* (Toulouse, 1980), 383–96; A. Latreille, 'Pratique, Piété et Foi Populaire dans la France Moderne au xixème et xxème siècles', in G. J. Cuming and D. Baker (eds.), *Popular Belief and Practice* (Cambridge, 1972), 282–7; W. A. Christian, *Person and God in a Spanish Valley* (London, 1972), 181–3; M. P. Hornsby-Smith, *Roman Catholic Beliefs in England: Customary Catholicism and Transformations of Religious Authority* (Cambridge, 1991), 9. We are grateful to Susan O'Brien for assistance on this point.

58 Altermatt, *Der Weg der Schweizer Katholiken ins Ghetto*; M. Wintle, *Pillars of Piety: Religion in the Netherlands in the Nineteenth Century* (Hull, 1987).

'pillarization' in which a Catholic network of schools, associations, and religious institutions provided an all-enveloping milieu for the faithful.[59] In fact, although this was the undoubted aspiration of many Catholic clergy, its extent should not be exaggerated. Even in the Low Countries and Britain where the trend towards Catholic segregation was most pronounced, the reality rarely accorded entirely with the ideal.[60] Nevertheless, the boom in Catholic confessional associations undoubtedly served as both the manifestation and the catalyst of a new more assertive Catholic identity.

Catholic political parties were at least in origin the corollary in the political sphere of the defensive mentality which had provided much of the impetus for the emergence of Catholic associations. Just as in so many areas of social and cultural life these associations were intended to protect the faithful from discrimination and corruption, so the parties acted as the guardians of Catholic interests in the national parliaments and municipal councils which had become the norm in much of Europe by 1900. Beginning with the establishment in the 1870s of the Centre Party in Germany and the Catholic Party in Belgium, the trend towards separate Catholic political representation gradually spread during the subsequent decades to the Netherlands, Austria, Switzerland, and, to a lesser extent, France and Italy. By 1914 only Portugal and Spain of the principal Catholic states of Europe lacked a distinct Catholic political grouping of some importance, while in Germany, Austria, and Belgium, Catholic political representatives already exercised substantial power.[61]

The Church rarely played a pre-eminent role in the creation and development of these parties. Though individual priests (such as Seipel in Austria or Sturzo in Italy) were often of considerable importance, national ecclesiastical leaderships and the Papacy tended to look with some suspicion on the active participation of the clergy in the political process. The attitude of the Papacy was, of course, much influenced by the particular circumstances of Italy where the Popes continued until 1929 to refuse to recognize the legitimacy of the post-unification Italian state.[62] Instead, it was more frequently the Catholic laity, and more especially men drawn from the expanding ranks of the Catholic bourgeoisie, who directed the new parties. Their primary motive—and the self-proclaimed justification of the parties—was to protect the Catholic Church and the faithful from anticlerical assaults. This often proved necessary. In Italy, France, Spain, and Portugal, the turn of the century was characterized by renewed anticlerical and, more particularly, anti-Catholic campaigns.[63] Nevertheless, the logic of participation in the parliamentary and electoral process also obliged Catholic parties to develop and articulate more wide-ranging political

[59] Whyte *Catholics in Western Democracies* 47–75. See also pp.195–6 and 221–6.

[60] S. Fielding, *Class and Ethnicity: Irish Catholicism in England 1880–1939* (Buckingham, 1993), 27–8.

[61] See pp. 39–40, 76–7, 157–8, and 191–2. Evans, 'Catholic Political Movements in Germany, Switzerland and the Netherlands', 97–107; J. W. Boyer, *Political Radicalism in Late Imperial Vienna: Origins of the Christian Social Movement 1848–1897* (Chicago, 1981), 122–83; M. L. Anderson, *Windthorst: A Political Biography* (Oxford, 1981).   [62] See p. 70.

[63] See pp. 39 and 131–2. D. L. Wheeler, *Republican Portugal: A Political History 1910–1926* (Madison, Wisc., 1978), 67–72.

platforms. In doing so, the parties went beyond a rhetoric of defence to present their solutions to the problems of society as a whole. This was not always easy. As early as the 1890s Catholic political groupings were already affected by differences of attitude and policy between their predominantly bourgeois leaders and 'Christian democrat' elements who called for greater attention to be paid to the needs of the working class.[64] Nevertheless, all Catholic elements could unite in opposition to the pernicious effects of liberalism which, as well as drawing the peoples of Europe away from loyalty to the Catholic faith, was held responsible for encouraging moral corruption and the evils of an individualist economic system. Anti-liberalism therefore provided the defining focus of pre-1914 Catholic parties and, in its place, they gradually came to develop a positive vision of a restored popular community, united by a common morality and by new socio-economic institutions—such as guilds—which would dissolve the class antagonisms of industrial society.[65]

The First World War accelerated the development of Catholic political action. The war's initial impact was to draw Catholics in combatant states such as France and Germany into national alliances with their erstwhile electoral foes but this new-found sense of common patriotic purpose was soon accompanied by a fear of the possible political consequences of the war. These apprehensions were amply fulfilled in the immediate aftermath of the war. The euphoria of military victory enabled national coalitions to remain in place in France and Belgium but in Central Europe and northern Italy the wave of social and political upheavals during 1918 and 1919 seemed to presage militant Socialist revolutions directly prejudicial to Catholicism. In fact, the revolutionary tide gradually receded but the political changes brought about by the war proved to be a more durable stimulus to Catholic political action. The establishment of the Weimar Republic in Germany and of the new nation-states in Central and Eastern Europe created democratic parliamentary regimes in which Catholics were obliged to unite politically in order to advance their interests. Similarly, in victorious countries such as Italy and Belgium, as well as in a number of neutral states including Switzerland and the Netherlands, reforms introduced after the war created a more democratic social and political system enhancing the need for Catholic political unity and action.[66]

The immediate post-war years therefore witnessed a rapid expansion in Catholic political movements. Long-established parties such as the German Centre Party, the Christian Social Party in Austria, and the Belgian Catholic Party were now joined by more recent groupings such as the RKSP in the Netherlands, the Italian Partito Popolare (PPI), the Partido Social Popular in Spain, the Christian Democrats in Lithuania, and the Parti Démocrate Populaire and the Fédération Nationale Catholique in France.[67] Political Catholicism was now indisputably a Europe-wide

[64] See pp. 37–9, 75–6, and 191–2; Misner, *Social Catholicism in Europe*.

[65] See p. 231; Mayeur, *Des partis catholiques à la démocratie chrétienne*, 10–11; Diamant, *Austrian Catholics and the First Republic*, 29–30.

[66] See pp. 77, 159–60, 193, and 227; Evans, 'Catholic Political Movements in Germany, Switzerland and the Netherlands', 103.

[67] See pp. 41–6, 77–81, 101–3, and 227–8; K. Von Klemperer, *Ignaz Seipel: Christian Statesman in a*

phenomenon and one which played an increasingly assertive role in parliamentary politics and government.

The upsurge in Catholic political organization also owed much to a new mood of confidence among the Catholic laity. The election of Pius XI in February 1922 brought to the head of the Church a Pope determined that Catholicism should play a more militant role in the modern world. As his initial encyclical, *Ubi Arcano Dei*, published in December 1922 illustrated, he believed that the Catholic faith must assert its ascendancy over the values and structures of State and society.[68] The centrepiece of his programme was the priority which he gave to movements of Catholic Action. Though the term had been used by his predecessors, it was Pius XI who gave great impetus to the development of these movements of the Catholic laity acting under the leadership of the clergy to bring about a recatholicization of modern life. Catholic Action movements were first established in Italy and then spread rapidly to other countries of Europe during the 1920s where they became the focus for the energies of a younger and more militant Catholic laity.[69]

The success of Catholic Action groups was one manifestation of this new mood of Catholic militancy. The rise in participation in pilgrimages, Marian processions, mass rallies, and spiritual associations were all further indications of a more ostentatious, or even triumphal, Catholicism which sought to challenge publicly the secular character of modern life. This Catholic renaissance was not universal. It was always strongest among those younger elements of the Catholic bourgeoisie who, partly as a consequence of the gradual expansion since the late nineteenth century of Catholic secondary and higher education, were influenced most directly by the declarations of the Papacy and of Catholic intellectuals. Universities played a central role in this process. Catholic universities such as those of Nijmegen in the Netherlands, Louvain in Belgium, Salamanca in Spain, and Coimbra in Portugal were often ancient institutions but it was at the end of the nineteenth century that they emerged as a major focus of Catholic intellectual life. They diffused Catholic social and political ideas and served as a focus for the energies of a new generation of Catholic militants. For these young enthusiasts, Catholicism seemed to provide an exclusive source of salvation for the ills of modern society. Nineteenth-century secular ideologies of liberalism, nationalism, and socialism had culminated in the horrors of the First World War and the barbarism of Soviet Russia and only some form of Catholic reconquest of society offered the prospect of a just social and political order.[70]

The impact of this militancy on Catholic political parties was ambivalent. On the

Time of Crisis (Princeton, 1972); V. S. Vardys (ed.), *Lithuania under the Soviets: Portrait of a Nation, 1940–1965* (New York, 1965), 30–2.

[68] Agostino, *Pie XI*, 71–6.

[69] Ibid. 114–18; Holmes, *The Papacy in the Modern World*, 80–1; Pollard, *The Vatican and Italian Fascism*, 5.

[70] Fouilloux, 'Courants de pensée', 117–21; M. Conway, 'Building the Christian City: Catholics and Politics in Inter-War Francophone Belgium', *Past and Present*, 128 (Aug. 1990), 117–27; M. Przeciszewski, 'L'Association catholique de la jeunesse académique "Odrodzenie" (La Renaissance): Aperçu historique', *Revue du Nord*, 70 (1988), 333–47; V. S. Vardys, *The Catholic Church, Dissent and Nationality in Soviet Lithuania* (Boulder, Colo., 1978), 31–6.

one hand, it encouraged Catholics to identify more strongly with their faith and to support its political representatives. On the other hand, there was an underlying tension between the priorities of the leaders of the Catholic political parties and the advocates of a new, more radical Catholicism. Pius XI himself felt that Catholic political parties were outmoded and, after Mussolini's acquisition of power in Italy in 1922, accepted the destruction of the Catholic Popolari as a political force.[71] For him, as for many of the young enthusiasts who rallied to Catholic Action, spiritual campaigns of reconquest were of primary importance and they looked with some disdain on the more modest aims of Catholic political leaders and on the compromises which they were obliged to conclude with non-Catholic political groupings. It was the youth organizations of Catholic political parties which were most directly affected by this mood of alienation among many younger Catholics. Some declined markedly in size, while others drifted towards the authoritarian right.[72]

The spiritual radicalism of these younger figures was not the only challenge faced by Catholic political parties. The general expansion in Catholic associations after the First World War also benefited Catholic working-class movements. The rise in membership of Catholic trade unions and other affiliated organizations as well as the emergence of the Jeunesse Ouvrière Chrétienne provided a new powerful voice for Catholic working-class demands. Some Catholic worker groups broke away to form their own political organizations or to seek alliances with socialist groupings, while Catholic parties tried not always successfully to incorporate Christian democrat aspirations without antagonizing their middle-class and rural electorates. The difficult balancing-act was one which often served to undermine the coherence of the parties, especially in the economic crisis of the early 1930s when working-class demands for employment measures clashed directly with the orthodoxies of financial retrenchment.[73]

Thus, by the 1930s, political Catholicism was both more omnipresent and more fractured than at any point during the previous half-century. The fortunes of Catholic political parties varied. In Belgium and the Netherlands, they remained influential coalition partners in government but elsewhere their influence was threatened not only by internal divisions but by the more general fragility of parliamentary political structures. Mussolini's seizure of power in Italy in 1922 had cut short the expansion of the Popolari in Italy and, though the Lateran Treaties of 1929 guaranteed a certain autonomy for Catholic organizations, Catholic Action groups were frequently the targets of government harassment during the subsequent decade.[74] In Spain, Primo de Rivera's coup in 1923 had similarly cut short parliamentary politics, but his fall from power in 1930 and the subsequent establishment of the Second

[71] See p. 81, Rhodes, *The Vatican in the Age of the Dictators*, 14–15.

[72] e.g. see pp. 109–16 and 200–1; E. L. Evans, *The German Center Party 1870–1933* (Carbondale, Ill., 1981), 256; id., 'Catholic Political Movements in Germany, Switzerland and the Netherlands', 116; J. Beaufays, *Les Partis catholiques en Belgique et aux Pays-Bas* (Brussels, 1973), 393–4 and 433.

[73] See pp. 163–5 and 196–8; Patch, *Christian Trade Unions in the Weimar Republic*; Diamant, *Austrian Catholics and the First Republic*, 91–8.

[74] See pp. 83–4.

Republic created a new impetus for Spanish Catholics to organize in the political domain. This led to the creation of the first mass Catholic Party in Spain, the CEDA, which combined—somewhat awkwardly—participation in a number of the governing coalitions of the Republic with a deep antipathy to its institutions and values.[75] The difficulties faced by Catholic political movements were nowhere more intense than in Germany where, though the Centre Party played a prominent role in the politics of the Weimar Republic, the party never identified fully with the post-war political system. Splits by left- and right-wing groups exacerbated the problems faced by the party which experienced a steady decline in its hold over Catholic political loyalties. The rise of the Nazi Party from the late 1920s onwards presented a further challenge for the party. The Catholic Church and the Centre Party opposed the Nazis both because of their 'pagan' nationalist and racialist ideology and, perhaps above all, because their policies seemed to threaten a return to the anti-Catholic *Kultürkampf* of the 1870s and Catholic electoral support for the Nazi Party was always below the national average. Nevertheless, in some areas, Catholics were attracted by the Nazi rhetoric of economic protest and national regeneration and the Centre Party proved unable to prevent either the Nazi seizure of power in January 1933 or the forced dissolution of the party which occurred soon afterwards.[76]

Perhaps the most significant development in European Catholic politics in the 1930s was the enthusiastic support given by Catholic groupings to the authoritarian regimes established in Portugal and Austria. In both cases, the demise of the democratic regimes was a complex process but one in which Catholic groups played a significant role. In Portugal, Salazar, who became the head of the government in 1932 and who replaced the republican constitution by the authoritarian Estado Novo (New State) in the following year was a young academic from the University of Coimbra who had long been active in Catholic spiritual and political campaigns.[77] In Austria, Dollfuss, the architect of the new non-democratic constitution promulgated in May 1934 was similarly a Catholic political leader whose explicit reliance on papal teachings in his public declarations brought him extravagant praise from Pius XI as well as from numerous Catholic groupings elsewhere in Europe.[78]

Events in Austria and Portugal encouraged Catholic militants throughout Europe impatient to break with the defensive policies adopted by the established Catholic

---

[75] See pp. 110–16; M. Vincent, 'The Spanish Civil War and the Popular Front: The Experience of Salamanca Province', in M. Alexander and H. Graham (eds.), *The French and Spanish Popular Fronts: Comparative Perspectives* (Cambridge, 1989), 79–92.

[76] See pp. 167–171; R. Morsey, *Der Untergang des politischen Katholizismus: Die Zentrumspartei zwischen christlichem Selbstverständnis und 'Nationaler Erhebung' 1932–1933* (Stuttgart, 1977); T. Childers, *The Nazi Voter: The Social Foundations of Nazism in Germany, 1919–1933* (Chapel Hill, NC, 1983), 188–91 and 258–61; O. Heilbronner, 'The Failure that Succeeded: Nazi Party Activity in a Catholic Region in Germany 1929–1932', *Journal of Contemporary History*, 27 (1992), 531–49.

[77] See pp. 133–9; T. Gallagher, *Portugal: A Twentieth Century Interpretation* (Manchester, 1983), 51–110.

[78] F. L. Carsten, *Fascist Movements in Austria: From Schönerer to Hitler* (London, 1977), 229–48; Weinzierl, 'Austria: Church, State, Politics and Ideology', 5–30; Gellott, 'Defending Catholic Interests in the Christian State', 571–89; Rhodes, *The Vatican in the Age of the Dictators*, 148.

parties. The early 1930s was a period of unprecedented volatility in Catholic politics as new groupings came to the fore inspired by opposition to what they perceived to be outmoded democratic parliamentary systems and eager to bring about Catholic-inspired social and political reforms. It was the young and, more especially, students and intellectuals who were to the fore in these movements. Groups such as the Christus Rex (Christ the King) movement led by Léon Degrelle in Belgium, the Blue Shirts in Ireland, the youth groups of the SKVP in Switzerland, and even at this time some of those intellectuals associated with the French periodical *Esprit* were all products of distinct national circumstances but they shared a militant rhetoric of Catholic revolution derived from neo-Thomist theology and papal teachings such as the highly influential encyclical *Quadragesimo Anno* issued by Pius XI in 1931. Their common goal was to bring about a truly Catholic political system which would, they claimed, provide a 'third way' for Europe between the twin evils of liberal democracy and fascist and communist totalitarianism.[79]

How far such Catholic groups constituted a distinct political movement in Europe in the 1930s has been the subject of some historical debate. Writers such as Zeev Sternhell have seen *Esprit* and similar groups in France as manifestations of a unitary fascist phenomenon, while a number of other historians have sought to underline the differences between Catholic radicals and secular movements of the radical right.[80] In fact, much depended inevitably on national circumstances. If events in Austria, for example, conspired to draw a distinct line between Catholic groups and other elements of the non-democratic right, in Spain a shared antipathy to the Second Republic led many Spanish Catholics to ally themselves closely with the emerging coalition of right-wing and fascist groupings which in 1936 supported the National-ist military revolt against the Republic.[81]

Efforts to put forward a distinct Catholic political alternative, did, however, gradually become more difficult during the 1930s. In Austria Dollfuss was assassin-ated in a Nazi-inspired revolt in 1934 while Salazar's regime in Portugal gradually distanced itself from its initial Catholic inspiration.[82] Elsewhere, Nazi persecution of Catholic organizations in Germany gathered pace after 1933, prompting Pius XI to issue the encyclical *Mit brennender Sorge* in 1937 which roundly condemned the ideology and policies of the Third Reich. In Belgium, the Rexist movement reacted to electoral reverses by adopting the trappings of Nazism while in France the election

---

[79] See pp. 47–8, 201–3, and 288–9; Winock, *Histoire politique de la revue 'Esprit'*; R. O. Paxton, 'France: The Church, the Republic and the Fascist Temptation 1922–1945', in Wolff and Hoensch (eds.), *Catholics, the State and the European Radical Right*, 67–91; A. Coutrot, *Un courant de la pensée catholique: L'Hebdomadaire 'Sept' (mars 1934–août 1937)* (Paris, 1961); M. J. Cronin, 'The Blueshirts in Ireland: the movement and its members 1932–5', D. Phil. thesis, Oxford 1994; Ruffieux, *Le Mouvement chrétien-social en Suisse romande*.

[80] Z. Sternhell, *Neither Right nor Left: Fascist Ideology in France* (Berkeley and Los Angeles, 1986); Wolff and Hoensch (eds.), *Catholics, the State and the European Radical Right*; B. Comte, 'Emmanuel Mounier devant Vichy et la Révolution Nationale en 1940–1941: L'Histoire réinterprétée', *Revue d'his-toire de l'Eglise de France*, 71 (1985), 259–62; Conway 'Building the Christian City', 117–51.

[81] See pp. 118–19.

[82] See pp. 138–9, F. L. Carsten, *The First Austrian Republic 1918–1938* (Aldershot, 1986), 212–14.

of the Popular Front government in 1936 restored the traditional battle-lines between the Socialist and Republican supporters of the Third Republic and their right-
wing opponents.[83]

It was the Spanish Civil War which symbolized the problems faced by Catholic
political groupings. The war presented an awkward dilemma for many European
Catholics. Though some Catholics supported the legitimate Republican government, many others—from a wide variety of backgrounds—joined their Spanish co-
believers in giving their tacit or declared support to General Franco's crusade against
atheistic communism.[84] Above all, the Spanish Civil War demonstrated the wider
difficulties faced by all Catholic political movements as they were obliged to choose
between the emerging rival camps of the democratic Western powers and the
German–Italian Axis alliance. As Europe moved towards a general war, any third
way—both in domestic and international politics—was increasingly difficult to find
and Catholics were obliged to choose between two camps neither of which fully
represented their aspirations. The Western powers—France and Britain—symbolized the despised secular values of liberalism while the anticlerical actions of the
German and Italian regimes during the 1930s served to harden Catholic attitudes
throughout Europe against the evils of 'totalitarian' fascism.[85]

Unlike in 1914, the declaration of war in September 1939 was met with little
enthusiasm in Europe. Catholics, in common with the vast majority of their fellow
citizens, rallied behind their governments while hoping that Europe would still be
saved from a return to the horrors of the previous conflict. The Papacy reiterated its
neutrality and sought to act as an intermediary in negotiations between France and
Britain and dissident elements within the Third Reich.[86] Peace, however, could not
be resurrected and the German western offensive in May and June 1940 and the subsequent entry of Italy into the war embroiled most European Catholics (except
neutral Switzerland, Ireland, Spain, and Portugal) in the sufferings—and political
choices—of the war. The rapid and seemingly irreversible German military victory
in the summer of 1940 obliged Catholics in the Low Countries and France to adapt
to the new political situation. In Belgium and the Netherlands, Catholics were prominent in efforts to create new political groupings and institutions which accepted
the reality of German hegemony and sought to introduce a vaguely defined 'New
Order'.[87] A similar pattern of events occurred in France where, despite the trauma of

---

[83] See pp. 54, 174 and 203; Rhodes, *The Vatican in the Age of the Dictators*, 195–210.

[84] J. M. Sanchez, *The Spanish Civil War as a Religious Tragedy* (Notre Dame, 1987); T. Buchanan, *The Spanish Civil War and the British Labour Movement* (Cambridge, 1991), 167–95.

[85] *Re* Catholic hostility to totalitarian fascism, see notably pp. 84–5, 175–6, and 234; Holmes, *The Papacy in the Modern World*, 61 and 65–6; Weinzierl, 'Austria: Church, State, Politics and Ideology', 23–5; A.-R. Michel, 'L'ACJF et les régimes totalitaires dans les années 1930', *Revue d'histoire de l'Église de France*, 73 (1987), 253–62; J. Gergely, 'A Magyarországi Katolikus egyhaz és a fasizmus', *Századok*, 121 (1987), 3–47.

[86] H. C. Deutsch, *The Conspiracy against Hitler in the Twilight War* (Minneapolis, 1968), 106–48 and 331–52; O. Chadwick, *Britain and the Vatican during the Second World War*, 86–100.

[87] See pp. 205 and 233–4.

the national defeat, both the Catholic Church and much of the Catholic laity rallied enthusiastically to the Vichy regime led by Pétain which appeared to offer the prospect of a government more sympathetic to Catholic interests and ideals than the Third Republic.[88]

Nor was it merely in Western Europe that Catholics were active participants in the new political circumstances created by the Nazi military triumphs. If German policies prevented the resurrection of a political process in Poland, elsewhere in Central and Eastern Europe, the war provided the opportunity for Slovakia and Croatia to become independent states under German tutelage. Catholicism had long formed an integral element of the identity of both nations and the Catholic Church and Catholic political figures featured prominently in the new states. In Slovakia, after its declaration of independence from the defunct Czechoslovak state in March 1939, a priest—Mgr. Tiso—became the first head of state and the new official party, the Slovak People's Party, enacted policies derived from an amalgam of Nazi and Catholic principles.[89] In Croatia, the Catholic influence was, if anything, even more emphatic. The new leader, Anton Pavelic, appointed with German support after the Nazi conquest of Yugoslavia in the spring of 1941, declared a constitution based on Catholic principles and the local Church hierarchy, led by Archbishop Stepinac of Zagreb, lent their enthusiastic support to the new regime. Church–State relations subsequently cooled but Pavelic was nevertheless received privately by Pius XII in May 1941 and Catholic activists remained prominent figures within his regime.[90]

Catholic support for the regimes of Slovakia and Croatia proved durable, but elsewhere in German-Occupied Europe Catholics soon retreated from participation in the efforts to construct a 'New Order' Europe. Their actions in 1940 had been based on the twin premisses that the war was to all intents and purposes at an end and that the Third Reich was willing to allow a certain degree of political freedom to the defeated populations. In the event, neither of these proved to be the case. The German failure to defeat Britain and the subsequent invasion of the Soviet Union in June 1941 revealed that the outcome of the war was far from certain while German actions in the Occupied territories demonstrated that plunder and repression were the principal determinants of Nazi policy. In these circumstances, political action seemed to be neither desirable nor necessary and Catholic participation in programmes of New Order political reform in Belgium and the Netherlands came to an end. Even in France, the Vichy regime proved to be a disappointment for Catholic hopes. Though Pétain's regime made much of its symbolic commitment to Catholic values, it proved to be a diffuse amalgam of different political tendencies, not all of which were

---

[88] See pp. 55–7; R. Bédarida, 'La Hiérarchie catholique', in J.-P. Azéma and F. Bédarida (eds.), *Vichy et les Français* (Paris, 1992), 444–62; N. Atkin, *Church and Schools in Vichy France 1940–1944* (New York, 1991); J. Hellman, *The Knight-Monks of Vichy France: Uriage 1940–1945* (Montreal, 1993).

[89] Y. Jelinek, *The Parish Republic: Hlinka's Slovak People's Party 1939–1945* (New York, 1976).

[90] S. Alexander, 'Croatia: The Catholic Church and Clergy 1919–1945', in Wolff and Hoensch (eds.), *Catholics, the State and the European Radical Right*, 31–66; Rhodes, *The Vatican in the Age of the Dictators*, 323–36.

sympathetic to Catholic interests. Support for Pétain always remained strong but Catholic attitudes towards the Vichy government had become more circumspect by 1941 and hardened markedly in subsequent years as the regime became primarily an agent of pro-Nazi collaboration.[91]

Despite the German attack in June 1941 on atheist Bolshevism as represented by the Soviet Union, instances of Catholic support for the Nazi cause during the latter years of the war were isolated. The Nazi crusade against Bolshevism did lead some to see a German military victory as essential for the survival of the Catholic faith. Though Spain did not formally ally itself with the Axis powers, Franco provided various forms of assistance to Germany and Spanish volunteers fought on the Eastern Front.[92] In Belgium, the pro-German Flemish Nationalists of the Vlaams Nationaal Verbond and the Rexist movement led by Léon Degrelle rallied some Catholic support while in France Catholic militants such as Philippe Henriot, the Vichy regime's influential Minister of Propaganda, and Paul Touvier, the head of the pro-German Milice in Lyon, bore witness to the tortuous path which led some erstwhile advocates of militant Catholicism to support for the Nazi cause.[93] These examples were, however, greatly outweighed by the instances of Catholics who were gradually drawn towards active opposition to Nazism. Catholic Resistance was a diffuse phenomenon which incorporated many different trends, some of which were more concerned to pre-empt Communist revolution than to defeat Nazism. But in the latter war years a wide range of Catholic groups emerged throughout Occupied Europe (as well as in Italy and to a limited extent in Germany) which sought to counter the actions and values of the Third Reich. Priests and laity participated in acts of individual valour protecting Resistance fighters, Catholic worker organizations were to the fore in efforts to help workers threatened with deportation to Germany while Catholic intellectuals participated in the burgeoning clandestine press.[94]

More significant, perhaps, than these actions was the change in political mentality which they represented. The sufferings of the war and experience of Nazi oppression destroyed much of the appeal which projects of authoritarian political reform had exercised over many Catholic militants during the previous twenty years. The notion of a true Catholic state in the mould of Dollfuss's Austria or Salazar's Portugal lost its charm and in its place the war years witnessed a renewed Catholic interest in democratic and participatory political structures. This change also reflected an evolution in the purposes of Catholic political action. If much of Catholic involvement in politics since the late nineteenth century had been devoted either to the protection of specific Catholic interests or to the achievement of a distinctly Catholic political order,

---

[91] See pp. 57–8; E. Fouilloux, 'Le Clergé', in Azéma and Bédarida (eds.), *Vichy et les Français*, 469–70; J. Duquesne, *Les Catholiques français sous l'occupation* (2nd edn. Paris, 1986), 111–82.

[92] P. Preston, *Franco: A Biography* (London, 1993), 374–450.

[93] See p. 205; M. Conway, *Collaboration in Belgium: Léon Degrelle and the Rexist Movement 1940–1944* (New Haven, 1993); H. R. Kedward, 'The Vichy of the Other Philippe', in G. Hirschfeld and P. Marsh (eds.), *Collaboration in France: Politics and Culture during the Nazi Occupation 1940–1944* (Oxford, 1989), 32–46; R. Rémond et al., *Paul Touvier et l'Église* (Paris, 1992).

[94] See e.g. pp. 57–9 and 84–5.

the Second World War encouraged a new openness in Catholic political attitudes. Especially among Catholic worker organizations and those intellectuals and other elements of the Catholic laity who participated in Resistance organizations, notions of the protection of a Catholic ghetto or of an offensive, triumphalist Catholicism gave way to a willingness to work with non-Catholic elements in a pluralist society in which Catholicism's influence would be more indirect but also perhaps more pervasive.

This change in the purposes and spirit of Catholic political action undoubtedly helped to lay the basis for the remarkable flowering of Christian Democrat political parties which occurred in much of Western Europe during the years following the Second World War. It would, however, be wrong to exaggerate the extent of this change. Geographically, it was limited to the Catholic heartlands of Western Europe. In Eastern Europe, the events of the Second World War and the predominant role of the Soviet Union created a very different political situation and one which was much less favourable to Christian democracy[95] while in Great Britain and the Irish Republic Catholicism remained deprived of direct political representation. Nor did Christian democracy spread to the Iberian peninsula—isolated from the effects of the war by the decision of Spain and Portugal to remain neutral—where Catholic political attitudes remained for the most part frozen in the triumphalist mentality fostered by the reliance of the regimes of Franco and Salazar on the trappings and structures of the Catholic faith to protect themselves against internal and external opposition.[96]

Nor should the extent of the change wrought in Catholic mentalities within Western Europe during the war years be overestimated. If some Catholics emerged from the war with a new willingness to collaborate with non-Catholic political groupings, the events of the war also served to reinforce more traditional Catholic attitudes. The rise in religious practice amidst the chaos and dangers of war encouraged a mood of religious optimism in which the Catholic faith once again seemed to offer the sole remedy to the evils of the modern age. The mood of spiritual crusade and reconquest spilled over into the immediate post-war years, fuelling a marked upsurge in pilgrimages, parades, and movements devoted to the Virgin Mary.[97] This also owed much to enhanced Catholic fears of atheistic communism in the ensuing Cold War. Both on an international level and within the domestic politics of countries such as France and Italy, Communist parties built upon their role in the anti-German resistance to emerge as a powerful political force after the liberation. Catholic fears of a Soviet invasion or of a Communist-inspired domestic uprising were a dominant feature of the post-war years and, strongly encouraged both by the Papacy and by national

[95] See, notably, M. Osa, 'Resistance, Persistance and Change: The Transformation of the Catholic Church in Poland', *Eastern European Politics and Societies*, 3 (1989), 268–99.

[96] See pp. 120–6 and 139–51.

[97] See p. 177; S. Laury, 'Le Culte marial dans le Pas-de-Calais (1938–1948)', *Revue d'histoire de la deuxième guerre mondiale et des conflits contemporains*, 128 (1992), 23–47; J.-D. Durand, *L'Église catholique dans la crise de l'Italie (1943–1948)* (Rome, 1991), 250–75; Perry and Echeverria, *Under the Heel of Mary*, 236–8.

ecclesiastical hierarchies, served to foster a defensive mentality among Catholic political groupings.[98]

Thus, fears of atheistic communism and the upsurge in religious devotion brought
about by the war were just as much features of Catholic wartime experience as were
the new ideas of Christian democracy. In these circumstances, it is therefore perhaps
not surprising that the Second World War failed to prove to be a decisive watershed
in the development of political Catholicism. Much did indeed change as a consequence of the war. The social, political, and ideological transformations it brought
about (or for which it served as a catalyst) inevitably had an impact both upon the
Catholic faith and its political expression. This was particularly so in the immediate
post-war years when innovations such as the 'worker-priest' movement in France
and Belgium and the left-wing Christian democrat groups in Germany and Italy appeared to herald a decisive break with the conservative affiliations of many European
Catholics.[99] But, with the gradual consolidation of the post-war political order and
the integration of the states of Western Europe into Cold War alliances, so more
traditional mentalities came to the fore and set the tone of Catholic political action
during the late 1940s and the 1950s.

This was particularly evident in the course followed by the Christian Democrat
parties of Western Europe. These marked in many respects a decisive new development in Catholic politics. The Christian Democrats of Germany and Italy, the
CVP/PSC in Belgium, and, perhaps most strikingly, the Mouvement Républicain
Populaire (MRP) in France were new political creations often founded by a younger
generation of Catholic figures whose political attitudes had been forged by the experiences of the war years. They broke with both the defensive separatist mentality
of the long-established Catholic parties and with the authoritarian Catholic tempta-
tions of the inter-war years in favour of a new personalist ideology which embraced a
democratic political system and a social market economy of free enterprise combined
with state intervention and enhanced welfare provision. In Germany, this change
was all the more radical because the new Christian Democrat Party was a cross-
confessional party, incorporating both Protestant and Catholic militants. This new
political programme was accompanied by a new attitude towards the Catholic
Church. Rather than presenting themselves as the defenders in the political sphere
of the Catholic Church, the new parties consciously stressed their independence
from clerical guidance and declared their wish to win the support of all voters regardless of their confessional or social background.[100]

These parties enjoyed considerable electoral success. In France, the MRP won
28.2 per cent of the vote in the elections of 1946, while in Germany, Italy, and Belgium, the Christian Democrats had established themselves by the end of the 1940s as

[98] *Re* the Papacy, see L. Papeleux, 'Le Vatican et l'expansion du communisme (1944–1945)', *Revue
d'histoire de la deuxième guerre mondiale et des conflits contemporains*, 137 (1985), 63–84; Durand *L'Église
catholique*, 373–404.

[99] See pp. 64–6, 85–6, and 178–9; O. L. Arnal, *Priests in Working-Class Blue: The History of the Worker
Priests (1943–1954)* (New York, 1986); Durand, *L'Église catholique*, 583–8.

[100] See pp. 59–64, 86–8, 178–85, and 207–9.

the largest single party and the dominant party of government. In part, this success was due to their policies which in the years after the liberation responded to the widely felt desire for social and political change. There were, however, other reasons for their broad appeal. Fear of a Communist revolution led many middle-class voters—regardless of their religious background—to see in the Christian Democrat parties the most effective guardian of their material interests. This was reinforced by the absence from the post-war political stage of many of the pre-war parties of the right. Discredited by their involvement in fascist or authoritarian adventures, the demise of these parties left many voters in post-war Europe without a political home. The Christian Democrats, with their marked anti-communism and commitment to private property, were the obvious point of refuge for these voters, prompting their left-wing opponents to accuse them of depending on the votes of erstwhile fascists. Finally, the support of the Catholic Church also contributed to Christian Democrat success. For all their protestations of autonomy, the parties benefited considerably from the Church's instructions to the faithful to vote for Christian Democratic parties, most notably in Italy where the Papacy used its considerable resources to the full to ensure Communist defeat and Christian Democrat success in the decisive parliamentary elections of 1948.[101]

Initial expectations that the Christian Democrats would be the agents of a programme of Catholic-inspired wide-ranging social and political reforms were therefore disappointed. Except in France, where the MRP went into rapid electoral decline after the elections of 1951, the Christian Democrat parties established themselves as parties of government, devoted to a Cold War political agenda of capitalist economics and defence of Western Europe against the Soviet Union. Only their commitment to the process of limited European integration, in which the Catholic political leaders De Gasperi, Adenauer, and Robert Schuman played a prominent though far from determinant role, remained as an indication of their initial reforming agenda.[102] The momentum of domestic reforms rapidly evaporated, provoking a mood of often bitter disappointment among Catholic trade unions and other working-class Catholic organizations. Instead, in matters of domestic policy, the Christian Democrat parties of the 1950s became advocates of a moderate conservatism or came to rely on the traditional Catholic rallying-calls of the defence of the Church and its institutions against the supposed anticlerical ambitions of liberal and socialist parties.[103]

This reorientation of the Christian Democrat parties was not, however, without its difficulties. Minority groups within all of the parties continued to press for them to adopt more radical agendas. More generally, the parties had difficulty in maintaining the support of an increasingly sophisticated and assertive Catholic electorate. Though Pius XII continued to present a vision of a hierarchical Catholic community,

---

[101] See p. 87; Durand, *L'Église catholique*, 641–94.

[102] P. Chenaux, *Une Europe Vaticane?* (Brussels, 1990).

[103] See pp. 209–13; G. Pridham, *Christian Democracy in Western Germany: The CDU/CSU in Government and Opposition, 1945–1976* (London, 1977), 56–104; R. Leonardi and D. A. Wertman, *Italian Christian Democracy: The Politics of Dominance* (London, 1989), 54–69.

it was one which was at variance with the reality of the more diverse and integrated society emerging in much of Western Europe. Despite the substantial network of Catholic confessional social and cultural institutions, it was impossible to maintain the separateness of the Catholic population. The rapid pace of social and geographical mobility, the unprecedented rise in living standards in much of Europe during the 1950s and the new educational and professional opportunities which economic development provided were all changes which undermined the homogeneity of Catholic communities with the consequence that the maintenance of a single Catholic political identity came to seem increasingly artificial.[104]

The death of Pius XII in 1958 and the decision of his successor John XXIII to summon the Second Vatican Council (1962–5) led to far-reaching theological and ecclesiastical innovations which inevitably had considerable consequences for the nature of political Catholicism. It would be wrong, however, to attribute all the responsibility for the changes which took place in Catholic political action during the 1960s to the impact of the Second Vatican Council. Though the Council's impact on the faithful was immense,[105] it was only one factor among several. At the heart of the transformations of the 1960s remained the driving-force of social and economic change which continued to erode Catholic distinctiveness and also led to a marked and sustained decline in levels of religious practice in many European countries.[106] This was reinforced by wider political changes which saw new political forces emerge and which prompted many liberal and socialist parties to abandon their anticlerical heritage. Deprived of their traditional adversaries, the forces of political Catholicism no longer possessed the same rationale for their own existence.

The impact of the Second Vatican Council was most evident in the change which it brought about in the attitudes of the ecclesiastical hierarchy towards Catholic political parties. Though John XXIII's successor, Paul VI, was in many respects a conservative figure who remained strongly supportive of the Italian Christian Democrat party, the dominant trend was for the clergy to abandon their efforts to direct the political action of the faithful. The bishops in the Netherlands and Belgium, for example, no longer instructed Catholics to vote for the 'official' Catholic party while even in Spain and Portugal a new generation of younger bishops and clergy, strongly influenced by the reforms of the Second Vatican Council, began to disentangle the Catholic Church from its close bonds with the Salazar and Franco dictatorships.[107] Even the hostility of the Papacy and of the Church towards communism began to give way to a more conciliatory posture. Concordats were signed with a number of East European states and in the 1970s the Italian Christian Democrats were drawn towards a historic compromise with the Communist Party.[108]

---

104 See e.g. U. Altermatt, *Katholizismus und Moderne*, 161–4.   105 See pp. 17–18.

106 See pp. 93 and 215; McLeod, *Religion and the People of Western Europe*, 134–5.

107 See pp. 126–8, 151–3, 216–17, and 245; J. A. Coleman, *The Evolution of Dutch Catholicism 1958–1974* (Berkeley and Los Angeles, 1978); P. Hebblethwaite, *Paul VI: The First Modern Pope* (London, 1993).

108 H.-J. Stehle, *Eastern Politics of the Vatican 1917–1979* (Ohio, 1981); P. Ginsborg, *A History of Contemporary Italy: Society and Politics 1943–1988* (London, 1990), 354–8.

This 'liberation' of the laity led to a flowering of new forms of Catholic political action. Socio-cultural organizations such as Catholic trade unions and youth organizations broke away and forged their own political allegiances, while Christian Democrat parties were obliged to seek new secular identities. Those that failed to do so—such as the MRP in France—disappeared, while others—such as the German, Dutch, and Belgian Christian Democrat parties—continued to prosper, thanks to a broad coalition of largely middle-class and rural voters. Though Catholic influences remained evident in their social and cultural policies, these parties were no longer primarily Catholic in inspiration or composition. Instead they gradually became predominantly centrist parties, committed to capitalist economics, welfare provision and European integration.[109]

Thus, the political, social, and economic changes which took place during the 1960s brought about the demise of the model of political Catholicism which had developed in Europe since the late nineteenth century. The Church no longer sought to control Catholic political activities while the laity no longer saw any automatic connection between their Catholic faith and a particular political allegiance. This in no sense indicated that Catholicism had withdrawn from the political realm. The Church continued to speak out on matters of particular concern, such as legislation on birth-control, while Catholic political movements and individuals remained prominent in European political life. What did largely disappear was the notion of political parties devoted to the defence of the particular interests and values of Catholicism. Instead, a new—and perhaps more truly Christian democrat—vision emerged of Catholics working as an active influence within a range of non-Catholic parties and movements. A particular form of political Catholicism had gone but the intimate connection between Catholicism and politics remained.

[109] Whyte, *Catholics in Western Democracies*, 100–11; R. E. M. Irving, *The Christian Democratic Parties of Western Europe* (London, 1979), 253–60.

1

France

JAMES F. McMILLAN

At the beginning of the twentieth century, the great majority of French Catholics were conservatives of one hue or another. Many still hankered after traditional monarchy. Others were neo-royalists, supporting the Action Française, the royalist, anti-republican, anti-Semitic, and virulently nationalist league founded at the time of the Dreyfus Affair. Headed by Charles Maurras, who was himself a non-believer, it nevertheless attracted Catholic support because of its outspoken defence of the Church's claims to a privileged place in national life in the face of anticlerical attempts to create a secular state and social order. Only a minority of French Catholics heeded Pope Leo XIII's appeal in the early 1890s to rally to the Republic in the movement known as the *ralliement*, which by the early 1900s was represented politically by the Action Libérale Populaire, a republican but still conservative party led by Jacques Piou and Albert de Mun.

Between the end of the First World War and the opening of the Second Vatican Council, however, the close link between Catholicism and traditional right-wing politics was broken. By 1960 not only had Catholics come to embrace the principle of political pluralism but it was even possible to discern the advent of a new Catholic left as a significant element on the French political scene. Developments in political Catholicism were not solely responsible for this transformation, but they played a crucial role. Hence the emphasis in this chapter on the opening to the left, particularly in the inter-war period. Building on the solid foundations laid in the years before 1914, the years 1919–39 can be seen in retrospect as a watershed, more so than the period after 1940.[1]

At the same time, however, it is hoped to show that the equation between Catholicism and conservatism itself requires to be nuanced. The alliance was never as straightforward as it appeared, since on the Catholic side it was prompted less by

[1] The best treatments of French political Catholicism are R. W. Rauch, Jr., *Politics and Belief in Contemporary France: Emmanuel Mounier and Christian Democracy, 1932–1950* (The Hague, 1972) and J. M. Mayeur, *Des partis catholiques à la démocratie chrétienne, XIXᵉ–XXᵉ siècle* (Paris, 1980). A. Dansette, *Destin du catholicisme français 1926–1956* (Paris, 1957) remains valuable, as does R. Rémond's contribution to A. Latreille (ed.), *Histoire du catholicisme en France*, ii (Paris, 1962). See also F. Dreyfus, *Les Forces religieuses dans la société française* (Paris, 1965) and the work of E. Poulat, esp. *Église contre bourgeoisie: Introduction au devenir du catholicisme actuel* (Paris, 1977). For the wider religious background, the standard overview is now G. Cholvy and Y.-M. Hilaire, *Histoire religieuse de la France contemporaine*, 3 vols. (Toulouse, 1985–8), though the 19th cent. is well served in English by R. Gibson, *A Social History of French Catholicism 1789–1914* (London, 1989).

common social and economic goals than by a religious outlook which identified the Republican and Socialist left as the enemies of the Church. If French political Catholicism was distinguished by its diversity, one thing all its adepts shared was an attachment to the principle of *catholicisme d'abord*—Catholicism first and foremost. Unlike the Action Française, which preached the doctrine of *politique d'abord*, political Catholics were people who put their religion first.[2]

The feature of French political Catholicism which distinguishes it from the experience of most other countries of Catholic Europe was its failure to develop the kind of mass Catholic Party to be found in, say, Belgium, Italy, or Spain. There was no Catholic Centre Party, or Zentrum, as was the case in Germany. Only the MRP, the Christian democrat party founded at the end of the Second World War, ever looked as if it might assume the role of a mass Catholic Party, and then only for a brief moment. Instead, in France, political Catholicism came in many different shapes and sizes. In one guise, it might be predominantly a movement of religious defence, as was the case of the Fédération Nationale Catholique (FNC) between the wars. More significantly, it manifested itself as Christian democracy, represented in party-political terms by the Parti Démocrate Populaire (PDP) and the Jeune République (JR) in the 1920s and 1930s before flowering as the MRP after 1944. In the French case, however, it needs to be stressed that Christian democracy embraced a wide variety of Catholic social organizations, including trade unions, workers' associations, and youth groups, in addition to political parties. Thus the Confédération Française du Travail Catholique (CFTC), the Action Catholique de la Jeunesse Française (ACJF), and the Jeunesse Ouvrière Chrétienne (JOC) are as vital to the story of Christian democracy in France as the foundation of the PDP, the JR, or even of the MRP. A further constituent element of French political Catholicism was the activity of Catholic intellectuals and journalists, who helped to define and to diffuse doctrines of political action inspired by Christian principles. Figures such as Emmanuel Mounier, Francisque Gay, and Robert Cornilleau, along with reviews such as *Sept* and *Esprit* and newspapers like *L'Aube*, *La Vie catholique*, and *Le Petit Démocrate* all helped to shape the form taken by French political Catholicism in the mid-twentieth century.

The absence of a Catholic Party in France owed much to the historic divisions between left and right which dated from the time of the French Revolution and which, at the end of the nineteenth century, were expressed primarily in terms of a conflict over religion. Anticlerical Republicans, in pursuit of their ideal of the secular state (the *état laïc*), passed a series of anticlerical laws in the 1880s (the *lois laïques*) and renewed their attack on the Church in the early 1900s, the culmination of their efforts being the Law of 1905 which separated Church and State. Catholics and conservatives, for their part, refused to accept the 'godless' Republic but were fearful of forming an overtly clerical party which they thought might encourage their opponents to even greater excesses. Many therefore continued to defend the ideal of an alliance of

---

[2] An interesting exploration of this theme is Y. Tranvouez, *Catholiques d'abord: Approches du mouvement catholique en France XIXe–XXe siècle* (Paris, 1988).

Throne and Altar, which allowed the Royalists to claim that they were the Catholic Party in France.

Moreover, if Catholics liked to imagine their country as one of the most favoured and fervent of Christian nations, 'the eldest daughter of the Church', the reality was that France was much less Catholic than they made out. In consequence, the potential support for a Catholic Party was nowhere near as great as its proponents supposed. Levels of religious practice varied considerably, according to region, gender, and social class.[3] Throughout the nineteenth century and into the twentieth century, there were areas which were more or less dechristianized. The countryside around Paris, the Centre, the Limousin, and the Charentes were all places where at best 15 per cent of the population of both sexes fulfilled their obligation to confess and receive communion at least once a year at Eastertime. The situation was only marginally better along the Mediterranean littoral. By contrast, in the mountain villages of the Massif Central, in Brittany, French Flanders, Alsace-Lorraine, the Franche-Comté, the Basque country, and the area around Lyons, religious observance was high. Thus at Saint-Brieuc in Brittany some 95 per cent of the adult population of both sexes went to confession and received the sacrament at Easter in 1912. In class terms, apart from the peasants of such areas of fervent Catholicism, it was aristocrats and bourgeois who were regular church-goers, rather than workers, though it is important not to exaggerate the extent of working-class dechristianization by concentrating attention exclusively on the radical artisans of the cities and the metal-workers of the Paris 'Red Belt' to the ...glect, say, of the more pious textile workers of the Nord and Alsace. Without exception, however, whether in Christian or dechristianized areas, women were more visible than men in Church-related activities. Thus in 1900 in dechristianized Chartres only 1.5 per cent of men and 15 per cent of women made their Easter Duties, while in Nantes the comparable figures were 82.4 per cent and 95.7 per cent. Since under the Third Republic all French women were denied the vote, their commitment to Catholicism could not be translated into any political advantage at the ballot box for a Catholic Party like the Action Libérale Populaire. In general, the cause of the Church was not a banner to which the masses were likely to flock in a society where indifference to religion was widespread. Overall, around 1900, only about 25 per cent of the adult population could be counted as practising Catholics, the majority of them women.

1. Origins

It is impossible to understand twentieth-century political Catholicism in France without some appreciation of its roots in nineteenth-century French 'social Catholicism'. The term denotes the doctrines, programmes, and methods adopted by Catholics to address the 'social question'—the complex of problems emanating from the advent of industrialization and a liberal capitalist state—in the light of the social

---

[3] This paragraph is based on Gibson, *Social History* and Cholvy and Hilaire, *Histoire religieuse*, ii. 171–218.

teaching of the Church.[4] Social Catholicism had its beginnings in the period before 1848, when such figures as Frédéric Ozanam and Buchez formed a minority democratic wing alongside the more traditionalist, paternalist, and hierarchical organizations set up by the likes of Villeneuve-Bargemont and Armand de Melun. By the third quarter of the nineteenth century, the conservative strain clearly predominated. A crucial influence was the social theory of Frédéric Le Play (1806–82), which stressed the fundamental importance to society of both religion and the patriarchal extended family (*famille souche*). His counter-revolutionary thought encouraged activists such as Albert de Mun, who founded the Œuvre des cercles catholiques d'ouvriers in 1871 and the Action Catholique de la Jeunesse Française (ACJF) in 1886. The former were study clubs intended to reconcile workers and the upper-class élites by working for the resuscitation of an idealized Christian corporate society. The latter aimed at the reconversion of youth to Catholic Christianity through the formation of a spiritual élite. In addition, Catholic industrialists like Léon Harmel, Augustin Cochin, and Benoist d'Azy pioneered various welfare schemes for their own employees.

In France, as elsewhere, publication of Leo XIII's famous encyclical *Rerum Novarum* in 1891 gave a massive boost to a wide range of social Catholic initiatives.[5] Among the more significant was the creation of a French Catholic trade-union movement, which prepared the ground for what in 1919 became the CFTC. New organizations were founded to diffuse social Catholic doctrine: for example the Jesuit Action Populaire, started in 1903, and the Semaines sociales, created in 1904 as a kind of summer school for social Catholic militants. Also important in this regard was the role of a social Catholic press, best represented by the *Chronique sociale de France*, edited from Lyons. One particularly noteworthy feature of turn-of-the-century French social Catholicism was the active participation of women, who founded their own study circles such as Jeanne Chenu's Action Sociale de la Femme, workers' settlements, *colonies de vacances* and, in 1911, an École Normale Sociale to train an élite of social Catholic women.[6]

As in Belgium, one of the most striking developments of the 1890s was the rise of Christian democracy.[7] In France, this was hailed as the 'second Christian democracy',

---

[4] The standard histories of French social Catholicism are J. B. Duroselle, *Les Débuts du catholicisme social en France (1822–1871)* (Paris, 1951) and H. Rollet, *L'Action sociale des catholiques en France*, 2 vols. (Paris, 1951–8), but they need to be supplemented by J. M. Mayeur, *Catholicisme social et démocratie chrétienne: Principes romains, expériences françaises* (Paris, 1986), which argues for the wider definition of social Catholicism adopted here.

[5] On *Rerum Novarum*, see P. Furlong and D. Curtis (eds.), *The Church Faces the Modern World: Rerum Novarum and its Impact* (Winteringham, 1993) and J. M. Mayeur, 'Aux origines de l'enseignement social de l'Église sous Léon XIII', in *Catholicisme social et démocratie chrétienne*, 47–65.

[6] J. F. McMillan, 'Women in Social Catholicism in Late Nineteenth and Early Twentieth-Century France', in W. J. Sheils and D. Wood (eds.), *Studies in Church History*, xxvii. *Women in the Church* (Oxford, 1990), 467–80; S. Fayet-Scribe, *Associations féminines et catholicisme: De la charité à l'action sociale XIXe–XXe siècle* (Paris, 1990).

[7] See in general M. Montuclard, *Conscience religieuse et démocratie: La Deuxième Démocratie chrétienne en France, 1891–1902* (Paris, 1965) and R. Rémond, *Les Deux Congrès ecclésiastiques de Reims et de Bourges*

the first being that associated with the Catholic utopian reformers of 1848. Essentially, turn-of-the-century Christian democracy was one particular manifestation of the wider phenomenon of social Catholicism, representing that section of the movement which wished to foster the growth of social democracy, and in some cases, political democracy. Prominent among its adherents was a new generation of clerics soon known as the *abbés démocrates*, who became passionately involved in not just social but also political issues. Two of their number, the abbé Lemire and the abbé Gayraud, were elected to the Chamber of Deputies.[8] In 1896 the nascent movement founded a Christian democratic party at Reims. At the same time, a younger generation of lay Catholics was encouraged to break with the traditionalist conceptions of the *cercles* and to launch more radical initiatives, the most daring of which was Marc Sangnier's Sillon, founded in 1899.[9] The overtly political orientation of such groups troubled both integrist Catholics in France and the Holy See. In his encyclical *Graves de communi* of 1901, Pope Leo XIII sternly pointed out that the term 'democracy' should in no way imply any particular kind of regime. Rather, 'Christian democracy' meant only 'beneficial Christian action among the people'. As one Silloniste pointed out, it was therefore possible to be a Christian democrat without being a democrat.[10] It was because of its continuing commitment to political democracy and to religious pluralism that the Sillon was condemned by Rome in 1910.

Defeated in the short term, the second Christian democracy, and in particular the Sillon, left their mark on subsequent developments. The precise influence of the Sillon remains difficult to quantify because, as Sangnier insisted, the group was first and foremost a friendship. But, even if serious internal divisions arose on account of Sangnier's over-masterful personality, few who passed through its ranks remained unaffected by the extraordinary openness, enthusiasm, and generosity of spirit which they encountered. The Sillon also awakened a sense of mission and, as will be seen, experience of militancy in the group was often a formative one for many of the partisans of French political Catholicism in the years after the First World War.[11] The condemnation of 1910 by no means put an end to Sangnier's own commitment to Christian democracy. In 1912 he founded the Ligue de la Jeune République to carry on where Sillon had left off and succeeded in reviving much of the latter's familial atmosphere and mystique. Deliberately refusing to turn itself into a conventional political party, Jeune République viewed itself as a league for the promotion of

(1896–1900) (Paris, 1964). For the account of a participant, see also P. Dabry, *Les Catholiques républicains: Histoire et souvenirs, 1890–1903* (Paris, 1905).

   8 On the abbé Lemire, see J.-M. Mayeur, *Un prêtre démocrate, L'abbé Lemire, 1853–1928* (Paris, 1968).
   9 J. Caron, *Le Sillon et la démocratie chrétienne, 1894–1910* (Paris, 1967); J. de Fabrègues, *Le Sillon de Marc Sangnier* (Paris, 1964); M. Barthélemy-Madaule, *Marc Sangnier (1873–1950)* (Paris, 1973); M. Launay, 'La Crise du *Sillon* dans l'été 1905', *Revue historique*, 245 (1971), 393–426.
   10 R. W. Rauch, Jr., 'From the *Sillon* to the *Mouvement Républicain Populaire*: Doctor Robert Cornilleau and a Generation of Christian Democrats in France, 1910–1940', *Catholic Historical Review*, 58 (1972), 25–66.
   11 Among the witnesses to the formative influence of the *Sillon* are E. Pezet, *Chrétiens au service de la cité, de Leon XIII au Sillon et au MRP* (Paris, 1965) and Raymond-Laurent, *Le Parti Démocrate Populaire 1924–1944: La Politique intérieure et extérieure de la France 1919–1939* (Le Mans, 1965).

civic education with the objective of liberating France from old-style party politics and rivalries and ending the dichotomy 'between the morality of public and private life'. For Sangnier and Georges Hoog, his faithful lieutenant and secretary-general of the League, the formation of citizens was more important than winning elections, but it is worth noting that the JR advocated a programme of advanced reforms which included proportional representation, women's suffrage, the adoption of the British system for the dissolution of parliament, and the referendum.[12]

Another achievement of the pre-1914 period which laid the groundwork for later developments was the creation of a Catholic press of Christian democratic tendencies. By far the most important organ was *L'Ouest-Eclair*, founded by the abbé Trochu and Désgrées du Loû, the son of an old Breton noble family who was galvanised into political action by Leo XIII's call for a *ralliement* to the Republic and who campaigned on behalf of Christian democracy in the west of France.[13] A collaborator on, and future editor of, the paper was Henri Teitgen (1882–1969), who before moving to Brittany had been active in the Sillon in his native Lorraine. His name alone is indicative of the continuities between pre-First World War Christian democracy and the full flowering of French political Catholicism in the post-Second World War period. Also significant for the future was *Le Petit Démocrate de Saint-Denis*, a weekly started in 1912 by Robert Cornilleau, a former Silloniste from Le Mans, which would become the unofficial party newspaper of the PDP in the 1920's.[14]

It remains true, however, that both before and after 1914 France had no Catholic Party. Not even the anticlerical onslaught of the left in the early years of the twentieth century, which finally ended the century-old Concordat between Church and State in 1905, succeeded in bringing Catholics together in a single political grouping. Some of the reasons for this have already been suggested. Papal opposition was undoubtedly a factor: Albert de Mun's attempt to form a Catholic Party in 1885 had been blocked by Leo XIII,[15] while Pius X, obsessed with threats to orthodoxy both from within and without the Church, tolerated only movements which were devoted either to the defence of religion or to spiritual ends, and only then when they were subject to the control of the hierarchy. Some French bishops tried to establish the kind of diocesan unions which the pontiff favoured, but without much success.

The nearest approximation to a Catholic Party in the pre-war period was the Action Libérale Populaire, founded in 1902 with the aim of continuing Leo XIII's *ralliement* and of combating the anticlerical legislation introduced by the united forces of the Left in the early twentieth century. Led by Albert de Mun in the Chamber of Deputies and organized nationally by Jacques Piou, the party benefited financially from 'laundered' funds from dissolved religious orders and by the end of 1904 had a membership of 160,000 divided among some 700 local committees. It also

---

[12] Rauch, *Politics and Belief*, 28–32; G. Hoog, *Histoire, doctrine, action de la 'Jeune-République'* (Paris, 1925).

[13] P. Delourme, *Trente-cinq années de politique religieuse ou l'histoire de 'l'Ouest-Eclair'* (Paris, 1936).

[14] Rauch, 'From the *Sillon* to the *Mouvement Républicain Populaire*'.

[15] H. Rollet, *Albert de Mun et le Parti catholique* (Paris, 1947).

received valuable support from Catholic women, in particular from those who were members of the Ligue Patriotique des Françaises. After the Separation Law of 1905, the party was disappointed to win only sixty-four seats in the elections of 1906. At the height of the struggle between Church and State, it was evident that, except in the most Catholic and conservative areas of the country, the electorate was not ready to support a party that was seen to be too confessional and 'clerical'. Nevertheless, for the first time under the Third Republic the French Chamber of Deputies contained in its midst a significant group of Catholic deputies.[16]

2. Between Two Wars

Some historians view the inter-war period as a 'second *ralliement*', a time of reconciliation between French Catholics and the modern world which carried on and completed the work first begun by Pope Leo XIII in the 1890s.[17] Certainly, there were encouraging signs of abatement in the religious quarrels which had been inherited from the nineteenth century and which had bedevilled relations between Catholics and Republicans in the pre-war period. During the First World War itself, despite the 'infamous rumour' put about by anticlericals accusing Pope Benedict XV of being a secret supporter of the Central Powers, Catholics had rallied loyally to the Union Sacrée. More than 30,000 priests served in the armed forces, not just as chaplains or stretcher-bearers but as fighting men. Many members of the religious orders, expelled from their country by the laws passed against the congregations between 1901 and 1904, returned voluntarily to enlist.[18] In the immediate aftermath of the war, in the elections of 1919, some 200 Catholics were among the deputies of the Bloc National which swept to power in the most resounding electoral victory obtained by the right since 1870. The new government made no secret of its desire for religious pacification and refused to apply the 'laic laws' to the provinces of Alsace-Lorraine recovered from Germany. It also set about re-establishing diplomatic relations with the Vatican, and, in a further gesture of goodwill towards Rome, sent an official delegation to be present at the festivities attendant on the canonization of Joan of Arc in 1920. Delicate negotiations were opened with the hierarchy on the thorny subject of the legal framework within which the Church should carry on its activities under the terms of the Separation Law of 1905, and these eventually bore fruit in 1924.

[16] On the ALP, see M. Fogarty, *Christian Democracy in Western Europe, 1820–1953* (London, 1957), 331–2; B. F. Martin, *Count Albert de Mun, Paladin of the Third Republic* (Chapel Hill, NC, 1978); J.-M. Mayeur, *La Vie politique sous la Troisième République 1870–1940* (Paris, 1984), 193–6. For the Ligue Patriotique des Françaises, see J. F. McMillan, 'Women, Religion and Politics: The Case of the *Ligue Patriotique des Françaises*', in W. Roosen (ed.), *Proceedings of the Annual Meeting of the Western Society for French History*, xv (Flagstaff, 1988), 355–64.

[17] cf. H. S. Paul, *The Second Ralliement: The Rapprochement between Church and State in France in the Twentieth Century* (Washington, 1967).

[18] On the First World War period, see J. Fontana, *Les Catholiques français pendant la Grande Guerre* (Paris, 1990); J.-M. Mayeur, 'La Vie religieuse en France pendant la Première Guerre Mondiale', in *Histoire vécue du peuple chrétien*, ii (Toulouse, 1979); and J. F. McMillan, 'French Catholics, "Infamous Rumours" and the Sacred Union', in M. S. and F. Coetzee (eds.), *Authority, Identity and the Social History of the Great War* (forthcoming).

The notion of a second *ralliement*, however, needs to be nuanced. Although this chapter wishes to argue that the inter-war period was indeed a time of important new initiatives in the field of French political Catholicism, it should be appreciated that continuities were as much in evidence as change.[19] It is certainly misleading to portray Pius XI as the Pope of a second *ralliement*, or as any kind of progressive. True, he condemned Action Française in 1926, thereby depriving it of a considerable portion of its following in the French Catholic community: but he also connived at the suppression of Sturzo's Popular Party in Italy and concluded concordats with Fascist Italy (1929) and Nazi Germany (1933). The larger project of the pontiff was always to revive and revitalize an intransigent and ultramontane version of Catholic Christianity. As the Pope of Catholic Action, he hoped that the laity might become apostles for Christ alongside the clergy—though always subject to the authority of the hierarchy. What Pius XI wanted was not a reconciliation between the Church and the modern world but a holy crusade against it in the name of Christ the King.[20]

Atavistic instincts also survived in other quarters. In May 1924 an alliance of the left (the Cartel des gauches) returned to power in a cabinet dominated by Radicals and headed by the veteran Radical leader Herriot. Faced with financial problems which he could hardly begin to understand, the premier preferred to divert attention on to the more congenial territory of the 'clerical threat'. Plans were announced to close the embassy at the Vatican, to extend the Separation regime to Alsace-Lorraine and to apply the letter of the laws on association of 1901 and 1904 against the regular clergy. Militant anticlericalism may have gone into decline, but, political anticlericalism, it appeared, remained as tempting as ever in order to consolidate the alliance of Republicans and Socialists.

In these circumstances, it is hardly surprising that the most striking manifestation of political Catholicism in the 1920s was a movement of religious defence of a recognizably traditional kind, with close links to the French parliamentary right. The Fédération Nationale Catholique was founded in 1924 as a direct response to the policies of the Cartel des gauches government.[21] Its leader, General Castelnau, was hand-picked for the task by the Catholic hierarchy and his brief was to organize a movement which would conform to papal teaching (especially that of Pius X) on Catholic Action. All over France, parish, cantonal, and diocesan unions were formed. Lectures, public meetings, mass rallies and demonstrations were rapidly organized. The character of the movement owed much to the imprint of its leader, whose zeal for religion was matched only by his patriotic ardour. Born in 1851 in the Aveyron into an old Catholic and noble family, Castelnau was a veteran of the Franco-Prussian War as well as of the First World War. The father of twelve children, he lost three sons

---

[19] cf. O. L. Arnal, *Ambivalent Alliance: The Catholic Church and the Action Française 1899–1939* (Pittsburgh, 1985).

[20] M. Conway, 'Building the Christian City: Catholics and Politics in Inter-War Francophone Belgium', *Past and Present*, 128 (1990), 117–51.

[21] On the FNC, see J. F. McMillan, 'Catholicism and Nationalism in France: The Case of the *Fédération Nationale Catholique*', in N. Atkin and F. Tallett (eds.), *Catholicism in Britain and France since 1789* (forthcoming): General Y. Gras, *Castelnau, ou l'art de commander 1851–1944* (Paris, 1990).

in the slaughter of 1914–18 and thereafter remained a die-hard Germanophobe. As a categorical believer in the myth of the Masonic plot, he believed that France in general was in the hands of the Freemasons and that the Herriot government in particular took its orders from the Masonic lodges.

When Herriot fell on 17 April 1925 Castelnau tried to claim the credit for the FNC, though in reality it was the premier's inability to solve the country's chronic financial problems which precipitated his resignation. Nevertheless, there was delight among FNC supporters when Herriot's successor, Painlevé, announced that the embassy at the Vatican would be maintained and that the Separation Law would not be applied to Alsace-Lorraine. Rather than disband the organization on the morrow of victory, however, Castelnau kept it in being as the agency for furthering his designs to restore a Christian social order. While taking care to emphasize that the movement was non-party-political and would not field candidates of its own in elections, he devised a programme for the elections of 1928 to be presented to all candidates which focused on 'freedom of education and association and the maintenance of the religious orders'. FNC supporters were invited to vote only for those candidates who endorsed the programme.

Yet by the late 1920s the FNC's aspirations to be identified as the embodiment of papal doctrines of Catholic Action were being undermined. Castelnau's protestations of political neutrality fooled no one, including Pius XI. While refusing, certainly, to establish his own political party, the General made no secret of his desire to draw Catholics away from 'that somnolent passivity which had cost them so dear between 1870 and 1910'.[22] If not a Catholic Party, the FNC had become a formidable political pressure group, whose terrain, as Castelnau put it, was 'that of *la voie publique*'.[23] The distinction between politics and public life was too subtle for most people, for it was clearly impossible to have an impact on national life without recourse to some kind of political action. As late as December 1929, on the occasion of the enthronement of the new cardinal-archbishop of Paris, Cardinal Verdier, the Vatican once again described the FNC as the 'principal axis' of Catholic Action in France and Castelnau as the 'guide of the laity'.[24] But the time was fast approaching when the Pope would make plain the extent to which Castelnau's notions of Catholic Action differed from his own. Renewing the stress on the need for an apolitical stance and emphasizing the benefits to be obtained from forming specialized groups under the control of the hierarchy, Pius XI gave orders for new organizational arrangements to be in place by 1932. A clash between the FNC and Rome became unavoidable, and symbolically, Castelnau was obliged to change the title of his newspaper from *Action catholique de France* to *La France catholique*.

Thereafter, tensions between the FNC and the Holy See continued to accentuate on account of the Vatican's attachment to the kind of pro-League of Nations foreign policy promoted in France by Foreign Minister Aristide Briand, while Castelnau and the FNC remained wedded to the nationalism of the conservative right. In the 1930s

---

[22] Quoted by Gras, *Castelnau*, 349.   [23] Ibid. 399.   [24] Ibid. 404.

the FNC was far from a spent force—indeed, as the incarnation of intransigent Catholicism and Catholic nationalism it did much to prepare its supporters for the 'National Revolution' which was to accompany the establishment of the Vichy regime. On the other hand, the FNC could no longer claim to be the foremost representative of French political Catholicism, since other, newer, and very different organizations had emerged to contest its primacy.

Not the least of the countervailing forces was that of Christian democracy, which had emerged rejuvenated at the end of the First World War, despite inevitable disruptions and the tragic loss of militants of the calibre of Sangnier's close associates Henry du Roure and Amédée Guiard. Much of the credit for keeping the flames of Christian democracy alive could be claimed by Ernest Pezet, yet another follower of Sangnier, who in 1917 launched a newspaper called *L'Âme française* in an effort to forge links between the 'second Christian democracy' and the different elements of social Catholicism (ACJF, Semaines sociales, and Catholic trade unions). Pezet and his collaborators, who included Robert Cornilleau and Jean Raymond-Laurent, thus became the moving spirits in an attempt to synthesize the political ideals of the Sillon and the social ideals of the social Catholics which was eventually to be realized in the creation of a new political party, the Parti Démocrate Populaire (PDP), in 1924.[25]

On the morrow of the war, the prospects for a renewal of Christian democracy seemed to be enhanced by Sangnier's reconstitution of La Jeune République in 1919, while in the Paris region the group of Republican-Democrats animated by Raymond-Laurent established the Fédération des Républicains-Démocrates de la Seine in June 1919, which had the *Petit Démocrate* as its mouthpiece. Similar networks existed in Finistère, the north, the south-east, and elsewhere, while a new Christian democratic impulse was supplied by the recovery of Alsace, where the German Catholic Centre Party had developed under the Occupation.[26] The success of the right in the parliamentary elections of 1919 brought about thirty deputies 'of Christian democratic inspiration' into parliament and it was the hope of men like Pezet that Sangnier would take the lead in uniting all the different elements into a single movement. He, however, remained suspicious of the conservative tendencies of the Catholic social movement and preferred to devote himself to the twin causes of pacifism and Franco-German reconciliation. Thus it fell to the likes of Pezet and Raymond-Laurent to take the initiative in organizing a new political party of the centre-right out of the combined forces of social Catholicism, the rump of the ALP, and parliamentarians sympathetic to Christian democracy (who, after the elections of 1924, numbered a mere fourteen, most of them from Alsace-Lorraine). The Parti Démocrate Populaire, founded in November 1924, was the result.

[25] Pezet, *Chrétiens au service de la cité*, 49 ff. The essential work on the PDP is now J.-C. Delbreil, *Centrisme et démocratie-chrétienne en France: Le Parti Démocrate Populaire des origines au MRP, 1919–1944* (Paris, 1990).

[26] M. Vaussard, *Histoire de la démocratie chrétienne*, i. *France–Belgique–Italie* (Paris, 1956), 86 ff.; C. Baechler, *Le Parti catholique alsacien 1890–1939: Du Reichsland à la République jacobine* (Paris, 1982); D. P. Silverman, 'Political Catholicism and Social Democracy in Alsace-Lorraine, 1871–1914', *Catholic Historical Review*, 52 (1966), 39–65.

The choice of name was significant, and arrived at only after considerable debate. The Breton group favoured the title of 'Parti Démocrate', while others, like the Alsatians and figures such as Marcel Prélot, were partisans of the label 'Parti Populaire', for its international echoes and obvious reference to Sturzo's Italian Popular Party, the PPI. The final compromise was intended to signal that the PDP was neither a specifically Catholic Party nor an official Christian democrat party. On the contrary, the party accepted the reality of the secularization of society and strongly affirmed its republicanism.[27]

On the other hand, if not a Catholic Party, the PDP was certainly a party of Catholics, and of Catholics inspired by social Catholic teaching and committed to the ideals of Christian democracy. It is worth stressing that their conception of democracy was as much social as political. The family was identified as the bedrock of society. Protective legislation on behalf of children, measures to stimulate the birth rate, social insurance schemes, and legislation on housing were notable features of its programme. The party was likewise committed to Christian trade-unionism and to developing professional organizations among both the working classes and the middle classes. But the PDP also went beyond conventional social Catholic teaching in its vision of a new kind of democracy inspired by the 'Popularism' of Sturzo, who personally was involved in the development of its doctrine through his collaboration in exile from Italy with the semi-official party review *Politique*, founded in 1927 by Marcel Prélot, an academic lawyer, ex-secretary-general of the ACJF and his leading French disciple and translator. In place of the *étatisme* of Jacobin democracy and the collectivism of Marxist social democracy, Sturzo advocated a 'popular' democracy which would be based on 'intermediary bodies', such as the family, the profession, the commune, and the region, which would act as a 'buffer' between the State and the individual. Another intellectual influence on the doctrinal position of the party was the 'personalist' philosophy of Paul Archambault, director of the review *Les Cahiers de la nouvelle journée* and another former Silloniste. Archambault's personalism affirmed that the greatest of all earthly values was the human person while denying that the individual was the most important element in society. Rather, he argued, there had to be a point of equilibrium between the individual and the social. Archambault's personalism differed somewhat from that of the subsequently much better-known Catholic personalist philosopher Emmanuel Mounier, with whom he engaged in a series of polemics, but it helped to inform the organicist and institutionalist theses defended by the PDP.[28]

In the estimation of some authoritative contemporaries, the PDP was a party of the right.[29] It would be more accurate, however, to view it as a party of the centre, albeit of the centre-right.[30] Refusing to accept the traditional left–right split in the country, it favoured republican concentration in a new and enlarged republican

27 Delbreil, *Centrisme et démocratie chrétienne*.
28 On the Archambault–Mounier controversy, see Rauch, *Politics of Belief*, 112 ff.
29 cf. A. Siegfried, *Tableau des partis en France* (Paris, 1930).
30 This is the thesis of Delbreil, *Centrisme et démocratie chrétienne*.

party. In this respect, it was a continuation of the *ralliement*, as Robert Cornilleau and others openly acknowledged. At its inception, it opposed the Cartel des gauches, but at the same time it repudiated the extra-parliamentary leagues (Action Française and others such as Taittinger's Jeunesses Patriotes). Likewise, the PDP kept its distance from Louis Marin's Fédération Républicaine, the principal parliamentary party of the right, objecting especially to its conservatism on social issues (though some electoral deals were negotiated for the elections of 1928). The PDP was closer to the centre-right Alliance Democratique, and notably to its more liberal wing (Flandin rather than Reynaud), which advocated a 'laïcite tolérante'.

On the other hand, relations with the other Christian democrat grouping, Sangnier's Jeune République, were not good. For Sangnier, the PDP was a re-incarnation of the ALP, and too wedded to the right. He himself had become pre-occupied primarily with international affairs and with his work on behalf of the League of Nations, disarmament, and Franco-German *rapprochement*. To promote peace, he established an annual Congrès démocrate international, which in 1926 succeeded in bringing together representatives of thirty nations at Bierville. Out of this he created a new pacifist group known as Les Amis de Bierville and in 1932 he gave up the presidency of the Jeune République in order to devote himself to editing a new pacifist newspaper, *L'Éveil des peuples*, and to encouraging the development of youth hostels, or *auberges de jeunesse*.[31] At this point, some of his followers elected to break with him and turned Jeune République into a formal political party, one which located itself markedly to the left of centre.

Sangnier's strictures on the PDP were not entirely justified. Some of its leaders, like Cornilleau, hoped to establish points of contact with the moderate left, provided that the old clerical bogey could be laid to rest. In an article first published in the *Petit Démocrate* of 23 January 1927 entitled 'Pourquoi pas?' he argued that there were no objections to collaborating with elements in the socialist tradition, since they shared the PDP's commitment to social progress and to spiritual values.[32] At the same time, the PDP refused to contemplate participation in any 'union of the right', particularly if such a coalition were to include the Action Française. For the PDP, Maurras was a sworn enemy, and in turn the party was virulently denounced by Action Française. Likewise, for the conservative and nationalist right, the party remained something of a *bête noire*. In 1929 it was denounced as a party of 'Christian Reds' by Auguste Cavalier, director of *L'Intérêt français*, on the grounds that it had not given adequate support to Catholic and Nationalist candidates in the elections of 1928 and that it not only refused a united front along with 'patriotic Catholics' in favour of the defence of the country and the social order but also supported a pact with socialism and advocated a conciliatory foreign policy towards Germany.[33]

The PDP's attitude to the FNC was more complicated.[34] Some like Pezet,

[31] cf. Rauch, *Politics of Belief*, 32: P. Farrugia, 'French Religious Opposition to War, 1919–1939: The Contribution of Henri Roser and Marc Sangnier', *French History*, 6 (1992), 278–302.

[32] The article was repr. in R. Cornilleau, *Pourquoi pas? Une politique réaliste* (Paris, 1929).

[33] A. Cavalier, *Les Rouges-Chrétiens?* (Paris, 1929).

[34] Delbreil, *Centrisme et démocratie chrétienne*, 174 ff.

favoured a strategy of 'entryism', so as to build upon links which existed between PDP members and the Federation. Henri Teitgen, for example, spoke at FNC rallies, as did the celebrated orator abbé Desgranges, a future deputy closely associated with the PDP.[35] Pezet himself was general secretary of the FNC and contributed a regular column to its bulletin *Credo* until May 1926. Other PDP chiefs were more overtly hostile to the FNC. Charles Flory, for instance, suspected that it harboured ambitions of becoming the French *parti catholique*. Similarly, some local leaders of the PDP who were also FNC members—for example Facque in the Seine-Inférieure—were unwilling to limit themselves to the official Castelnau line of purely religious defence. Pagès was highly critical of both the monarchist tendencies within the FNC and its extravagant chauvinism. Disputes over international politics, indeed, produced sharp exchanges between the *Echo de Paris*, in which Castelnau was a regular columnist, and *L'Ouest-Eclair*, which supported the League of Nations and efforts at international reconciliation.

In electoral terms, the PDP never became a major force in French politics between the wars. After the elections of 1928, it had some seventeen deputies, most of whom were favourably disposed to the modernizing conservative government of André Tardieu in 1930. The elections of 1932 were a disappointment, reducing the number of deputies to sixteen. In the even more polarized situation of the elections of 1936, parliamentary representation shrank to thirteen. Party membership at this time was around 13,000. Moreover, after 1932 it was evident that the party was itself divided into a right and a left in what was also largely a conflict of generations.[36] The rightist tendency, around Alfred Bour, resented the influence of *L'Aube*, the daily newspaper founded in 1932 by Francisque Gay, and the strengthening of links with the Jeune République. The leftist tendency, represented by Bidault, was keen to see the party distance itself further from the right and founded its own youth movement, the Jeunesses Démocrates Populaires, in 1934. But the party was unambivalent in its republicanism. After the riots of 6 February 1934, the serious disturbances outside the Chamber of Deputies which left fourteen people killed and another 236 wounded after clashes between the police and right-wing demonstrators, the party rallied to the new prime minister Doumergue, who assumed the reins of government after the resignation of the Radical Daladier. At the same time, it maintained its hostility to the Fascist leagues and was notably suspicious of Colonel de la Rocque's Croix de Feu, regarded by the left as the most dangerous of the leagues, despite their shared outlook on social questions. (The minority of PDP members who were more charitably disposed to de la Rocque preferred to see him as simply the leader of another apolitical veterans' association.)

Whatever their shortcomings, the Christian democrats of the PDP (and of course, even more so, those of the smaller JR) represented a break with the tradition, still embodied by the FNC, which assimilated Catholics to the politics of the right. The

---

[35] For the abbé Desgranges, see abbé Desgranges, *Journal d'un prêtre député, 1936–1940* (Paris, 1961) and Chânoine Dutroncy, *L'abbé Desgranges, conférencier et député (1874–1958)* (Paris, 1962).

[36] Delbreil, *Centrisme et démocratie chrétienne*, 306 ff.

impact of Christian democracy was significantly reinforced by the founding of a number of new Catholic reviews and newspapers, many—but not all—of which specifically aligned themselves with the Christian democratic tradition, or 'spiritual family', and contributed further to the detachment of Catholics from reactionary politics. Among the most influential of these journals were certain publications of the Dominican Order. *La Vie intellectuelle* was launched as a monthly in 1928 by the Dominican Père Bernadot (with the strong support of Pius XI), and became a bi-monthly from 1931. Although its circulation was small (5,000–6,000 in 1934), it drew upon an outstandingly talented team of contributors—men like Etienne Borne, Henri Guillemin, and Pierre-Henri Simon—who were to establish themselves as some of the leading lights of Parisian journalism. According to the historian René Remond, it played 'an incomparable role' in the evolution of Catholic ideas in the period before 1939.[37] *Sept*, also published by the Dominicans, had a much wider circulation (printing up to 100,000 copies) and a likewise significant impact in its short three-year history between 1934 and 1937 on account of its strong support for the internationalism represented by the League of Nations and its stance against Mussolini's aggression in Ethiopia in 1935 (undertaken even at the risk of alienating a considerable body of its readership).[38] Similarly, *Sept* resisted the French right's attempts to portray the Francoist uprising in Spain as a 'Holy Crusade'. It also supported the Popular Front, the electoral alliance of the combined left (including Radicals, Socialists, and Communists) which swept to power in the elections of 1936, giving France for the first time a Socialist Prime Minister in the person of Léon Blum. On the other hand, it rejected the *main tendue*, the outstretched hand of friendship proferred to Catholics by Communist Party leader Maurice Thorez in a radio broadcast of 17 April 1936. In February 1937 *Sept* caused a furore by not only publishing an interview with Blum but also by suggesting that his government was entitled to the loyal support of Catholics. In the wake of denunciations to their superiors, the Dominicans of *Sept* were obliged to cease publication, but its work was carried on by a team of laymen headed by Stanislas Fumet who relaunched the review under the name of *Temps Présent*.

Esprit, launched in 1932, was equally devoted to the project of ending the traditional Catholic association with the politics of the right, but it certainly cannot be regarded as simply another representative of the Christian democratic tendency.[39] Its youthful editor, Emmanuel Mounier, a former member of the ACJF and *agrégé* in philosophy, had no time for conventional politics and conventional political parties and refused to allow his movement to become merely the left wing of Christian democracy. Thus, whereas many Christian democrats associated with the PDP and

[37] R. Rémond, *Les Catholiques dans la France des années 30* (Paris, 1979) (1st pub. as *Les Catholiques, le communisme et les crises 1929–1939* (Paris, 1960), 261–2).

[38] A. Coutrot, *Un courant de la pensée catholique: L'Hebdomadaire 'Sept' (mars 1934–août 1937)* (Paris, 1961).

[39] On Mounier see Rauch, *Politics and Belief*; J. Hellman, *Emmanuel Mounier and the New Catholic Left, 1930–1950* (Toronto, 1981); M. Kelly, *Pioneer of the Catholic Revival: The Ideas and Influence of Emmanuel Mounier* (London, 1979); and M. Winock, *Histoire politique de la revue 'Esprit', 1930–1950* (Paris, 1975).

other organizations drew inspiration from Mounier's writings, he never returned the compliment, consistently ridiculing their efforts to find a *modus operandi* under the Republican regime. He and his team, he proclaimed, were revolutionaries, 'but in the name of the Spirit'. In his keynote article in the first issue of *Esprit*, Mounier announced his ambition to 'remake the Renaissance' in accordance with Jacques Maritain's dictum of the 'Primacy of the spiritual'. By contrast with the the right, which wished to link religion to the defence of property, family, and country, *Esprit's* 'first duty', according to Mounier, was 'to dissociate the spiritual from politics and more particularly . . . from the right'.[40]

It would be a mistake, however, at least for the period of the 1930s, to represent Mounier as the quintessential incarnation of the 'new Catholic left'. After the Second World War, he was to be hailed as the pioneer of a new kind of Christian socialist humanism, but as John Hellmann has shown, in the early days of its existence, the politics of *Esprit* were more convoluted.[41] Some, indeed, of Mounier's collaborators, had fascistic sympathies with 'revolutionary' right organizations in France such as the group Ordre Nouveau (prominent members of which were Arnaud Dandieu, Alexandre Marc, and the historian Robert Aron) and Réaction (of Thierry Maulnier) and even entertained an admiration for anti-Hitlerite National Socialism of the Otto Strasser variety. In the spring of 1935 Mounier attended a conference in Rome on the fascist conception of the corporate state, though he came away convinced that the Italians had erred in making the State rather than the human person the primary value. Nevertheless, despite his explicit repudiation of the aims and methods of fascism, by the late 1930s Mounier was insisting on the need to keep one's distance from the left as much as from the right. Essentially, what *Esprit* was seeking was a 'third way' in politics which would be neither right nor left. If Mounier at no time condoned Hitlerism or anti-Semitism, he never wavered in his contempt for the 'established disorder' of the democratic regime under the Third Republic and in consequence, much to their dismay, was scathing about the efforts of Christian democrats to work for improvements within the system.

The group's official philosophy was personalism but it derived its appeal less from any doctrines than from the adoption of a style and attitude towards the world. Helene Iswolsky, an attender at *Esprit's* summer congresses, later testified to its openness, generosity, and idealism (the parallel with *Sillon* is striking) and also noted the role played by young Catholic women in the group.[42] Its ideas were diffused to a larger public in the late 1930s by a sister review, *Le Voltigeur français*, directed by Pierre-Aimé Touchard, which appeared twice monthly. Its opposition to Nazism was uncompromising. Immediately after the Munich Agreements, it published an article which concluded with the sentence: 'Today, let us refuse to "collaborate" with Nazism or Fascism, on pain of accepting a spiritual and material slavery.'[43] By April

---

[40] E. Mounier, 'Refaire la Renaissance', *Esprit* (Oct. 1932), repub. in *Œuvres* (Paris, 1961), i. 137–74.
[41] Hellman, *Emmanuel Mounier*, 5–8.
[42] H. Iswolsky, *Light Before Dusk: A Russian Catholic in France 1923–1941* (London, 1942), 107.
[43] P. Christophe, *1939–1940: Les Catholiques devant la guerre* (Paris, 1989), 53.

1939, having denounced Hitler's imperialism and racism, it declared that the only urgent problem to be resolved was how to define 'the tactic of resistance'.[44] Choices which were to become even more urgent under the Occupation were already being made before 1940.

More radical still than *Esprit* was *Terre Nouvelle*, which described itself as the 'organ of revolutionary Christians'. A monthly, founded in 1935, *Terre Nouvelle* was not an exclusively Catholic journal and benefited from the contributions of Protestants such as André Philip, the young Socialist deputy, and Paul Ricœur, the philosopher. Its editor and most dynamic figure, however, was Maurice Laudrain, a Breton Catholic born in Nantes in 1901 who became a skilled worker and a militant in the CFTC and Sangnier's Jeune République. Active in pacifist circles, in 1927, through the influence of Gaston Tessier, he was appointed personal secretary to Mgr. Chaptal, the auxiliary Bishop of Paris, and also became a member of the French Socialist Party, the SFIO. In 1931 he published *Vers l'ordre social*, a call to Christians to fight against the power of money, which appeared with a preface written by Mgr. Chaptal. Soon afterwards however, Laudrain was denounced by both Catholics and Socialists alike. The latter resented his denunciations of Socialist anticlericalism, while the papal nuncio Valeri secured his dismissal from Mgr. Chaptal's secretariat on account of his revolutionary tendencies. While unemployed, Laudrain wrote a book entitled *Socialiste parce que chrétien* which he published in Belgium under a pseudonym and which already contained most of the ideas which *Terre Nouvelle* was set up to propagate.[45] Essentially, the review tried to synthesize the ideas of Christianity and communism and was one of the few Catholic publications not to reject outright the offer of the *main tendue* from the French Communist Party, the PCF, in 1936.[46] Rapidly placed on the Index, it was deemed too radical even by Mounier. Not even *Esprit*, let alone the Vatican, was ready for any kind of Christian–Marxist dialogue in the era of the Popular Front and Stalin's Purges and *Terre Nouvelle* exercised at best a marginal influence.

Much more influential than Laudrain—indeed perhaps the most influential figure of all in the world of Catholic journalism in the inter-war period—was Francisque Gay, the founder of *La Vie catholique* in 1924, a weekly which had a sale of around 40,000 until it folded in 1938.[47] Born in 1885, Gay was yet another ex-Silloniste and had been a seminarian before finding his true vocation as a Catholic journalist and publisher in the cause of Christian democracy (he was a co-director of the firm Bloud et Gay). After Pius XI's condemnation of the Action Française, he committed *La Vie catholique* wholeheartedly to the papal position, at a time when other Catholic newspapers such as *La Croix* preferred to minimize its significance, in the process earning himself the undying hatred of Maurras and of the entire French right.[48] Gay was

[44] Ibid.   [45] A. Rochefort-Turquin, *Front populaire: Socialistes parce que chrétiens* (Paris, 1986).
[46] cf. F. J. Murphy, *Communists and Catholics in France, 1936–1939: The Politics of the Outstretched Hand* (Gainesville, Fla., 1989).
[47] E. Terrenoire, *Un combat d'avant-garde: Francisque Gay et La Vie catholique* (Paris, 1976).
[48] A selection of some of Gay's more important articles can be found in F. Gay, *Comment j'ai défendu le Pape* (Paris, 1927).

also, with Gaston Tessier, co-director of *L'Aube*, the new daily newspaper set up in January 1932 to be the voice of Christian democracy and a further witness to the break between Catholicism and Maurrassianism.[49] Whereas *La Vie catholique* was primarily a religious newspaper, *L'Aube*'s mission was explicitly political. As the 'organ of a spiritual family', the paper embodied a 'unity of orientation but diversity of tendencies'. Its overriding concern was to ensure that Catholics could not always be identified with the causes of nationalism and reaction and in consequence it looked for points of contact with the left in the search for social progress and international peace. Collaborators included prominent social Catholics (Marius Gonin of the Lyons *Chronique sociale*, Adéodat Boissard of the Semaines sociales, Joseph Zamanski of the Confédération française des professions) and some of the most talented journalists active in Christian democracy (Robert Cornilleau, Raymond-Laurent and Georges Bidault from the PDP, and Georges Hoog from Jeune République). Figures such as Paul Archambault and Jean Lacroix contributed more philosophical pieces.

With 12,000 subscribers in 1934, *L'Aube's* circulation was small, but its political and cultural impact was out of all proportion to these figures. Not only was its readership much larger than its subscribers, since many of the latter were institutional subscribers (schools, religious establishments, and others), but more importantly its views were regularly broadcast on the radio in the daily digest of press comment. With *Esprit* and *Sept*, it did much to dispel the association of Catholicism with right-wing nationalism, especially through its internationalism and rejection of militarism. Its response to Mussolini's ambitions in Ethiopia was to publish (simultaneously with *La Vie catholique*, *Sept*, *Le Petit Démocrate*, and *Esprit*) a 'Manifesto for Justice and Peace'.[50] Georges Bidault, the paper's leading commentator on foreign affairs, demanded the imposition of sanctions on Italy (as did the PDP's Ernest Pezet in the Chamber of Deputies). On the other hand, Bidault counselled non-intervention in the Spanish Civil War, while refusing to recognize the legitimacy of the Nationalist uprising against the Republican government. Without minimizing the atrocities committed by Republican forces against the Spanish Catholic Church, *L'Aube* also reported the crimes committed by the Nationalists in the name of religion and the nation, as did Francisque Gay in a separate publication of his own.[51] *L'Aube* also manifested a special sympathy for the Basques, staunch Catholics persecuted for their Republican sympathies, many of whom arrived in France as refugees. What made *L'Aube* even more notorious, however, was its consistent advocacy of resistance to Nazi aggression and its opposition to the Munich Agreements. Once again Gay sought to publicize the newspaper's position by reproducing its articles on the Czech crisis, along with relevant documents and other articles culled from *Esprit* and the Christian democrat press, in an edited work which he published in 1938.[52] The

[49] F. Mayeur, *L'Aube: Étude d'un journal d'opinion, 1932–1940* (Paris, 1966).
[50] The manifesto is reproduced in Rémond, *Les Catholiques*, 96–8.
[51] F. Gay, *Dans les flammes et dans le sang* (Paris, 1936).
[52] Id. (ed.), *La Tchécoslovaquie devant notre conscience et devant l'Histoire* (Paris, 1938).

stance that would lead many Christian democrats into the ranks of the French Resistance, and make Georges Bidault into one of its leading lights, was evident well before 1940.

If the rise of a significant Catholic press was fundamental to the progress made by Christian democracy between the wars, so too was the continuing vitality of social Catholicism. Social Catholics, particularly those with leadership experience in the ACJF, were at the forefront of the struggle against the Action Française and assumed key roles in the PDP (and later the post-war MRP) as well as writing for the likes of *L'Aube* and *Politique*.[53] The number of adherents to the CFTC increased dramatically, especially after 1936. Having resisted the call of the left-wing CGT (General Confederation of Labour) for syndical reunification and stuck to its own distinctive organization along professional lines as set out in its plan of 1935, it saw its membership soar from 150,000 to 400,000 in the late 1930s.[54] Many of these new members came from the ranks of the Young Christian Workers, the JOC (Jeunesse Ouvrière Chrétienne), the archetype of the reorganized and specialized Catholic Action encouraged by the Vatican in the 1930s. Founded by the abbé Cardijn in Belgium in 1925, the JOC began to operate in France in 1927. Its key idea was that the task of converting the working class to Christianity would be carried out by workers themselves. Jocistes brought a new sensitivity to working-class conditions in their work of evangelization and sought to find practical solutions to problems through the application of Cardijn's maxim: see, judge, and act. Their enthusiasm and openness were infectious, as was their courage in openly witnessing to their faith whether through badges, public prayers, or the downing of tools at 3 o'clock on the afternoon of Good Friday. Seeking to bring others to Christ through the spirit of friendship, they succeeded in reaching out to alienated young workers of both sexes and brought them back into contact with Catholic Christianity. At the same time, they taught such people that they did not have to tolerate harsh working conditions. Despite its overt apoliticism, it is no accident that Jocistes participated enthusiastically in the strike wave of 1936, the 'social explosion' triggered by the victory of the Popular Front coalition at the polls.[55]

The model of the JOC was successfully applied to other milieux in the 1930s, leading to the creation of Young Farmers' groups (JAC), Young Students groups (JEC), etc. and their female equivalents, all of which added to the impression of a new dynamism in the world of French social Catholicism. Enjoying the support and patronage of figures such as Cardinal Liénart of Lille and Bishop Dubourg of Marseilles, social Catholics were preoccupied primarily with their mission of rechristianization. In the process, however, particularly when they spoke of the 'new order' with which it was necessary to replace the existing society, they were taken by

[53] Y.-M. Hilaire, 'L'ACJF, les étapes d'une histoire (1886–1958)', *Revue du Nord* (Apr.–Sept. 1984).

[54] M. Launay, *La CFTC: Origines et développement 1919–1940* (Paris, 1986).

[55] On the JOC, see Dansette, *Destin du catholicisme français*; J. Débès and E. Poulat, *L'Appel de la JOC (1926–1928)* (Paris, 1986): P. Pierrard, M. Launay, and R. Trempé, *La JOC, regards d'historiens* (Paris, 1984); G. Cholvy, B. Comte, V. Feroldi, *Jeunesses chrétiennes au xxe siècle* (Paris, 1991).

French employers and the French right generally to be 'Red Christians'. A typical article written by Louis Bertrand in the *Revue des Deux Mondes* described them as extremely dangerous and as being the dupes of communism and anarchism.[56] That was a gross distortion, of course, but what was certainly true was that, like Mounier and *Esprit*, social Catholics were looking for a 'third way' which would avoid the excesses of capitalism and communism. As such, they could not easily be classified as orthodox conservatives.

It was the hope of Francisque Gay that the manifold initiatives on the part of Christian democrats and social Catholics in the 1920s and 1930s would have a decisive impact on the French political scene. Recognizing that unity among Catholics was a prerequisite for the fulfilment of his ambition, ever since the founding of *La Vie catholique* he strove personally to bring together different tendencies into one fold. By the mid-1930s, however, he admitted to considerable disappointment, since unity appeared to be more elusive than ever. In a 'Confidential Memoir' drawn up for some three hundred or so friends and allies, he posed the question as to why Catholics 'of our outlook [*esprit*] and even Catholics *tout court*' had not been able to exercise power under the Third Republic. Christian democrats in France, he suggested, had won widespread respect (except on the extreme right, where they were hated), but unlike the situation in other countries (Italy, Germany, Austria, Spain), they remained 'simple curiosities having little influence in the mass of the country'. A prime reason for this, according to Gay, was the fear of being taken for a confessional or clerical party—itself an understandable fear, but one consequence of which was an excessive timidity on the part of Catholics to stand up and be counted as champions of their faith. The right, by contrast, had no such inhibitions, even when its spokesmen were Catholics whose strictness of observance left much to be desired. Another problem was fragmentation, and the dissipation of energy into so many different channels, along with the distaste for conventional electoral politics manifested by Sangnier and some of his devotees. Gay also underlined how French political Catholicism suffered from the lack of a leader of the calibre of an O'Connell, a Windthorst, a Sturzo, or a Robles. Sangnier, who might perhaps have assumed the role, was himself part of the problem.[57] What Gay did not say was that he too was part of the problem, because of his own combative character, which alienated not just men of the Action Française but also elements of the PDP and other Christian democrats. Thus his candidature in the elections of 1936 at Cholet (Maine-et-Loire) was vigorously opposed by *Ouest-Eclair*, which had no love for *L'Aube* or its editor. His business partner Edmond Bloud also broke with him, while Gaston Tessier and other prominent social Catholics resigned from the paper's editorial team in October 1936.

Perhaps no event did more to highlight—and to exacerbate—the divisions in French political Catholicism than the Spanish Civil War. For those on the right, who probably spoke for the majority of French Catholics, the Nationalist rising was what

[56] Christophe, *1939–1940*, 12.

[57] F. Gay, *Pour un rassemblement des forces démocratiques d'inspiration chrétienne: Mémoire confidentiel* (Paris, 1935).

the Spanish bishops made it out to be: a holy crusade to defend the Church and Christian civilization against the sacrilegious depredations of the left which included the murder of priests and nuns and the burning of churches.[58] Franco, according to G. Bernoville in *La France catholique* of 9 May 1938, was 'an essentially religious, calm and meditative spirit', whose ideal was that of Christian civilization.[59] As we have seen, Christian democrats viewed the conflict in a different light, and made much of the fact that the Catholic Basques were on the side of the Republic. In *L'Aube* of 3 October 1936 Sturzo himself reaffirmed views which he had expressed in the English *Catholic Herald* that there was neither a crusade nor a holy war, and that atrocities had been committed by the Nationalist troops against unarmed civilians in Badajoz and elsewhere.[60] As an editorial in *Sept* on 7 August 1936 argued, civil wars are the dirtiest of all wars and those which engender the most heinous crimes. The insurgents who had backed the rebel generals and encouraged the mobilization of colonial troops against their fellow-countrymen were therefore as much in the wrong as the Republican anticlericals.[61]

Yet by 1939, however divided, French political Catholicism had established itself as a significant, if still minority, current in French political and intellectual life. The old connection with the traditional right, incarnated by the FNC, had by no means completely disappeared and was still a feature, for instance, of Cardinal Baudrillart's Institut Catholique in Paris.[62] It also flourished in overtly anti-republican articles in the *Revue des deux mondes* written by Catholic contributors like Louis Bertrand and Victor Guiraud. The latter vituperated against the regime's inability to distinguish between 'the first drunken batchelor to come along and a Castelnau, three times the saviour of France and the educator of twelve children' and deplored the 'tragic experiences of the Cartel and of the Popular Front'.[63] Moreover, in 1939 the new pope, Pius XII, lifted the ban on the Action Française, much to the delight of traditionalist French Catholics. Thus encouraged, some of the latter, like Mgr. Chollet, archbishop of Cambrai, and his amanuensis canon Jules Bouche, a former professor at the Theology Faculty of Lille and once a favourite pupil in Rome of the Action Française sympathizers Cardinal Billot and Father Henri Le Floch, took to denouncing *L'Aube* to the Vatican in the hope of having it condemned for repeating the errors of the Sillon. The newspaper, it was claimed, was the violent enemy of Mussolini's Italy and Franco's Spain and in French politics supported revolutionary ideas which attacked both the ruling classes and capitalism.[64]

On the other hand, such paranoid denunciations merely serve to illustrate the extent to which political Catholics had succeeded in making new openings to the centre and left of the political spectrum. Talk of *rouges-chrétiens* (apart from the revolutionaries of *Terre Nouvelle*), was greatly exaggerated, as Francisque Gay never tired of pointing out.[65] While the Christian democrats of *L'Aube* made no secret of their

---

[58] Rémond, *Les Catholiques*, 144–5.   [59] Ibid. 181–2.   [60] Ibid. 187.   [61] Ibid. 177–8.
[62] Revealing are the memoirs of the dean of the Faculty of Letters, Jean Calvet, *Mémoires de Monseigneur Jean Calvet* (Lyons, 1967).
[63] Christophe, *1939–1940*, 34.   [64] Ibid. 19 ff.
[65] F. Gay, *Pour en finir avec la légende 'Rouges-Chrétiens'* (Paris, 1937).

aversion for fascist leagues like the Croix de Feu, they were far from enthusiastic about the Front populaire, the Popular Front electoral alliance of the left which swept to power under Léon Blum, the leader of the Socialist Party, in the elections of 1936. In parliament, the PDP voted against the Blum government, and in that respect it had more in common with the FNC than with the Popular Front.[66] Nevertheless, the distance travelled from the old right was increasingly apparent, especially with the founding of the Nouvelles Equipes Françaises (NEF) in 1938.[67] Yet another initiative of Francisque Gay and the team around *L'Aube*, the NEF again looked back to the Sillon as its inspiration. A league rather than a political party, it set out its claims to occupy the centre ground between right and left and refused to accept that French politics inevitably required adherence to one or other of the traditional blocs. Arguing for a new political order, Georges Bidault and Charles Blondel issued a manifesto entitled *Aux hommes de notre esprit* which was designed to appeal to the broad spectrum of Christian democratic and social Catholic opinion and which succeeded in drawing favourable comment even from Mounier for its emphasis on the need for a fresh start. 'It is no longer a question of defending democracy,' asserted the manifesto. 'It is a question of establishing it.'[68] After only a few months, the NEF claimed to have a network of some 150 groups in different parts of the country, two of the most dynamic of them (apart from the Paris group) being Henri Fréville's at Rennes and Edmond Michelet's at Brive. Whether or not the NEF could have gone on to fulfil all the hopes of their founders it is impossible to tell, but what can be asserted with confidence is that, when France fell before the German *Blitzkrieg* in 1940, the activism of groups of political Catholics such as the NEF and *Esprit* bears witness to the dynamism of French Catholic life in the 1930s.

3. The War, Vichy, and Resistance

The catastrophic defeat of France in 1940 spread dismay and confusion among the Catholics of France as it did among the population as a whole. The country was divided into two zones: an occupied zone in the north and along the western seaboard which was directly under German control and a nominally sovereign French state in the south which had its seat of government in the spa town of Vichy. The great majority of Catholics followed the lead given by their bishops in accepting the Armistice and in recognizing the Vichy regime under Marshal Pétain as the established power. In the first few months following the collapse, the question of the legitimacy of Vichy hardly arose. On the contrary, the presence of the papal nuncio Valerio Valeri was a further sign of the regime's good standing with the Church.[69]

---

[66] Delbreil, *Centrisme et démocratie-chrétienne*, 313–27.

[67] On the NEF, see F. Mayeur, *L'Aube*, 186–211; Rauch, *Politics of Belief*, 198 ff.; Christophe, *1939–1940*, 24–5.

[68] Quoted by Rauch, *Politics of Belief*, 200.

[69] Y.-M. Hilaire, 'L'Été 1940: L'Effrondrement et le sauveur', in *Églises et chrétiens dans la IIe guerre mondiale, La France: Actes du colloque international tenu à Lyon du 27 au 30 janvier 1978 sous la direction de Xavier de Montclos, Monique Luirard, François Delpech, Pierre Bolle* (Lyons, 1982).

Most Catholics welcomed the end of the Third Republic and the sweeping away of a political class for whom anticlericalism had been an article of faith, and identified with the declared intention of the regime to organize a 'National Revolution' which would be based largely on a return to Christian moral values. The hierarchy, far from confining itself to recognizing Vichy as the established power, heaped adulation on the new head of state and represented him as the instrument of Divine Providence sent to lead the nation back to its Christian roots.[70] Many lay Catholics were excited by the prospect of playing a full part in public life in a recognizably Christian state. It was therefore no great surprise to find former militants of the FNC such as Xavier Vallat and Philippe Henriot in prominent positions at Vichy. Vallat was first the organizer of the Marshal's Légion des Combattants and then Vichy's notorious Commissioner for Jewish Affairs, responsible for framing and implementing the regime's anti-Semitic legislation. Henriot, the Secretary of State for Information, came to be known as the voice of Vichy Radio and in his broadcasts defended the same concept of a 'Christian civilization', menaced above all by Bolshevism, which he had championed at FNC rallies back in the 1920s. Jacques Chevalier, the Catholic philosopher and former teacher of Mounier at the University of Grenoble, was briefly Education Minister in 1940–1. Social Catholics were particularly attracted to the new order.[71] Eugène Duthoit, dean of the Faculty of Law at the Catholic University of Lille and president of the Semaines sociales, formerly a supporter of Sturzo and of trade-union rights and a declared enemy of Mussolini, agreed with Cardinal Baudrillart that there was no alternative to Pétain, the 'sublime old man who has sacrificed his glory for the country'.[72] Likewise leaders of Catholic youth movements like the Jesuit Père Doncœur looked to the Marshal to restore a sense of the sacred in public life and to prepare the way for a Christian renaissance. Robert Garric, of the Équipes sociales, was enthusiastic about Vichyite youth organizations, while François Valentin, ex-president of the ACJF in Lorraine, headed the pro-Vichy Légion des Combattants. The Jesuit Père Desbuquois, director of the Action populaire, though anti-Nazi, was strongly in favour of a *politique de présence* at Vichy and contributed to the elaboration of Vichy's Labour Charter. Coming from an anti-liberal and traditionalist background, nostalgic for a former social order supposedly founded on religious values, and admirers of authoritarian Catholic regimes such as Salazar's Portugal, many social Catholics readily identified with Vichy and for the first year of its existence, at least, chose to regard it as the embodiment of their own aspirations for a Christian state.

Even some of the more advanced elements in pre-war political Catholicism succumbed to the promise of national regeneration under Vichy. Emmanuel Mounier,

[70] J. Duchesne, *Les Catholiques français sous l'Occupation* (Paris, 1966): cf. R. Bédarida, 'La Hiérarchie catholique' and E. Fouilloux, 'Le Clergé', in J.-P. Azéma and F. Bédarida (eds.), *Vichy et les Français* (Paris, 1992).

[71] P. Droulers, 'Catholiques sociaux et Révolution Nationale (été 1940–avril 1942)', in *Églises et chrétiens*, 213–25. cf. R. O. Paxton, 'The Church, the Republic and the Fascist Temptation, 1922–1945', in R. J. Wolff and J. K. Hoensch (eds.), *Catholics, the State and the European Radical Right, 1919–1945* (Boulder, Colo., 1987). [72] Christophe, *1939–1940*, 80.

for example, despite the misgivings of some of his collaborators, relaunched *Esprit* as early as November 1940, on the grounds that the time was ripe to cultivate the qualities of leadership along with renewed emphasis on community and spiritual values. Some of his pre-war entourage and admirers occupied important positions at Vichy: for example René Gillouin and Robert Loustau (both ex-Ordre Nouveau) were among Pétain's speechwriters, while the economist François Perroux advised the Marshal on family affairs and youth policy. Mounier himself lectured at the École Nationale des Cadres at Uriage, set up to form a new, more moral, and more vigorous élite.[73] Similarly, some of the leading lights of the CFTC, such as the metalworker Jean Pérès, opted for Vichy and endorsed the regime's Labour Charter.[74] Eleven out of thirteen PDP deputies voted full powers to Pétain in July 1940 and Christian democrats were among the most active militants in Vichy's family, youth, and agricultural organizations. Some of their number went further down the road to pro-German collaborationism (newspapers like *Ouest-Eclair* and the Pau-based *Le Patriote des Pyrénées* being cases in point).[75]

Outright collaboration with the Nazis on the part of Catholics (as opposed to adherence to Vichy and the Marshal) was exceptional, but by no means unknown. The most prominent example was Henriot, who used his position at Vichy Radio to make propaganda for the Milice, the French police force founded in 1943 to combat the Resistance alongside the Gestapo. Most of the upper ranks of the Milice were recruited from Catholic circles where the conviction was strong that in the 1920s and 1930s French Catholicism had become poisoned by the spread of democracy through the machinations of 'red Christians'. The Savoy region was a prime example, its most notorious, but by no means sole, Catholic leader being Paul Touvier.[76] Born in 1915 the eldest of a large and strictly pious Catholic family from Chambéry, he imbibed the views of a father whose intransigent Catholicism was reinforced by his devotion to counter-revolutionary politics (to his dying day he remained convinced of the guilt of Dreyfus). As a modest railway clerk, Touvier joined Colonel de la Rocque's Parti Social Français in the late 1930s, and after the defeat of 1940, became a staunch Pétainist, joining the local Légion de Combattants and then its offshoot, the Service d'Ordre Légionnnaire (SOL), established under the general direction of the extreme nationalist Joseph Darnand with a mission to harass Jews, Communists, and Freemasons. When the SOL became the Milice in 1943, Touvier rose to be an increasingly powerful figure in the organization, ending up as one of its chiefs in the Lyons area. In his subsequent defence of his wartime activities, he claimed that it was the Church which had shown him the road to follow and that his guiding principle was always fidelity to the faith of his ancestors.[77] Certainly, after the Liberation, it was a network of clerics which helped him to escape and campaigned

---

[73] Hellman, *Emmanuel Mounier*, 158–88. He exaggerates, however, in entitling his chapter 'Personalism in Power'.

[74] M. Launay, 'Le Syndicalisme chrétienne et la Charte du Travail', in *Églises et chrétiens*, 189–212.

[75] J.-C. Delbreil, 'Les Démocrates populaires, Vichy et la Résistance, 1940–1942', ibid. 117–26.

[76] R. Rémond (ed.), *Paul Touvier et l'Église: Rapport de la Commission historique instituée par le cardinal Decourtray* (Paris, 1992).   [77] Ibid. 52.

for his rehabilitation. Twice sentenced to death, in 1946 and 1947, he received a presidential pardon from Pompidou in 1971, but was forced to remain in hiding because of the opprobium that continued to attach to his name. He was finally arrested in 1989, having been tracked down to a monastery of reactionary monks in Nice.

At the opposite pole of the political spectrum to Touvier and his ilk, there were political Catholics who were among the first Frenchmen to constitute themselves into an active resistance to the Nazi occupation. In particular, the originality, precocity, and spiritual dimensions of Christian democratic resistance deserve to be underlined, since they bear witness to the degree to which pre-war attitudes determined the stance taken in 1940 and after.[78] As we have seen, Christian democrats were alive to the menace of Nazi barbarism and aggression well before the outbreak of war. The existence of their pre-war networks centred on journals such as *Sept*, *Temps présent*, and *L'Aube* made possible the publication and diffusion of an underground press after 1940 (which included newspapers such as *Temps nouveau*, *Liberté*, and, most famously, *Témoignage chrétien*, the Jesuit-produced organ of opposition to Nazi racial policy which first appeared in November 1941).[79] In September 1940 the printing presses of Francisque Gay were used to produce *La France continue* while those of Marc Sangnier were the source of a wide range of Resistance propaganda before his arrest in February 1944.[80] The first Christian clandestine newspaper, *La Voix du Vatican*, appeared as early as July 1940. Distributed in Marseille, it was produced by a network of schoolteachers at the Jesuit school at Avignon made up of former readers of *Sept* and *Temps présent* as well as militants of the ACJF. The four-page sheet reminded its readers of Pius XI's encyclical *Mit brennender Sorge*, which spelled out the incompatibility of Nazism with Christian principles, and reproduced messages broadcast on Vatican Radio denouncing Nazi atrocities in Poland.[81] At the heart of the resistance of *La Voix du Vatican* and that of other Catholic groups which resorted to clandestine activism was the profound conviction that Nazism represented the powers of darkness, and posed a dire threat not only to liberty but to the survival of Christianity itself. As Edmond Michelet, a former NEF militant who was to be deported to Dachau concentration camp for his Resistance activities, recalled: 'My position was in some ways more religious than political . . . (because) Nazism affected essential things'.[82]

Resistance, therefore, was not merely a reaction to defeat but more a continuation of an anti-Nazi crusade that was already under way. During the 'phoney war' period, Christian democrats tried to counter all talk of defeatism and refused to contemplate breaking with allies of France who were determined to stand up to Hitler. After the military collapse, they wanted to fight on.[83] On 17 June 1940 Edmond Michelet

---

[78] cf. H. R. Kedward, *Resistance in Vichy France* (Oxford, 1978).

[79] R. Bédarida, *Les Armes de l'esprit: Témoignage chrétien, 1941–1944* (Paris, 1977).

[80] Rauch, *Politics of Belief*, 236.   [81] Christophe, *1939–1940*, 107–10.

[82] J. Charbonnel, *Edouard Michelet* (Paris, 1987), 46; cf. the memoirs of P.-H. Teitgen, *'Faites-entrer le témoin suivant', 1940–1958: De la Résistance à la ve République* (Paris, 1988).

[83] Christophe, *1939–1940*, 146 ff.; Rauch, *Politics of Belief*, 236 ff.; Delbreil, 'Les Démocrates populaires'.

prepared a pamphlet for the citizens of Brive, urging them to ignore Pétain's call for an armistice. Maurice Schumann, a convert from Judaism and a militant of the Jeune République, joined General de Gaulle in London and became the best known broadcaster on behalf of the Free French. Other JR militants started the underground group Valmy in January 1941, which was broken up in October 1942. Among the eighty parliamentarians who refused to vote full powers to Marshal Pétain on 10 July 1940 were two PDP deputies (Pierre Trémintin and Paul Simon) and a PDP senator (Auguste Champetier de Ribes, who was to be arrested in 1942), along with Philippe Serre and Paul Boulet of the *Jeune République*. From 1940 François de Menthon was the editor of the clandestine newspaper *Liberté*, which was distributed by Christian democrats such as Pierre-Henri Teitgen in Montpellier, Etienne Borne in Toulouse, Charles d'Aragon in the Lower Pyrenees, and Edmond Michelet in Brive. Eventually, the group fused with *Combat*, the network headed by Henri Frenay and Claude Bourdet and whose members came to include Emmanuel Mounier and Georges Bidault, who in 1943 succeeded Jean Moulin as president of the National Resistance Council (CNR). In northern France, which was occupied by the enemy from 1940, Christian democrats were likewise among the earliest resisters, as, for example, in the group of the rue de Lille, organized by Emilien Amaury of the PDP and including figures such as Ernest Pezet and Raymond-Laurent. Others joined Résistance Nord and a few even found their way into Front National, which was one of the principal organs of Communist resistance.

Christian trade-unionism, another expression of Christian democracy, had its own distinguished Resistance record.[84] Gaston Tessier was one of the founders of Libération-Nord and represented the CFTC on the National Resistance Council. From the first, militants like Paul Vignaux were determined to maintain an independent trade-union movement in the face of Vichy's corporatist tendencies, and above all to resist the imposition of a single and obligatory union as stipulated by the Labour Charter. In the southern zone, links were forged with the CGT and its general secretary Jouhaux in the underground Mouvement Ouvrier Français, which was particularly strong in Lyons and Toulouse.

The specialized groups of Catholic Action were another rich source of Resistance activity. If the JAC adhered to Vichy's Corporation paysanne, students in the JEC tried to counter Vichy's anti-Semitic laws by distributing anti-Nazi and anti-racist tracts, and notably the text of *Mit brennender Sorge*. The introduction of compulsory labour service in Germany in February 1943 met with protests from the ACJF and the JOC. Militant Jocistes, indeed, decided to show their solidarity with the deportees by joining them in exile: some 10,000 cells and 70 federations were established in 400 German cities, which, as in the case of Marcel Callo and others, frequently led to persecution and martyrdom. Abbé Guérin, founder of the JOC was arrested, and the organization's cells in Paris closed down. Other Jocistes, rather than accept deportation to work in Germany, joined fellow workers in taking to the Maquis.[85]

---

[84] Launay, 'Le Syndicalisme chrétien'; M. Branciard, *Histoire de la CFDT: Soixante-dix ans d'action syndicale* (Paris, 1990).   [85] Cholvy and Hilaire, *Histoire religieuse*, iii. 85–9.

While still engaged in the struggle against Nazism, Resistance leaders began to turn their minds towards the shape which France should take at the Liberation.[86] Combat, for example, established a study group in 1942, the Comité générale d'études, with a journal *Les Cahiers politiques*, to examine proposals for reform of the social and economic structures of the country. Members, who included Bidault and François de Menthon as well as the socialists Robert Lacoste and André Philip, met together in Paris at the house of Francisque Gay. Bidault also canvassed the idea of launching a new, broad-based political movement, without being very specific about its character. If any single individual can be credited with giving a decisive push to the creation of such an organization, it was the young JEC militant Gilbert Dru, a disciple of Mounier and admirer of Péguy, who energetically combated Nazi ideas and Vichy in the student milieu in Lyons in his *Cahiers de notre jeunesse*. The suppression of his journal in 1943 spurred him to even greater activism on behalf of what he called 'the Movement', which he conceived of as an amalgamation of the forces of Christian democracy and the French republican tradition. Study and discussion of Dru's project took place in Resistance circles consisting largely of former PDP and social Catholic militants (not all of whom shared Dru's vision of a vast new revolutionary grouping, preferring instead the establishment of a more conventional but viable Christian democratic party) and led to a meeting at the house of Raymond-Laurent on 16 January 1944, where it was decided in principle to launch a new political organization. Initially called the Mouvement Républicain de Libération (MRL), under the direction of André Colin and René Simonnet of the ACJF it prepared a ringing manifesto which called for a revolution at the Liberation to free France not just from the Nazis and Vichy but also from the power of money and the capitalist system. In addition, it endorsed the sweeping changes envisaged by the Resistance Charter drawn up by the CNR. In practice, what was anticipated was a programme of nationalizations, enlargement of the role of the state in the management of the economy, and the establishment of a welfare state, along with the restoration of a democratic republic.[87] Gilbert Dru did not live to see what became of his dreams for a total renewal of his country: on 17 July 1944 he was captured by the Gestapo in Lyons and on 27 July publicly executed. Whether he would have approved of the direction taken by the reform movement must remain a moot point. For by November 1944 the MRL had become the MRP.

4. Post-1944

The Constituent Assembly of the MRP was held on 24/25 November 1944 with all the currents of French Christian democracy represented—the two parties of the inter-war years, the PDP and the JR, the ACJF and the specialized groups of Catholic Action, along with the workers of the CFTC.[88] Thus, the delegates present

---

[86] On this subject generally, see A. Shennan, *Rethinking France: Plans for Renewal 1940–1946* (Oxford, 1989).

[87] J.-M. Domenach, *Gilbert Dru, celui qui croyait au ciel* (Paris, 1947): Rauch, *Politics of Belief*, 240 ff.

[88] On the founding of the MRP, see the memoirs of R. Bichet, *La Démocratie chrétienne en France: Le*

were conscious of representing not only the new spirit of the Resistance but a v;ener-
able tradition which, as Maurice Guérin told them, stretched back to Lamennais and
L'Avenir and embraced the whole history of social Catholicism in France.[89] Continuity was symbolized by the presence at the proceedings of Marc Sangnier, who received rapturous applause when he rose to speak and was elected honorary president
of the new organization. The prospects of the party seemed excellent. Its very newness appeared to offer the possibility of a new broom in French politics. On account
of its Resistance record, it occupied a role at the centre of national political life which
had always been denied the PDP and the JR. Georges Bidault was appointed minister of foreign affairs in the provisional government formed by de Gaulle in September 1944, while other MRP leaders—François de Menthon, Pierre-Henri Teitgen,
and Maurice Schumann—were fellow ministers. Participation in the Resistance also
reinforced the image of the MRP as a genuinely republican party, which boosted its
credibility on the left. At the same time, given that the old right-wing parties had
been completely discredited, the MRP was initially the repository of conservative
and Catholic votes, which more than any other factor accounted for its astonishing
electoral success in 1945 and 1946. In the elections of 21 October 1945, the party
polled 4,580,222 votes (23.9 per cent of the votes cast) and won 150 seats. In June
1946 it fared even better, polling 5,589,213 votes (28.2 per cent of the votes cast). In
November 1946 it dropped to 4,988,609 votes (25.9 per cent of the votes cast) but
won 173 seats as opposed to 166 in June. In the immediate post-war period, the MRP
thus emerged, alongside the Socialists and the Communists, as one of the key players
in a tripartite division of political power.

Party militants hoped to remake France in the image of Christian democracy. As
Albert Gortais put it: 'the doctrine which inspires the policy of the MRP . . . is
founded on a spiritualistic conception of man, on a completely humanistic conception of society'.[90] Society was seen as being made up not of atomized individuals but
of natural social groups, which it was the business of the State to protect and to regu-
late. This communitarian ethic was perhaps the most distinctive and controversial
element in the party's doctrine, repudiated on all sides by those who refused to speak
its special language. Nevertheless, as developed by theorists of the calibre of Etienne
Gilson and Etienne Borne, the doctrine of the MRP amounted to more than vague,
high-sounding pieties. Rather, it urged, in Bidault's phrase, a *révolution par la loi*
which would complete political democracy with social democracy and steer a middle
course between liberalism and Marxism. Idealistic and altruistic, the MRP presented itself as a centre party which rejected the old politics of two opposing blocs in
favour of reconciliation and renewal.

Though never officially a Catholic Party, the MRP was unmistakeably the principal

Mouvement Républicain Populaire (Besançon, 1980). The standard history is still R. E. M. Irving, *Christian Democracy in France* (London, 1973). See also, E.-F. Callot, *Le Mouvement Républicain Populaire: Origine, structure, doctrine, programme et action politique* (Paris, 1978).

[89] M. Einaudi and F. Goguel, *Christian Democracy in Italy and France* (Notre-Dame, Incl., 1952), 109.
Continuity is also stressed by Pezet, *Chrétiens au service de la cité*, 82.
[90] Einaudi and Goguel, *Christian Democracy*, 126.

incarnation of political Catholicism in post-war France. Of the 204 deputies elected to parliament in the first three elections after the war, more than half came from a background of militancy in Catholic Action. A similar proportion had previously been members of either the PDP or the JR, while around 15 per cent had been active in the CFTC. The Catholic connection with the party remained strong throughout its existence. Thus, in 1959 seven out of thirteen members of the National Bureau were products of Catholic Action, while all the other members had links to some other Catholic organization. Similarly, thirty out of thirty-nine members of the National Executive Committee had previous experience of activism in Catholic groups. In electoral terms, the party was strongest in the most Catholic parts of France—in the West, Champagne, Alsace-Lorraine, and the South-East. It also benefited strongly from the arrival of a female electorate (French women having finally obtained the right to vote in 1944). A survey in 1952 found that two-thirds of the practising Catholic female population claimed to vote for the MRP.[91]

Yet for all its enthusiasm and idealism, the MRP failed to break the mould of French politics. By 1947 it was already clear that the dream of renewal and *révolution par la loi* was not to be realized. Goodwill on the part of the MRP was not enough to transform the French political scene while other, more potent, forces were at work: the onset of the Cold War, the expulsion of the Communists from government in 1947 and the creation of General de Gaulle's RPF, the Rassemblement du Peuple Français or 'Rally of the French People', in the same year. Disgusted by what he viewed as a return to the party politics of the Third Republic, de Gaulle made no secret of his ambitions to replace the new-born Fourth Republic with a more authoritarian, presidential regime headed by himself. Overnight, the MRP lost the special status it had claimed as the 'party of fidelity' to de Gaulle, a loss reflected in the desertion to the RPF of leading lights such as Edmond Michelet and Louis Terrenoire, the son-in-law of Francisque Gay. At the same time, it lost a significant portion of its electorate among conservatives who had only supported the party *faute de mieux*. In the municipal elections in Paris in 1947 the party lost about 75 per cent of the votes which it had obtained the previous year. The damage was less severe in the legislative elections of 1951, but the party's vote slumped nevertheless to 2,370,000 votes (12.6 per cent of the votes cast) and 95 seats. The comparable figures in the legislative elections of 1956 were 2,366,000 votes (11.1 per cent of the votes cast) and 83 seats.

In the opinion of Francisque Gay, it was a serious error on the part of the MRP leadership to have opted to remain in government in the circumstances which obtained after 1947, and which resulted in the party's identification with the 'Third Force' (the ruling coalition of MRP, Socialists, Radicals, and moderates formed to contain the threat from both the PCF and the RPF) and in consequence with the politics of immobilism so characteristic of the Fourth Republic.[92] In their defence, however, it should be said that the MRP leaders took their commitment to a democratic republic seriously, and were determined to see off the challenge of both

[91] The figures in this para. are taken from Irving, *Christian Democracy*.
[92] F. Gay, *Les Démocrates d'inspiration chrétienne à l'épreuve du pouvoir* (Paris, 1951).

extreme left and extreme right. A more serious charge might be that they failed to adapt their doctrine and programme to the challenges of the times. The party manifested a remarkable lack of flexibility in its almost obsessive pursuit of a genuine centre ground in French politics, appearing ready to go to almost any lengths to prevent the re-emergence of the historical right–left division. Hence its unwavering commitment to the Third Force, and, if needs must, the politics of immobilism. Simply by remaining a government party it underwent a significant shift to the right. To placate the Radicals and moderates, the party was obliged to jettison its more advanced ideals on social and economic questions, all the more so when the MRP's determination to see Catholic schools subsidized by the State as stipulated by the Barangé Law of 1951 embittered relations with the Socialist Party and led it to support the government formed in 1952 by the conservative Antoine Pinay.

Even more disastrous was the party's influence in the sphere of colonial policy, over which it presided for much of the period of the Fourth Republic. At the Ministry of Overseas France, MRP ministers were responsible for some of the most indefensible and damaging policies of the regime: the war in Indo-China, savage repression in Madagascar between 1947 and 1949 which cost the lives of 100,000 people, and the coup against the Sultan of Morocco in 1953. Until 1958 the party upheld the idea of *Algérie française*, though it also favoured reform, and it was to defend this cause that Georges Bidault and others on the right of the party eventually broke away to form their own *Démocratie chrétienne* group which not only remained implacably hostile to de Gaulle's plans for Algerian independence but even supported OAS terrorism. The MRP's commitment to hard-line colonialism is difficult to reconcile with its general ideology and traditions. Idealistically, the party's liberals spoke of spreading economic, social, and political progress throughout France's overseas possessions, but the right of the party remained strongly attached to the traditional 'civilizing mission' of French colonial policy which aimed to assimilate the peoples of the Empire rather than prepare them for independence. Moreover, the Empire had historically been a vehicle for the spread of Catholicism through missionary activity. Even Gambetta, the early Third Republican leader who promoted the secularization of the French state and society, had stipulated that anticlericalism was not for export. A public opinion poll in 1946 discovered that practising Catholics were more in favour of the maintenance of the colonies than other Frenchmen.[93] Faced with the pressing problems of decolonization which developed after 1945, the MRP failed to look at the situation with a fresh eye. Bidault represented the extreme case of its inability to move with the times. Undoubtedly gifted, he suffered from an over-confidence in his own ability as well as from an addiction to alcohol, both of which left him in many ways a victim of his own past. Continuing to interpret contemporary events in the light of Munich and 1940, he equated any compromise with the Algerian nationalists of the FLN with capitulation to the Nazis.[94]

---

[93] N. Ravitch, *The Catholic Church and the French Nation 1589–1989* (London 1990) 137.
[94] A critical biography of Bidault is a notable lacuna in the historiography. To date there is only the hagiographical B. Ott, *Georges Bidault: L'Indomptable* (Annonay, 1975).

In the area of foreign policy, however, the party arguably showed itself in a better light, though here again it was obliged to abandon many of the aspirations it had entertained in the immediate aftermath of the war. Just as it opposed the formation of two hostile blocs on the domestic front, so too the MRP opposed the division of the world into two camps and aspired to see France emerge as an independent power, bolstered by the resources of its colonial empire. Initially, it sought to maintain Germany in a position of weakness, so as to increase French preponderance in Western Europe. Once again, however, the onset of the Cold War compelled the party to abandon its grand designs, cherished above all by Bidault, but in this instance, largely thanks to the influence of Robert Schuman, who occupied the Quai d'Orsay in ten successive governments between 1948 and 1953, it succeeded in evolving an attractive alternative vision in the form of the European idea. Based essentially on Franco-German reconciliation, European integration became the goal of MRP policy after 1950 and achieved tangible expression in the creation of the European Economic Community in 1956. Born in Luxemburg in 1886, raised in German Lorraine and trained in German law before embarking on a political career in France after the First World War, Schuman epitomized the European idea in his own person, viewing it as a logical extension of his own commitment to a Christian civilization which was threatened by Soviet domination and Communist subversion.[95] If 'Europeanism' was stymied by the return to power of de Gaulle in 1958, it was to be taken up enthusiastically by his successors (and in particular by François Mitterrand) and the MRP can therefore rightly be credited with having blazed a trail which others would follow long after the party had ceased to exist.

Already unable to mobilize more than 8.8 per cent of the electorate in 1956, the MRP, like the Fourth Republic itself, was condemned to death by the establishment of the Fifth Republic in 1958. Under the new presidential regime established by de Gaulle, the role of all political parties was diminished, but for a party of the centre ground like the MRP life became simply impossible. However much the party criticized de Gaulle's more authoritarian regime and his nationalistic foreign policy, once the Gaullists succeeded in establishing themselves as the representatives of conservatism, potential Christian democrat voters preferred them to the MRP rather than risk giving victory to the left. In the elections of November 1962, only 5.3 per cent of the electorate voted for the the party (as opposed to 8.3 per cent in 1958) and at the second ballot a substantial number defected to the Gaullists. Most militants accepted that the party had outlived its usefulness. Some, like Pflimlin and especially Maurice Schumann, opted to merge with the new conservative majority in the hope of acting as a Christian democratic leaven within it. Others followed the lead given by Jean Lecanuet and Joseph Fontanet in 1963 in setting up a new opposition party, the Centre Démocrate.[96]

The protracted death and not always glorious life of the MRP should not, however, detract from its very real achievements. Shortcomings it had in plenty. If the

---

[95] The Christian dimension of Schuman's policy is stressed by R. Poidevin, *Robert Schuman* (Paris, 1988). [96] cf. Irving, *Christian Democracy*, 231 ff.

religious training of the leadership fostered a certain idealism and camaraderie, it failed to provide genuine political experience and encouraged a tendency towards cliquishness and sentimentality. Moreover, the Catholic orientation of the party was a weakness as well as a strength, since it confined its support largely to traditionally Catholic parts of the country and saddled it with a confessional image which it found difficult to shed. But the most serious problems encountered by the MRP were hardly of its own making. As a party of the centre, it found itself out of joint with the configuration of both domestic and international politics after 1945. Thus, the high hopes entertained in the Liberation era were never capable of realization and should not be used as the yardstick by which to measure the party's lack of success. Doubtless, the MRP would have done better to try to make genuine openings to the left rather than allow itself to become first the prisoner of the moderates and Radicals and then the victim of the Gaullists. But, for a monument, at least the party could point to its pioneering work in the field of European policy. It could also take pride in its contribution to the creation of a comprehensive system of social security in the post-war period and the establishment of a very generous system of family allowances during Robert Prigent's tenure of the health ministry in 1946. Moreover, in electoral terms, the MRP had an impact which significantly surpassed that of the PDP in the period between the wars. In the countryside, it made a certain amount of progress at the expense of the old right, while in urban areas, if its appeal was above all to middle-class professionals, it was able nonetheless to convince at least significant numbers of working people, in the Nord and in Alsace-Lorraine in particular, that a Catholic Party need not be their enemy. 12 per cent of the MRP's deputies elected in June 1946 were themselves of working-class origin.

The MRP was only the principal, not the sole, representative of political Catholicism in post-war France. Indeed, other groups, starting with Mounier and *Esprit*, were highly critical of its role and adopted positions much further to the Left. The first review to reappear in Liberated France (in December 1944), *Esprit* no longer maintained its pre-war 'neither right nor left' position but strongly identified itself with a philosophy of personalism which it claimed was directly descended from nineteenth-century French utopian socialism.[97] In Mounier's view the time was ripe for both moral regeneration and a political revolution that would sweep away the capitalist economy and bourgeois society. The revolution, of course, did not take place, but for a time personalism enjoyed a vogue as the most prestigious intellectual current within French Catholicism, which helped to make Catholic socialism a valid political ideology. Ideally, Mounier would have liked to see the formation of a French Labour party, capable of uniting all the democratic forces in the country between the PCF and the extreme right, and much of his resentment of the MRP derived from its opposition to such a project. Relations with the Communist Party were the thorniest problem of Mounier's last years (he died in 1950). Greatly strengthened by its Resistance record, the PCF was undoubtedly the party which spoke for the great

---

[97] Hellman, *Emmanuel Mounier*, 202 ff.

mass of the French proletariat in the immediate post-war years and Mounier recognized that there could be no revolution in France without its participation. At the same time, he was not blind to the crimes of Stalinism. He therefore attempted to engage in dialogue with the PCF and refused to indulge in the kind of crude Communist-bashing characteristic of the Cold War era, only to find himself misunderstood and attacked by Communists and the right alike.[98] Here again Mounier was a precursor, opening up pathways down which others would follow later.

Some elements of the Catholic avant-garde had a more positive view of communism even in the 1940s.[99] The Union des chrétiens progressistes, founded in 1947 by André Mandouze and other intellectuals, was a fellow-travelling organisation which refused to abandon the ideals of Gilbert Dru and the Resistance and was soon the object of ecclesiastical sanctions in 1949.[100] Another group, the Jeunesse de l'Église, animated by the Dominican Maurice Montuclard and his brother Paul, dated back to 1936 and had been active in the Resistance. It, too, turned towards Marxism in the search for a more dynamic and communitarian Christianity which would appeal to the working-class.[101] Yet another Dominican, Père Henri Desroches, a member of the study group *Economie et Humanisme* established by his Dominican confrère Père Lebret, aimed at a theoretical reconciliation of Christianity with Marxism in the interests of promoting international peace.[102] The peace movement also attracted other 'red priests', such as the abbé Jean Boulier, who helped Frédéric Joliot-Curie draft the celebrated *Appel de Stockholm* and was subsequently laicized for his collaboration with Communists.[103] All these groups had little time for, and in turn were regarded with suspicion by, the MRP, though it should be noted that the party itself had its dissidents on the left who objected to its increasingly virulent anticommunism. Men like Paul Boulet, Charles d'Aragon, and the abbé Pierre represented a left-wing tendency which eventually led to their expulsion in 1954, while from within the fold others such as Léo Hamon continued to remind the leadership of the MRP's original ideals and kept up the friendships they had forged with Communists in the days of the Resistance.[104] The advanced wing of the MRP also had an influential mouthpiece in the newspaper *Témoignage chrétien*, which criticized the party for its stance on Catholic schools and colonial policy.[105]

Political Catholicism's shift to the left was reinforced by developments within the social Catholic movement. By far the most dramatic initiative was the worker-priest experiment, begun during the Occupation when a number of young priests opted to join the workers conscripted into the German labour force.[106] Their discovery of

---

[98] Rauch, *Politics of Belief*, 252 ff.

[99] On the Catholic avant-garde generally, see J.-M. Domenach and R. de Montvalon, *The Catholic Avant-Garde: French Catholicism since World War II* (New York, 1967).

[100] Rauch, *Politics of Belief*, 289–91.   [101] Ibid. 285–6.   [102] Ibid. 287.

[103] J. Boulier, *J'étais un prêtre rouge: Souvenirs et témoignages* (Paris, 1977).

[104] Einaudi and Goguel, *Christian Democracy*, 171–2.   [105] Irving, *Christian Democracy*, 83.

[106] cf. O. L. Arnal, *Priests in Working-Class Blue: The History of the Worker-Priests (1943–1954)* (Mahwah, 1986). An interesting memoir is *Priest and Worker: The Autobiography of Henri Perrin*, trans. Bernard Wall (London, 1965).

the dechristianized working class tallied with the findings of a report carried out by two priests at the behest of Cardinal Suhard, the Archbishop of Paris, which was published as *France, Pays de Mission?* in 1943 and advanced the thesis that new, missionary-type, techniques were necessary if the French Church was to stand any chance of renewing links with the proletariat.[107] The establishment of the Mission de Paris, a mission to the working classes of the Paris region, followed swiftly in 1944 and brought young priests and seminarians into direct contact with workers on the shop floor. Other dioceses such as Lyons and Marseilles lent their support, as did various religious orders, notably the Jesuits and the Dominicans.[108] But problems arose when some of the priests identified with the workers to the point where they joined in strike movements and in political activities orchestrated essentially by the Communist Party. Right-wing Catholics and employers were outraged and campaigned relentlessly to have the experiment suppressed. For a time the French bishops succeeded in protecting the priests from the anti-Communist die-hards in the Roman Curia, but in 1953 the Holy See put a stop to further recruitment. The movement began to break up as some priests preferred ecclesiastical censure and excommunication to the abandonment of their working-class comrades. Stifled in the short run, the spirit of the worker-priests, however, undoubtedly contributed to the renewal that was to take place under Pope John XXIII and the Second Vatican Council.

Catholic Action itself underwent considerable changes in the post-war period.[109] While some members continued to view their commitment in strictly religious terms, others began to insist on the need for transformations in political, social, and economic structures as a pre-condition for an enriched spiritual life. Catholic Action was divided into two groups according to gender in 1945: Action Catholique Générale Hommes (ACGH) and Action Catholique Générale Femmes (ACGF). These adult groups, however, were less dynamic than the specialized youth groups, which initially remained branches of the ACJF. By raising the age limit for membership, the JOC (known after 1950 as Action Catholique Ouvrière) and the JAC made headway in winning new recruits. The latter, for instance, numbered 300,000 in the mid-1950s and by 1961 had taken control of the Fédération Nationale de Syndicats d'Exploitants Agricoles (FNSEA), the principal farmers' organization. It was the youth movements (with the exception of the JOC) which increasingly insisted on addressing the problems of the temporal realm and in consequence they found themselves at odds with the Church hierarchy who wished them to refrain from meddling with the affairs of Caesar. Torn apart by internal quarrels, the ACJF disbanded in 1956.

The evolution of the trade-union organization the CFTC took place along similar lines. After 1945 the minority Reconstruction current sought to 'de-confessionalize'

---

[107] H. Godin and Y. Daniel, *France, pays de mission?* (Paris, 1943).

[108] cf. D. Perrot, *La Fondation de la Mission de France* (Paris, 1987).

[109] A good guide is W. Bosworth, *Catholicism and Crisis in Modern France: French Catholic Groups at the Threshold of the Fifth Republic* (Princeton, 1962). See also J. Debes, *Naissance de l'Action Catholique Ouvrière* (Paris, 1982).

the organization and to work for the creation of a socialist society. Sharply critical of the MRP, it opposed subsidies for Catholic schools and steadily increased its support within the union to the point where in 1964 it succeeded in having its name changed from the CFTC to the Confédération Française Démocratique du Travail (CFDT).[110]

Yet another manifestation of the shift from right to left was the new direction taken by the Catholic Scout movement. A conservative body in the period before the war, after a flirtation with Vichy and the experience of the Resistance, scouting inspired the creation of the group La Vie Nouvelle in 1947, which not only propagated the personalist ideas of Mounier but increasingly took on a left-wing political orientation over the course of the 1950s.[111] The same trajectory can be traced in the story of the Mouvement Populaire des Familles (MPF), founded in 1942 as a fusion of the male and female branches of the Ligue Ouvrière Chrétienne (LOC), an offshoot of Catholic Action which before the war had carried on the work of the JOC among the adult population.[112] During the Occupation, however, it had become increasingly drawn into the politics of the Resistance and after 1945 it was denied recognition as a Catholic Action organization. In 1949 it changed its name to the Mouvement de Libération du Peuple (MLP) in confirmation of its changed priorities. In the late 1950s the MLP, joined by most of the JR, formed part of the coalition of left-wing Christians, ex-SFIO Socialists, disillusioned Communists, former Mendésistes, and others who in 1960 constituted themselves into the Parti Socialiste Unifié (PSU). By 1960 the 'new Catholic left' was clearly a reality.

Its importance, however, should not be exaggerated. Whatever the trends within the élites of Catholic Action, the bulk of the Catholic electorate, as in the past, continued to support the parties of the right. In 1952 only 8 per cent of practising Catholics voted for the left: the rest divided their allegiance between the MRP (54 per cent), Independents (20 per cent), and the Gaullist RPF (18 per cent).[113] After 1958 the central political reality was the resurgence of the Right in the formidable shape of Gaullism, which, as we have seen, thwarted the ambitions of the MRP to mobilize Catholics behind the banner of Christian democracy as in Italy or Germany. The passing of the Debré law in 1959, which provided extensive State assistance to public schools, encouraged the great majority of the Catholic electorate to identify with the Gaullist party as the one best able to defend their interests. The political demise of the General in 1969 in no way arrested the tendency of practising Catholics to side with the right: as late as 1980 an opinion poll showed four-fifths of their number to be so inclined.[114]

Similarly, the rise of a Catholic left should not obscure the survival of a die-hard reactionary Catholic right. Men like Xavier Vallat sought to maintain the alliance between integral Catholicism and integral nationalism.[115] The latter ideology,

---

[110] G. Adam, 'De la CFTC à la CFDT', *Revue Française des Sciences Politiques*, 15 (1965), 87–103.
[111] Rauch, *Politics of Belief*, 321–2. [112] Ibid. 316–17; Dansette, *Destin*, 372–8.
[113] J. F. Sirinelli (ed.), *Histoire des droites en France*, iii. *Sensibilités* (Paris, 1992), 671. [114] Ibid.
[115] cf. X. Vallat, *Le Nez de Cléopâtre: Souvenirs d'un homme de droite 1918–1945* (Paris, 1957).

discredited at the Liberation, made a steady comeback under the Fourth Republic in the wake of the colonial wars in Indo-China and Algeria, as embittered army officers and their press spokesmen blamed French failures on Communist subversion at home. Newspapers which represented the integral nationalist current such as *L'Observateur catholique* reserved some of their strongest invective for the abuse of 'Christian Stalinists', and throughout the 1950s French Catholic reactionaries bombarded the Holy Office in Rome with denunciations of their co-religionists (like the worker-priests or activists in the peace movement) who appeared to be colluding with the Communist enemy.[116] Integrism, indeed, was to survive even the Second Vatican Council, and resurfaced powerfully in the 1970s in the schismatic movement headed by Archbishop Lefebvre.

Thus French Catholicism remained deeply divided, and in the 1960s its potential was further diminished by a steep decline in religious practice, which finally convinced social Catholics that their original project of re-creating a new Christendom was hopelessly unrealistic. Instead, they began to settle for witnessing to their faith in a predominantly non-Christian world. Yet if political Catholicism in France never enjoyed the more spectacular successes it scored in countries where it gave birth to a mass Catholic Party, in its richness and diversity of expression it nevertheless contributed much to French political life in the twentieth century. Above all, the shift to the left brought Catholics out of the right-wing ghetto where they had been confined at the turn of the century, and in this way served to make France a more genuinely pluralist, tolerant, and democratic society.

[116] Y. Tranvouez, 'Entre Rome et le peuple (1920–1960), in F. Lebrun (ed.), *Histoire du catholicisme en France du xvᵉ siècle à nos jours* (Toulouse, 1982), 476–7.

2

Italy

JOHN POLLARD

1. Introduction

The history of political Catholicism in modern Italy stands apart from that in most other European countries for a number of reasons: the long history of Catholic hostility to the State, the key role which the Papacy played in the ideological and organizational development of Italian political Catholicism, and the completeness of its triumph in the parliamentary arena in the post-war period, which has allowed the Catholic Party uninterrupted dominance of governmental power until very recently. Yet that history has otherwise much in common with the history of political Catholicism elsewhere, so that in this survey of the development of political Catholicism in Italy between 1918 and 1968 many of the themes will be the same as those which feature in other chapters. In particular, emphasis will be placed on the relationship between the ecclesiastical hierarchy, especially the Papacy, and the various organizational forms which political Catholicism took in this period, and on the interaction between the Italian Catholic movement in general and the political activities of Italian Catholics. After 1918 this meant essentially Catholic Action and the Partito Popolare Italiano (PPI) and after 1945 Catholic Action and the Democrazia Cristiana (DC).

Another very important strand is the ideological development of Italian Catholic activism, both in terms of the input of papal social teaching and the response of Catholic political thinkers and politicians to non-Catholic and even anti-Catholic sources of economic, social, and political ideas. Similarly, the geographical and social bases of Italian Catholic political activism, and especially of its electorate, from 1905 onwards, require careful analysis, as do the relations between overtly party-political forms of Catholic activism in Italy, and its social and economic manifestations, especially the Catholic trade unions and peasant leagues.

Finally, Catholic political pluralism, both inside and outside the mainstream Catholic movement, with a recurrent tension between the intransigent and more conciliatorist tendencies, are a characteristic of the development of Italian political Catholicism in this period. It also needs to be stressed that Italian political Catholicism has a long pre-history prior to the end of the First World War. For this reason, considerable attention will be devoted to the origins and development of the Italian Catholic movement in the late nineteenth and early twentieth centuries. Without this background, it is almost impossible to understand the development of political Catholicism between 1918 and 1968.

2. The Origins of Political Catholicism in Italy: From the Opera dei Congressi to the Giolitti–Gentiloni Pact

Modern Italian political Catholicism was called into being by the Holy See in a special set of circumstances for clearly defined purposes, in essence as the agent of the Papacy in its struggle against the Liberal State in the nineteenth century. The processes of national liberation and state-building carried out by the moderate liberal political class during the course of the Risorgimento steadily ate away at both the territorial sovereignty of the popes in the Papal States of central Italy, and the legal privileges, landed property, and social influence which the Church enjoyed elsewhere in the peninsula. The final destruction of the temporal power of the Papacy came with the occupation of Rome in September 1870 and its proclamation as the capital of Italy. The response of Pius IX was to breathe anathemas and excommunications against the 'subalpine usurpers' (the Savoyard royal family) and all others who had assisted in the despoliation of the Church. Thus was born the 'Roman Question', as the Church–State conflict was called, which was to poison Italy's internal politics and complicate its foreign relations for several decades.[1]

More practical methods of protest were also adopted: already in 1864 the Roman Curia had issued the *Non Expedit*, a decree forbidding Catholics to vote or offer themselves as candidates in the elections of the Kingdom of Italy. This had the effect of reducing the already tiny electorate by half, and depriving the new state of the talents of some of its most gifted citizens. But the most effective form of protest, and of defence against the secularism and anticlericalism of the Liberal State, was the creation of a Catholic movement, starting with the Società della Gioventù Cattolica (Catholic Youth Association) in 1868.[2]

The first forms of Italian political Catholicism were thus essentially 'anti-system'; obedience to the Pope took the form of the most intransigent hostility to the Liberal State and all its works. In their newspapers, in their youth and recreational groups, and at their regular congresses, which gave the original Catholic movement its name, the Opera dei Congressi, Catholic leaders, clerical and lay, inveighed against the evils and iniquities of both political and economic liberalism. Capitalistic individualism was the object of particular criticism, and on this basis the Catholic movement shifted naturally towards the organization of the Catholic masses, especially in the countryside. Even before the publication of Leo XIII's social encyclical *Rerum Novarum* in 1891, the movement was seeking to organize the Catholic masses and insulate them from liberal anticlericalism. The next step would be to create more specifically eco-

---

[1] C. A. Jemolo, *Church and State in Italy, 1850–1950* (Oxford, 1960), chs. 1 and 2. For a general history of Italy covering the period of this study, see M. Clark, *Modern Italy, 1871–1982* (London, 1983).

[2] On the origins of the Catholic movement, see R. A. Webster, *The Cross and the Fasces: Christian Democracy and Fascism in Italy* (Stanford, 1960), ch. 1; G. De Rosa, *Storia del movimento cattolico in Italia* (Bari, 1966), vol. i, chs. 1–5; and C. Seton-Watson, *Italy from Liberalism to Fascism* (London, 1967), ch. 6.

nomic institutions for paternalistic, benevolent purposes: peasant co-operatives, *casse di risparmio* (credit banks) and eventually embryonic organizations for Catholic workers.

As a result of its intransigence, the Italian Catholic movement adopted the psychology and rhetoric of an alienated subculture. Not surprisingly, therefore, during the 'end-of-century crisis' of the 1890s, when Italy was racked by recurrent economic difficulties, and resulting social distress and disorder, many Catholic leaders found themselves tarred with the same brush as their counterparts in the other alienated subculture struggling to emerge in Italy at this time: the working-class movement. Several Catholic organizers, including priests, such as the intransigent leader Don Davide Albertario, were thrown into prison as subversives along with Anarchist, Socialist, and Republican leaders.[3]

From its inception in the 1860s, the strength of the Italian Catholic movement lay in the North: in Venetia, north-eastern Lombardy, and southern Piedmont, in that order. More specifically, it was concentrated in the provinces of Belluno, Padua, Treviso, Vicenza and Verona, Bergamo, Brescia, Como, Sondrio, and Cuneo. Outside these 'white' areas, as they were known, there were some isolated enclaves of Catholic strength in central Italy, such as the Marches on the Adriatic coast, the province of Lucca in Tuscany, and in the South the province of Lecce (Apulia), the eastern coastal strip of Calabria, and parts of the interior of Sicily. All these provinces were primarily rural and agrarian: the Catholic movement rarely had a strong following in the great industrial or regional capitals. Milan, the centre of a particularly strong Catholic tradition, the Ambrosian Church, was the exception to this rule, and only then in a partial fashion because, as a result of industrialization, the rival working-class movement there grew rapidly in strength. The strength of the Catholic movement in its heartlands can be explained by a number of factors, the first of which was the efficiency of the Habsburg and, to a lesser extent, Piedmontese educational systems which ensured the emergence of an educated rural and small-town middle class on which the leadership of the network of Catholic organizations came to depend. These same cadres were eventually to provide the bulk of the local leadership of the PPI in the 1920s. Also very important was the fact that Catholic culture in Lombardy and Venetia during the Risorgimento was predominantly nationalist due to the presence of the national enemy, Austria, whereas in the Papal States it was strongly anti-nationalist given the stance of Pius IX. Thus Emilia-Romagna and Umbria developed a strong anticlerical tradition by way of reaction. Finally, in the white provinces, the parochial clergy was closer to the peasantry because it was largely recruited from its ranks. It is, therefore, no accident that of the six Italian popes this century, five—Pius X, Pius XI, John XXIII, Paul VI, and John Paul I—came from the peasantry or rural nobility of Lombardy and Venetia. By way of contrast, in most parts of the South ecclesiastical patronage was exercised by the local landowning élites and the parochial clergy were thus identified with their patrons in the minds of the peasantry. The future leader of the Catholic Party in the 1920s, Fr. Luigi Sturzo, had to

[3] Seton-Watson, *Italy*, ch. 5.

Table 2.1. Regional distribution of Popolari and Christian Democrat support, 1913–1979

Region	Popolari–Christian Democrat														Core areas
	1913*	1913†	1919	1921	1924	1946	1948	1953	1958	1963	1968	1972	1976	1979	
Piedmont	2.7	0.2	19	22	11	35	48	40	41	36	40	40	36	34	Cuneo
Liguria	7.4	0.3	20	24	13	32	46	39	40	32	35	35	34		
Lombardy (VdA)	14	11	30	26	17	39	52	46	45	40	45	44	41	40	Bergamo–Breiscia–Sondrio
Veneto	25	14	36	36	23‡	49	60	53	55	53	52	52	51	50	Padua. Vicenza
Fruili	—	—	—	3.2	8.2	47	57	50	44	43	43	43	42	37	Udine
Trent (Triest)	—	—	—	6.5	23‡	57	50	45	43	39	38	38	33	31	Trento
Emilia	—	4.4	18	19	8.0	23	33	30	30	26	28	27	28	27	
Tuscany	0.9	0.4	20	19	5.4	28	39	34	35	30	31	31	32	30	Lucca
Marches	—	5.2	27	30	10	31	47	42	43	38	39	39	39	38	Macerata
Umbria	—	—	17	16	5.3‡	26	36	31	33	30	29	30	30	29	
Latium	—	—	26	22	5.3‡	33	52	37	38	33	40	35	36	37	Frosinone
Abruzzi	—	—	7.2‡	7.2‡	1.7‡	42	52	41	46	45	49	48	44	46	Chieti
Molise	—	—	7.2‡	7.2‡	1.7‡	40	56	46	55	51	50	55	51	55	Campobasso
Campania	—	0.1	18	14	1.6	34	50	36	42	40	43	40	40	42	Caserta
Apulia	—	—	10	10	6.7	33	49	38	44	43	44	42	42	43	Lecce
Basilicata	—	4.5	—	4.2	3.3‡	31	48	41	47	42	49	49	45	44	Potenza
Calabria	—	—	18	19	3.3‡	34	49	41	47	44	42	39	39	43	Cosenza
Sicily	—	3.6	12	13	4.5	34	48	36	43	39	39	39	42	44	Catania
Sardinia	—	—	12	11	5.6	41	51	42	47	42	43	42	40	38	Nuoro
TOTAL	6.0	4.2	20	20	9.0	35	48	40	42	38	39	39	39	38	

* Conservatore cattolico.
† Cattolico.
‡ Part of a larger electoral district.
SOURCE: P. Farneti, *The Italian Party System: 1945–1980*, S. E. Finer and A. Mastropaolo (eds.), Francis Pinter, London, 1985.

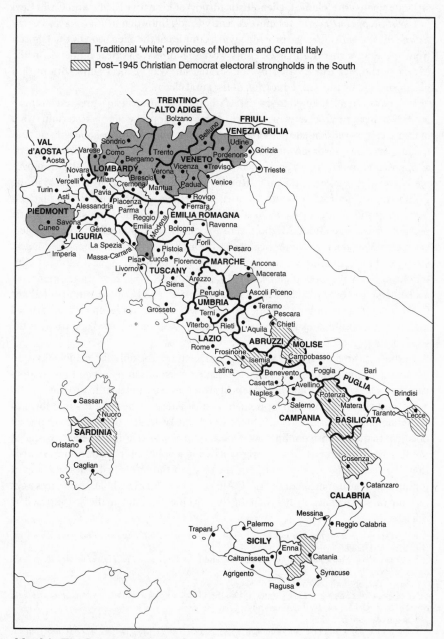

Map 2.1. The Catholic heartlands of Italy.

Source: P. Farneti, *The Italian Party System: 1945–1980*, S. E. Finer and A. Mastropaolo (eds.), Francis Pinter, London, 1985

struggle against the 'clerical, clientelistic torpor' of his native Sicily[4] and Carlo Levi in *Christ Stopped at Eboli*, and more recently Frank Snowden in *Violence and Great Estates in the South of Italy*,[5] provide vivid examples of the alienation of the Church from the Southern rural masses. This weakness of ecclesiastical influence in the Mezzogiorno was exacerbated by the strong survival of local superstitions and paganism, and by the poor education of the rural clergy.

It is, however, not enough to say that Catholic associationalism's greatest strength lay in Northern rural society; in practice, its greatest appeal was only to certain strata of that society—the landed aristocracy, the small-town professional bourgeoisie, and the property-owning or tenant peasantry and some of the *mezzadri* or sharecroppers, as opposed to the *braccianti* or day-labourers. This also explains the Catholic move-ment's relative weakness in Emilia-Romagna and most of Tuscany, and also in the Lombard provinces of Milan and Mantua, where the rural, wage-earning proletariat was strong and where it gave its loyalty to agrarian socialism. Even so, charismatic peasant leaders like Guido Miglioli were able to attract support from rural, prolet-arian elements, such as the *braccianti* on the rich dairy-farms, hence the modest strength of the Catholic peasant leagues in the province of Cremona. Catholic trade-unionism also made modest gains; in 1914, for example, the 'white' trade unions had a membership of over 100,000 whereas the socialist General Confederation of Labour (CGL) counted six times as many supporters.[6] Catholic trade-union strength lay mainly among professionals, for example teachers, and women workers, whereas the CGL drew support from workers in heavy industries.[7]

In the last three decades of the nineteenth century, the only discernible division within the Catholic movement had been that between intransigents and conciliator-ists, that is between the rigid upholders of abstentionism and hostility to the Liberal State, and those like bishops Bonomelli and Scalabrini who sought some form of accommodation with liberalism.[8] On the whole, the lay leaders of the Opera remained obedient to the intransigent line; even social reformists like Filippo Meda insisted at the turn of the century that they were following a policy of 'preparation in absten-tion'. Nevertheless, the experience of the crisis of the 1890s had had the effect of toning down the intransigence of the Catholic movement as a whole. More stress was now put on social issues, rather than the Roman Question, and on the threat posed by Socialism.

[4] P. Misner, *Social Catholicism in Europe: From the Onset of Industrialisation to the First World War* (London, 1991), 249.

[5] C. Levi, *Christ Stopped at Eboli* (London, 1982) and F. M. Snowden, *Violence and Great Estates in the South of Italy: Apulia, 1900–1922* (Cambridge, 1986), 79–86.

[6] Seton-Watson, *Italy*, 299 n. 2.

[5] C. Levi, *Christ Stopped at Eboli* (London, 1982) and F. M. Snowden, *Violence and Great Estates in the South of Italy: Apulia, 1900–1922* (Cambridge, 1986), 79–86.

[6] Seton-Watson, *Italy*, 299 n. 2.

[7] For a survey of Catholic trade-unionism, see S. Agocs, *The Troubled Origins of the Italian Catholic Movement, 1878–1914* (Detroit, 1988), chs. 7, 8, and 9; Misner, *Social Catholicism*, 255–61; and N. Pernicone, 'The Italian Labour Movement', in E. Tannenbaum and E. P. Noether (eds.), *Modern Italy: A Topical History* (New York, 1974).

[8] Seton-Watson, *Italy*, 219–34; and Jemolo, *Church and State*, 71–3.

There had already emerged in the Catholic world an influential lay movement which, in journals such as *Annali cattolici, Rivista universale,* and the *Rassegna nazionale,* struggled against the restrictions imposed by the 'Syllabus of Errors' and the *Non Expedit* in an attempt to insert Catholics into the political life of Italy, by means of a 'national, conservative party' that would embrace both Catholics and Liberals of goodwill.[9] The national conservatives were drawn in the main from the Catholic *haute bourgeoisie* and landed aristocracy especially, but not exclusively, of northern and central Italy. Indeed, in the last decades of the nineteenth century and the first of the twentieth, the Catholic bourgeoisie was building up powerful interests in the financial sector of the economy, especially banking and insurance; in agriculture; and to a lesser extent, manufacturing industry. In addition, they acquired a controlling influence over the Catholic press and therefore the Catholic movement as a whole.[10] They also became the leaders in those political activities permitted to Catholics by the *Non Expedit,* notably local government, and when the ban was relaxed at a national level in 1904 they were among the first Catholics to enter Parliament. Committed to a clerico-moderate position, that is to alliances with the less avowedly anticlerical elements of the Liberal establishment, they were to become, as Capitani D'Arzago, a Milanese political notable observed in 1908, to all intents and purposes merely the Catholic wing of the Liberal ruling class.[11]

The Italian invasion of Libya in 1911, which was strongly supported by Catholic financial interests clustered around the Bank of Rome and through the newspapers which they controlled, brought some clerico-moderates, as they were by now called, closer to the extreme right-wing Nationalist Association. When the majority of the clerico-moderates voted for Italian intervention in the First World War in 1915, all the ideological preconditions for the later Catholic conservative alliance with Fascism had already been fulfilled.[12]

Catholic intransigence, on the other hand, took a different direction. Those intransigents of a social reformist bent founded the Christian democracy movement. They were inspired by *Rerum Novarum* and by Pope Leo XIII's other major encyclical *On the Christian Constitution of States.* A further influence were the writings of the Catholic sociologist Giuseppe Toniolo, whose Milan *Programme of Catholics vis-à-vis Socialism* was predictably paternalistic, stressing the duty of work, the social function of property, supporting the formation of labour unions but condoning the use of the strike weapon only as a last resort. Led by two priests, Romolo Murri and Luigi Sturzo, the Christian democrats eventually elaborated a programme of economic, social, and political reform which, in the event of a Catholic entry into national politics, aimed at a radical transformation of the Liberal State. The Turin Programme of 1899 advocated proportional representation, the need to encourage

[9] O. Confessore, *I cattolici e 'la fede nella libertà'* (Rome, 1989).

[10] J. F. Pollard, 'Catholic Conservatives and Italian Fascism: The Clerico-Fascists', in M. Blinkhorn (ed.), *Fascists and Conservatives: The Radical Right and the Establishment in Twentieth Century Europe* (London, 1990), 38–40. See also M. G. Rossi, *Le origini del Partito Cattolico in Italia* (Rome, 1977), ch. 6.

[11] A. Caroleo, *Le banche cattoliche* (Milan, 1976), 42.

[12] For this important episode see Webster, *The Cross and the Fasces,* ch. 2.

small property-formation, and administrative decentralization, all policies that were to remain hallmarks of political Catholicism in Italy until long after the Second World War.[13] In the short term, the Christian democrats concentrated on the further development of Catholic economic and social organizations, especially the trade unions and the peasant leagues, as part of direct action to help the Catholic masses.[14]

If the Christian democratic programme was different from that of the clerico-moderates, then so was their membership, which broadly represented the Catholic small-town and rural bourgoisie—small businessmen and professionals, parochial clergy, and the organizers of the Catholic trade unions and peasant leagues—with a sprinkling of more prominent intellectuals. By 1903 they had captured effective control of the Opera, but the new pope, Pius X, feared both their radical reform programme and the heretical, modernist, tendencies of Murri. This induced him to break the hold of the Christian democrats by dissolving the Opera and reorganizing the Catholic movement into various associations more directly dependent on the hierarchy.[15] After this setback the Christian democratic leadership dispersed: Guido Miglioli continued to work for his beloved peasants; Don Sturzo moved over to head the major organizational legatee of the Opera and forerunner of Catholic Action, the Unione Popolare; and Murri drifted further and further into disobedience to the Papacy, becoming a radical member of Parliament.

The election of Pius X marked an important milestone in the history of Italian political Catholicism in another sense. Impressed by the success of Catholics in defending the interests of the Church in local government in his native Venetia and alarmed by the rise of the working-class movement, whose militancy reached a peak in the general strike of 1904, the pope decreed the suspension of the *Non Expedit* on a limited basis for the general elections of 1905. Catholics in some key northern constituencies were permitted to vote either for acceptable Liberals or even to stand as parliamentary candidates themselves, in order to keep out the Socialists. The result was to establish a pattern of clerico-moderate alliances with the Liberals, the 'party of order', and to permit the entry of Catholics into national political life for the first time. Catholics stood and were elected in 1904 and 1909, and in 1913, with the introduction of virtual universal adult male suffrage, twenty-nine Catholics were returned.

This development did not, however, signify the emergence of a Catholic Party in Parliament. From the outset the Vatican, which controlled Catholic political activity through the Unione Elettorale, stressed the distinction between *cattolici deputati*, that is deputies who happened to be Catholics, and *deputati cattolici*, i.e. deputies who saw themselves as officially representing Italian Catholics. The latter was emphatically ruled out. In any case, the disparate nature of the Catholic parliamentary group, which included both clerico-moderates and others of a more Christian democratic orientation, meant that they rarely voted as a block. Nevertheless, their

[13] For the Milan and Turin programmes see Misner, *Social Catholicism*, 241–2.
[14] Seton-Watson, *Italy*, 228–37; Webster, *The Cross and the Fasces*, ch. 1; and J. M. Molony, *The Emergence of Political Catholicism in Italy* (London, 1977), 22–3.
[15] Seton-Watson, *Italy*, 228–37, and Webster, *The Cross and the Fasces*, ch. 2.

participation in the parliamentary process was to prove a useful experience for future representatives of the PPI.[16]

Even more significant for the future was the outcome of the 1913 general elections. As a result of the pact between Giolitti and Count Gentiloni, the president of the Unione Elettorale, dozens of Liberal candidates sought and obtained Catholic electoral support according to a set of conditions laid down by the Unione, in order to protect their seats against an expected Socialist onslaught. Gentiloni actually claimed that over two hundred Liberal MPs owed their election to Catholic support.[17] Certainly, Giolitti's parliamentary majority was saved thanks to Catholic support, and it is clear that a mass electoral base existed for a future Catholic Party even before the outbreak of the First World War.

3. The First Catholic Party: The PPI, 1918–1926

Though the Papacy, and some sections of the Italian Catholic movement, had opposed Italy's intervention in the First World War, Italian Catholics played their part loyally in the war effort, both at home and at the front.[18] The patriotism of Catholics thus removed one of the last major obstacles to their direct and successful participation in Italian politics, for it gave the lie to charges that Catholics were unpatriotic. But the Italy in which the PPI was born, had been dramatically changed by the war itself. The Italy of 1918 was one of radical economic, social, and above all, political change. The PPI was one of the major organizational representatives of this new mood.

The emergence of the first Catholic Party onto the Italian political stage in 1918 inevitably required the approval of the Holy See. That this was reluctantly, grudgingly, given is clear from the testimonies of Benedict XV and his secretary of state, Cardinal Gasparri. As Gasparri later explained, he saw the PPI as merely the 'least bad' of all parties.[19] The Vatican was seriously concerned about the political dangers posed by a Catholic Party with a priest, Don Luigi Sturzo, at its head. Perhaps, more fundamentally, the Vatican feared the consequent loss of direct control over mass, Catholic political activities. Its worst fears on this score were to be realized in 1920 when the new party refused to enter into those traditional clerico-moderate alliances with the Liberals which the Church hierarchy believed to be necessary in the fight against the Socialists at the crucial local government elections of that year. This failure of the Popolari to do their 'duty' lost them much sympathy both among the local episcopacy and in the Vatican.[20]

To appease the Vatican's concerns, Sturzo and his colleagues insisted on describing their new party as 'aconfessional', i.e. not as a Catholic Party but simply one based on Christian principles and open to all 'free and strong men'. This position, however, outraged the members of the intransigent faction which emerged at the party's

---

[16] The first serious study of the Catholic deputies is to be found in G. Formigoni, *I cattolici-deputati (1904–1918)* (Rome, 1989), 13–103.

[17] Clark, *Modern Italy*, 156–7.

[18] Webster, *The Cross and the Fasces*, ch. 4.

[19] Molony, *Emergence of Political Catholicism*, 47–8.

[20] Ibid. 56.

founding congress in 1919. It also failed to convince the secular press, which insisted on portraying the party as the secular arm of the Church. It could be argued that the Church got the worst of both worlds: on the one hand, all the mistakes and failings of a party led by a priest were laid at its door, on the other hand, the aconfessional party's commitment to the defence of the Church's interests seemed less than enthusiastic. The 1919 party programme devoted only six lines to those interests, and managed to avoid mentioning the Roman Question at all.[21] The party's relationship with the Vatican was, therefore, from the outset, a difficult one.

The January 1919 appeal of the founding committee, and the programme adopted at the Bologna congress contained no other elements of which the Holy See could have disapproved. On the contrary, they were fully in line with papal teaching on the family and freedom of education, and with mainstream Catholic thinking on economic and social questions. They were also very close in spirit to the original, end-of-the-century Christian democratic programmes, placing a strong emphasis on the need to protect small property, the need for tax reform and agrarian development, and, given the Sicilian origins of Sturzo, the commitment to Southern development is not surprising. Nor is the inclusion of proposals for administrative decentralization, proportional representation, female suffrage and the election of the Senate, which typified the spirit of *dicianovesimo*, that is the radical reformism that affected all parties in the aftermath of the war. Similarly, the PPI was explicitly Wilsonian in its foreign policy proposals though this was to become rather more muted when the Treaty of Versailles was actually signed and the Pope made public his objections to the peace settlement.[22]

The 'take off' of the new party was dramatic: within a few months of Sturzo's first appeal, it had received the virtually unanimous support of the Italian Catholic world, the newly independent Catholic trade-union organization (CIL) and the Catholic peasant leagues, the Catholic press, most of the affiliated organizations of the Unione Popolare (which was renamed 'Catholic Action', to avoid confusion) especially those of youth, all the Catholic deputies in Parliament, and the bulk of the parochial clergy.[23] Only the episcopal bench remained rather more cautious in its attitude. Moreover, the results of the 1919 general elections, conducted under proportional representation and full universal male suffrage for the first time, confirmed the strength of support for the Popolari in the country at large—the party won 20 per cent of the votes and 100 out of the 508 seats in Parliament, making it the second largest parliamentary party after the Socialists.[24]

The election results also confirmed that the party's electoral base was to be found in the traditional heartlands of Italian Catholicism. Venetia, with 35 per cent, and

[21] The text of the PPI programme is in P. Scoppola, 'L'affermazione e crisi del P.P.I.', in G. Sabbatucci (ed.), *La crisi italiana del primo dopoguerra: La storia e la critica* (Rome, 1976).

[22] For the foreign policy of the PPI see I. Giordani, *La politica estera del P.P.I.* (Rome, 1924) and G. Gualerzi, *La politica estera dei popolari* (Rome, 1959).

[23] Molony, *Emergence of Political Catholicism*, 53–8, and G. De Rosa, *Storia del Partito Popolare Italiano* (3rd edn., Rome, 1974), 9–10, 15–16.

[24] E. Caranti, 'Il Partito Popolare nelle elezioni del primo dopoguerra', *Civitas*, 12 (1965), 9–10.

Lombardy, with nearly 31 per cent, gave the party its highest electoral scores. In the 1921 general elections the north-eastern province of Trento, acquired under the terms of the Treaty of Versailles and the home base of Alcide De Gasperi, later to be Sturzo's successor as leader of the PPI, also polled a very high vote for the party. Outside the North-East only Le Marche (27.3 per cent) and Latium polled in excess of the party's national average. In the South, no region achieved this level of support, and in some regions like Lucania it barely reached 5 per cent of the vote. It is hard to tell how far this electorate was specifically Catholic, there being no sociological studies of the electoral base of the PPI, but it is precisely the concentration of Popolare votes in the white provinces that suggests that this was largely the case.[25]

Ironically, the breadth of support for the PPI in both the Catholic movement and the Catholic electorate was to prove a weakness as well as a strength, for the party was always to be highly heterogeneous, spanning virtually the whole arc of the ideologies and interest groups to be found in the Italian Catholic world. In particular, it brought together in an unnatural and short-lived alliance great landowners at one extreme, and landless labourers at the other. This alliance quickly fell apart under the impact of agrarian fascism in northern and central Italy in 1921 and 1922.[26] The party divided into recognizable factions from the the the start. On the right there were the intransigents grouped around Padre Gemelli, friend of Pius XI and later rector of the Catholic University of Milan. On the centre-right were the clerico-moderate grandees like Grosoli, Santucci, and Crispolti who effectively controlled the Catholic press. The centre, led by Luigi Sturzo, was the dominant force in the party, including most of the torchbearers of early Christian democracy and the bulk of the white trade-union leadership. And on the left were men like Guido Miglioli whose socialist leanings had inspired him to suggest the name 'Party of the Christian Proletariat' at the Bologna congress. It is interesting to note that some men of Miglioli's inclinations could not accept the policy of the party and in the 1921 general elections the dissident Popolari and the Cristiani del Lavoro won 30,000 votes between them in Lombardy and Venetia.[27]

As time went on, not even the charismatic leadership of Sturzo, who as a priest and as the last historic leader of the original Christian democratic movement commanded unrivalled authority in the party, was able to hold these divergent factions together. Indeed, the fact that Sturzo was a priest was a source of weakness to the party, for as such he was forced to lead the party from outside Parliament and his priestly status was ultimately to prove the Achilles' heel of the PPI, because he was subject to the canonical sanction of the ecclesiastical authorities.

Despite its weaknesses, and its relative newness to parliamentary life, the new party was called upon to play a key role in Italian politics following the 1919 general elections. While it had probably robbed the Socialist Party of a greater electoral victory than it actually achieved in 1919 (the latter won 150 seats and therefore became

[25] Webster, *The Cross and the Fasces*, 61–4.
[26] P. Corner, *Fascism in Ferrara, 1915–1925* (Oxford, 1975), 127–8.
[27] Caranti, 'Partito Popolare', 10.

the largest party in Parliament), what was more significant was that the PPI, by monopolizing the Catholic vote, also deprived the Liberals of their parliamentary majority. The Socialists, true to the decision taken at their 1912 congress, refused to participate in 'bourgeois politics'; thus no government could now be formed or sustained without the support of the Popolari. Each of the six cabinets formed between July 1919 and October 1922, and including Mussolini's first government, contained at least two Popolare ministers and several under-secretaries of state.[28] Finance and/ or the treasury were usually in the hands of the Popolari as well as agriculture, and in 1921, in a move unprecedented in the history of Liberal Italy, a Catholic became minister of justice.

In February and July 1922, as the parliamentary crisis of the Liberal State deepened, Filippo Meda, veteran Catholic politician and the leader of the parliamentary caucus of the PPI, was asked by the King to take the premiership. Much to Sturzo's dismay, Meda refused because of his unwillingness to shoulder the burdens of high office. Meda's refusals deprived his party of the opportunity to play a dominant role in politics, and probably also the last real chance to preserve Italian democracy.[29]

The party's experience of parliamentary politics was not an entirely happy one: the demands of a modern, mass party, with a fixed programme, did not square with the traditional, transformist tactics of the Liberal notables who headed Italian governments in this period. Governments came and went with increasing rapidity partly because of the bitter rows between the Popolari and a succession of Liberal premiers —Nitti, Giolitti, Bonomi, and Facta—over the failure of the latter to implement policy commitments made when the governments were formed.

By the beginning of 1922, the failure of the Liberal State to grapple with the many economic and political problems facing it, and in particular its failure to deal with the spread of Fascist squadrist violence in the northern and central regions of Italy, had provoked a serious parliamentary crisis. In the summer Bonomi's newly formed government fell precisely because of an explosion of violence in Guido Miglioli's home town, Cremona. By October Luigi Facta's first government had also fallen, and it was at this point that the King in his desperation had turned to Meda. But rampant Fascist violence in the provinces was not only paralysing Italian parliamentary life, it was also having a divisive effect on the PPI. The fissiparous tendencies in the party manifested themselves in pro-Fascist manœuvres by the party's right-wing. The party's intransigent tactics during the ministerial crises of 1922, which led to the downfall of the first Facta government and the still birth of another, that of Giolitti, alienated Catholic conservative opinion. In June the Marquis Cornaggia-Medici made his first attempt to establish a conservative alternative to the Catholic Party by founding the short-lived Unione Costituzionale. In July Prince Francesco Boncompagni-Ludovisi resigned the Popolare whip and joined the Nationalists, and in September the eight Popolare senators protested to Sturzo about the party's

[28] M. Missori, *Governi, alte cariche dello Stato e prefetti del Regno* (Rome, 1973), 258–67.
[29] Pollard, 'Catholic Conservatives', 33–5.

alleged flirtations with the Reformist Socialists. The direction in which the Catholic conservatives, both inside and outside of the PPI, were moving was that of Popolare participation in a government of 'National Concentration', headed by a Liberal leader such as Giolitti and including all centre and right-wing groups, the Fascists not excepted.[30]

The Vatican was also becoming more openly critical of the PPI. The election of Pius XI in February 1922 had accelerated this trend, for he was even less sympathetic towards the party than his predecessor had been. Thus, during the parliamentary crisis of October, which culminated in the Fascist March on Rome at the end of the month, the Vatican clearly regarded the entry of the Fascists into government as an absolute necessity if political stability was to be restored, and as a result pressurized the Popolari into supporting the government which Mussolini formed at the beginning of November. As Mussolini set about consolidating his power during the next two years, the Vatican increasingly threw in its lot with Fascism, motivated by the belief, which was obviously encouraged by Mussolini, that he could solve the Roman Question, which the PPI had signally failed to do. In the spring and summer of 1923 the Vatican encouraged Catholic political pluralism by giving the nod to the emergence of another pro–Fascist, Catholic, conservative political grouping, the Unione Nazionale, and in July it dealt a powerful blow to the PPI by ordering Sturzo to resign as party leader.[31]

Very quickly, the PPI fell apart. In July fourteen right-wingers broke ranks, thus allowing the passage of the Acerbo Law, Mussolini's electoral legislation which abolished proportional representation and awarded two-thirds of the seats to the party which polled the largest number of votes in excess of a quarter plus one. As Santarelli has pointed out: 'If the Popolari had not split . . . proportional representation would not have been abandoned, and in that case Mussolini might not have been able to make use of those lists of "national concentration" which in the elections of 1924 permitted him to consolidate his power.'[32] The collapse of the PPI was, therefore, a major factor in the eventual triumph of Mussolini and Fascism.

When Parliament was dissolved in March 1924, a quarter of the Popolare deputies elected in 1921 had either been expelled or had seceded, and the entire Popolare contingent in the Senate also defected, taking with them those Catholic newspapers controlled by Grosoli's Trust. In the ensuing elections, thirteen Catholic candidates (mostly ex-Popolari) stood in Mussolini's 'big list' and a strong appeal to Catholics to vote for Fascism was made through Grosoli's newspapers.[33] The Vatican's abandonment of the PPI was completed during the Matteotti Crisis of 1924, when the reformist Socialist leader was abducted and murdered by Fascist thugs. In the ensuing political maelstrom, the attempt by the Popolari to exploit the last chance of removing Mussolini by forming a coalition government with Matteotti's party and

---

[30] A. Lyttelton, *Seizure of Power* (2nd edn., London, 1987), 131.

[31] Pollard, 'Catholic Conservatives', 34.

[32] E. Santarelli, *Storia del movimento e del regime fascista*, i (Rome, 1967), 359.

[33] Pollard, 'Conservative Catholics', 36.

others, was publicly denounced by Pius XI.[34] By the end of 1926 the PPI, along with the other democratic, anti-fascist opposition, was dissolved and the new Fascist dictatorship forbade its reconstitution.

4. The Fascist Interlude

With the dissolution of the PPI, Pius XI and his secretary of state, Cardinal Gasparri, had achieved two long-sought-after aims, the re-establishment of papal control over the Italian Catholic movement and the re-establishment of a direct interlocutory relationship with the Italian state, free from the embarrassing complications created by the existence of a Catholic political party. They were thus able in the period 1926 to 1929 to bring to a successful conclusion negotiations for the resolution of the Roman Question which culminated in the signing of the Lateran Pacts. As a quid pro quo, they instructed Italian Catholics through Catholic Action to vote for the single Fascist list in the 'plebiscite' of 1929, thus effectively returning to the policy of Pius X when he relaxed the *Non Expedit* twenty years earlier. Though the Vatican's 'marriage of convenience' with Fascism was disturbed by disputes over the precise competence of Catholic Action in the youth, labour, and recreational fields in 1929, 1931, and again in 1938, when the introduction of the Racial Laws added a further cause of conflict,[35] there was, nevertheless, a high degree of convergence between the Church and Fascism in the areas of economic, social, and even foreign policy until 1938.[36]

In these circumstances, and given the totalitarian ambitions of the regime, there was very little space for autonomous political activity by Catholic laymen. After the demise of the PPI, the only Catholic groups which managed to retain a place, albeit marginal, in Italian politics were the two clerico-fascist organizations, the Unione Nazionale which was essentially an aristocratic clique, and the Centro Nazionale Italiano, which continued to be active in Parliament, loyally endorsing the legislation on which the Fascist dictatorship was built between 1925 and 1929. After 1929, however, both organizations were brutally discarded. Thereafter, clerico-fascist politicians, like Stefano Cavazzoni for example, found a new role as mediators between Fascism and Catholic financial interests.[37]

Full-blooded Catholic anti-fascism was even less successful than clerico-fascism. Only a handful of Popolare leaders followed Sturzo into exile (De Gasperi was caught trying to leave Italy, arrested, tried, imprisoned, and eventually released into the custody of the Vatican). In any case, the differences between Sturzo, Ferrari, Donati, and Miglioli—whose strange odyssey eventually took him to Moscow—prevented the formation of a Popolare party-in-exile on the lines of the Communist, Socialist,

---

[34] Lyttelton, *Seizure of Power*, 243.

[35] For these disputes, see J. F. Pollard, *The Vatican and Italian Fascism, 1929–1932: A Study in Conflict* (Cambridge, 1985), chs. 3 and 6.

[36] J. F. Pollard, 'A Marriage of Convenience: The Vatican and the Fascist Regime in Italy', in J. Obelkevich, L. Rope, and R. Samuel (eds.), *Disciplines of Faith: Studies in Religion, Politics and Patriarchy* (London, 1987), 511–13.

[37] Pollard, *The Vatican and Italian Fascism*, 31–42.

or the radical-reformist Giustizia e Libertà organizations. Sturzo's anti-Fascist activities in Britain and America had a minimal influence on Catholics in Italy.

The majority of the ex-Popolare politicians retired into a private life relatively undisturbed by police harassment. Only two overtly anti-fascist organizations succeeded in attracting significant Catholic support during the years of the regime: the Allianza Nazionale (National Alliance) of Lauro De Bosis, which was not strictly Catholic in ideological orientation and was quickly crushed by the police in 1931, and the Movimento Guelfo D'Azione (Guelf Action Movement) of Piero Malvestiti. The latter was unique in being the only truly Catholic anti-fascist movement to be indicted before Mussolini's Special Military Tribunal.[38] Catholic anti-fascist activity was also carried on inside the associations of Catholic Action, indeed Catholic Action became the focus of most Catholic 'political' activity from the mid-1920s onwards, as the Vatican had intended it to be. But it was a very different Catholic movement now from the one that Sturzo had presided over on the eve of the First World War. The dissolution of the PPI in 1926 had been followed very shortly by that of the Catholic trade-union confederation. And despite the financial resources and political influence of its clerico-fascist proprietors, the bulk of the Catholic daily press also went under in the mid- and late 1920s; by 1929 only Catholic newspapers under diocesan control managed to survive. With the trade unions went a lot of the other economic and social organizations—especially the peasant leagues and the co-operatives—and the financial effects of Mussolini's revaluation of the lira in 1926 had a devastating effect on Catholic banks and credit unions, which in turn was one of the causes of the decline of the Catholic press.[39] By 1929 the Catholic presence in Italian civil society had been significantly reduced, even in the rural heartlands, and Catholic Action, the core of the Catholic movement was suffering a haemorrhage of its membership.

The Vatican seems to have been more or less acquiescent in the other 'demolitions' of Fascism, but when the embryonic regime laid violent hands on the Catholic youth organizations, the Pope became alarmed. It was precisely in order to save these organizations that the Vatican took the initiative to open negotiations for a comprehensive settlement of the Roman Question in August 1926.

Article 43 of the resulting Concordat of 1929 was of crucial importance to the future development of political Catholicism in Italy, for it ensured the survival of Catholic Action as the only autonomous, non-Fascist organization in Mussolini's so-called totalitarian state. In the short term, Mussolini sought to restrict the activities of Catholic Action further, especially during the crisis in relations between the Vatican and the regime in 1931, which was partly prompted by the activities of the ex-Popolari. The youth organizations were also the target of Fascist wrath, but in the subsequent reconciliation of September 1931, they survived. Thus FUCI, the

[38] For an account of the Catholic role in the anti-Fascist movements of the 1930s, see C. F. Delzell, *Mussolini's Enemies: The Italian Anti-Fascist Resistance* (New York, 1974), ch. 3 and the essay by Wolff on Italy in R. J. Wolff and J. K. Hoensch (eds.), *Catholics, The State and the Radical Right in Europe, 1919–1945* (Highland Lakes, NJ, 1987).

[39] Pollard, *The Vatican and Italian Fascism*, 31–42.

Catholic students' organization, and Movimento Laureati, the graduate movement, were to provide under the moral and spiritual direction of Mgr. G. B. Montini (later Paul VI) the nursery for much of the post-war Christian Democratic leadership. As Renato Moro has demonstrated, the post-war Catholic élite of trade-union leaders, party secretaries, ministers, and prime ministers including P. E. Taviani, G. B. Scaglia, Aldo Moro, Emilio Colombo, Guido Gonella, Beniamino Zaccagnini, Giulio Andreotti, and Mariano Rumor, was largely the product of these organizations.[40] But the autonomous space for debate and development of Catholic social and political ideas was very restricted. Catholic Action was under constant police surveillance. As a result, the price of survival was to pay lip-service to the policies of the regime: corporatism, imperialism, and racialism. Whereas in 1929 Catholic Action had instructed Catholics in rather general terms simply to vote in the elections of that year, five years later it ordered, 'Go to the polls and vote for the government of the Honourable Mussolini'.[41] There was, however, a pseudo-debate on corporatism, or rather on the corporative institutions which Fascist Italy had created between 1925 and 1939. Though Pius XI had implicitly criticized Fascist corporatism's 'monopoly privilege' as being incompatible with Catholic social teaching in his encyclical *Quadragesimo Anno*, academics at the Catholic University of Milan like Amintore Fanfani and Francesco De Vito supported Fascist corporatism in their publications, and like Fr. Brucculeri of the Jesuit journal *La civiltà cattolica*, they tentatively suggested ways in which the system might be improved and made to accord more fully with Catholic principles.[42] Again, though the Vatican strongly opposed Mussolini's alliance with Hitler, and his subsequent entry into the Second World War on the side of Nazi Germany in June 1940, Italian Catholic lay opinion was more divided.

Politically conscious Catholics began to prepare for the post-Fascist future long before Mussolini was toppled from power in July 1943. Sturzo in exile and De Gasperi in the Vatican library had ample time to meditate on the short-lived and unsuccessful experience of *popolarismo*: both came to the inescapable conclusion that its fatal weakness had been its poor relations with the Vatican, a lesson that De Gasperi was to apply successfully after 1945. FUCI continued its vigil and in 1936 the Movimento Laureati began its Religious Culture Weeks at Camaldoli, from which emerged new ideas for the future of social Catholicism.[43] Thus, as elsewhere in Europe, the 1930s and early 1940s provided the crucial, formative period for the emergence of the post-war Italian Catholic intelligentsia.

Just as active Catholic participation in the First World War had been one of the prerequisites for the emergence of the PPI in 1919, so Catholic participation in the armed Resistance against the Nazi occupiers and the Fascist Social Republic from

---

[40] Ibid. 161–7 and ch. 7; and R. Moro, *La formazione della classe dirigente cattolica, 1929–1937* (Bologna, 1972).

[41] *Bollettino ufficiale dell'Azione Cattolica*, 1–2 (1934).

[42] Webster, *The Cross and the Fasces*, ch. 12; and P. Ranfagni, *I Clerico-fascisti: I giornali dell'università cattolica negli trenta* (Florence, 1977), chs. 4 and 5.

[43] R. Leonardi and R. Wertman, *Christian Democracy in Italy: The Politics of Dominance* (Basingstoke, 1989), 35–7.

September 1943 to May 1945 helped to wash away the 'sin' of collaboration between the Church and Fascism, and gave a patriotic chrism to the re-emerging Catholic political forces. Few Catholics gave serious support to Mussolini's Social Republic, whereas in the Veneto, Friuli, Lombardy and Piedmont, and Emilia-Romagna regions there was widespread support from both the parochial clergy and the peasantry for the partisans. A variety of Catholic groups and individuals raised, trained, and led partisan bands—the Osoppo Brigades in Friuli for example, were the creation of elements from the local Movimento Laureati, the Fiamme Verdi Tito Speri brigade in Brescia was organized by local Catholic Action, Piero Malvestiti played a crucial role in the Comitato di Liberazion (CLN), the ruling council of the Resistance in Milan, and Enrico Mattei ended up commanding a small army of partisans under the Christian democratic banner. Italian Catholics thus paid their passage and earned a secure place for their leaders, with De Gasperi at their head, in the first Resistance Unity government of 1944.[44]

5. The Rebirth of Italian Political Catholicism, 1943–1945

At its rebirth along with the other major anti-Fascist parties after the fall of Fascism in 1943, Italian political Catholicism exhibited strong signs of pluralistic tendencies. Though the core of the reborn Catholic Party gathered around Alcide De Gasperi, the historic leader of political Catholicism and nuclei of other former Popolare leaders like S. Jacini and Migliori in Milan, and Spataro, Cingolani, and Scelba in Rome, other new groups with divergent ideological positions had appeared on the scene. The emerging cadres formed by Montini in FUCI and Movimento Laureati were not so divergent in their ideas from old-style Popolarismo, though their guiding principles, as enshrined in the Code of Camaldoli, differed in some significant respects from De Gasperi's programme for the Democrazia Cristiana (the Christian Democrats), published in 1944, which became the founding charter of the new party.[45] The ideas of *ex-guelfisti* like Piero Malvestiti and other Catholics who took part in the Resistance tended towards a more consciously Catholic 'third way' between capitalism and communism (though without any corporatist overtones) and were later to be incorporated into the Republican constitution.

A more advanced position was represented by another Catholic active in the Resistance, Enrico Mattei. Together with the leaders of the re-emerging Catholic trade-union movement, Gronchi and Grandi, he gave the most explicit commitment to the need for the State to intervene in the economy in the interests of social justice. The position of Giorgio La Pira, university professor and later mayor of Florence, was even more radically different. Inspired by the belief in the need for a profound religious and moral transformation of society as the true basis for social justice, La Pira

---

[44] For the role of Catholics in the Armed Resistance, see Delzell, *Mussolini's Enemies*, chs. 5 and 7 (esp. pp. 293–4), and 11 (pp. 489–90), and for a broader history of Italy between the fall of Fascism and the end of the war, see D. Ellwood, *Italy 1943–1945* (Leicester, 1985).

[45] For the text of the programme see F. Malgeri (ed.), *Storia della Democrazia Cristiana*, v (Rome, 1981), 418–28.

was committed to a Catholic integralist view of politics, which required the active and dominant participation of the Church. But the most extreme of all Catholic political groups to emerge in the aftermath of Fascism were the Christian Socialists of Leghorn and the Christian left or Communists of Rome. Influenced by their contacts with the mainstream, Marxist left, they advocated a workers' revolution as a social expression of the Gospel. Neither movement secured a mass base for its activities, and the members of the Rome group were excommunicated by Pius XII in 1949.[46]

Ironically, when faced by the difficulties of Italy's immediate, post-war economic situation, its dependence on US capital and the DC's lack of a competent economic élite, all the various social theories of the Catholic Party were forced to give way to the *laissez-faire* policies of an old-fashioned liberal, Luigi Einaudi, who was co-opted by De Gasperi to organize Italian reconstruction.[47]

The political pluralism latent in all this ideological diversity was not to take any significant organizational form after 1945, though it was later to manifest itself in the emergence of factions inside the Catholic Party—particularly after the death of De Gasperi in 1954. The various groups in fact very quickly coalesced into an essentially compact and united Christian Democratic Party, thus providing De Gasperi with the organisational base to bring about the triumph of Christian Democracy between 1945 and 1948. De Gasperi's clever tactical manœuvring was also assisted by the confused politics of the CLN, which laid claim to the government of post-Fascist Italy. Another, vital, factor was the concern of both the Vatican and the USA about the threat from the Communist Party, which had assumed the dominant role in the Resistance. The DC leader's first stroke of luck was to be chosen as a compromise candidate for the premiership when Ferrucio Parri's administration was brought down by the conservatives in December 1945. As the first 'Catholic' prime minister, and also as minister of the interior, the key ministry controlling the prefects or provincial governors and the police, De Gasperi was able to exploit the enormous political and ultimately electoral advantage which these two great offices gave an Italian politician. His hand was greatly strengthened by the tactically neutralist role which he insisted that his party should play in the contentious referendum on the monarchy which took place in June 1946, and the DC emerged at the accompanying general elections as the largest of the three mass parties (the others being the Socialists and the Communists) with 35 per cent of the vote.[48]

The role of the Vatican was crucial to the success which the new Catholic Party achieved. After the collapse of Fascism, and even more so after the abolition of the monarchy, the Catholic Church was the strongest surviving national institution in Italy, a phenomenon that Federico Chabod appropriately compared to the situation following the fall of the Roman Empire.[49] Along with the USA, with which the

---

[46] Webster, *The Cross and the Fasces*, chs. 10, 11, and 12; and Leonardi and Wertman, *Christian Democracy*, ch. 2.

[47] J. L. Harper, *America and the Reconstruction of Italy, 1945–1948* (London, 1986), chs. 6 and 8.

[48] N. Kogan, *A Political History of Italy: The Post-war Years* (New York, 1983), ch. 2; and P. Ginsborg, *A History of Contemporary Italy: Society and Politics, 1943–1988* (London, 1990), chs. 2 and 3.

[49] F. Chabod, *L'Italia contemporanea, 1918–1948* (Turin, 1961), 125.

Vatican had established a close working relationship during the course of the War, the Vatican was one of the two arbiters of Italy's fate in the immediate post-war period. But the support of the Vatican for the DC was by no means guaranteed in 1945. There is clear evidence that Pius XII and some of his closest advisers, influenced by the troubled history of the Partito Popolare in the 1920s, were not convinced of the need or desirability of committing themselves to a Catholic Party. Only the insistent lobbying of Mgr. Montini, and the DC's 1946 electoral success weaned them away from earlier plans to resuscitate a clerico-moderate alliance between the Catholics and a leading liberal politician such as Orlando. It was not until 1947 that the Vatican finally dropped its reservations. The defenestration of the Socialist and Communist parties from government, and De Gasperi's success in inserting a clause into the republican constitution which confirmed the Lateran Pacts against fierce opposition from the Socialists and other lay parties, finally convinced the Vatican that the DC was the only reliable instrument for the defence of its interests in Italy.[50]

It was also Vatican diplomacy which won acceptance for De Gasperi and the DC and smoothed the way for De Gasperi's highly successful visit to Washington in 1947.[51] As the Cold War situation developed, it became clear that the DC was the only credible answer to the challenge from the Communists and the Socialists, and thus it won financial and moral support from both the Vatican and the USA in the crucial elections of April 1948.[52] In particular, thanks to a Vatican policy of total commitment, the very substantial forces of Catholic Action were thrown into the contest on the side of the DC. Having survived the Fascist era intact, whereas the organizations of the working-class subculture had had to be virtually rebuilt from scratch, Catholic Action was by now Italy's largest and most effective voluntary organization, with branches in every single one of the peninsula's 24,000 Catholic parishes. Through the Civic Committees of Luigi Gedda, the Catholic vote was in this way mobilized on a massive scale.[53]

There was also another obvious reason for the success of the DC in 1948—the fear of Communism. In the shadow of the Prague coup and under a massive propaganda barrage, the DC was seen as the ark of salvation by much of Italy's middle class. The 1948 general elections therefore witnessed a kind of Giolitti–Gentiloni pact in reverse, with hundreds of thousands of voters forsaking the Liberal and other right-of-centre parties to put their faith in the DC. As a result, the party won 48 per cent of the vote and, due to a quirk of the system of proportional representation, over 50 per cent of the seats in the Chamber of Deputies. In the short space of less than fifty years Italian political Catholicism had made the transition from being an anti-system

[50] P. Scoppola, *La proposta politica di De Gasperi* (Bologna, 1977), ch. 3, esp. pp. 121–9.

[51] A. Varsori, 'De Gasperi, Nenni, Sforza, and their Role in Post-War Italian Foreign Policy', in J. Becker and F. Knipping (eds.), *Power in Europe? Great Britain, France, Italy and Germany in a Post-war World, 1945–1950* (Berlin, 1980), 90, 93, 94.

[52] Ginsborg, *Contemporary Italy*, 115–8, Kogan, *Political History*, 39–40; and D. Keogh, 'Ireland, the Vatican and the Cold War: The Case of Italy', *Historical Journal*, 34/4 (1991), 931–52.

[53] G. Poggi, 'The Church in Italian Politics, 1945–1950', in S. J. Woolf (ed.), *The Rebirth of Italy, 1943–1950* (London, 1972), 146–52 and Ginsborg, *Contemporary Italy*, 116–18.

movement to being the dominant party of government, and remained so until the early 1990s.

The support of the Vatican, however, proved to be a mixed blessing for De Gasperi and the DC. Catholic success in the 1948 elections gave rise to a spirit of Catholic triumphalism, to a climate of confessional intolerance which led one historian to describe Italy in the 1940s and 1950s as 'the Papal State of the Twentieth Century'.[54] Thanks to Italy's Napoleonic, highly centralized, administrative system, Catholic power at a national level was effectively replicated at the level of local government, creating a repressive atmosphere for both political and religious minorities,[55] and the Italian Catholic world sought to match political dominance with the establishment of cultural hegemony over Italian society as well. In these circumstances, Pope Pius XII tended to see the DC as merely the long, secular arm of the ecclesiastical hierarchy. Without a solidly established organizational base of its own, the DC under De Gasperi had to fight hard to escape the more extreme demands of the pope and his advisers, including one that would have resulted in a legal ban on both the Communist and Socialist parties, and during the 1952 local elections in Rome, De Gasperi was only able to avoid being forced into an alliance with the reviving forces of neo-Fascism by a technical loophole.[56]

6. The DC after De Gasperi: Fanfani and the New Model Party

The period of DC triumph was, in any case, to be of short duration. Within less than five years of its massive 1948 election victory it was clear to all that such a feat could not be repeated. Though the rigours of the Cold War had not abated, large sections of the middle classes had become alienated from their erstwhile saviours. In particular, the application of the DC's reforming policy in the South, through the passage of a land redistribution measure, enraged local élites. To counter the growing threat from both the right and a resurgent Communist Party in 1952 De Gasperi reluctantly pushed through Parliament an electoral law amendment which would give the party, or coalition of parties, with the largest number of votes in excess of a quarter 51 per cent of the seats. This 'swindle law', as it was dubbed by its Socialist and Communist opponents, bore an unfortunate resemblance to Mussolini's Acerbo Law of 1923, and this was probably another reason why the DC lost votes when the elections were held.[57] With its vote reduced to just over 40 per cent in the 1953 elections, the DC was condemned to rule for another ten years with a precarious, unviable parliamentary majority provided by support from the small centre parties—the Social Democrats, the Liberals, and the Republicans. The consequences for De Gasperi personally were more serious in the short term: he failed to form a government and

[54] Webster, *The Cross and the Fasces*, 214.

[55] V. Bucci, *Chiesa e Stato: Church and State Relations in the Constitutional Framework* (The Hague, 1969), 60–5; and D. Settembrini, *La Chiesa nella politica italiana, 1944–1963* (Milan, 1973), 322–30 and 489–93. See also A. C. Jemolo, *Società civile e società religiosa* (Turin, 1959), 73.

[56] For an account of this episode see G. Zizola, *Il microfono di Dio* (Milan, 1990).

[57] Kogan, *Political History*, 64.

was relegated to the sidelines as party secretary. His death the following year was a further serious blow to the Catholic Party.

Amintore Fanfani sought to take over the mantle of De Gasperi's authority without any enduring success and the DC has subsequently never had an undisputed national leader. It thus become more and more of a coalition of party factions. Faced by the risk of further electoral decline, Fanfani also sought to create a new model party built around an autonomous party organization with an electoral base independent of the Church and Catholic Action and with sources of party funding other than from Confindustria, the private sector employers' association with which the DC had been closely associated. As Giorgio Galli, the leading authority on the post-war Catholic Party has put it, Fanfani no longer wanted the DC to be 'the servant but the leader of the (Italian) Catholic world'.[58] Fanfani's project had only limited success as far as the party's structure and electoral base were concerned, but the pursuit of funding from the public-sector companies had more success and initiated the process whereby they became incorporated into a system of state clientelism. The creation of a ministry of state holdings in 1956 and the withdrawal of the state companies from membership of Confindustria in 1957 brought the state sector more directly under the control of the politicians. In this way, in the longer term certainly, the DC was to become more independent of both the Church and organized Italian capitalism.

By 1953 the Christian Democrats' electoral base already possessed characteristics that were significantly different from those of the PPI in the 1920s. The hard core of electoral support for the Catholic Party remained the Catholic subculture of northeastern Italy and the other white areas, and it still relied heavily on the capacity of Catholic Action and collateral organizations like the Catholic trade unions and Coldiretti (the powerful farmers' association) to mobilize the vote elsewhere. But the electoral success of 1946, when the DC won 35 per cent of the vote as opposed to the 20 per cent which the PPI achieved in 1921, is explained by another factor—the introduction of female suffrage in 1945. It has been estimated that in the 1950s and 1960s more than 60 per cent of DC votes in local and national elections came from women.[59] In addition, as has been seen in the 1948 elections especially, the DC benefited from desertion of the parties of the centre-right by middle-class voters.

Another important feature of the 1946 and 1948 elections was the unprecedented support which the DC won in some southern regions. In particular, the party managed to establish small strongholds in Abruzzi and Molise, and in Basilicata, the latter being a region where the Popolari had hardly existed as an eléctoral force in 1921. This new support can largely be explained in terms of the DC's success in exploiting the 'Southern political system', that is in tapping into the more traditional electoral resources of clientelism and mafia, by means of the ministry of the interior and the prefects.[60] History was repeating itself; just as in 1861, when the local landowning élite had joined forces with the new Northern moderate Liberal unifiers of Italy in a

[58] G. Galli, *Storia della D.C.* (Rome, 1978), 168.
[59] Leonardi and Wertman, *Christian Democracy*, 166.
[60] Ginsborg, *Contemporary Italy*, 176–81.

'tacit alliance'[61] and in 1924 when the Southern notables jumped on the bandwagon of Fascism, thus giving the Fascists 80 per cent of the vote whereas they had hardly been represented at all in 1921, so in 1946 and 1948 substantial elements of the southern landed élites chose to throw in their lot with Christian Democracy which, as the party of the prime minister, seemed to offer the best defence of their class interests. The success of the DC in stabilizing these new sources of electoral support was to depend upon the capacity of local leaders to put down solid, enduring roots in their areas. Despite the setback in 1953, this they largely succeeded in doing, using control of the ministry of public works, the Southern land reform agency, the Cassa per il Mezzogiorno (the development agency for the South), and such other institutions as the ministry of posts and telegraphs and the ministry of transport (state railways) which provided an almost unlimited source of jobs for southern constituents. Like the Socialists, the Social Democrats, and the Republican Party in the 1960s, from 1948 onwards the DC in the South became a largely clientelistic party and also one deeply penetrated by organized crime: the Mafia in Sicily, the 'Ndrangheta in Calabria, and the Camorra in Naples.[62]

Even more novel and more fruitful were the DC's attempts to exploit the massive state sector inherited from Fascism for electoral purposes. As a result of the operations of IRI—the Industrial Reconstruction Institute established during the Great Depression to bail out 'lame duck' industries and banks—according to Ricossa, 'after 1936, the Italian state owned a proportionately larger part of industry than was the case in any other European state with the exception of the Soviet Union'.[63] Though Enrico Mattei had been given the task of dismantling this massive state sector, beginning with AGIP, the petrol distribution firm, by capitalizing on the discovery of natural gas in the Po Valley, he added a massive new dimension to that holding—ENI, the State Hydrocarbon Agency. This he used to intervene in the restructuring and modernization of Italy's economic system, with greatly beneficial effects during the economic miracle in the late 1950s and early 1960.[64] Thus, after the Second World War, the Italian state had a controlling interest in economic activities ranging from transport (railways and airlines), to engineering, chemical, energy, and food-producing industries. In addition, the State controlled, directly or indirectly, the lion's share of Italy's major banks. It is also clear that Mattei was the first Christian Democratic politician to use systematically the funds of a state-controlled industry to influence internal party struggles, largely, it should be said, in order to promote the interests as he saw them of the industries themselves.[65]

[61] Seton-Watson, *Italy*, 24.

[62] J. Walston, *The Mafia and Clientelism: Roads to Rome in Post-War Calabria* (London, 1988), esp. 85–6 and 193–8; G. Servadio, *Mafioso: A History of the Mafia from its Origins to the Present Day* (London, 1976), ch. 9; P. Arlacchi, *Mafia Business: The Mafia Ethic and the Spirit of Capitalism* (Oxford, 1968), chs. 3 and 7; and J. Chubb, *Patronage, Power and Poverty: A Tale of Two Cities* (Cambridge, 1982).

[63] G. Ricossa, 'Italy, 1920–1970', in C. Cipolla (ed.), *The Fontana Economic History of Europe, i. Contemporary Economies* (Glasgow, 1972), 287.

[64] M. V. Posner and S. J. Woolf, *Italian Public Enterprise* (London, 1967), 55–6 and 68–9, and Ginsborg, *Contemporary Italy*, 163–5.

[65] See G. Galli, *La sfida perduta: Biografia politica di Enrico Mattei* (Milan, 1976), 249–50.

In fact, the Fascists had already pioneered the use of jobs in the state bureaucracy, the party, the corporations, and possibly in the state economic sector too, for the purpose of 'manufacturing consensus'.[66] In the 1950s and 1960s Fanfani and his Christian Democratic allies followed suit on a larger scale, colonizing industrial undertakings, banks and credit institutions, and the media industries with their appointees in order to reward political favours, win electoral support, and guarantee access to new sources of party funding.[67] In consequence, voting behaviour in Italy has been increasingly conditioned by personal, clientelistic relationships between the voters and the parties. In this way, the DC became, like Fascism before it, a kind of 'party of the State' or 'regime', and one which by 1968 had been in power uninterruptedly for longer than Fascism.

Whatever the long-term implications of the strategies outlined above, in the short term, that is from 1953 to 1963, the DC found itself in an increasingly difficult, seemingly untenable position in Parliament, and one that was not significantly alleviated by the results of the 1958 elections. A narrow and fragile parliamentary majority of the DC and the centre parties condemned Italy to short-lived, ineffective coalition governments. The exploitation of the Cold War card, the continued reliance on appeals to the fear of Communism, provided no escape from this situation: on the contrary, the Communists actually gained in electoral strength in this period.[68] Only a more radical strategy, namely an 'opening to the left', with a splitting of the alliance between the Communists and the by now thoroughly discontented Socialists, and the absorption of the latter into the governing majority offered any realistic chance of escape from this situation. But this initiative was blocked by conservative elements in the DC, the US administration, and above all by the intransigent hostility of the Church hierarchy. Under the leadership of Pius XII they refused to countenance any compromise with the still Marxist-orientated PSI.

Relief came with the death of Pius XII and the election of John XXIII in 1958. Papa Roncalli's new course on the international plane, the first tentative steps towards Vatican Ostpolitik, paralleled the DC's opening to the left in Italian, domestic politics. More important even than that, was John XXIII's determination to disengage the Church from his predecessor's policy of total involvement in Italian politics. Though obstructed by conservative elements in the Italian episcopate, and even in the Roman Curia itself,[69] the Pope managed to establish the principle that Italian Catholic lay politicians had the right and even the duty to make fundamental changes of direction by themselves. His encyclical *Pacem in Terris* was the final green light for the experiment in a centre-left coalition which, even if it was to prove largely un-

---

[66] Ginsborg, *Contemporary Italy*, 146–7.

[67] Ibid. 178–81; G. Galli, *Storia della D.C.*, chs. 9 and 10; R. Filizzola, *Amintore Fanfani* (Rome, 1988), 39–41; and P. A. Allum, *Politics and Society in Post-war Naples* (Cambridge, 1973), 172–3. For an overall view see P. Farneti, 'Patterns of Changing Support for the D.C. in Italy: 1946–1976', in B. Denitch (ed.), *Legitimation of Regimes* (London, 1979).   [68] Kogan, *Political History*, 5.

[69] See P. Hebblethwaite, *John XXIII: Pope of the Council* (London, 1984), ch. 17 for an account of curial machinations; and also P. Furlong, 'The Changing Role of the Vatican in Italian Politics', in L. Quartermaine and J. Pollard, *Italy Today: Patterns of Life and Politics* (Exeter, 1987), 64–5, where he analyses the continuation of disengagement in the reign of Paul VI.

successful in its objective of bringing much-needed economic and social reforms to Italy, at least unblocked the immobilism that had prevailed since the 1950s, and extended the life of Christian Democratic political hegemony. Under a succession of prime ministers who were mostly veterans of FUCI, starting with Aldo Moro, and with the blessing of their former mentor Montini, who was elected as Pope Paul VI in 1963, the DC succeeded in splitting the left and reducing the Socialist Party to the status of a dependent governmental ally.[70]

The failure of the reformist project of the Centre-left can be explained by a number of factors, but there are those who argue that it was a result of a deliberate choice on the part of the DC, which was afraid that the effects of reform would be to upset the precarious balance of social forces on which its electorate was built.[71] Whatever the explanation, there can be no doubt that the trend towards state clientelism accentuated from the mid-1960s onwards, the DC strengthening its links with a 'state bourgeoisie' composed of finance speculation and parasitic bureaucratic elements, all feeding on the patronage resources provided by control of the governmental apparatus, be it national, regional, or local, and the vast public sector.

7. The DC and the Beginnings of Secularization: Vatican II and the Economic Miracle

John XXIII's other great initiative in the *aggiornamento* of the Catholic Church, the Second Vatican Council (1962–6), was also to have a powerful impact on the future of political Catholicism in Italy. Its stress upon freedom, the role of the laity—both in the liturgy and in other ecclesial matters—, and above all the primacy of the individual conscience, led to a brief flowering of Catholic political pluralism. At one level, it encouraged new ventures in community—*communità di base*—and a resurgence of Catholic intellectual freedom which expressed itself in the *cattolici del dissenso* (dissident Catholics) and was to reach its culmination in Catholic opposition to the referendum against the divorce law in 1974.[72]

The most important example of autonomous, Catholic lay activism is provided by the ACLI—the Associations of Italian Catholic Workers. Founded as a point of reference and guidance for Catholic workers inside the unified Italian General Confederation of Labour, which was born out of the Resistance unity in 1944, the ACLI spearheaded the eventual break-up of the confederation and the return to a separate Catholic trade union confederation, the CISL, three years later. In the 1960s the ACLI increasingly moved away from the positions of the parent body, Catholic Action, and from the authority of the ecclesiastical hierarchy, and under the

[70] Kogan, *Political History*, ch. 11.

[71] G. Galli and A. Nannei, *Capitalismo assistenziale* (Milan, 1976), 60; see also A. S. Zuckerman, *The Politics of Faction: Christian Democratic Rule in Italy* (London, 1979), 84.

[72] F. Spotts and T. Wieser (eds.), *Italy: A Difficult Democracy* (Cambridge, 1986), 258; P. A. Allum, 'Uniformity Undone: Aspects of Catholic Culture in Post-War Italy', in Z. Baranski and R. Lumley (eds.), *Culture and Conflict in Post-War Italy: Essays on Mass and Popular Culture* (Basingstoke, 1990), examines the impact of Vatican II on Catholic culture in Italy in broader terms.

leadership of Livio Labor it had established a wholly autonomous role for itself by the end of the decade. In the 1972 general elections, Labor was to launch the first major experiment in Catholic political pluralism since the war by offering an alternative list of left-wing Catholic candidates under the name of the Movimento Politico dei Lavoratori (Catholic Workers' Political Movement), but had no success in winning seats.[73] The impulse towards Catholic political pluralism also took a more dangerous form, as far as the DC was concerned, with the tendency of increasing numbers of Catholics to ignore the instructions of the eclesiastical hierarchy and to vote instead for the Socialists and Communists. The near-monopoly of the Catholic electorate by the DC had finally been broken.

These tendencies, and an even broader cultural crisis of Italian Catholicism, were also encouraged by momentous changes which had been taking place in Italian society as a whole since the mid-1950s—the effects of the economic miracle, and of the cultural conquest of Italy by Anglo-American influences. The miracle had set in motion profound economic and social changes—industrialization, urbanization, and an accompanying migratory shift from countryside to town and from the South to the North, all of which helped to break or at least to transform radically the ties between the Church and hundreds of thousands of Italian Catholics.[74] The traditional values of Italian Catholic culture—'frugality, private property, family and the subordinate position of women, the myth of the land, acceptance of one's social status and the virtue of obedience, and the castigation of atheists, sinners and revolutionaries'[75]— were also challenged by the bombardment of Italy by Anglo-American consumerist and essentially secular culture through the cinema, television, and popular music resulting in a diminishing acceptance of these values, especially among women and young people.

Thus even before the student upsurge of 1968 and the trade-union agitation of the 'Hot Autumn' of 1969, which were to set in train a decade of social unrest, spawning new social movements, it is clear that Italian society was already going through processes of radical social change. The impact on the Catholic world was dramatic; attendance at mass slumped, from 69 per cent of the population in 1956 to only 48 per cent in 1968. There was an equally dramatic slump in support for Catholic associationalism, membership of Catholic Action falling from 3.3 million in the mid-1960s to 1.65 million in 1970.[76] Perhaps even more significant than these figures was the outcome of the 1974 referendum: the substantial majority in favour of divorce clearly demonstrated that the Church's ability to influence Italian civil society was in decline. As a result of secularization, the base of the Christian Democratic electorate in the Catholic community was beginning to shrink. The process had thus already begun whereby the DC was to be transformed into a more conventionally middle-class, conservative party.[77]

---

[73] Kogan, *Political History*, 245 and 263.

[74] For the impact of these changes see Ginsborg, *Contemporary Italy*, 239–45.

[75] P. A. Allum, 'Uniformity Undone', 82.   [76] Clark, *Modern Italy*, 371.

[77] For an analysis of this process, see P. Furlong, *The Italian Christian Democrats: From Catholic Movement to Conservative Party* (Hull Papers in Politics, 26; Hull, 1982).

8. Conclusion

It is clear that the Papacy played a crucial, determining role in the evolution of political Catholicism in Italy both before and during the period under discussion. It was the Papacy which called it into being, permitted it to enter the parliamentary arena, and grudgingly allowed it to take the shape of an organised mass political party, yet effectively destroyed the chances of the survival of the party between 1922 and 1924. During the Fascist interlude, it was Pius XI who prepared for the post-Fascist future by preserving FUCI and the Movimento Laureati in the 'island of separateness' that was Catholic Action. And having failed to Christianize and clericalize Fascism as he intended, he at least was able to ensure that Catholics, in the shape of the emerging cadres of those organizations, would be in a strong position to fight for the political succession after the fall of the regime.

Similarly, the rebirth of political Catholicism in the post-Fascist era, and its electoral triumph in 1948, would have been impossible without papal intervention and support. There is no parallel between this situation and the history of political Catholicism elsewhere in Europe. This is hardly surprising: the role of the Catholic Church in Italian politics has always been determined by a factor which is obviously missing in every other Catholic country—the presence of the Papacy. Given that presence, the Catholic Church in Italy speaks with a greater and more direct authority than elsewhere, for at the risk of stating the obvious, its head is no mere cardinal primate, but the Bishop of Rome, the Vicar of Christ, and the infallible head of the Church throughout the world. And the Church–State conflicts of the Risorgimento period, and especially the Roman Question, bound the Papacy and Italian Catholics very closely together. As Falconi has described it, the Papacy has always regarded the Italians 'as an essentially levitical people', at the service of the 'Servant of the Servants of God'.[78]

For this reason, until the election of John XXIII in 1958, *all* the popes in the period under discussion showed great reluctance to concede real political autonomy to the Italian Catholic laity. Until 1929 the organized, mass Catholic movement was seen as an invaluable *forza di manovra*, a lever to be used in the Vatican's tortuous but improving relations with the Italian state, and particularly in the pursuit of the Papacy's major goal up to this point—a reversal of the losses of territory, property, legal privileges, and social influence which it had suffered during the Risorgimento. This policy came into increasing conflict with the growing cultural and political maturity of Italian Catholics, the sharpest examples being in 1904 when Pius X effectively proscribed the first Christian democratic movement and, even more brutally, in the mid-1920s when Catholics were forced to accept papal policies that contributed to the downfall of Italian democracy.

On the other hand, the Vatican's revivification and reorganization of the Unione Popolare into Catholic Action, was ultimately to provide both a line of retreat for many ex-Popolari after the demise of their party, prompting bitter rows between the

---

[78] C. Falconi, *The Popes in the Twentieth Century* (London, 1967), 292–3.

Vatican and the regime over their political activities in 1929, 1931, and 1938, as well as providing a launching pad for a new Catholic Party in 1943. That experience of Catholic Action did, however, produce a new breed of Catholic politicians who, crushed between the theocratic authoritarianism of Pius XI and the totalitarian intolerance of Mussolini, were arguably more conformist, and more obedient to ecclesiastical authority, than their predecessors in the PPI had been.

The DC was also more heavily dependent upon Catholic Action than its precursor, relying upon that organization for the continued recruitment of its cadres and the mobilization of the Catholic electorate. Fanfani's efforts to build up a party organization and electoral base independent of Catholic Action resulted in a dilution of the Catholic nature of the party as Cold War tactics and clientelistic operations began the process of transforming the DC, a typical religion-based, inter-class party, into one that was more broadly representative of the middle and lower middle classes. It can therefore be argued that the PPI, despite its self-proclaimed aconfessionality and its difficult relations with the ecclesiastical authorities, was a more genuinely Catholic party during its short existence than was the DC.

The determining influence of the Papacy is less clearly discernible in the development of the ideologies of Italian political Catholicism, except in so far as it crushed the Marxist tendencies of the extreme left-wing margins of the Catholic movement in the early 1920s and 1940s. The formative spiritual and ideological influences of Montini on the FUCI and Movimento the Laureati in the 1930s and early 1940s, and in particular his introduction of many future leaders of the DC to the ideas of Jacques Maritain, was achieved despite serious misgivings on the part of the Vatican authorities.[79] In the same period, Fascism acted as a catalyst for a general rethinking of political ideas and tactics on the part of many Catholic activists: the most obvious examples being Sturzo and De Gasperi, but of great importance also were the political theorizing of Piero Malvestiti and the Guelf movement and of La Pira and his friends in Florence. The experience of Fascism also ensured the effective abandonment of corporatist ideas, even by some of their most notable proponents, such as Fanfani and Paolo Emilio Taviani. Given the intellectual ferment that had preceded the refounding of the Catholic Party, it is especially ironic that after 1946, faced by the realities of government, of electoral politics, of Italy's economic plight and powerful US influences, the DC developed a working ideology of pragmatism. The ideas of social Catholicism have increasingly been relegated to parliamentary and conference oratory and to the rhetoric of periodical journalism. Since then, the Christian Democrats seem to have come to terms with the reality of international, and Italian, neo-capitalism. If the Catholic concept of social solidarity survives in practice in Italy then it is in the form of widespread and endemic clientelism. And if *Pacem in Terris* provided the ideological justification for the opening to the left, it appears to have had very little effect upon the evolution of DC policy in the 1960s other than, perhaps, to justify the continuation of a large public sector.

---

[79] Moro, *Formazione della classe dirigente cattolica*, 234.

As Webster has pointed out, 'It is always a mistake to write of Catholics in Italy, or elsewhere, as a block. Within the general limits of obedience to the Holy See there is room for all but the most radical differences.'[80] Very wide differences there were indeed inside Italian political Catholicism, and they would probably have been wider and more radical but for papal intervention against such radicalism, usually it has to be said, radicalism of the left. In the early 1920s, as we have seen, Catholic political pluralism was positively encouraged, as the Vatican sought to undermine the PPI's monopoly of the Catholic electorate, but once the Vatican had decided to make the DC its agents in Italy, such freedom was prohibited in the name of the political 'Unity of Catholics'.

The dilution of the ideological patrimony of Italian political Catholicism was, as we have seen, largely the result of new electoral strategies. The geographical and social bases of Italian political Catholicism remained essentially the same until 1946. Electorally speaking, the PPI never succeeded in attracting very much support beyond the traditional geographical and social boundaries of the Catholic movement out of which it had developed. Only the party's restricted success in winning votes from landed élites in the Campagna, Apulia, and Sardinia gave any hint of the spectacular electoral success that the DC was to win for itself in the South after the Second World War.[81] Indeed, this success was partly responsible for making the DC a national party in a way in which the PPI emphatically was not. Bearing in mind the DC's other success in attracting broader middle-class support through anti-Communism and clientelism, it could therefore be argued that by 1968 it had realized the dream of many Catholic political activists of the last decades of the nineteenth century, namely the creation of a national conservative party.

[80] Webster, *The Cross and the Fasces*, 20.   [81] Pollard, 'Catholic Conservatives', 40.

3

Spain

MARY VINCENT*

On 31 May 1919 King Alfonso XIII consecrated Spain to the Heart of Jesus. Unveiling a new monument, which depicted the Spanish nation prostrate before Christ's Sacred Heart, Alfonso led his government in the act of reparation, lamenting those who 'cast you aside, scorning your commandments'. Together, king and government implored God to ensure that 'the world from pole to pole' resounded with praise for 'the divine Heart, through whom we have reached salvation'. This 'enthronement' on the Cerro de los Angeles—a hilltop just outside Madrid which marks the geographical heart of Spain—was the culmination of a long campaign to have images of the Sacred Heart erected in every public place in the land. These statues, with their concomitant cults of reparation for the ingratitude of the modern world, came to represent the aspirations of those who desired an integral, totally Catholic society, where Church and State were as one. Carved into the base of the statue which now adorned the Cerro were the words 'You will reign in Spain'.[1]

The conflation of earthly and heavenly kingship apparent in this ceremony was characteristic of contemporary Spanish catholicism. Enthronements of the Sacred Heart were invariably accompanied by the sound of the royal march, which was also played at the elevation of the host during mass. Just as Jesus Christ was to reign in the hearts and minds of Spaniards, so the house of Bourbon was to reign in Spain, protecting the Church against the ravages of republicanism, separatism, and socialism. The principle of monarchy went unchallenged amongst Catholics: those who did not look to Alfonso to secure the position of the national Church were Carlists rather than republicans, supporters of the Bourbon pretender rather than the Bourbon incumbent.[2]

To those taking part in the elaborate ceremony held on the Cerro there was only

* I would like to thank Frances Lannon and Paul Heywood for their comments on an earlier draft of this article.

[1] A reference to the 'Great Promise'—that Christ's Sacred Heart would 'reign in Spain and with more veneration than in other countries'—revealed to Bernardo de Hoyos SJ in 1733. Quotations from 'Acto de Consagración al Sacratísimo Corazón de Jesús', repr. *Boletín Eclesiástico del Obispado de Salamanca* (1936), 204.

[2] The Carlists were originally the followers of Don Carlos, pretender to the throne of Isabella II (1833–68). By the end of the Second Carlist War (1872–6), support for this counter-revolutionary cause was largely confined to Navarre; it survived into the 20th cent. as a regional movement, until revived in the 1930s. See M. Blinkhorn, *Carlism and Crisis in Spain 1931–1939* (Cambridge, 1975), ch. 1.

one way of being Spanish and that was to be Catholic. The construction of a totally Catholic nation was a constant aspiration for the generations of polemicists, preachers, and politicians who carried the Church's banner in the public life of twentieth-century Spain. In general, these men and women assumed that this would be assured by a benevolent confessional state. Political agitation was a last resort, used only in adverse circumstances, such as those created by the Second Republic (1931–6). Under the Catholic monarchy, however—as under the Catholic dictatorship of Franco—the great majority of the faithful were content to hymn the eternal values guaranteed by the State.

Yet, even in 1919, and despite the self-confidence apparent among the notables on the Cerro de los Angeles, theirs was a beleaguered position. The map of Spanish Catholic practice revealed extremes of both adhesion and alienation.[3] In most parts of northern Spain more people than not attended church on a regular basis. In the Basque regions, Catholic practice was overwhelming, as much a part of the local identity as was language, or scenery; among the peasant smallholders on the plains of Castile, or in the foothills of Aragon, catholicism was also ubiquitous, automatically entrusted with communal and family ritual, even if mass-going was not so predominant as among the scrupulous Basques. Further south, numbers shaded off. In the huge, latifundia-dominated, dioceses of Extremadura, New Castile, and Andalusia, non-practice was usual and anticlericalism common. Nor was geography the only variable affecting religious practice among Spaniards: throughout the land, more women than men were to be found swelling the ranks of the faithful. The image of the pious woman, be she mantilla-clad *beata* or the priest-ridden harridan of anticlerical fable, was a familiar cliché. Although in parts of the north as many men as women could be found in the pews, some discrepancy—in forms of practice if not in actual attendance—was common.[4]

Class proved a sterner determinant of Catholic identities than did either geography or gender. Proletarian districts, even in the great Basque city of Bilbao, saw far fewer of the faithful filling the pews on Sundays. In part, this reflected a lack of pastoral structures in industrial areas. No new parishes were established in Barcelona, the largest city in Spain, after 1877; in 1907 some of the city's parishes contained over 60,000 souls. Similarly, by 1935 the Madrid parish serving working-class Vallecas contained an impossible 80,000 people. The Catholic nation was not to be found here: pastors caring for industrial flocks gave vivid testimony of working-class indifference and hostility. Maximiliano Arboleya, canon of Oviedo cathedral in the mining region of Asturias, wrote to his bishop in January 1922 about parishes where,

---

[3] See F. Lannon, *Privilege, Persecution, and Prophecy: The Catholic Church in Spain 1875–1975* (Oxford, 1987), ch. 1.

[4] Duocastella found that in 1962 in the Basque diocese of Vitoria, 84.2% of men as well as 86.3% of women attended Sunday mass, 'Géographie de la practique religieuse', *Social Compass*, 12 (1965). Anthropological observers have, however, regularly commented on women's greater readiness to receive the sacraments, even in northern Spain, e.g. W. Christian, *Person and God in a Spanish Valley* (rev. edn.; Princeton, 1989), S. Tax Freeman, *Neighbors: The Social Contract in a Castilian Hamlet* (Chicago, 1970), and C. Lisón Tolosana, *Belmonte de los Caballeros* (repr. Princeton, 1983).

despite an abundance of children, the priest could not count on 'even one little girl for First Communion'.[5]

It was neither coincidence nor accident that those urban areas which were well provided with Catholic churches, schools, and hospitals were those occupied by the bourgeoisie. The Church's capacity to save souls seemed dependent upon the privilege and protection offered by both the upper classes and the Spanish state. In the words of the Jesuit trade-union organizer Gabriel Palau, 'We have the idea that all Spain is Catholic and can never cease to be so. . . . Many Catholics believe that only governments have a duty to defend religion.'[6] The fates of Throne and Altar were thus inextricably intertwined.

Like Arboleya, Palau was actively engaged in the reconversion of industrial society. Catholic trade unions were the favoured instruments of these urban evangelists and by 1918 a clear distinction had emerged between the patronal syndicates established by Palau and his fellow Jesuits, and the 'free' or independent unions founded by Arboleya and the Dominican fathers Gerard and Gafo. Whereas the first were paternalist and confessional bodies, mirroring the natural order of society in their distinction between 'protected' and 'protectors', both of whom were welcomed as members, the second were workers-only unions which imposed no religious criteria for membership and acted independently of employers.[7] Both initiatives failed. In Asturias, for example, Arboleya's persistent efforts to establish independent workers' syndicates were consistently defeated, not least by the opposition of local Catholic employers, while Father Palau's unions were seen by other workers as a breeding ground for blackleg labour, and by the employers as 'a prophylactic against socialism'.[8] Throughout northern Spain, Catholic unions were regarded as 'yellow'. In Barcelona, concerted efforts to evangelize the working class, led by Palau, created a body reviled by other unions as 'a sacristy of scabs'. The city's only free syndicates degenerated into free-shooting *pistoleros*, often in the service of military authority.[9]

Only in the Basque Country did Catholic industrial unions experience any lasting degree of success. Founded in 1911—and later affiliated to the Basque Nationalist Party—Basque Workers' Solidarity (SOV) appealed largely to white-collar workers, and its membership rose steadily, if not spectacularly. By the time of the Second

[5] D. Benavides Gómez, *El fracaso social del catolicismo español* (Barcelona, 1973), 529–31. For Vallecas in the 1930s see the account by the incumbent, F. Peiró, *El problema religioso-social en España* (Madrid, 1936). Other figures from A. Shubert, *A Social History of Modern Spain* (London, 1990), 151; Lannon, *Privilege, Persecution, and Prophecy*, 16–17.

[6] Quoted E. de Vargas-Zúñiga, 'El problema religioso en España I', *Razón y Fe* (1935).

[7] There is a succinct account of Catholic unionism in Benjamin Martin, *The Agony of Modernization: Labor and Industrialization in Spain* (Ithaca, NY, 1990), ch. 6; Lannon, *Privilege, Persecution, and Prophecy*, ch. 6 places the unions in their wider church context.

[8] A. Shubert, *The Road to Revolution in Spain: The Coal Miners of Asturias 1860–1934* (Illinois, 1987), 113–14; id., 'Entre Arboleya y Comillas: El fracaso del sindicalismo católico en Asturias', in *Octubre 1934: Cincuenta años para la reflexión* (Madrid, 1985), 243–52; J. Andrés-Gallego, *Pensamiento y acción social de la Iglesia en España* (Madrid, 1984), 321–7; Benavides Gómez, *El fracaso social*, 44–53 emphasizes the Jesuits' hostility to independent unionism.

[9] See C. Winston, *Workers and the Right in Spain* (Princeton, 1985) and, more widely, J. J. Castillo, *El sindicalismo amarillo en España* (Madrid, 1977).

Republic the SOV recorded between 37,000 and 40,000 members, though it had still made few inroads into industrial Vizcaya.[10] The SOV's relative strength, however, owed much—if not everything—to nationalism. Rather than breaking the mould, the Basque union did little to allay the impression of failure conveyed by the history of Catholic unions in Spain.

To some extent, the project of Catholic unionism was rent by contradiction from the very outset. Leo XIII's encyclical *Rerum Novarum* (1891), which had endorsed Catholic syndicalism, rejected outright the notion of class struggle, maintaining that

it is a great mistake to imagine that class is spontaneously hostile to class . . . Just as the different parts of the body unite to form a whole so well proportioned as to be called symmetrical, so also nature has decreed that in the state these twin classes should correspond to each other in concord and create an equilibrium.

This fundamentally corporative vision of organic harmony meant that Catholic unionists never admitted the possibility of conflicting class interests, still less capital–labour dialectics.[11] Yet, the very real nature of such struggles—which were well defined by 1919—determined the ultimate failure of confessional unionism in Spain; if internal conflicts weakened the Catholic unions, external conflicts decided their fate.

While Catholic trade unions ossified, Catholic agrarian syndicates thrived. Religious practice was high throughout most of the northern countryside, which was lauded by Catholic propagandists as a repository of unchanging values. More practically, much was made of papal teaching on private ownership. Property—clearly understood to be land—was the key to social harmony; the acquisition of 'some little property' would enable workers to become small proprietors, thus ensuring that 'class would move closer to class'.[12] The National Catholic Agrarian Confederation (CNCA), founded in 1917, oversaw a network of agricultural syndicates, rural savings banks, co-operatives, and insurance schemes which spread throughout northern and eastern Spain. The CNCA created a formidable apparatus of agrarian defence, albeit one which failed to make any impression on the latifundia districts of the south.[13] Amongst Catholic smallholders, however, loyalty to the Confederation proved strong, not least because of the technical and insurance services it provided. This fidelity persisted, despite the markedly paternalistic character of the CNCA, which had been profoundly influenced by the Society of Jesus. Papal doctrine on the sanctity of property undoubtedly found an echo among peasant proprietors, particularly once the Confederation instigated some much-vaunted redistribution schemes.

---

[10] J. P. Fusi, *El País Vasco: Pluralismo y nacionalidad* (Madrid, 1984), 43–60; id., *Política obrera en el País Vasco* (Madrid, 1975), esp. 193–203.

[11] *Rerum Novarum*, §14, §16, §43; see also *Quadragesimo Anno* (1931).

[12] *Rerum Novarum*, §47.

[13] J. Cuesta, *Sindicalismo católico agrario en España (1917–1919)* (Madrid, 1978); J. J. Castillo, *Propietarios muy pobres: Sobre la subordinación política del pequeño campesino en España (La Confederación Nacional Católico-Agraria, 1917–1942)* (Madrid, 1979).

The CNCA came into existence in the year in which labour unrest, regionalist grievance, and military discontent threatened not only the incumbent government but also the monarchical system itself.[14] Though in 1917 the immediate crisis was averted, the complex and corrupt system of power-sharing which had developed since the Restoration of the Bourbons in 1875 had entered its death-throes. The Restoration system was dependent upon the brokerage of local patrons, or *caciques*, and was thus increasingly threatened by the burgeoning forces of mass politics. While there were some attempts to come to terms with this changing political arena—the Conservative leader Antonio Maura, for example, attempted to introduce a project of 'revolution from above', at least in rhetorical form—these had little impact. Constitutional agitation, agrarian unrest, and the rapid growth of republican and socialist alternatives all testified to the crisis of the Spanish state.[15]

In such circumstances—with the Catholic nation apparently threatened with dissolution—news of Don Luigi Sturzo's foundation of the Italian People's Party (PPI) in 1919 was received with some interest. The Catholic daily *El Debate* commented favourably on the news, although it feared the PPI's political programme would undoubtedly 'give scandal' to many of 'our friends'. *El Debate*'s influential editor, Angel Herrera Oria, was president of an élite Catholic lay organization, the National Catholic Association of Propagandists (ACNdeP), which had long harboured ambitions of uniting Spanish Catholics in a single political grouping. The Propagandists—who were immensely influential in the CNCA—were impressed by Sturzo's acceptance of modern political methods but found his party's progressive policies and aconfessional nature far less appealing.[16]

Unsurprisingly, when a Spanish version of the PPI emerged belatedly in 1922, its mentors were not to be found among the ranks of the ACNdeP. The People's Social Party (PSP) was, instead, formed around Severino Aznar's Christian Democrat Group, established in 1919 as a forum for debate and discussion. The Group had brought together leading social Catholics—including Aznar himself, Arboleya, Gafo, and the like-minded Augustinian Bruno Ibeas—in an attempt to provide a coherent, Christian analysis of Spain's social problems. Both Jesuits and Propagandists were conspicuous by their absence; Herrera Oria, for instance, refused to put his name to the group's manifesto.[17] If conservative responses to the Christian Democrat Group were tepid, the integrist reply was far more heated. These factional followers of the Carlist pretender—for whom the 'social reign of Jesus Christ' was an attainable political reality—claimed the word 'democrat' smacked of 'forbidden fruit'. Yet, the concept of democracy espoused by the Group's members would have been virtually unrecognizable to post-Second World War Christian democrats. Far

[14] See J. A. Lacomba Avellán, *La crisis española de 1917* (Madrid, 1970).

[15] R. Carr, *Spain 1808–1975* (2nd edn.; Oxford, 1982), ch. 12; M. Suárez Cortina, *El reformismo en España* (Madrid, 1986).

[16] J. Tusell, *Historia de la democracia cristiana* (2 vols.; Madrid, 1974), i. 55–7, 104; Benavides Gómez, *Democracia y cristianismo en la España de la Restauración 1875–1931* (Madrid, 1978), 359; see also O. Alzaga, *La primera democracia cristiana en España* (Madrid, 1973), 120–3.

[17] Issued on 7 July 1919 and discussed in Tusell, *Historia de la democracia cristiana*, i. 100–4.

from reflecting pluralist political ideology, the term 'democrat' was chosen only to reflect the Group's ambition to reconcile Catholicism and the modern world. Used in this sense, the expression dated back to Leo XIII, who had firmly declared the term to be devoid of any political significance, a ruling reaffirmed by Pius X in 1910.[18]

However, the 1922 grouping firmly declared itself to be a political party—rather than a federation or a union—and so adopted the language of liberal democracy, still viewed askance by many on the Catholic right. This self-definition meant that the PSP represented the first attempt Spain had seen to establish a modern conservative political party. The PSP forms a key point in what may be seen as a modern historiographical project to search for the roots of Christian democracy in pre-Franco Spain. The work of historians such as Domingo Benavides and Javier Tusell explores the ideology of non-integrist Catholics, suggesting continuities with later conservative movements. The standard work on the PSP is by Oscar Alzaga, who went on to an active political career in Adolfo Suárez's Unión de Centro Democrático (UCD) during Spain's transition to democracy, before establishing his own small Christian democrat party in July 1981. He cites the opinion of PSP veterans, such as Manuel Giménez Fernández—reformist minister of agriculture under the Second Republic and later a leader of the Christian democrat opposition to Franco—as to the PSP's uniquely Christian democrat nature.[19]

Yet, during its brief political life the PSP never amounted to more than an amorphous grouping of essentially disparate elements, brought together through common concern at threats to the established order. Notwithstanding its brave espousal of the language of party, the PSP had more in common with the old Catholic leagues and unions than with modern political machinery. Although some Propagandists—notably Giménez Fernández and Gil Robles—availed themselves of the 'full liberty' the ACNdeP gave its members to collaborate with the new party, Gil Robles, for one, preferred to regard what appeared to be 'a constituted party' as a 'meeting of "men of goodwill" '.[20] Similarly, Carlists like Salvador Minguijón and Víctor Pradera viewed the PSP, in Pradera's words, as providing the possibility of 'a minimum programme of association or coincidence for rightist elements'. Rather than represent 'an ultra-democratic coterie', the party's slogan should be 'everything by and for the union of Catholics'. In stark contrast to this corporatist caution, the PSP's leader, Angel Ossorio y Gallardo, spoke of 'fervent democratic action' and truly representative parliaments. The new party, he declared, should be aconfessional, democratic, and popular.[21]

[18] H. Jedin (ed.), *The Church in the Industrial Age* (London, 1981), 233–45, 473–6; Tusell reckons that only the radical clerics Arboleya and Ibeas were democrats in the political sense, *Historia de la democracia cristiana*, i. 103.

[19] Interview with G. Fernández quoted Alzaga, *La primera democracia cristiana*, 14; on Alzaga's political career, see P. Preston, *The Triumph of Democracy in Spain* (London, 1986), 209–10.

[20] J. M. Gil Robles, *La fe a través de mi vida* (Madrid, 1975), 82–4. The 'heterogeneity of the component elements' led him later to see the PSP's demise as inevitable, ibid. 87–8.

[21] Alzaga, *La primera democracia cristiana*, 149; Tusell, *Historia de la democracia cristiana*, i. 107, 114; *El Debate*, 19 June 1923. Carlist collaborators with the PSP were followers of the corporatist thinker Juan Vázquez de Mella: Blinkhorn, *Carlism and Crisis*, 21–7, 35–6.

However, Ossorio was far from being a representative figure. Several PSP party orators spoke in corporative terms of 'the organic reconstruction of society', and the rejection of liberal laicism in Spain, where Catholicism served as both 'social and political law'.[22] The PSP leader's view of religion as a private emotion found little echo; the great majority of Spanish Catholic leaders shared the monolithic vision articulated by Pradera. Spain should be recognized as a totally Catholic society, with the Church's unique position as sole purveyor of the truth confirmed by law. Hence, when in September 1923 King Alfonso XIII acquiesced in General Miguel Primo de Rivera's abrogation of the constitution, the resulting military regime was greeted with jubilation by virtually all sectors of the Spanish Church. The coup was a fatal blow for the PSP which, in Manuel Azaña's words, broke up on its 'first real encounter with reality', providing enthusiastic collaborators for the new regime.[23] In the words of *El Debate*, 'national life' had to triumph over 'formal legality'; democracy was simply government by quantity rather than by quality.[24]

The Restoration Monarchy's legacy of corrupt government and violent social disorder ensured that the prospect of a military regime engendered widespread optimism. Many on the Catholic right would have welcomed any form of authoritarian solution: *El Debate*, for instance, insisted that the new government be 'of dictatorial type'.[25] Under the patriotic guidance of the army, the new state would ensure the Church's privileged position, enabling it to carry out its mission for the salvation of Spain. Ten bishops were guaranteed seats in Primo's corporatist-inspired National Assembly, a body greeted with enthusiasm as a way forward from the internecine party squabbles of liberalism. The new regime also guaranteed Catholic standards of public morality and, more importantly, education: religion and patriotism became the watchwords for both teachers and pupils.[26]

Catholics were not only the educators and moralists of this new state, they were also its politicians. Primo de Rivera's new agent of political mobilization, the Patriotic Union (UP)—envisaged as a single mass party on the Italian model but defined as an official 'anti-party', in which all members were required to be practising Catholics—provided ample opportunity for Herrera and his Catholic Propagandists.[27] As *El Debate* had predicted, '[w]hen Spain is reborn, it will be our men and our organizations who occupy the new channels of citizenship.'[28]

---

[22] Reports of PSP rallies, *El Debate*, 24 Mar., 11 May, 19 June 1923. Ossorio's prominence in the PSP was especially mistrusted by Herrera Oria: Gil Robles, *La fe a través de mi vida*, 85; Tusell, *Historia de la democracia cristiana*, 112.

[23] M. Azaña, *Obras completas* (4 vols.; Mexico, 1966–8), i. 481–3. Ossorio, in contrast, remained in opposition.

[24] *El Debate*, 22, 23, 25 Sept.; 2 Oct. 1923.

[25] Ibid., 14 Sept. 1923.

[26] See S. Ben-Ami, *Fascism from Above: The Dictatorship of Primo de Rivera in Spain* (Oxford, 1983), 102–8.

[27] J. L. Gómez Navarro, *El régimen de Primo de Rivera* (Madrid, 1991), 207–60; Ben-Ami, *Fascism from Above*, 129–60.

[28] Quoted Tusell, *Historia de la democracia cristiana*, i. 121–2; see also Gil Robles, *La fe a través de mi vida*, 88.

The ACNdeP's first aim was to provide political leadership in defence of the Spanish Church. In the words of the Association's founder, Angel Ayala SJ,

religion and politics cannot be separated. If politics is the art of good government, how can religion want no part in that government on which depends material and religious prosperity, men's temporal and eternal welfare? In this sense, religion is essentially political.[29]

Though his own Association was to remain an élite, under Primo Herrera immediately began to create 'a broad movement of citizenship', comprising 'unions . . . of men of goodwill, concerned above all else with municipal and provincial problems'.[30] Building skilfully on the network of agrarian syndicates established by the CNCA, the Propagandists achieved in the UP the first effective mobilization of Spanish Catholics at local level.[31] The most fervent supporters were to be found among the small and medium proprietors of northern Spain, though anti-separatism severely limited the UP's appeal among the Basques. Typically, local 'unions' were led by members of the Catholic bourgeoisie, already prominent in the agrarian syndicates but, on the whole, new to politics.

In the 1920s the ACNdeP, though still discreet in operation and small in numbers, became the commanding presence on the Catholic political stage. The new men of the UP would not simply retire from public life when Primo fell from power. This new political class was not, as yet, interested in party politics; the ACNdeP was typical in its commitment to any government that 'guaranteed public order and the principle of authority'.[32] The first Patriotic Unions were to give depth to the dictatorship rather than lead to a full-scale Catholic political mobilization, something which would only happen in opposition to a secularizing republic. But, some of the foundations for such a mobilization were laid under Primo. The language of anti-communism and anti-parliamentarism became common currency among the Spanish right, which rapidly espoused the watered-down corporatism advocated by Primo on the Italian and Portuguese models.[33]

Anti-liberalism, together with a confessional addiction to corporative theory, had also led more radical Catholics to welcome Primo's regime. Canon Arboleya, for instance, had hoped and believed that the dictatorship would provide state-sanctioned opportunities for implementing social Catholic teaching. Yet, by the time of his fall, it was widely agreed that the general's rule had been a wasted opportunity for social Catholicism.[34] The new corporative agencies had provided little more than patronage structures and similar charges could be laid against the UP. The political and

---

[29] A. Ayala, *Formación de selectos* (Madrid, 1940), 407–8, quoted G. Hermet, *Los católicos en la España franquista* (2 vols.; Madrid, 1985), i. 249.

[30] A. Herrera Oria, 'En la muerte del Padre Ayala', *Obras* (Madrid, 1963), 840–9; memoirs of José María Gil Robles and Fernando Martín-Sánchez Juliá, quoted M. Fernández Areal, *La política católica en España* (Madrid, 1970), 94–5.

[31] A process examined in detail in J. L. Gómez-Navarro, 'Unión Patriótica: Análisis de un partido del poder', *Estudios de Historia Social*, 32–3 (1985).

[32] Herrera's presidential address 1925, repr. *ACNdeP* (Boletín de la Asociación Católica Nacional de Propagandistas) (1950), 459–60.

[33] For the ideological development of the regime, see Ben-Ami, *Fascism from Above*, 174–89.

[34] See M. Arboleya Martínez, *Sermón perdido* (Madrid, 1930).

administrative personnel had altered, but the most dramatic change in the country's political climate was the now deafening clamour for democracy and a republic. Yet, among Catholics, the number of democrats was as exiguous as ever. By 1930 the Church's political spokesmen were younger, more professional, and more widely heard, but their political message was still inextricably intertwined with monarchical privilege.

The only exceptions were to be found in the Basque Country and Catalonia where, under the governance of a centralizing dictatorship, the regional churches became significantly more dissident. While the Basque episcopate raised no protest at Primo's Castilianizing policies, the dictator's bloodless persecution of the signs and symbols of the Basque nation did much to alienate—and democratize—young Basque Catholics, among them the Propagandist José Antonio Aguirre, future president of an autonomous Basque republic.[35] In Catalonia, Cardinal Françesc Vidal i Barraquer of Tarragona—second in importance only to the primatial see of Toledo—led his fellow bishops in determined opposition to the government's injunction that all Church business be conducted in Spanish.[36] In both regions, the experience of centralizing dictatorship created an oppositional current of Catholic politics which was to become genuinely democratic. Even before Primo's dictatorship, calls for regional autonomy had become increasingly clamorous; in his wake, the groundswell in favour of devolution became unstoppable. By the time Primo—now a discredited and solitary figure—resigned in January 1930, Catalonia was overwhelmingly republican. When his ineffectual successor, General Dámaso Berenguer, called municipal elections for the following April in a doomed attempt to oversee a return to constitutional government, even the local Catholic newspaper, *El Matí*, declared, in Catalan, that it was 'completely indifferent' to their outcome.[37]

In contrast, *El Debate* declared parliaments to be decadent institutions and warned that a change of regime would open the floodgates to 'an epoch of anarchy' and 'Russian experiments'.[38] Even in the face of the crushing republican victory—which, as Gil Robles subsequently recalled, came as 'a bitter surprise' for 'the world of the [P]ropagandists'[39]—Herrera's paper argued vehemently against seeing the election result as a plebiscite in favour of the king's abdication. Such a momentous decision should only be taken by the nation. Superior to, and greater than, the plebs, the nation 'signifies, in spiritual terms, ideas, feelings, traditions, interests, hopes . . ., [a] hundred values that one word decided by the masses, with more or less careful reflection, cannot destroy in a moment'.[40] This distinction between nation and people echoed the contemporary Catholic emphasis on national, as opposed to popular, will.

[35] See J. A. Aguirre y Lecube, *Entre la libertad y la revolución 1930–1935* (2nd edn.; Bilbao, 1976); Tusell, *Historia de la democracia cristiana*, ii. 13–18.

[36] See R. Muntanyola, *Vidal i Barraquer, el cardenal de la paz* (Barcelona, 1971); Ben-Ami, *Fascism from Above*, 199–202; J. Massot i Muntaner, *L'església catalana entre la guerra i la postguerra* (Barcelona, 1978), 10–12.

[37] H. Raguer, *La Unió Democràtica de Catalunya i el seu temps* (Montserrat, 1976), 37–8, 80–1; Tusell, *Historia de la democracia cristiana*, ii. 127–38. [38] *El Debate*, 14 Feb., 12 Mar., 10 Apr. 1931.

[39] Gil Robles, *La fe a través de mi vida*, 97–8. [40] *El Debate*, 14 Apr. 1931.

In Catholic political thought, the general good determined political action; popular sovereignty was a misguided notion which gave rise to the atomization of liberal democracy. As the general good found expression in the nation—understood as a continuing historical process, even a providential destiny—so the interests of the national community overrode those of individual citizens. But, in the heady days of April 1931, popular sovereignty held sway. The new regime was swept in on a massive popular vote, leaving erstwhile monarchists contemplating the harsh reality of failure.

The first question to be asked was, of course, why they had lost. Surprisingly, however, very few Catholic representatives seemed willing to pose the question. A rare exception to this reluctance to look inwards to explain the republican victory was a report, prepared for the Holy See, which baldly declared: 'In Spain religion is dying little by little under the protection of the State'. Under the monarchy, 'The official nature of Catholicism in Spain', instead of being 'of undeniable advantage for the Church, obscures the religious reality of the country'.[41] The ritual splendours of Restoration Catholicism contrasted sharply with the extraordinarily low levels of practice which characterized many parts of Spain. José Gafo, in a rare public analysis of the April revolution, declared,

Excellent things are *novenas, processions, pilgrimages, enthronings* [of the Sacred Heart], *statues, flags*, all the *symbols* of Catholicism, the splendours of the *cult, solemn confessions of faith*, the *legal recognitions* and *official acts* of religiosity, in which Catholic activities have predominantly, almost *exclusively* concerned themselves, and which now suffer the same fate as the *symbols* of the Monarchy; but there are more fundamental, more solid . . . and more productive things which should not have been abandoned as they were.[42]

Dramatic proof of this confusion of symbols occurred on 11 May 1931 when—in response to a monarchist provocation—churches, convents, and religious schools were burnt in Madrid as a wave of incendiarism spread to other Spanish cities. In retrospect, this violent popular attempt to extirpate the signs of the old order was portrayed as the occasion for a concerted Catholic entry into politics, in particular, that of the ACNdeP.[43] In fact, Herrera's Propagandists had been active for some weeks before; the coming of the Republic might have left its opponents ideologically paralysed but the organizational response was immediate.[44] The Association had created a permanent machinery, effective at both national and provincial level. The expertise and leadership—not to mention the propaganda organs—for any new Catholic initiative were already in place.

As early as June 1930, in a lecture to the Madrid Propagandists' study circle, Herrera Oria had articulated Pope Leo XIII's doctrine of accidentalism: all power came from God and all constituted authorities were therefore worthy of respect.

[41] M. Batllori and V. M. Arbeloa, *Arxiu Vidal i Barraquer: Església i Estat durant la Segona República Espanyola 1931–1936* (4 vols.; Montserrat, 1971–7), ii. 72–83.

[42] *La Ciencia Tomista* (May/June 1931), 397–412.

[43] e.g. *Ya*, 17 May 1959, reprod. in F. Areal, *La política católica*, 99–100.

[44] On the early weeks of the Republic, see P. Preston, *The Coming of the Spanish Civil War* (London, 1978), 27–34.

Legislative character was far more important than legal form and Catholics should work for their beliefs within the constituted legality.[45] Though doctrinally scrupulous, accidentalist dogma was essentially pragmatic. If the form of regime were irrelevant, all Catholics could work together in defence of fundamental principles. Accidentalist leaders made overtures to fellow Catholics in the Alfonsist and Carlist 'catastrophist' camps—who rejected any co-operation with the Republic—in the hope of establishing a mass political presence.[46] *El Debate* launched National Action (AN)—an 'organization of social defence'—simply as a vehicle for those who had campaigned against the Republic. The new group's monarchist inheritance was apparent in its motto, 'Religion, Fatherland, Order, Family, Property'. The word 'monarchy' was deliberately omitted for pragmatic reasons. Herrera and his circle were aiming for as wide an 'anti-republican concentration' as possible: 'Above all Spain; or, in the words of Leo XIII, "the general good".'[47]

Though scrupulously avoiding the language of party—which was not only tainted by liberalism but might also suggest that the entire Catholic religion could be reduced to a single manifesto—National Action, soon renamed Popular Action (AP), could not retain catastrophist loyalties, although co-operation, particularly at a local level, remained common.[48] To both Carlists and Alfonsists, not only was the dynastic question fundamental, but also—and more importantly—the Republic would never be defeated by legal means. The Carlists had taken up arms against the First Republic and were, even in 1931, training their militia, the Requeté, to do so again against the Second.[49] The difference between the accidentalist and catastrophist camps was, however, essentially tactical. Both were fundamentally hostile to the Republic. *El Debate* quickly substituted the term 'anti-revolutionary' for 'anti-republican', but it was clear that, although AP was prepared to work within the law to achieve its aims, it was no loyal opposition.[50]

Even before the church-burnings of 11 May, Republican Spain was believed by many Spanish Catholics to be at the mercies of Soviet Communism. True Spain was laid low; the victory of anti-Spain at the polls in April was given concrete reality by the following month's arson attacks. This simple distinction between Spain and anti-Spain proved a fruitful source of rhetoric for the new accidentalist right. Not

---

[45] A. Herrera Oria, *Obras Selectas* (Madrid, 1963), 11–15; see also Leo XIII, *Immortale Dei* (1885), *Cum Multa* (1882), and *Au milieu des sollicitudes* (1893). Leonine political teaching is summarized in R. Aubert, *The Church in a Secularised Society* (London, 1978), 9–15, 41–5.

[46] 'Catastrophists' were so-called because of their conviction that the regime would only be changed by catastrophic, i.e. violent, means. [47] *El Debate*, 15, 21, 29 Apr.; 7 May 1931.

[48] e.g. the Carlist José María Lamamié de Clairac stood alongside accidentalists in Salamanca in all elections held under the Republic.

[49] A. Lizarza Iribarren, *Memorias de la conspiración: Cómo se preparó en Navarra la Cruzada, 1931–1936* (Pamplona, 1953); M. Blinkhorn, 'Right-Wing Utopianism and Harsh Reality: Carlism, the Republic and the "Crusade" ', and P. Preston, 'Alfonsist Monarchism and the Coming of the Spanish Civil War', in M. Blinkhorn (ed.), *Spain in Conflict 1931–1939: Democracy and its Enemies* (London, 1986), 160–82, 183–205.

[50] A contrary view is put in R. A. H. Robinson, *The Origins of Franco's Spain: The Right, the Republic and Revolution, 1931–1936* (Newton Abbot, 1970); against Robinson, see Preston, *Coming of the Spanish Civil War*.

only did such terms have a political resonance—explaining, among other things, the April defeat—they also echoed the near-Manichaean division between good and evil, the Church and the world, the spirit and the flesh, which characterized so much contemporary Spanish piety. One Jesuit-run pious magazine, for instance, summed up political choice in the crude question 'Rome or Moscow?'.[51] The language of Christ and Antichrist could also be employed against those who sought to blur the distinctions, and present both political and religious choices in less simple a manner.

The elections of July 1931 returned an overwhelming Republican majority to the Constituent Cortes, which could only have been won with at least some Catholic votes.[52] At national level, Miguel Maura's Conservative Republicans were proclaiming the compatibility of Catholicism and democratic pluralism and similar options were proving viable locally. Three Catholic deputies elected for Catalonia chose to sit with the Esquerra—the broad left Catalan group on the government benches—rather than join the Catholic opposition groups, even though these included the Basque Nationalists. Even in Castile, Segovia elected the Republican canon Jerónimo García Gallego, while Avila returned the great medieval historian Claudio Sánchez-Albornoz who, unusually, combined Catholicism with membership of Manuel Azaña's Republican Action.

In the face of this unacceptable confusion of what were, to the old monarchist right, antithetical positions, the accidentalists and their allies sought to equate republicanism and anti-religion. In so doing, they were undoubtedly helped by the crude anticlericalism of the republican constitution, which looked to eliminate Catholicism from the public sphere by removing crucifixes from schoolrooms, banning processions, and secularizing cemeteries. Such moves—along with those directed against the religious orders—were opposed by all Catholic politicians.[53] Catholic Republicans, however, were prepared to accept the constitutional separation of Church and State and the introduction of freedom of worship, both of which were bitterly opposed by the self-styled defenders of the faith.

All cherished integrist ideals of the construction of a totally Catholic nation were laid to waste by the constitution. In a determined rearguard action, the self-proclaimed Catholic deputies used the debates on the constitution to show, repeatedly, their refusal to accept political and cultural pluralism.[54] When, as was inevitable, the religious clauses of the constitution were passed, they walked out in protest. Several of the constitution's provisions were scarcely compatible with those democratic liberties it otherwise enshrined—a contradiction that was pointed out again and again by Catholic republicans.[55] However, for the majority of Catholic politicians,

---

[51] *La Estrella del Mar* (Organo de la Confederación Mariana de España), 24 Aug. 1931, p. 427.

[52] As was recognized by J. M. Gil Robles, *No fue posible la paz* (Barcelona, 1968), 32–3.

[53] With the rare exceptions of Sánchez-Albornoz and Nicolau d'Olwer.

[54] *Diario de Sesiones de las Cortes Constituyentes de la República Española* (Madrid, 1933), 664–6, 764–70, 951–2, 1528–36, 1548–55. See also F. de Meer, *La cuestión religiosa en las Cortes Constituyentes de la II República Española* (Pamplona, 1975) and Lannon, *Privilege, Persecution, and Prophecy*, 181–6.

[55] Maura resigned from the government on 14 Oct.; the three Catholic Esquerra deputies crossed the floor during the constitutional debates.

the constitution was the inevitable consequence of parliamentarism. As both acci-dentalists and catastrophists frequently observed, there was no such thing as a con-servative republic. Even before the offending document had been passed formally by the Cortes, Herrera's Propagandists launched a campaign ostensibly calling for a re-vision of the constitution on religious grounds. Yet, the campaign's organizers and orators were equally opposed to the articles allowing for the creation of autonomous regions and, in particular, the redistribution of property. Those protesting against the constitution were, in effect, mobilizing against the Republic itself.[56]

As the men of AP set about creating Spain's first mass party of the right, religion proved their most potent rallying cry. Their first concerted appeal was to the newly enfranchised women of Spain, who were widely seen as a 'natural' source of sup-port.[57] Untainted by collaboration with Primo, Catholic women came into politics to show how the campaign against the constitution represented a new epoch in Spanish electoral life. The spokeswomen of AP presented themselves as apolitical creatures, driven into the public sphere by the secularizing onslaught of the Republican government. For both male leaders and female followers, the mobilization of women was an emergency response to an emergency situation. Female branches were cus-tomarily involved in catechesis and charity work, a reflection of the proper concerns of Catholic womanhood. Though the main agenda of these mothers and home-makers remained domestic, female labour—usually unpaid, though not necessarily unskilled—was essential to the creation of a modern party machine. AP's women workers built up voting registers; they organized and electioneered, campaigning tirelessly against civil marriage, divorce, and secularization. Such issues were per-ceived as particularly important to women, but their use of the religious question as shorthand for a whole series of other moral and political choices reflected the way in which the Catholic right used the banner of defence of the faith to spearhead a far wider attack on the economic and political bases of republicanism.

Economic issues came to the fore in mobilizing the agrarian bedrock of Catholic politics. AP's ambitious young leader, José María Gil Robles, was also national secretary of the CNCA and his vehement defence of property rights struck a chord with the Castilian smallholders who made up the bulk of the CNCA's membership. Already suffering economically, these peasant farmers were alarmed at the legal weakening of property rights—the terms of which were regularly exaggerated by CNCA orators—and alienated by the incompetent implementation of agrarian re-form. Intended to alleviate conditions in the south rather than the north, the Repub-lic's agrarian reform law offered nothing to the Castilian peasantry while the worsening economic conditions and spiralling social unrest affected them greatly. In such circumstances, it was unsurprising that support for AP continued to grow,

[56] Preston, *Coming of the Spanish Civil War*, ch. 2, esp. pp. 35–6.

[57] J. R. Montero, *La CEDA: El catolicismo social y político en la II República* (2 vols.; Madrid, 1977), i. 656–708; see also the case study by M. Vincent, 'The Politicization of Catholic Women in Salamanca 1931–1936', in F. Lannon and P. Preston (eds.), *Élites and Power in Twentieth-Century Spain* (Oxford, 1990), 107–26. Women were given the vote in the 1931 constitution.

particularly given the new party's skilful manipulation of agrarian rhetoric and CNCA organization.[58]

By November 1933, the date of the next elections, the CNCA's bulletin could declare: 'Fortunately, all the forces which defend the principles of social catholic doctrine (religion, family, property and order), upheld by our organization are united'.[59] In these Catholic Agrarian eyes, such forces were united in the CEDA (Spanish Confederation of Autonomous Right-Wing Groups), founded under Gil Robles's leadership in February 1933. CEDA was a permanent, rather than an *ad hoc*, electoral organization committed, like its predecessor AP, to affirming 'the principles of Christian civilization', and thus the revision of the Republican constitution. Looking to lead the Spanish right into the age of mass politics, CEDA maintained its open-door policy, announcing that it would welcome all 'rightist organizations that agree fundamentally with Popular Action's ideology and tactics'.[60]

This umbrella structure not only ensured that such well-established regional sectors of the accidentalist right as Luis Lucia Lucia's Valencian Regional Right (DRV) maintained their autonomous identities, but also continued AP's appeal to as broad a cross-section of the Catholic population as possible. '[I]n the political-religious order', declared the CEDA, it could have no other programme than 'the doctrine of the Catholic Church'. The 'principal aim and fundamental reason for its existence' was to work for 'the empire of the principles of Christian public law in the governance of the State'.[61] This rather presumptuous statement was characteristic of the way in which AP/CEDA unwaveringly categorized its actions and manifestos as 'Catholic'. Despite their scrupulous avoidance of party rhetoric, the Propagandist leaders of AP clearly harboured ambitions of becoming the faithful's only acceptable electoral choice.

Although the new confederation dismissed the idea of party as 'a rigid fiction', the run-up to the parliamentary elections of November 1933 showed it to have possibly the most successful party organization in Spain.[62] Various Propagandists—including Gil Robles and Herrera Oria—had made research visits to Italy and Germany, often under the aegis of *El Debate*.[63] Their observations of the 'new movements' in these fascist states helped inspire the CEDA to swamp entire localities with election publicity in the autumn of 1933. The scale of the campaign was unprecedented; CEDA was the only party of the right seen to be mounting an effective campaign against the Socialist Party (PSOE).

[58] Castillo, *Propietarios muy pobres*, 361–89; Preston, *Coming of the Spanish Civil War*, 30–41; and esp. A. López López, *El boicot de la derecha a las reformas de la Segunda República: La minoría agraria, el rechazo constitucional y la cuestión de la tierra* (Madrid, 1984), 153–207 on the opposition to art. 44 of the constitution, which allowed for the expropriation of property.

[59] *Revista Social y Agraria*, 31 Oct. 1933.

[60] 'Reglamento del congreso de Derechas Autónomas de febrero–marzo de 1933', in Montero, *La CEDA*, ii. 618–21; see also 'Estatutos de la CEDA', ibid. 637–8.

[61] 'Programa votado por el primer congreso de la CEDA (febrero–marzo de 1933): Conclusiones aprobadas', ibid. 621–36.

[62] *CEDA* (Organo de la Confederación Española de Derechas Autónomas), 1 (20 May 1933).

[63] Montero, *La CEDA*, 651–2; A. Viñas, *La Alemania nazi y el 18 de julio* (Madrid, 1974), 143–50.

The CEDA made much of this Christian–socialist dichotomy. Claiming the elections as a confrontation between redemption and revolution, CEDA orators sought to present all republican options as communist while keeping the Catholic label exclusively for themselves. Thus, Miguel Maura's Conservative Republican party was referred to as 'those who consent to Spain being lit by burning churches'; Sánchez-Albornoz was accused of hypocrisy and corruption by the Avila branch of the AP/CEDA youth movement (JAP); and, in neighbouring Salamanca, the provincial Catholic daily mounted vituperative attacks on two centrist deputies, one of whom was both a practising Catholic and a Conservative Republican.[64] In the increasingly polarized political world of the Second Republic, personal faith had come to seem an inadequate definition of Catholicism.

After the elections, the CEDA was the largest single party in the Cortes; though not asked to form a government, it occupied a hegemonic position on the right of the parliamentary spectrum. This position—together with the federal structure which allowed an unusually wide range of opinions to gather together in one party—partly explains why some scholars have sought to carve a niche for the CEDA in the history of Spanish Christian democracy. Richard Robinson, for instance, has argued, not only that Gil Robles turned the CEDA into 'a republican party in all but name', but also that it 'was really the Spanish counterpart of other European Christian-democrat parties. Its first loyalty was to the Church and the question of the form of government was unimportant.'[65] Leaving aside the question of the extent to which Christian democrat parties existed anywhere in Europe before 1945, the presumed indifference of democrats to forms of government seems distinctly odd. Such an interpretation relies essentially upon a literal, even a credulous, reading of CEDA rhetoric. In contrast to Robinson's view, the limits of accidentalism are accepted by other historians who, though anxious to trace Christian democrat continuities into and from the CEDA, follow the schema discerned by Giménez Fernández and Gil Robles. Both protagonists remembered the CEDA as fragmented; while there was a reformist wing—and, according to Gil Robles, an initial Christian democrat impulse—this was defeated by those landowning groups within the party whose prime concern was with the defence of property rights. The deliberate scuppering, by exactly those elements, of various moderate and papally inspired agrarian reform measures put forward by Giménez Fernández during his time at the ministry of agriculture was widely cited in support of this analysis.[66]

The existence of a Christian democratic tendency within the CEDA is seldom disputed, although a cursory examination of those who are deemed to have comprised this reformist wing reveals far less unanimity. Javier Tusell follows Gil Robles in

---

[64] *JAP* (Periódico quincenal de la JAP de Avila) and *La Gaceta Regional* (Salamanca), Nov. 1933 *passim*.

[65] R. A. H. Robinson, 'The Parties of the Right and the Republic', in Carr (ed.), *The Republic and the Civil War in Spain* (London, 1971), 46–78, esp. 70.

[66] Gil Robles, *No fue posible la paz*, 199–200, id., *La fe a través de mi vida*, 94–6; memoir of Giménez Fernández given in C. Seco Serrano, 'Estudio Preliminar', in Gil Robles, *Discursos parlamentarios* (Madrid, 1971), p. xlix. See also E. Malefakis, *Agrarian Reform and Peasant Revolution in Spain* (New Haven, 1970), 347–63; Tusell, *Historia de la democracia cristiana*, i. 282–312.

arguing that, if the CEDA had split, or at least rid itself of reactionary elements, it would have provided the basis of a true Christian democrat party; historians like José Montero and Paul Preston argue, in contrast, that such a label is, at best, applicable only to a reduced nucleus around Giménez Fernández and Lucia Lucia.[67] Giménez Fernández himself, writing in 1971, looked to those who 'followed the line of . . . Herrera', thereby extending the definition to encompass the Propagandist-inspired party mainstream.[68]

The case for seeing the CEDA—at least in part—as heir to the PSP and fore-runner of the early anti-Franco opposition is strengthened by the fact that some indi-viduals can be traced through all three groups, notably Giménez Fernández and Gil Robles. But, although such men had weighty social Catholic credentials, their past—if not their future—careers as democrats were chequered. Gil Robles's pre-war commitment to democracy was particularly tenuous. Visions of a Christian democrat CEDA core, stripped of all contrary or apathetic elements, and with the potential to develop into a modern conservative party, may have found favour among historians, but there is little evidence that such plans would have appealed to the CEDA leader. Gil Robles never contemplated restricting party membership to convinced demo-crats, nor in the 1930s did he accept the prospect of political pluralism. As one, ad-mittedly hostile, observer has put it, Gil Robles, 'distanced from the philosophy of the rights of man, . . . was outside the ideological preoccupations common to the founders of the Republic'.[69]

Essentially the CEDA was an anti-republican party, and its anti-republicanism translated into anti-pluralism. Though, like Catholic parliamentary groupings throughout Europe, it looked to fill the conservative space in the political arena, the weakness of the moderate conservative tradition in Spain meant that the CEDA soon careered rapidly to the right. The common currency of the CEDA was not Christian democracy but Christian corporatism. In the wake of the impetus provided by *Quadragesimo Anno*, Catholic intellectuals spent much time on corporative theory and the practical examples offered by the new European dictatorships.[70] Such con-cerns became more general after the left's electoral defeat in 1933, which finally allowed Catholic politicians to envisage a time when, once again, the State would be theirs. Visions of a new order informed the rhetoric not only of the CEDA but also of small fascist groupings which in February 1934 united under José Antonio Primo de Rivera as the Falange Española de las JONS.

Rather than rule Catholic fascism as illegitimate a political option as Catholic re-publicanism, CEDA leaders depicted the Falange simply as misguided. To those who shared the new, Catholic, corporatist vision of the State, fascism was not pernicious,

---

[67] Tusell, *Historia de la democracia cristiana*, i. 362–6; Preston, *Coming of the Spanish Civil War*, ch. 6; Montero, *La CEDA*, vol. ii, ch. 8.

[68] Quoted I. Molas, *El sistema de partits polítics a Catalunya (1931–1936)* (Barcelona, 1972), 38–9.

[69] J. Becarud, 'La acción política de Gil Robles (1931–36)', *Cuadernos de Ruedo Ibérico*, 28–9 (1970–1), 59–66.

[70] e.g. various series of articles by Narciso Noguer SJ, *Razón y Fe*, Mar., May, June, Aug., Sept., Nov. 1934; May, July–Aug., Sept. 1935.

simply unnecessary.[71] Anti-Marxism, a thirst for immediate social justice, and a corporatist vision of the State were not unique to the Falange. JAP, the CEDA youth movement, baptized its bulletin with the banner headline 'We want a new state'; its programmatic '19 points' included an explicit declaration of 'Anti-parliamentarism' and its members gave half-Roman salutes, professed unquestioning devotion to the *jefe*—who 'never makes mistakes'—and demonstrated their loyalty, discipline, and patriotism at mass rallies.[72] There were many who saw fascism in the JAP. José Antonio responded to Gil Robles's call for a purge of 'Judaizing Freemasons' with the words, 'these are fascist principles; he may reject the name, but the name is not the thing'.[73] Similarly, when the JAP rejected charges of fascism by asserting 'we are ourselves', at least one *falangista* understandably asked for a more precise differentiation.[74] Such goading could not disguise the great success of the JAP. Larger and more united than the Falange, the JAP, unlike the fascist party, had a genuine national presence and drew from the same potential membership.[75] The similarities between the two groups were thrown into stark relief in the spring of 1936 when, having failed to achieve 'all power for the *jefe*' through the ballot box, *japistas* exchanged their green shirts for blue ones in a general exodus to the Falange.

Gil Robles later admitted that the patriotic 'anti-politics' of the JAP had, in fact, resulted in 'totalitarian politics'. Yet, as a comparatively young man himself, he was convinced that leading Spain towards the new order was a youthful task. 'Who knows', he asked, 'if, in the inscrutable plans of providence . . . the hard task of harmonizing new political trends with the immortal principles of our Christian religion' might not fall to the JAP.[76] In this quest for a new order, which would reconcile traditional Catholic values with the apparatus of the modern state, increasing numbers of CEDA sympathizers—young and old—looked towards Dollfuss's Austria. The government assault on the Austrian Socialist Party in February 1934 was greeted with particular approval in the Spanish Catholic press; according to *El Debate*, it was 'a lesson to us all'.[77]

Authoritarian solutions to problems of 'disorder' were widely quoted, particularly among those who regarded the Austrian fighting as a prelude to what would inevitably succeed in Spain.[78] Liberal democracy was disintegrating; communist violence

---

[71] See e.g. the dialogue, 'JONS ¿Para qué?', between Eduardo Jiménez del Rey and the JONS leader Onésimo Redondo, *La Gaceta Regional* (Salamanca), 2, 8, and 14 Dec. 1933 and the supplementary article, 'Los puntos de la FE son los nuestros', 3 Jan. 1934. Both Jiménez and Redondo were Propagandists.

[72] e.g. those held El Escorial, Apr. 1934, and Uclés, May 1935; *JAP* (Organo nacional de las Juventudes de Acción Popular de España), 27 Oct. 1934, and 1 June 1935. Manifestos are given in Montero, *La CEDA*, ii. 642, and the '19 points' in Robinson, *Origins of Franco's Spain*, 169–70.

[73] Quoted Preston, *Coming of the Spanish Civil War*, 214.

[74] *FE* (Organo de Falange Española), 1 Feb. 1934; *JAP*, 25 May 1935; *Arriba* (Seminario de la Falange), 13 June 1935.

[75] Blinkhorn, 'The Iberian States', in Detlev Mülberger (ed.), *The Social Basis of European Fascist Movements* (London, 1987), 320–48.

[76] Gil Robles, *No fue posible la paz*, 196, 207–8; on his return from Germany, he had declared his admiration for fascism's 'youthful enthusiasm', 'Antidemocracia', *La Gaceta Regional* (Salamanca), 8 Sept. 1933.   [77] *El Debate*, 14–17 Feb. 1934.

[78] e.g. *La Gaceta Regional* (Salamanca), 15 Feb. 1934; see also *El Debate*, 11–14 Feb. 1934.

lay in wait. When in October 1934 the Spanish Socialist Party led an ill-conceived insurrectionary general strike—in part, a response to the announcement of three CEDA ministers—Gil Robles's party was clamorous in its demands for swift and stringent action. The JAP orchestrated a movement of civil defence as the defiant Asturian coalfields—the only area of determined proletarian resistance—were subjected to brutal military repression. In these circumstances, *El Debate*'s December call for a corporative constitution had an ominous resonance. The previous month Gil Robles had outlined his vision of an organic state in which power would be reinforced, governmental stability increased, and popular assemblies restricted to specific legislative functions.[79] Even the most socially conscious *cedistas* seemed unconcerned with civil rights. Giménez Fernández, for instance, had no qualms about closing PSOE offices in Badajoz, the province he represented in the Cortes.[80] He also joined his two fellow CEDA ministers in resigning from the cabinet when it voted to commute the death sentences passed by an army tribunal on two Socialist deputies.

A recent biographical study argues persuasively that Giménez Fernández, in marked contrast to most of his accidentalist CEDA contemporaries, was a convinced republican.[81] To distinguish between accidentalism and republicanism, however, does not necessarily address the wider issue of democracy. Certainly, if the question is construed in terms of democratic rights for socialists, then there was little to separate Giménez from his monarchist co-religionaries. His reputation as the Christian democrat conscience of the CEDA rests on the basis of his time at the ministry of agriculture. The defeat of Giménez Fernández's agrarian reform proposals was, according to Edward Malefakis, 'one of the central tragedies of the Republic. The transformation of the CEDA into a socially conscious Christian democratic party, which was [G]iménez's central purpose, was never accomplished.' Yet, the furious, obstructive response of the landowning right must have been anticipated. More damaging was the local opposition the minister encountered, notably in Seville, his native province, and Badajoz.[82] Rather than revealing proto-Christian democrat support, the minister's proposals split the party at every level. Indeed, the only CEDA grouping which unanimously accepted his reform plans was the JAP.[83]

The Christian democrat nature of Giménez Fernández's proposals often goes unquestioned. Yet, no legislative proposals should be divorced from their political context. Though appointed beforehand, Giménez only took office at the ministry of agriculture in the wake of the October rising. He analysed Spain's agrarian problems in religious terms, as befitted a professor of canon law. The landless should become landholders, though not necessarily outright owners. Such reform would lead, in

---

[79] *El Debate*, 22, 23 Dec. 1934; interview with Gil Robles, reproduced *JAP*, 24 Nov. 1934.

[80] He had favoured suppressing the local branch of the socialist FNTT during an earlier strike in 1934; I am grateful to Dr Timothy Rees for this information.

[81] J. Tusell and J. Calvo, *Giménez Fernández, precursor de la democracia española* (Seville, 1990), 38, 44, 116.

[82] Malefakis, *Agrarian Reform and Peasant Revolution*, 355; Tusell and Calvo, *Giménez Fernández*, 99–100 and 162–5 on his deselection in Badajoz and difficulty in finding another seat.

[83] *JAP*, 24 Nov. 1934; 27 Apr., 1 July 1935.

papal terms, to that 'reform of morals' without which no restoration of society could be accomplished.[84] The minister's proposals thus had a moral rather than an economic premiss, as was evident in his emphasis on the obligation of landlords to act in the common good. They were seen as part of a post-Asturias strategy which would ensure order through a policy of repression while wooing workers away from socialism with a programme of social legislation.[85]

The minister's agrarian proposals also had to be seen in corporative terms. *Quadragesimo Anno* explicitly set out in 1931 a corporative reorganization of State and society as the way forward from evils of individualism and the consequent class struggle between capital and labour.[86] Just as, in *Rerum Novarum*, access to property had seemed to offer a way between liberalism and socialism, so the current interest in corporatism was presented as a way forward from the competing creeds of capitalism and communism. Such alternatives would steer between the Scylla and Charybdis of warring classes, protecting the community against either absorption by the State or dissolution in the face of liberal individualism. The illegitimacy of liberalism as a political option for Catholics perhaps does most to explain Giménez Fernández's refusal to accept a place on the Republican slate which contested the 1933 elections in Seville. Nor was he driven out of the CEDA in the wake of the agrarian reform fiasco. A Propagandist first and foremost, he consulted Angel Herrera as to his situation and agreed with the ACNdeP president that his personal position was secondary to 'social Catholic representation'.[87] Party cohesion was to be put before all else.

Only when the right was defeated in the elections of February 1936 which brought the Popular Front to power, did Giménez Fernández and his fellows attempt to strengthen centrist links in support of the now-threatened Republic.[88] From the end of March Giménez Fernández and Lucia were in contact, not only with their co-religionaries Miguel Maura and Claudio Sánchez-Albornoz, but also with Azaña and the Socialists Besteiro and Prieto in a vain attempt to establish a national government.[89] Even had the CEDA deputies been able to establish preliminary dialogue at governmental level, they now had no following to bring with them. Luis Lucía, who had once commanded a strong regional power base in Valencia, retained only a nominal leadership of the DRV, which had become the first CEDA organization to embrace direct action, organizing a clandestine militia, and from May making direct contact with military conspirators.[90] As Lucía was well aware of developments in Valencia, his attempts to forge a Republican solution to the problems of spring 1936 were futile.

---

[84] *Rerum Novarum*, §27, 59; *Quadragesimo Anno* (1931), §15, §127–9.

[85] See e.g. Jiménez del Rey's editorials in *La Gaceta Regional* (Salamanca), 13, 14 Oct.; 7 Dec. 1934.

[86] *Quadragesimo Anno*, §81–7, 91–8.   [87] Tusell and Calvo, *Giménez Fernández*, 43, 112.

[88] Similarly, only in this context did some *cedistas* point to a lack of social content in the party programme.

[89] Tusell, *Historia de la democracia cristiana*, i. 357–9; Preston, *Coming of the Spanish Civil War*, 192–3; J. Avilés Farré, *La izquierda burguesa en la II República* (Madrid, 1985), 305. Azaña dismissed Giménez Fernández as a 'conservador utópico, . . . destinado al fracaso y la soledad, sobre todo entre las clases conservadores', *Memorias políticas de guerra* (2 vols.; Barcelona, 1981), ii. 20.

[90] R. Valls Montés, *La Derecha Regional Valenciana (1930–1936)* (Valencia, 1992).

Lucía's and Giménez Fernández's desire to replace the—in their eyes—calamitous reality of a Popular Front government with a national coalition also suggests an idiosyncratic definition of the democratic process. Even in 1936 the left wing of the CEDA is better defined as social Catholic than Christian democrat. And social Catholicism was far removed from democratic political assumptions. For example, the Dominican doyen of Catholic trade-unionism, José Gafo, was genuinely neutral towards the Republic and had in January 1934 written of how, to those on the right, 'Any social reform, which has necessarily to imply sacrifices, is termed *socialist*'. Yet, despite clearly occupying a position on the Catholic left, Gafo's name appeared alongside those of die-hard monarchists on the manifesto for Calvo Sotelo's Bloque Nacional, a corporatist initiative launched by far right elements in December 1934. Gafo was attracted by Calvo Sotelo's vision of a new, integrative state which would ensure historical continuity and enforce 'a distributive social justice'. A true concern for his fellow men had never altered Gafo's opinion of an inorganic suffrage, the 'essential vice of parliamentarism, classical liberalism and false democracy'.[91]

Throughout the Second Republic, only minority Catholic groups, principally in the northern peripheries of the Basque Country and Catalonia, were exploring explicitly democratic political options. Here local Catholic republican parties developed, although only the Basque Nationalist Party (PNV)—which was founded in 1895—maintained a national presence after 1933. Conservative in moral and religious matters, the PNV sat with other Catholic opponents of the new regime in the Constituent Cortes. Yet, the PNV was passionately committed to regional autonomy, a subject which was anathema to most *cedistas* and reduced Alfonsists to apoplexy. The frustration of regional aspirations under Primo's dictatorship had left a legacy of distrust among the Basques which the Castilian Catholic right did little to allay. The well-known links between catastrophist groups and the Spanish army—not to mention the military hero-worship which swept through the Catholic press in the wake of the Asturian revolt—caused further disquiet.

As the CEDA veered to the right under the Republic, so the PNV moved to the left. By February 1936 the two parties were clearly on different sides; in this final electoral confrontation between Spain and anti-Spain, the PNV stood alone.[92] Although the Carlists retained some residual support, the majority of Basque Catholics voted for the PNV. Such unanimity was not apparent in Catalonia—which had far lower levels of religious practice—despite similarities between the two regional churches. After 1931 most Catalan Catholics, including Cardinal Vidal, supported the Lliga Regionalista, a conservative nationalist grouping whose deputies voted with the right on religious questions and with the left on regional ones. Established in an age of faction rather than party, the Lliga never fully succeeded in defining a modern role for itself.[93] The popular vote was taken by the broad left Esquerra

[91] *La Ciencia Tomista*, Sept. 1933, and Jan./Feb. 1934; R. A. H. Robinson, 'Calvo Sotelo's *Bloque Nacional* and its manifesto', *University of Birmingham Historical Journal*, 10 (1966), 160–84.

[92] Tusell, *Historia de la democracia cristiana*, ii. 106–19.

[93] See I. Molas, *Lliga Catalana: Un estudi d'Estasiologia* (2 vols.; Barcelona, 1972).

Republicana, which enjoyed a hegemony in Catalan politics lasting as long as the Republic.

The perceived inadequacies of the archaic Lliga, together with the secularism of the Esquerra, led to the foundation of the Unió Democràtica de Catalunya (UDC) in November 1931. The UDC had very little electoral strength. Its single parliamentary affiliate, Manuel Carrasco i Formiguera, had been elected for the Esquerra and was not returned when he stood for the UDC in November 1933. Only Pau Romeva, a deputy in the Catalan regional assembly, the Generalitat, successfully fought an election for the UDC. Yet, despite these very real limitations, the party represented a new development in Catholic politics. It was not explicitly confessional, nor was it founded to defend the Church against the Republic, a task the Lliga had claimed as its own. Rather, the new grouping was nationalist, democratic, and republican, standing on a platform of autonomy, liberty, and social reform—including recognition of the legitimate rights of the Church.[94]

The UDC and PNV were most sharply differentiated from their Castilian counterparts by their acceptance of democratic pluralism. Both parties, of course, belonged to regional subcultures, which, particularly in their use of local languages, already demanded the recognition of cultural pluralism in Spain. The UDC fostered the use of Catalan, and looked outside Spain for its intellectual inspiration. The party's founders were inspired, not only by early Catalan nationalists like Bishop Torras i Bages and Joan Maragall, but also by G. K. Chesterton—whose collected works were translated by Romeva—and the French Thomist thinkers Jacques Maritain and Emmanuel Mounier.

These intellectual influences were also apparent in José Bergamín's Madrid journal, *Cruz y Raya*, which first appeared in April 1933 and whose ideological frame of reference was much wider than was commonly seen in Spanish Catholic publications of the time. It featured work by Chesterton—in Azaña's translation—, Pablo Neruda, and Luigi Sturzo while, most importantly, the journal acted as a Spanish forum for Mounier's *Esprit* group. *Cruz y Raya*'s political concerns were equally unusual: from its pages, Bergamín mounted a fierce attack on the repression that followed the Asturias revolt while other columnists condemned Nazism, commenting particularly on the attraction it seemed to have for so many Spanish Catholics.[95] In contrast to the ideas of *raza* and *hispanidad* being developed by right-wing ideologues,[96] or the belief in Basque lineage, first articulated by the xenophobic Sabino Arana, which still informed much Basque political thought, *Cruz y Raya* condemned racism as unchristian and immoral. The editors' philosophical and cultural concerns were thus far removed from those found in the anti-Semitic right-wing circles which dominated Catholic politics under the Republic.

---

[94] Manifesto given in Raguer, *La Unió Democràtica de Catalunya*, 89–92. See also ibid. 249–89; Tusell, *Historia de la democracia cristiana*, ii. 123–204.

[95] *Cruz y Raya*, May and Aug. 1933; Feb., Oct., Nov. 1934.

[96] Esp. Giménez Caballero, *Genio de España* (Madrid, 1932); R. de Maeztu, *Defensa de la Hispanidad* (Madrid, 1934).

Unsurprisingly, those few Catholics who stayed loyal to the government in the Civil War belonged to precisely these pluralist, republican groups. The PNV and the UDC were the only Catholic political parties to remain with the Republic, and the Basques provided the legitimate government with its only significant popular Catholic support. Theirs was not an easy decision.[97] The first weeks of the war had seen the unleashing of a fearful wave of anticlerical violence which was to cost the lives of 13 bishops, 4,184 diocesan priests, and 2,648 religious—283 of them female.[98] Despite republican claims to the contrary, these men and women were killed simply because of the office they held. Most were murdered, in the first days of fighting, by hit-squads whose activities ceased as the government regained control of law and order. But, the infamous Paracuellos massacres of November 1936—when the gaols of Madrid were emptied in the belief that the city was about to fall—claimed the lives, not only of José Gafo, but also of the Brothers of St John of God who had cared for the inmates of the region's mental asylum. Church property was desecrated; the bodies of nuns were disinterred and displayed on the streets of Barcelona; the towering statue of the Sacred Heart on the Cerro de los Angeles was ritually executed by a republican firing squad.[99] In the face of such atrocities, it is hardly surprising that Catholics became bitter opponents of the Republic. Some Catalan clergymen, for instance, were forced to conclude that the Republic was their persecutor, even though they had voted for it in 1931.[100]

Not all churchmen who reached this conclusion perceived Franco as their saviour. Vidal i Barraquer, for instance, had been smuggled out of Catalonia in grave danger from the violence which claimed the life of his auxiliary bishop, but later refused to sign the collective pastoral letter drawn up by Cardinal Gomá y Tomás which roundly declared that God was on Franco's side.[101] Only Bishop Múgica of Vitoria had joined Vidal in refusing to endorse the July letter. A conservative prelate, who had been exiled by the Republic, Múgica was sympathetic to Basque nationalist aspirations and had been horrified by the execution of fourteen Basque priests by insurgent troops in October 1936.

In quantitative terms, fourteen priests are scarcely significant when compared to the 6,845 priests and religious killed by the other side. But, none the less, shooting ordained Catholic clergy is a curious activity for those fighting in the name of God. Múgica's gradual disillusionment with Franco's crusade was not unique. The massacre of Republican prisoners at Badajoz in August 1936, the sustained repression of dissidents in the Nationalist zone, above all the bombings of the Basque towns of Durango and Guernica, led some Catholics to distance themselves from, and even to condemn, the Nationalist cause. In Spain, Ossorio y Gallardo and Bergamín were among those protesting at massacres shrouded in incense. They were joined by the

---

97 See J. de Iturralde (pseud.), *La guerra de Franco, los vascos y la iglesia* (San Sebastián, 1978).

98 A. Montero Moreno, *Historia de la persecución religiosa en España 1936–1939* (Madrid, 1961).

99 R. Fraser, *Blood of Spain* (London, 1979); R. Carr, *Images of the Spanish Civil War* (London, 1986).

100 F. Lannon, 'The Church's crusade against the Republic', in Preston (ed.), *Revolution and War in Spain*, 35–58.

101 J. Iribarren, *Documentos colectivos del episcopado español 1870–1974* (Madrid, 1974), 219–42.

French writers Mauriac and Bernanos, as well as Jacques Maritain, who insistently rejected neo-Thomist identifications of Franco's crusade with Aquinas's 'just war'. Though less influential, the English voices of Greene and Attwater were among those raised in protest at the Condor Legion's indiscriminate bombing of civilian targets. This spectrum of dissident opinion encompassed both antipathy towards Franco and active support for the Republic.[102] Its small, and often stifled, dissident voice was crying in the wilderness in the 1930s but was to inherit the kingdom after the 1960s.

In 1936, however, the great majority of Catholics acclaimed Franco as the paladin of their Church, protecting Christendom from the ravages of communism. In Spain, this majority was overwhelming. With the outbreak of hostilities, true Spaniards could once again look forward to the day when a Catholic head of state would wield the absolute authority conferred by outright victory. In Cardinal Gomá's words, '[t]he war cannot be ended by compromise, by arrangement, or by reconciliation . . . Pacification is only possible by arms.'[103] Franco's crusade was a war of conquest; territory was taken, but the cost was heavy and, as in all wars, the price was paid by the young. Boys abandoned their Catholic youth groups for the militias; girls forsook philanthropy for voluntary war work. In general, they took up their duties with enthusiasm, convinced that they were part of God's purpose. A new society was being forged by the war: even at the front, young soldiers were exhorted to conduct themselves as 'armed apostles', observing a minute's prayer for the dead, for instance, rather than the 'emptiness' of a minute's silence. These new crusaders were to be 'the most valiant, the most obedient', worthy heirs to the mantle of St James the Moorslayer.[104]

Those who fell were not simply heroes, they were martyrs. Their names became litanies, their lives, the stuff of pious legend. The last moments of the clergy killed in the revolutionary violence of July and August were recounted—and minutely illustrated—by hagiographers, as was the physical damage inflicted on ecclesiastical buildings.[105] Yet, out of suffering came redemption. Spain would be purified by the blood of its martyrs who were, in the words of one young nun, the 'living stones' of the new monument the Heart of Jesus was building in Spain.[106] For this young woman, daughter of a fiercely integrist family, the social reign of Jesus Christ was becoming a reality. In those, largely Traditionalist, circles nurtured on apocalyptic prophecies and visions—such as those that occurred in the Basque village of Ezquioga in 1931—the Crusade had a clearly millenarian purpose.

[102] A. Ossorio y Gallardo, *La guerra de España y los católicos* (Buenos Aires, 1942); J. Bergamín, *Detrás de la cruz* (Mexico City, 1941); G. Bernanos, *Les Grands Cimetières sous la lune* (Paris, 1938); Maritain's introd. to A. Mendizábal, *Aux origines d'une tragédie* (Paris, 1837); *Tablet*, July–Aug. 1937. See also Lannon, 'The Church's Crusade against the Republic', 35–58.

[103] Address to International Eucharistic Congress, Budapest (May 1938), quoted J. Chao Rego, *La iglesia en el franquismo* (Madrid, 1976), 35.

[104] *Signo* (Organo de la Juventud de Acción Católica), 4 and 20 Nov. 1936.

[105] e.g. A. Castro Albarrán, *La gran víctima* (Salamanca, 1940).

[106] M. T. Camarero-Nuñez, *Mi nombre nuevo "Magnificat": María del Pilar Lamamié de Clairac y Alonso ACJ 1915–1954* (Madrid, 1960), 193.

Though integrist millenarianism was the province of a minority of Spanish Catholics, the determination to construct a new, post-war society was universal. Like all civil wars, the Spanish conflict was a vicious, fratricidal struggle to determine the future shape of the nation. In the Republican zone, Franco's crusaders saw a competing and antithetical vision of society: the anti-Spain which had to be extirpated if the true Spain were to flourish. Secularism and party politics were consigned to the past as Franco marched victorious into Madrid in April 1939, once again asserting the triumphant existence of the Catholic nation. Spanish Catholics attended mass rosaries rather than mass rallies, celebrating their *caudillo*'s triumph with Te Deums in every church in the land. The ancient hymn of thanksgiving rang out again when Franco was anointed, at the hands of the cardinal primate, in a ceremony of consecration which combined the medieval liturgy of the kings of Castile with devotion to the Christ of Lepanto, at whose feet Franco's sword was laid.[107] Centuries of Christian history apparently culminated in the *caudillo*, whose reign would ensure the preservation of the Spanish Church. Secure in the new identification of Church and State, Spanish Catholics abandoned politics, often with relief. Even the Propagandists now eschewed the public world of politics: Herrera Oria had entered a seminary and Gil Robles was an exile in Portugal. The ultimate failure of their tactic under the Republic had traumatized the ACNdeP; the new president, Fernando Martín-Sánchez Juliá, vowed that he would 'not join any political party nor occupy any public office'.[108]

Paradoxically, the Franco regime represented both the end and the culmination of the Catholic political option. Certainly, Catholic political parties were banned along with all others, but the party strategy had only ever been adopted as an emergency measure against the Second Republic. Carlists and Falangists were forcibly merged into the Francoist 'Movement', much against the will of their leaders. Most members, however, happily gave Franco their fervent support as did virtually all others who had long yearned for the reassertion of the Catholic nation. State service now replaced party loyalty: whatever their original political affiliation, Franco's bureaucrats, administrators, publicists, and ministers were all Catholics.[109]

During the first decades of the Franco regime, Catholicism was the common currency of its adherents. Some Catholics were particularly loyal servants: eleven members of the ACNdeP held cabinet posts during the war and its immediate aftermath, doing much to ameliorate the international ostracism which followed the Second World War. While Spain was reviled as a pro-fascist power, the Propagandists forged links with foreign Catholic groups in a systematic attempt to improve Spain's standing abroad. For example, Pax Romana—an international Church organization originally founded by Martín-Sánchez Juliá—was persuaded to hold a congress in Spain as early as 1945. Some historians, notably Javier Tusell, have restricted the Catholic label to precisely these groups of Propagandists, working to bring Spain

---

[107] P. Preston, *Franco* (London, 1993), 330; *Tablet*, 3 June 1939.
[108] *ACNdeP*, 224 (1938); see also F. Areal, *La política católica*, 96.
[109] The only exceptions were those few Falangists inspired by national syndicalism.

back to the international fold.[110] Not only did their efforts help to rehabilitate the regime but their contacts with the outside world also brought some of them—particularly Joaquín Ruíz Giménez—into the Christian democratic current which dominated the post-war mainstream of Catholic politics in Europe. Yet, the Spanish Church's utter reliance on State protection re-emerged in the 1940s and 1950s just as strongly as under the Restoration. Far from being a dissident tendency within the early Franco regime, Propagandist diplomats—among them Joaquín Ruíz Giménez—negotiated the 1953 Concordat with the papacy, which not only confirmed Spain's return to the international community but also marked the high point of post-Civil War Church–State relations.[111]

The Concordat began by recognizing Catholicism's unique and privileged position in Spain. The Church was to be the moral guide of the new state, and was exempted, to a certain extent, from its censors. In return, Franco retained anachronistic presentation rights in regard to the Spanish episcopate. The identification of Church and State was completed to the satisfaction of all parties. Far from being simply a pseudo-fascist embarrassment, Spain had been recognized as a truly Catholic nation—the 'spiritual reserve of the West'. In this sense, the Concordat was the culmination of the rechristianization campaigns that had swept post-war Spain. The first aim had been to make good the enormous physical damage sustained by the Spanish Church during the war: desecrated chapels were scrubbed by pious volunteers—some refusing to yield the task to 'Marxist' prisoners—, works of art were returned to religious buildings, and liturgical items were donated by foreign congregations.[112] New recruits flocked into the depleted seminaries, while mission fathers, often Jesuits, travelled the country reconverting lapsed communities.[113] These intense and emotional visitations would culminate in a spectacular, if short-lived, display of popular religiosity. A similar effect was achieved in the mass pilgrimages of the time: one went to offer the blood of '7,000 martyrs of the Crusade' to the Virgin of the Pillar, spiritual patron of the Reconquest, another led 18,000 pilgrims to Franco's birthplace, El Ferrol del Caudillo, while regular homages were paid to the Sacred Heart on the Cerro de los Angeles, rebuilt immediately after the war.[114]

Any notion that Catholicism and 'Spanishness' were not synonymous was stifled by this surge of liturgical triumphalism. The faithful were urged to rechristianize every aspect of Spanish life, thereby finally creating a totally Catholic society.

[110] J. Tusell, *Franco y los católicos* (Madrid, 1984).

[111] G. Hermet, *Los católicos en la España franquista* (2 vols.; Madrid, 1985), ii. 197–242; Tusell, *Franco y los católicos*, 227–83. The Holy See's relations with Franco were more circumspect than the oft-cited public pronouncements may suggest, A. Marquina Barrio, *La diplomacia vaticana y la España de Franco (1936–1945)* (Madrid, 1983). Text of the Concordat given in R. García-Villoslada (ed.), *La iglesia en la España contemporánea* (Madrid, 1979), 755–70.

[112] *ACNdeP*, 225, 227 (1938); *Tablet*, 22 and 29 Apr. 1939, 25 May 1940.

[113] Against a low point of *c*.7,500 in 1934, the number of seminarists rose to 16,317 in 1947, 18,536 in 1951, and 24,179 in 1961, S. Aznar, *La revolución española y las vocaciones eclesiásticas* (Madrid, 1949), 74. The Jesuit province of León organized 38 missions in 1931, 64 in 1939, 131 in 1941, and 174 in 1942, *Bodas de Plata de la Provincia de León SJ 1918–43* (n.p. [Léon?], n.d. [1943?]).

[114] *Signo*, 31 Aug. and 7 Sept. 1940; *Bodas de Plata de la Provincia de León SJ*. See also G. di Febo, *La santa de la raza* (Barcelona, 1988) and A. Oresanz, *Religiosidad Popular Español, 1940–1965* (Madrid, 1974).

Republican legislation on divorce, civil marriage, and lay education was all repealed as, of course, was the Catalan wartime statute on abortion. Campaigns for the moralization of contemporary society dominated post-war Catholic activity, particularly among women.[115] Self-sacrificing, modest, and devout, the true Christian woman was to ensure morality and piety, first in her family and then in society at large. Her greatest task was that of motherhood: she was exhorted to create Christian families, to foster vocations among her sons and to reinstate traditional pious practices. Church and State worked together on pronatalist campaigns which would restock the race, make good the awful damage inflicted by the war, and allow women to find true fulfilment.[116]

Under Franco, and in marked contrast to the Republican period, Catholic women were confined firmly to the domestic sphere. Within six months of its first issue in 1941, even *Medina*, the Falangist women's magazine, had eschewed ideological comment for beauty tips. Though most pronounced—and earliest—among women, this political anaesthetization was soon apparent among the whole population.[117] Though partly a response both to the still-vivid memory of the war and the hunger and privation which followed, this alienation from the political process also reflected the brutal fact that Franco's new state, complete with rechristianization project, depended upon vicious repression.

Franco's victory speech had warned that the spirit of the 'anti-Spanish revolution' still breathed in 'many a breast': 'We welcome to our camp all who have repented and wish to collaborate in the greatness of Spain; but if they sinned yesterday they must not expect applause until they redeem themselves by deeds.'[118] In fact, erstwhile sinners were redeemed by imprisonment, exile, and, not infrequently, death. Prisoners were 'spiritually cultivated': Women's Catholic Action established a subsection for prison visitors while the Society of Jesus provided chaplains for many gaol camps.[119] In this systematic policy of repression, which lasted into the 1960s, the danger of recidivism was constantly emphasized, not least by references to the international conspiracy of Marxists, Masons, and Jews. The struggle of Spain and anti-Spain continued; peace had merely brought a change of front.[120]

As this good fight was no longer to be waged in the political sphere, Catholics looked to other areas, most notably education. The Francoist education law of 1938 recognized Church schools and ensured that state schooling would be Catholic. In 1943 religious education was even made compulsory for university students. This

[115] See F. Blázquez, *La traición de los clérigos en la España de Franco: Crónica de una intolerancia (1936–1975)* (Madrid, 1991), 63–89.

[116] *Senda* (Revista mensual del Consejo Superior de Mujeres de AC de España), 1–7 (1941), *passim*; M. Nash, 'Pronatalism and motherhood in Franco's Spain', in G. Bock and P. Thane (eds.), *Maternity and Gender Politics* (London, 1991), 160–77.

[117] A. López Piña and E. Aranguren, *La cultura política de la España de Franco* (Madrid, 1976), 63–72.

[118] Speech broadcast 20 May 1939, text given *Tablet*, 27 May 1939.

[119] e.g. Juan Lamamié de Clairac SJ was responsible for the 'spiritual cultivation' of a staggering 50,000 Republican prisoners in León, 1937–9. He was transferred, somewhat abruptly, in 1940: *Bodas de Plata de la Provincia de León SJ*.

[120] See e.g. 'La cruzada no terminó con el último disparo', *Signo*, 12 Mar. 1939.

Catholicizing of the Spanish education system was only made possible by the purging of all Republican and otherwise unsuitable teachers. The challenge of meeting the resulting shortfall in an already inadequate service was undertaken by various Catholic groups, including the Propagandists, who set about the conquest of university chairs with their customary assiduity and achieved their customary success, most notably in law. The project of élite formation continued, although new cohorts were now formed by professors rather than politicians: the ACNdeP organized a university section in 1942 and opened its first *colegio mayor*—a students' residence with some teaching and pastoral functions—in Madrid in 1950.[121] This colonization of higher education continued unabated, but the ACNdeP did not find the field free for very long. New competitors were emerging, notably that most characteristic organization of post-war national Catholicism, Opus Dei.

Nominally established in 1928, Opus Dei only emerged in its public form after the Civil War. While its aims were, in some respects, similar to those of the ACNdeP, the Opus represented both a new model of lay Catholicism and a new form of the religious life, becoming known as a Secular Institute.[122] Though the membership included priests—and two categories, *numerarii* and *oblati*, enjoined celibacy—the Opus was primarily concerned with the secular sphere. Its tenets were set out in *El camino* (*The Way*; 1939), a handbook of maxims penned by the founder, José María Escrivá. Most members, the *supernumerarii*, did not live in community but were free to marry and lead family lives, though they were reminded that such an option was 'for the foot-soldiers, not for the General Staff of Christ'.[123] All members were exhorted to pious, unquestioning obedience and, notoriously, to 'discretion'.[124] *La obra* combined child-like pietism and theological conservatism with professional training and an enthusiasm for business. All members were expected to enter education and many had higher degrees, often in scientific subjects. Like the ACNdeP, the Opus was to provide leaders; unlike the Propagandists, however, some *opusdeístas* lived in community and all took vows. Moreover, the constitutions, membership, and inner workings of the Opus were all veiled from public scrutiny.[125]

Like the ACNdeP, the Opus launched its bid to form the lay leaders of post-war Spain from the universities. Members of both associations competed for professorial posts under rules which favoured governmental candidates. The Opus opened *colegios mayores* all over Spain and in 1952 founded an institute of higher education in Navarre, recognized as a university in 1961–2.[126] Opus Dei did not, however, restrict itself to academic leadership. Indeed, its preferred fields were vocational and

[121] *ACNdeP*, 295 (1942); 449 (1950). [122] *Provida Mater Ecclesia* (1947).

[123] *El Camino* (27th Sp. edn.; Madrid, 1973), maxim 28.

[124] Ibid., maxims 53, 457, 614–29, 639–56, 832, 941.

[125] The 'secret' nature of the Opus has attracted much attention in a large and polemical literature. D. Artigues (pseud.), *El Opus Dei en España, 1928–62* (2nd edn.; Paris, 1971); J. Ynfante, *La prodigiosa aventura del Opus Dei: Génesis y desarrollo de la Santa Mafia* (Paris, 1970), and M. Walsh, *The Secret World of Opus Dei* (London, 1989) are all highly critical. In contrast, see D. Le Tourneau, *El Opus Dei* (1986) and R. Gómez Pérez, *El franquismo y la iglesia* (Madrid, 1986), 251–63, 300–1.

[126] Artigues, *El Opus Dei*, 43–60; N. Cooper, *Catholicism and the Franco Regime* (London, 1975), 24–5, 27.

technical: the University of Navarre became distinguished for business studies and journalism. Individual members achieved notable success in business and commerce and, although the Opus strenuously denied constructing a financial empire, a syndicate of Opus Dei members took control of the Banco Popular Español in the early 1950s and, in the same decade, built up a substantial publishing empire. When Opus Dei ministers finally entered Franco's government in 1957, it was on a specific programme of state-controlled economic modernization.

Of all Catholic institutions, the Opus Dei was most closely associated with the Franco regime. Categorized by the German theologian Hans Urs von Balthasar as the most important repository of modern integrism, the Opus remained faithful to a regime its members clearly found congenial.[127] The *generalísimo*'s penultimate prime minister and appointed successor, Admiral Carrero Blanco, was widely recognized as an Opus fellow-traveller. Indeed, the Institute proved a fruitful source of politicians and public figures throughout Franco's lengthy rule and, unlike other Catholic bodies, never became a source of dissidents.

The same could not be said of the Opus's rivals in the Society of Jesus, nor of its precursor, the ACNdeP. Even in the immediate post-war years, when Francoist triumphalism was at its height, some Propagandists were dissidents. José Antonio Aguirre, ex-president of the short-lived Basque Republic, was, of course, in exile, as was Gil Robles, who did not return from Portugal until 1953. Returning to his monarchist roots after the war, Gil Robles attempted to construct a conservative anti-Franco opposition around the Bourbon pretender, Don Juan. Gil Robles's antipathy to Franco, though genuine, was undoubtedly related to his own thwarted political ambitions; far from embracing democracy, his proposed corporative constitutional monarchy was inspired by Salazar's dictatorship.[128] Within Spain, Giménez Fernández also drew away from his initial, unquestioning support for Franco. As with Gil Robles, personal experience had taken its toll. Immediate adhesion to the crusade had not persuaded the local Falange that Giménez Fernández had abandoned his idiosyncratic brand of republicanism; only General Queipo de Llano's intervention saved him from the firing squad. Critical of the hollowness of triumphalism, Giménez developed his own rapidly evolving political thought in response to papal encyclicals and the work of foreign theologians, including Maritain and Mounier. As his opposition to the dictatorship crystallized, so did his commitment to democracy and in 1957 the ex-CEDA minister finally accepted the leadership of a small Christian democrat party.[129]

Earlier in the same decade, some Catholic intellectuals—among them the Propagandist José Luis Aranguren—had begun exploring the concepts of political and

---

[127] Quoted J. Georgel, *El franquismo: Historia y balance 1939–1969* (Paris, 1971), 201.

[128] J. M. Gil Robles, *La monarquía por la que yo luché: Páginas de un diario (1941–1954)* (Madrid, 1976). The, always very small, Catholic monarchist opposition is exhaustively studied in J. Tusell, *La oposición democrática al franquismo* (Barcelona, 1977).

[129] Tusell and Calvo, *Giménez Fernández*, 225–85; Tusell, *La oposición democrática al franquismo*, 327–36; interview with Giménez Fernández in S. Vilar, *La oposición a la dictadura: Protagonistas de la España democrática* (Barcelona, 1976), 455–66.

cultural pluralism, particularly in the context of Spanish history.[130] The ACNdeP had never abandoned dialogue: the study circle at Alcoy had discussed Cardinal Gomá's pastoral 'The lessons of war and the duties of peace' even after it had been banned by the government.[131] Similarly, as minister of education after 1951, Ruíz-Giménez used his position to liberalize the universities, introducing appointment criteria similar to those employed under the Second Republic and elevating Pedro Laín Entralgo—whose scholarly work was committed to cultural heterogeneity—to the rectorship of Madrid University. These early signs of intellectual dissent took on a political complexion after February 1956, when a skirmish between Falangist and anti-Falangist students at Madrid University led to police intervention. In the aftermath of this first instance of bourgeois protest against the regime, Ruíz-Giménez was removed from office.

The year gave its name to the so-called 'generation of 56', that age-cohort which had not fought the civil war but which nevertheless lived in its shadow. Reared amid the suffocating orthodoxies of crusade Catholicism, these young men and women were to be profoundly attracted by the universal Church headed by John XXIII.[132] In 1956, however, the innovations of French pastoral practice and German theology were largely unknown in Spain. The national Church was intensely insular. Its history was that of the crusade: on the eve of the Second Vatican Council most Spanish bishops were over 75 years old and 90 per cent had been ordained before 1936.[133] In contrast, the clergy was among the youngest in the world.

It is no coincidence that those Catholics who first seemed uncomfortable with the conformities of national Catholicism were those with links outside Spain. It was while in Rome as ambassador to the Holy See from 1948–51 that Ruíz Giménez realized that Spanish Catholicism was merely a province of the universal Church: 'there were other, far more open, ways of living as a Catholic'.[134] Others were reaching the same conclusion. Lili Alvarez, a former Wimbledon champion and the only woman to feature prominently in this early debate, had pleaded that priests cease to treat the laity as 'little children, in need of continuing tutelage'.[135] Yet, despite these early critics the impetus for *aggiornamento* came from outside the national Church. The summoning of the Second Vatican Council in January 1959, the publication of *Mater et Magistra* in 1961, and, particularly, the opening of the first session of the Council in October 1962, initiated an extraordinary period of *apertura* (opening) in the Spanish Church. The resonance of Vatican II could not be muffled by state censors; starved of change, and greedy for news, the 'generation of 56' fell upon conciliar pronouncements, particularly *Pacem in Terris* (1963), as manna in the desert.[136]

[130] See Blázquez, *La traición de los clerigos*, 120–5; E. Díaz, *Pensamiento español en la era de Franco (1939–1975)* (Madrid, 1983), 52–8, 62–86.

[131] *ACNdeP*, 274 (1941); *Tablet*, 21 Oct., 9 and 16 Nov. 1939.

[132] C. Floristan, introd. to J. Chao Rego, *La iglesia en el franquismo* (Madrid, 1976), 15–16.

[133] N. Cooper, *Catholicism and the Franco Regime* (London, 1975), 30.

[134] Interview with Ruíz Giménez: Vilar, *La oposición a la dictadura*, 404.

[135] Alvarez, 'Examen de conciencia', *Senda*, Jan. 1958.

[136] Lannon, *Privilege, Persecution, and Prophecy*, 246–52; Díaz, *Pensamiento español*, 116–23. On the Vatican Council, see H. Jedin (ed.), *The Church in the Modern Age* (London, 1981), 96–151; Aubert,

Yet, the appetite for change which was so apparent among these Spanish Catholics was very much the product of their own experience. Many were concerned with what they perceived as a discrepancy between rhetoric and reality. Ruíz Giménez's time at the ministry of education, for example, had shown him that, despite promises of reconstruction, there was no money to build schools and little interest in doing so.[137] Similar concerns were voiced by those involved in pastoral work at a less exalted level, particularly among the young activists in the JOC (Catholic Workers' Youth) and HOAC (Workers' Brotherhoods of Catholic Action). Always concerned with social issues, these increasingly militant organizations were involved in wage disputes and strike action from the early 1950s. This stance brought JOC and HOAC into direct conflict with the State, particularly as their activists became increasingly vocal critics of human rights abuses and the lack of social justice in Spain.[138] At the same time, Catholic sociologists, influenced by the French school of Gabriel Le Bras, were finding that, despite the years of rechristianization, the missions, the pilgrimages, and the triumph of the Catholic arms of Franco, the Spanish working class was as indifferent or as hostile to religion as ever. In 1955, an early survey of the Catalan textile town of Mataró found that a mere 14 per cent of workers were practising Catholics and only 5 per cent attended Sunday mass. As one lay commentator pointed out, after years of effort, Spain had proved not to be different after all.[139]

In the late 1950s and early 1960s concern at the real state of Spanish Catholicism became more widespread. Sociological surveys, pastoral concerns, and the biblical emphasis of the post-1945 liturgical movement combined to make many Spaniards conscious of the shortcomings of their national Church. This was particularly true in Catalonia and the Basque Country, where clandestine nationalist sentiment was a potent force. The great Benedictine abbey at Montserrat emerged as a focus for Catalan nationalism from the late 1950s while, in the Basque Country, an increasingly radical secular clergy began on a path of opposition which was soon to lead to confrontation with the State.[140] The separatist terrorist group ETA had developed out of Catholic youth groups; many of its members were known to those priests who sheltered them or refused to co-operate with the security forces searching for them.

Yet, taking Spain as a whole, full-scale dissent only truly emerged in response to Vatican II. As Ruíz Giménez remembered, abandoning Franco's regime was very difficult for those who recalled the anticlerical horrors of the Civil War. He resolved this personal 'crisis of conscience' only while a lay observer at the Council.[141] In effect, a higher authority had undermined many of the basic tenets of Francoism and,

The Church in a Secularised Society, 624–38; W. M. Abbot (ed.), *The Documents of Vatican II* (London, 1967).

[137] Interview in Vilar, *La oposición a la dictadura*, 410.

[138] For an account by a protagonist, see J. Castaño i Colomer, *La JOC en España (1946–1970)* (Salamanca, 1977).

[139] A. L. Marzal, 'España es diferente', *Cuadernos para el Diálogo*, 4 (1964).

[140] Stanley Payne dates the beginning of clerical opposition to a protest letter of May 1960, signed by 339 Basque priests: Payne, *The Franco Regime 1936–1975* (Madison, Wisc., 1987), 500. See further, Lannon, *Privilege, Persecution, and Prophecy*, 106–13.   [141] Vilar, *La oposición a la dictadura*, 409.

like many of his contemporaries, Ruíz Giménez responded with a call for dialogue, both within and without the Church. In 1963 he founded the journal *Cuadernos para el Diálogo* (*Notes towards Dialogue*) which, although published in Paris, became an important forum in Spain's cultural transition. The new periodical was intended 'to facilitate the communication of ideas and feelings between men of different generations, beliefs and basic attitudes'; its editorial stance was 'open, progressive, in the postconciliar tradition . . . respecting the religious liberty of all men'. In a word, this new intellectual forum, open to Catholics and non-Catholics alike, was democratic.[142]

In the 1960s important sectors of the Spanish Church finally embraced the notion of plurality. The idea of religious liberty was hardly revolutionary to North American Catholics, nor, perhaps, to their northern European cousins, but in Spain, before the conciliar deliberations leading up to *Dignitatis Humanae* (1965), such a notion was simply unthinkable. Of all the conciliar decrees and constitutions, this ruling on religious freedom had the most impact. Generations of Spanish Catholics had fought— with words, with votes, and eventually with arms—for an absolute and unique truth. In the words of the Jesuit periodical *Aún*, 'until now we have won our battles by eliminating the adversary or ignoring him. From now on we will have to win them by recognizing and accepting him. And we will have to see in him the dignity of a son of God.'[143]

Aún greeted the new developments, particularly the much-vaunted process of dialogue, with palpable excitement. It called for ecumenical dialogue within the Church and opened a formal discussion in its pages on the conduct of the Spanish bishops in Rome. The world, according to the editorial column, 'had been opened to dialogue'. Some columnists, notably Eduardo Manrique, even looked to open the way for a dialogue with communism, a project which had already been undertaken in practice by various militants in JOC and HOAC.[144] Indeed, as Alfonso Comín recognized in an article in November 1965, talking to communists seemed simpler than talking to conservative Catholics.[145] Wide-ranging though the post-conciliar project of dialogue was, it always failed to encompass the right, as *Aún* found out to its cost the following year when a special issue calling for dialogue with the episcopate led to its closure by the State. Targeting the concepts of authority and obedience had brought these turbulent priests up against the limits of dialogue in Franco's Spain.

Throughout this time of *apertura*, some sections of the Spanish Church kept their ears closed. While some members of religious orders, especially Jesuits and Dominicans, travelled the long way from crusade to council, others remained faithful to their *caudillo*, who was himself genuinely convinced that Vatican II was the work of Freemasons. Not all Spanish Catholics had greeted news of the council with enthusiasm: Women's Catholic Action, for instance, had declared that it was a 'question for

---

[142] *Cuadernos para el Diálogo*, 1 (1963); Vilar, *La oposición a la dictadura*, 415; Díaz, *Pensamiento español*, 112–5.　　　　　[143] 'Miedo a la libertad religiosa', *Aún*, 65 (1964).
[144] *Aún*, 55 (1963), 57 and 58 (1964). On Catholic–Communist dialogue, see Manrique's articles, *Aún*, 52 (1963), 59 (1964); A. Comín, *Cristianos en el partido, comunistas en la iglesia* (Barcelona, 1977); S. Balfour, *Dictatorship, Workers and the City: Labour in Greater Barcelona since 1939* (Oxford, 1989), 22–30, 69–83.　　　　　[145] 'Un diálogo difícil', *Aún*, 68–9 (1965).

the Hierarchy and theologians' in which the faithful had simply to wait 'with a spirit of submission'.[146] Many Spanish Catholics felt no need to look beyond the certainties of national Catholicism. At its most extreme, this loyalty to the past led to the bizarre schism of the self-styled 'Gregory XVII' at the apparition site of Palmar de Troya in Seville.[147] Very few Francoists, however, became schismatics. Most remained, like their political counterparts, in an ideological bunker defined by the divisions of the Civil War.

After Vatican II, the Spanish Church was broadly divided into traditionalists and critics. Franco's difficult relations with Pope Paul VI helped to accentuate this cleavage, which finally killed any surviving notions of political Catholicism. However strenuously those in the bunker denied it, the old absolutes were gone for ever. There was now no single Catholic position. Aware that sincerely religious men and women were to be found in all political groups, from the Falange to the underground communist party, Spanish Catholics largely gave up the attempt to define a particular political space for the Church. Ruíz Giménez even refused to use the term 'Christian democrat'; he was, he said, simply 'a Christian and . . . a democrat'.[148] By 1965 there was no longer a political Catholicism in Spain although, in the decade leading up to Franco's death in 1975, there were to be more political Catholics than ever before.

[146] *Senda y Alba*, July 1959.
[147] R. Perera, *Las creencias de los españoles: La tierra de María Santísima* (Madrid, 1990), 185–93.
[148] Vilar, *La oposición a la dictadura*, 416.

4
Portugal
TOM GALLAGHER

Portugal is venerated by many European Catholics because it is a centre of the world-wide cult of Mary which developed after the apparition of Our Lady at Fátima in 1917. Moreover, for nearly forty years, its political destinies were in the hands of an austere dictator who convinced conservative Catholics everywhere that in Portugal a genuine attempt had been made to shape government policy around Catholic social principles. But even before his retirement in 1968, Dr Salazar had revealed himself to more percipient Catholics as a personal autocrat who had insisted on a compliant church and whose policies were proving immensely harmful to the standing and long-term prospects of the Church.

In return for accepting the protection of the authoritarian state, the Church lost the freedom of action to play the active role in politics and society that other national churches have pursued with varying degrees of success in the last seventy years. The story of twentieth-century Portuguese Catholicism has been one of increasing ghettoization where its failure to translate residual regional strength into national influence is increasingly marked. Church leaders emphasized devotionalism and piety but offered no sustained encouragement to political movements and parties which claimed a Catholic inspiration for their activities or sought to implant Catholic values in public life. During the long embargo on political activity between 1926 and 1974, the Church was also lukewarm in support of movements, essentially social or spiritual in orientation, that had cause to take a public stand. Thus, unlike its counterparts in the other major Catholic states of Western Europe, the Portuguese Church set its face against a politically engaged Catholicism. No durable Catholic opposition existed and when political freedoms returned in 1974, the time for advancing a Christian democratic alternative to the left or to secularism had long passed.

It was Portugal's authoritarian ruler, Dr Salazar, who imposed strict limits on the ability of the Portuguese Church to intervene in national affairs, ones that were adhered to by a hierarchy grateful not to be faced by a state openly hostile to religious interests. A long bruising engagement with the forces of political liberalism forged the Portuguese Church into a defensive and reactive institution ill-equipped to use modern political means to advance its cause and prepared to enlist behind the banner of a political dictator whose Catholic nationalist imagery evoked memories of medieval Portugal when the Church and monarchy had operated in tandem. To begin to explore the institutional malaise of twentieth-century Portuguese Catholicism, it is therefore necessary to take into account the difficulties under which it had laboured during the previous 150 years.

In 1918 Portuguese Catholicism was emerging from a long period of crisis and doubt in which it had ineffectually sought to combat secularizing trends in Portuguese society as well as encroachments by the State on its privileges and traditional sources of influence. Ever since the reforming rule of the Marquis of Pombal (1750–77), who suppressed the Jesuits, Church–State relations were marked by hostility to the wealth and influence of the Church[1] and, in particular, of the religious orders. The Church paid dearly for backing the reactionary Miguelistas in the civil war of 1832–4, when the victorious rebels seized its property and estates in the south. This was a backlash from which Portuguese Catholicism has never recovered in the province of the Alentejo where religious devotion fell steeply in the remainder of the nineteenth century.[2] In this underpopulated region, parish structures were weak and it had been the religious orders who had ministered to the population. Meanwhile, in the north which contained the bulk of the population, diocesan clergy were far more numerous and the *paroco* (parish priest) was an integral element of most local communities.

In the Catholic North the landholding system had a profound and lasting effect on social relations. The prevalence of *minifundia*, or dwarfholdings, meant that the gulf between want and plenty, noticeable in the south, was less marked north of the Tagus river which flows across the centre of Portugal and is the key geographic dividing line. Ownership of some land, however meagre, predisposed the peasantry against challenging the traditional order and, in an atmosphere of social cohesion, the Church flourished in many areas of the north.[3]

In the absence of its northern redoubt, the Portuguese Church would have been ill-equipped to resist the third and greatest challenge to its authority, mounted by urban middle-class republicans. Republican sentiment had steadily mounted in the face of economic problems and the failure of the State to compensate for these by pursuing a policy of colonial expansion in Africa. The Ultimatum of 1890 delivered by Britain to prevent Portugal encroaching into present-day Zimbabwe was a grievous blow to the standing of the constitutional monarchy and the oligarchical liberalism which had prevailed since 1851. Though their base was a narrow one, Republicans were able to depict themselves not just as the party of lower-middle-class social radicalism but as the patriotic party keen to end Portugal's demeaning position as a colonial satellite of Britain.

By 1910 the constitutional monarchy was so isolated and enfeebled that it was able to put up scant resistance before a civilian Republican revolt which broke out in the capital. Most of the beneficiaries of the previous order transferred their allegiances to

[1] S. G. Payne, *A History of Spain and Portugal*, ii (Madison, Wisc. 1973), 410.

[2] For religious conditions in the Alentejo during the mid-20th cent., see J. Cutileiro, *A Portuguese Rural Society* (Oxford, 1971), 249–70.

[3] T. Gallagher, 'Peasant Conservatism in an Agrarian Setting: Portugal 1900–1975', *Journal of Iberian Studies*, 6/2 (1977), 60.

the new Republic or adopted a wait-and-see attitude. The existence of republican systems in Brazil and France, the countries with which Portugal enjoyed the closest ties, initially dispelled anxieties about Portugal's radical departure among those whose economic interests or social outlook predisposed them against bold political experimentation. By 1910 there was a widespread feeling, at least in urban Portugal, that the monarchical regime had run its course and could not be resuscitated in any convincing way.

Portugal's *petit bourgeois* rulers were greatly influenced by French norms and cultural values. Six years after the effective separation of Church and State in France, Portugal's anticlerical rulers followed suit. But the State's restrictions on the Church imposed in a lightning series of decrees during 1911 were far more sweeping and came to be regarded as persecution beyond the ranks of those who bore their brunt.[4] All Church property was nationalized, the faculty of theology at the University of Coimbra was closed and the chair of canon law abolished, holy days were made into normal working ones, and the number of seminaries was sharply cut back, the remaining ones being placed under government control.[5] There were severe restrictions on worshipping after sunset, bell-ringing, religious processions, and clerical freedom of movement. The Jesuits were once more sent packing along with many foreign religious orders, all foreign and foreign-trained priests were barred, and ecclesiastical pronouncements were subject to censorship. Divorce was introduced, the marriage ceremony was made civil, and religious teaching was disallowed in schools. Upon the enactment of these laws, the majority of bishops were expelled or went into exile and in 1913 diplomatic relations with the Holy See were broken off.

The Church had been more closely identified with the constitutional monarchy than any other institution, which had already made it the target of hostile Republican propaganda before 1910. Its privileged role in the monarchical order, allied to its weakness and unpopularity in Lisbon, where the bulk of political power lay irrespective of what political tendency or system prevailed, left it open to attack in the event of a radical political upheaval. Of the various vested interests bound up with the toppled regime such as the southern landowners and the upper echelons of the army, the Church was the easiest one to penalize. It was also the only obvious target the Republicans had to hand since they were not so radical that they wished to reconstruct the economic order.

In its brief flowering Portuguese Jacobinism was socially radical but economically conservative and the anticlerical offensive was pitched to suit the tastes of the urban lower middle class which would act as the regime's only reliable power-base. Freemasonry was the secular creed of this numerically weak but influentially located group in Portuguese society. Dismantling the clerical privilege which prevented Portugal from taking its place as a modern, progressive nation able to stand alongside

---

[4] A. J. Telo, *Decadência e Queda da 1 República Portuguesa*, i (Lisbon, 1980), 81.

[5] R. Robinson, 'The Religious Question and the Catholic Revival in Portugal', *Journal of Contemporary History*, 12 (1977), 352–3; T. C. Bruneau, 'Church and State in Portugal: Crisis of Cross and Sword', *Journal of Church and State*, 18 (1976), 466–7.

its French mentor was to prove one of the few objectives behind which most Republicans were able to close ranks.

Radicals behaved and spoke as if organized religion was a pitiful relic of a failed past to which no serious consideration need be shown even as their fragile regime was beset by problems inherited from its predecessor as well as new ones induced by the factionalism which quickly undermined the Republican experiment. In 1911 their champion Afonso Costa, the most purposeful of the Republic's many prime ministers, had no qualms about forecasting an end to Roman Catholicism in a few generations, when speaking in the northern town of Braga, the religious seat of Portugal.[6] But if this was a prize Costa really desired, Republicanism was too ephemeral and opportunistic a movement to secure it. Within a short time the parliamentary republic would be preoccupied with internal power struggles and with staving off mounting challenges from conservative forces that would eventually overwhelm it in the 1920s.

The anticlericalism which ran its course from 1910 to 1914 was largely an intellectual or middle-class affair in which enthusiastic mass involvement was not a factor. Popular anticlericalism, manifesting itself in the church-burning that occurred during periods of social unrest in neighbouring Spain, was absent even though Portugal already possessed an urban and rural southern proletariat that was deaf to religious appeals. Neither was there any grass-roots backlash in the Church's northern strongholds to impede the modernizing tendencies of urban liberals, that could compare with the rural resistance movements spearheaded by the Carlists in Spain or by the Cristeros in Mexico after its 1910 revolution.

Faced with what seemed like a state-sponsored drive against organized religion itself rather than just clerical authority, a purposeful response did, however, arise from young Catholic intellectuals who managed to find both their voices and a receptive audience during the turbulent early years of the republic. In 1912, a Catholic student group known as the *Centro Academica da Democraçia Cristão* (CADC) was revived by Catholic students at the University of Coimbra. These activists, drawn from fairly modest but devout homes in the north, were well placed to mount a defence of Catholic interests. Being located in the smallholding northern half of the country, Portugal's major educational institution was influenced by the traditionalist outlook of the surrounding region. Moreover, the student body at Coimbra had always been an influential group destined for posts in the public administration, the legal profession, and politics so this was important terrain in which to promote the Catholic viewpoint and assert the right of Catholics to operate in public life.

Manuel Gonçalves Cerejeira (1888–1977) and António de Oliveira Salazar (1889–1970) emerged as the leading figures in this Catholic student nucleus. Both were emblematic figures in the CADC: from frugal but respectable provincial rural backgrounds seeking to make careers in conservative institutions which had in the past afforded openings for conventional and hardworking young men from the provinces.

---

[6] D. L. Wheeler, *Republican Portugal: A Political History 1910–26* (Madison, Wisc. 1978), 69.

In later years, their careers at the helm of Church and State would parallel one another to a striking extent, but in the initial years of the Republic, the prospects for a new generation of politically engaged and ambitious Catholics must have seemed bleak. Cerejeira, a future primate of the Portuguese Church, carried a Mauser pistol during tense periods when Republican and conservative students were engaged in street battles.[7] At issue was the right of *Imparcial*, the CADC journal, to be sold openly. Cerejeira, its editor, worked hard to ensure that Catholics, monarchists, and members of the newly founded Integralist movement, closed ranks to defend a conservative platform.[8] By 1914 student conservatives (with Catholics at the forefront) were on the way to gaining the upper hand in Coimbra, the first Catholic victory against Republican secularism.

'Piety, Study, Action', the motto of the CADC, suggests that it was regarded more as a pressure group designed to restore lost Church influence than as a politically engaged movement ready to participate in the muscular politics of the First Republic. The priorities of the CADC were conservative unity, moral regeneration, and the rechristianization of Portugal. It maintained friendly relations with almost all the forces on the political right, *Imparçial* being a focal point for debates and interventions.[9]

Salazar, the CADC's most gifted intellectual, was a lecturer in economics at Coimbra University after 1915. Both he and Cerejeira steered the CADC away from overt commitment to the standard right-wing campaigns, particularly monarchical restoration. In 1914, with the Republic still looking fairly secure, Salazar declared 'democracy to be a historic phenomenon and by now irresistible'.[10] He and his cohorts subscribed to the Christian democratic perspective that had been licensed by the Vatican in order to enable Catholics to compete in the political arena in what was seen as the start of a turbulent age of mass democracy. But almost a decade later (and possibly much earlier), his outlook had changed, Portugal having gone through a series of upheavals that devalued the democratic option to an even greater extent than was occurring elsewhere in Catholic Europe. In 1922 Salazar declared that 'we are drawing near to that moment in political and social evolution in which a political party based on the individual, the citizen or the elector will no longer have sufficient reason for existence'.[11] By now, liberalism and secularism were rapidly losing support. It took no great effort of will for the forces of the right to win the battle of ideas. Anti-parliamentary ideas were bound to prove attractive in the midst of widespread electoral chicanery and administrative misrule. When Guerra Junqueiro, the famous anticlerical Republican poet, returned to the practice of Catholicism before his death in 1923, it was a telling sign that the validity of the radical secular cause,

[7] M. G. Cerejeira, *Vinte Anos de Coimbra* (Lisbon, 1943), 222.

[8] A. J. Telo, *Decadência e Queda da 1 República Portuguesa*, ii (Lisbon, 1980).

[9] A. Matos Ferreira, 'La Peninsula Iberique', in J.-M. Mayeur (ed.), *Histoire du Christianisme des origines à nos jours*, xii (Paris 1990), 406.

[10] H. Kay, *Salazar and Modern Portugal* (London, 1970), 24.

[11] P. C. Schmitter, 'The Impact and Meaning of "Non-Competitive Non-Free and Non-Significant" Elections in Authoritarian Portugal', in G. Hermet (ed.), *Elections without Choice* (London, 1970), 150.

unchallenged for a century or more, was being questioned even by some of its stal-
warts.[12] Another sign that the tide had turned in the Church's favour came in 1921
with the enthronement of a new archbishop of Lisbon: António José de Almeida,
Portugal's head of state, and an old Jacobin who had poured withering invective upon
the Church two decades earlier, presided at the ceremony and professed his respect
for the Church.[13]

Despite the strength of devotionalism in the north, a mass Catholic Party failed to
emerge in Portugal as it would in several other countries (starting with Germany in
the 1880s) marked by a clash of religious and state interests on a similar scale. Leaving
aside the fact that electoral malpractice by the strongest Republican grouping, the
Democrats, made the electoral option an unrewarding one for Catholics hoping to
secure change via the ballot box, other factors made this course an impractical one.
Women and illiterate citizens were deprived of the vote by the Republican electoral
law. This prevented Catholics from turning the devotionalism of the northern peasant to political advantage or of staging a revival in urban centres by relying on the
women's vote. Besides, absent from the scene was a strong Catholic social movement
sponsoring co-operatives, Friendly Societies, and labour associations. Some efforts
in this direction had occurred in the north at the turn of the century, but they were
not sustained and they did not spread to areas of growing social tension in the south.

Having neglected the social sphere before 1910, the Church thereafter was too em-
battled to give much time to cultivating the variety of lay vocational groups emerging
under clerical direction in other countries. Nevertheless, an explicitly Catholic
movement, known as the *Centro Católico Portuguesa* (CCP) had emerged by 1917 and
would participate in the remaining elections that were held under the Republic.[14]

From the outset the CCP insisted that it was not a party which aspired to exercise
political power but an association without a party character that sought to represent
the viewpoint of Catholic civil society. It was taking part in the electoral struggle not
as an end in itself but in order to bring about the rechristianization of laws and
customs in Portugal.[15] But a close study of the CCP reveals that its parish organizations only came to life during pre-election periods and that, except for conferences
on Catholic social teaching, little in its behaviour could distinguish it from conservative bodies which did accept the party label.[16]

The CCP won seats at every parliamentary election held after 1918, mainly in
northern districts such as Minho and the Beiras which had withstood the anticlerical
storm. It had the explicit backing of the hierarchy and even the Papacy.[17] It was seen
as an instrument designed to change the situation which permits 'the existence of a

[12] E. Prestage, 'Reminiscences of Portugal', in H. V. Livermore *Portugal and Brazil: An Introduction*
(Oxford, 1953), 6 n. 1.   [13] Telo, *Decadência e Queda*, i. 89.
[14] A certain amount of confusion has arisen about the founding year of the CPP. It is given as 1919 in
Telo (ibid. 90); 1915 is the date cited in R. Robinson, *Contemporary Portugal: A History* (London, 1979),
45; while the much likelier date of 1917 is given by M. Braga da Cruz, in his exhaustive study, *As orígens da
democracia cristã e salazarismo* (Lisbon, 1980), 264.
[15] Braga da Cruz, *As orígens da democracia cristã*, 307, 324, 326.
[16] Ibid. 340.   [17] Matos Ferreira, 'La Peninsula Iberique', 406.

parliament basically opposed to Roman Catholicism that is elected by a people which remains essentially Catholic'.[18] Many bishops and possibly most clergy and lay leaders, while continuing to favour the monarchical regime, saw as their priority the need to restore the Church as an active force in national life. When diplomatic relations were restored with the Holy See under the authoritarian conservative regime of General Sidónio Pais who ruled Portugal for a year until his assassination at the end of 1918, it was clear that progress in this direction was possible even in the republican context. Portugal's entry into the First World War in 1916 had already eased much of the State pressure on the Church as the goal of national unity took precedence over ideological vendettas. In order to establish a consensus behind intervention, the moral sanction of the Church was vital, so permission was granted to send chaplains with the troops and to remove obstacles in the way of the Church's missionary role in the colonies.[19]

António Lino Neto, the main promoter of the CCP, exemplified the cautious *modus vivendi* that arose between Church and State during the latter half of the First Republic's tempestuous existence. He was an energetic and moderate politician who opposed the rising tide of right-wing authoritarianism of which Salazar would be the eventual beneficiary. In 1923 he expressed his fears in Parliament that the strained atmosphere in Portugal might give rise to a home-grown Mussolini or Primo de Rivera.[20] Soon afterwards he was contradicted by *A União* (the *Union*), the CCP's own press organ which, in an editorial, exalted dictatorship 'as a vital reaction from society against insupportable anarchy ready to asphyxiate it'.[21] This is a clear sign of the prestige that anti-democratic views enjoyed in influential Catholic ranks, but in 1924, with the rudderless Republic suffering further discredit, Neto reiterated his previous view: he argued that all dictatorships are disastrous; that parliamentary institutions, though undoubtedly defective, have a necessary role in political life; and that the army is not, by nature, equipped to understand Portugal's complex political and administrative problems.[22]

Perhaps the punishment it had received from liberal republicanism made the CCP overestimate the strength of the regime even as it was staggering towards collapse. The CCP's moderation earned it the criticism of full-blooded reactionaries who expected Portugal's traditional interests to make common cause to drive out the Republicans. But serious divisions not just over tactics but forms of government weakened the right and may have given the discredited Republic a stay of execution of a few years. Chief among these was whether to restore the monarchy or continue with the republican form of government. From 1919 the CCP and the CADC were making it clear that they were partisans neither of the Republic nor of the monarchy and that preoccupation with the outward form of government was not the answer to Portugal's manifold problems. The CADC preoccupied itself with moral and

---

[18] *Imparçial*, 249 (8 Mar. 1917), quoted ibid. 405.   [19] Ibid. 406.
[20] Braga da Cruz, *As origens da democracia cristã*, 316.
[21] *A União* (8 Nov. 1923), quoted ibid. 316.
[22] A speech in parliament delivered by Lino Neto on 9 Jan. 1924 and referred to, ibid. 318.

family questions in line with the official Church viewpoint that the root of Portugal's problems lay in the existence of a moral vacuum. To mark the recovery the Church had made in recent times, an impressive Eucharistic Congress was held in Braga in 1924 at which a range of addresses were given by prominent lay and religious figures; Salazar's contribution, entitled 'The Peace of Christ and the Working Class', was based on the need for the working class to cast aside its militancy and cultivate patience and passivity since its reign was not meant to be on this earth.[23]

The scale of Portugal's economic problems which were hitting the pockets of influential groups like the military dependent on the public purse, led to growing acceptance of the Catholic viewpoint that preoccupation with external forms of government was a wasteful distraction. The most obvious sign of the national Catholic revival in the twilight years of the Republic was the Lisbon diocese's launching of a Catholic daily paper, *Novidades*, in 1923 which soon enjoyed a respectable circulation. It was duplicated by the appearance of weekly and fortnightly local papers in the north with a clear Catholic orientation. In such outlets Salazar was writing about the need for a programme of action to cure Portugal's dire economic and financial problems; and since concrete suggestions about how to extricate Portugal from its plight were not plentiful on the right, it ensured that he was increasingly noticed.

A military coup launched on 28 May 1926 overthrew the parliamentary republic. It was to the Catholic world that military leaders, united in their detestation of the previous regime but unsure of what to do next, looked for political collaborators. Salazar briefly served as minister of finance in the provisional government hastily formed in June 1926. He resigned after sixteen days convinced that it was impossible to do worthwhile work in the face of continuing instability. A military dictatorship finally took shape over the summer which struggled to remain in charge against a background of continued plotting and near-financial insolvency. In April 1928 Salazar was taken back into government as minister of finance after insisting upon sweeping conditions which included the right to veto expenditure in all government departments. Beforehand he had used the Catholic press to promote his own economic ideas and repudiate those of the officer in charge of the ministry of finance.[24] This was a sign that he was operating in the political arena as an independent figure rather than as a representative of the Church. The failure of military efforts to correct the economy damaged their standing and increased the likelihood that the military-controlled regime would be a temporary arrangement until a new balance of power emerged.

Despite imposing stiff conditions, there were aspects of Salazar's political background which made the elevation of a civilian, soon behaving as a financial dictator, acceptable to important elements in the army. His Catholic background was likely to be reassuring since the Catholic lobby had behaved in a prudent and indeed

---

[23] Telo, *Decadencia e Queda*, ii. 81.

[24] This account of Salazar's rise within the ambit of the military dictatorship is derived from T. Gallagher, *Portugal: A Twentieth Century Interpretation* (Manchester, 1978), esp. ch. 3; also A. F. Nogueira, *Salazar*, ii (Coimbra, 1977), *passim*.

self-effacing manner in the 1910–26 period; fears of a return to full-blooded clericalism (though felt and expressed in some quarters), consequently had little impact. The credibility of those on the right who identified with Catholic interests was reinforced by the papal condemnation of Action Française on 29 December 1926.[25] The Pope's insistence that 'politique d'abord' be replaced by 'religion d'abord' as a guiding example for French Catholics, justified what had been the trend in the Portuguese Catholic world for some time. The hierarchy had been stressing the need for the unity of Catholics in order to accomplish the institutional restoration of the Church and had played down the importance of outward political forms as long as basic Catholic rights were respected. However demanding Salazar could be as a ministerial colleague, military figures had relatively little trouble reaching an understanding with the Catholic Church, an institution which like the army emphasized unity and discipline as necessary for its own well-being and that of the nation.

The emphasis on 'religion d'abord' was shown by the way in which the Church channelled its energies into encouraging a spiritual and devotional revival outside the secularized south and the cities. The driving force behind this revival was the growing devotion to Mary which stemmed from the series of apparitions Our Lady of Fátima made to three children, Lucia, Jaçinta, and Francisco, between May and October 1917 in the central Portuguese hamlet of Fátima. Fátima is situated in an intermediate zone just to the west of the River Tagus which divides north from south but could be said to separate religious Portugal from irreligious or indifferent Portugal. The hierarchy was initially circumspect about the impact that Fátima had on the faithful but in 1930 the local bishop was able to announce that the cult of Fátima had the authorization of the Vatican. From then on this flourishing Marian cult occupied a central place in the minds of the Catholic peasantry and Leiria, the capital of the district in which it was located, acquired a bishopric which it had previously lacked, the fulcrum of the Church shifting from the north to the centre of the country where its implantation had always been much weaker. The pilgrimages and celebrations associated with the cult of Fátima restored public visibility to a Church which had been required to retreat into the shadows in the time of the First Republic.[26]

Liberals were unable to make effective propaganda against Salazar due to an increasingly rigorous censorship. Salazar's careful accounting methods stopped the drain of the national finances and were equated with an economic miracle by a censored press which he was not adverse to manipulating to his own advantage. At an early stage, he made it clear that he was in government as a politically disinterested financial expert not as a representative of Catholic interests. He had outlined this position on the day he took office in April 1928 in an interview with *Novidades*: 'Tell

[25] A. Matos Ferreira, 'A Acção Católica—questões em torno da organização e da autónomia da acção da Igreja Católica (1933–1958)', in C. Rosas (ed.), *O Estado Novo: Das Origens Áo Fim Da Autarcia 1926–1959*, ii (Lisbon, 1987), 285.

[26] That the Fátima apparition remains controversial is shown by the comment in the standard history of Portugal, A. H. de Oliveira Marques *História de Portugal* (Lisbon, 1976 edn.), ii. 225 that 'in May 1917, the Church, or some of its local elements, organised—and certainly exploited—the so-called apparition of Fátima'.

the Catholics that the sacrifice I have made gives me the right to expect that they of all Portuguese, will be the first to make the sacrifices I may ask of them, and the last to ask for favours which I cannot grant.'[27]

The need to be responsive to Portugal's anticlerical traditions, as well as his own desire to be free of political obligations, explains why Salazar emphasized at the outset that he was not the representative of clerical interests. He knew that the Church lacked the means to intervene actively in shaping a new political settlement after the bruising experiences it had received at the hands of a hostile state in the previous decades. He was probably also aware that most Catholics would place few demands on him if he succeeded in vanquishing republicanism and liberalism and substituting them with a new Christian political settlement based on property, order, and the family. In 1929 the appointment of Manuel Gonçalves Cerejeira, Salazar's friend and ally from Coimbra, as archbishop of Lisbon resulted in the elevation as primate of the Church of someone with whom Salazar could work in tandem in subsequent decades.[28]

From the outset Cerejeira was careful to assert the autonomy of the Church from the State while striving to ensure that it enjoyed the influence befitting a national institution able to rely on unparalleled historical continuity and strong, if localized, popular devotion. But the churchman was under no illusion that Church–State relations would have to be handled with the utmost prudence to prevent the personal connection between himself and the *de facto* head of government being exploited by the enemies of all they stood for. Thus, in a letter to Salazar written in the autumn of 1930, Cerejeira warned against confounding the Church with the dictatorship in the way that it had been confounded with the monarchy before 1910.[29] At that time, he may have viewed the current regime as a short-term arrangement which would not necessarily evolve into full-blown and permanent authoritarianism. Shortly beforehand in September 1930, Cerejeira had written to President Carmona, suggesting that a wide-ranging political amnesty on the twentieth anniversary of the formation of the Republic, might be a gesture that could secure national reconciliation.[30]

Salazar reacted angrily, having not been consulted in advance about this initiative. It was one that Cerejeira did not repeat but when the terms of their relationship were discussed after Salazar became head of government in 1932, both men were anxious to define their respective spheres of influence. On being told by Salazar that he represented 'Caesar, just Caesar, and that he was independent and sovereign', Cerejeira responded that he represented 'God . . . who was independent and sovereign and, what's more, above Caesar'. A. Franco Nogueira, Salazar's biographer and the only person with untrammelled access to Salazar's voluminous correspondence, reckons that both men respected the other's sovereignty which made for a smooth, if increasingly formal and distant, relationship over the next four decades.[31]

---

[27] Novidades (27 Apr. 1928), quoted in Kay, *Salazar*, 43.
[28] Matos Ferreira, 'La Peninsula Iberique', 407.
[29] Id., 'A Acção Católica', 289.   [30] A. F. Nogueira, *Salazar*, ii. 95–6.
[31] Ibid. iv (Coimbra, 1980), 30–1.

Ever since editing *Imparçial* at Coimbra Cerejeira had worked for conservative unity and he is unlikely to have had any qualms about the creation in 1930 of the União Nacional (National Union). The birth of what became the regime's official political movement was proclaimed by Salazar himself and highlighted his growing pre-eminence. It was meant to draw together the main groups participating in the dictatorship—monarchists, conservative republicans, army officers, Catholics, and Integralists—so that the factionalism which at times had threatened the regime's survival could be formalized and defused. Its launch anticipated the dissolution of all other political bodies, including the CCP. Lino Neto, its president, and some others were reluctant to wind up their movement. The CCP had always claimed to be an association, without a party character, in existence to defend Catholic interests, not to engage in party warfare or electoralism for its own sake which were the features of the previous regime Salazar was determined would have no part in his new order. However, Salazar was adamant: in 1933, the year in which the provisional character of the regime was ended upon the proclamation of Portugal as a corporative and unitary republic, Salazar pointed out that 'an independent Catholic body working in the political realm would prove inconvenient for the march of the dictatorship'.[32] The CCP was duly wound up and most Catholic activists gravitated to, and were given places in, the newly created public bodies in which political activity was tolerated. By 1935 a national assembly was sitting for three months of each year and in 1939 a corporative chamber became the upper house of a new bicameral parliament. These were deliberative rather than legislative bodies whose membership and activities Salazar carefully monitored as he did with the National Union, the political framework being a façade behind which an informal personal dictatorship was constructed.

Most politically engaged Catholics were content to participate in a regime which had superseded liberalism and put an end to the vacuum at the heart of the state which had marked the agitated times of the First Republic. Lino Neto and the few others who, in their speeches and respect for constitutionalism, had viewed Christian democracy as the basis for a representative democracy and not just as a tactic for Catholic survival and recovery in a hostile political environment, remained aloof from Salazar's Estado Novo (New State).[33]

No fresh political innovations would emerge from Salazar during what was to stretch into a marathon personal dictatorship. Neither did the Portuguese Church reveal any capacity to innovate in ways which would bring its dream of staging a Catholic revival in Portugal nearer to accomplishment. Later than in most other European countries, Portugal witnessed the formation of Catholic Action even though its goals of defending Catholic interests and a rechristianization of society could be said to be in greater need of fulfilment in Portugal than in many other Catholic countries where the movement had sprung up earlier.

In the year 1933 the hierarchy authorized the formation of Acção Católico Português (Portuguese Catholic Action: ACP). Coming on the creation of Salazar's

---

[32] Speech of 23 Nov. 1932 quoted in Matos Ferreira, 'A Acção Católica', 283.
[33] Braga da Cruz, *As origens da democracia cristã*, 363–71.

New State has prompted one writer to describe it as an attempt by the Church to define a space for itself in the authoritarian state Portugal had become.[34] But the low profile which the ACP acquired during most phases of its active life over the next thirty years weakens such a view. The motivation behind it may have been nothing more than the need to bring the Portuguese Church in line with others by following the recommendations of the papacy to create a movement of the lay apostolate under clerical direction.

In the ACP there was a narrow definition of 'religious and pastoral activity' and an emphasis on tight hierarchical control even by the standards of inter-war Catholic Europe. Homilies and conference proceedings emphasized piety, good works, prayer, and personal example but there was no strategy of action which could harness this energy and bolster Church influence in areas of weakness. The ACP did see the formation of élites who would bring a Christian perspective to their public duties as part of its remit but it was prevented from playing this role by its own restricted agenda: few members had the opportunity to acquire skills in administration, public speaking, and conciliation of differences valuable for public affairs. The ACP's emphasis on piety and devotional and sacramental practice taken along with the regime's insistence on political uniformity and obedience meant that the Catholic Church was unable to produce an intellectual élite of any real distinction. Intellectuals in Portugal continued to be attracted by humanistic and rationalist doctrines and, in the university world, Marxism would acquire a powerful appeal among several generations of university students which it had not possessed during the Republican regime.

Under corporative legislation which promised an end to class conflict, the already precarious conditions of life of landless labourers and workers declined steeply which enabled the underground Partido Comunista Português (Portuguese Communist Party: PCP) to gain a powerful foothold in southern Portugal from the 1930s onwards. Few priests in the south were prepared to live close to the poor or to draw attention to the lack of social justice in their lives. One who did was Abel Varzim who by the late 1930s was prepared to question the efficacy of the corporativist doctrine in the National Assembly to which he then belonged. He mounted increasingly searching questions about the failure of the New State to protect the conditions of life and employment of the workers. This in turn brought him into conflict with his clerical superiors (who viewed his outspokenness as a danger to healthy Church-State relations) and with the state which suppressed his newspaper, *O Trabalhador* (The Worker).[35]

Communism was fiercely denounced by the Church once it became clear that it was no longer a distant threat but had become the alternative faith for large numbers of sullen and resentful Portuguese alienated from the New State. Bolshevism at home and the eruption of civil war in Spain which yielded up thousands of martyrs to the faith would have weakened any inhibitions possessed by Catholics about the lengths to which Salazar had gone in order to consolidate his rule. It is unlikely that

---

[34] Matos Ferreira, 'La Peninsula Iberique', 408. [35] Id. 'A Acção Católica', 292.

Cerejeira had envisaged in 1929 how radical and sweeping Salazar's plans were. The creation of a political police, the dissolution of working-class movements and secret societies, the introduction of pre-publication censorship, and the removal from public employment of those whose loyalty to the new order was suspect, were proof of Salazar's determination to break with the past in line with the drift to the authoritarian right elsewhere in Europe.

However, Salazar's Catholic and juridical formation made him wary of going down the totalitarian path which would involve the mobilization of the masses and the creation of a one-party state which viewed itself as the embodiment of all virtue. In 1934 he speculated about whether 'it might not bring about an absolutism worse than that which preceded the liberal regimes . . . Such a state would be essentially pagan, incompatible by its nature with the character of our Christian civilization and leading sooner or later to revolution'.[36]

Salazar counterposed the one-party states of Germany and Italy with the Portuguese New State 'which does not evade certain constraints of moral order which it deems vital to maintain as balances on its reforming programme . . . Our laws are less severe, our daily life less interfered with while the State is less absolute and does not proclaim itself as omnipotent'.[37]

It is significant that Salazar set the New State apart from full-blown fascism while he was grappling with the Blueshirts, an extreme-rightist body influenced by the rise of Nazism in Germany. This challenge from the radical right had been successfully overcome by 1934 which thereafter left Salazar with no qualms in saying that the ideological roots of the New State were to be found in the writings of traditional Catholic theorists and in the papal encyclicals (particularly those of Leo XIII) which proposed a Catholic solution to the problems of the modern age. Of course, Salazar was a gifted adapter who borrowed the repressive techniques of his own time as well as some of the symbolism of Italian Fascism to endow a regime based on order, tradition, and a respect for hierarchy with a modern veneer. Perhaps it was the dozen years he spent as a theorist of Catholic social thought and as an activist in the CADC and the CCP which did most to shape the political system he created after 1930: hostility to the party concept; lack of concern with the outward form of regime, whether monarchy or republic; and commitment to inter-class co-operation were central tenets of political Catholicism before 1926 which Salazar was able to draw on and refine as he constructed his own political order.

Education was probably the area of government where Catholic influence was to be felt the most. Salazar was mindful of the need to overturn the liberal, secular inheritance of the Republican era if future generations were to embrace positively the very different outlook of the New State. Accordingly, the education ministry was placed in charge of two longstanding Catholic activists, António Carneiro Pacheco (1936–40) and Mário de Figueiredo (1940–4) who shared Salazar's belief that education was

---

[36] A. O. de Salazar, *Doctrine & Action: Internal and Foreign Policy of the New Portugal*, trans. Edgar Broughton (London 1939), 231.

[37] A. Ferro, *Salazar: Portugal and her Leader* (London, 1939), 74–5.

a key aspect of social control able to revive and popularize traditional values. After 1936, the school curriculum was heavily politicized so that it became a prime source of New State propaganda. All schoolchildren were required to be enrolled in an official youth movement, the *Mocidade Portuguesa*. In the countryside, the regime was less in evidence but great care was taken to inculcate the values of nationhood, family, and attachment to one's locality. The school was deliberately used to keep the rural population where it was and to discourage emigration to the city. In speeches and interviews Salazar frequently referred to the social dangers posed by a growing population which between 1920 and 1940 increased by one-quarter to 7 million.[38] Unsurprisingly, the revival of a mystical brand of folk Catholicism centred on the Miracle of Fátima proved a boon for a regime intent on keeping the countryside frozen in a pastoral pre-industrial age and it was exploited openly by the regime's propagandists.

The continued parlous state of the Church in Lisbon showed that the Catholic revival in Portugal was a movement of cautious recovery and defence rather than expansion or renewal. In the early 1930s a diocesan population of one-and-a-half million was being served by only 320 priests, many of them 'old and worn-out clergy'.[39] On 8 December 1935 a pastoral letter issued by Cardinal Cerejeira painted an alarming picture:

Black Africa of the Pagans is at the very gates of Lisbon—the mother church of so many Christian churches in Africa, Asia, Oceania. Should things continue thus, the time will not be long coming when our Christian land will be turned completely into a cemetery of glorious Catholic and apostolic tradition like those brilliant dead churches in north Africa that were once illuminated by the genius of St Augustine.[40]

This was an admission by Portugal's leading churchman at the zenith of Salazar's national revolution that the Church was a slender minority presence in Portugal's capital. Against this background, it is difficult to talk about a 'Christian reconquest' in Portugal after 1926.[41] Indeed, under Salazar Portugal continued to have the lowest ratio of priests to Roman Catholics in Europe with 1 per 2,311 inhabitants in 1954 compared to 1 per 1,336 in neighbouring Spain.[42] Although primate of the Portuguese Church, Cerejeira's authority did not extend beyond his own diocese and it would not have been a straightforward exercise to transfer priests from better-supplied parts of the north. In 1931 the diocese of Braga had three times as many priests as Lisbon, while a small rural diocese like Vila Real had almost as many again, an imbalance that has continued down to the present day.[43]

The Church did not receive endowments or special concessions from the regime which might have enabled it to recoup partly its position in the capital. Even after gaining undisputed control of the country, Salazar remained wary of unduly close

---

[38] M.-F. Mónica, *Educação e Sociedade No Portugal de Salazar* (Lisbon, 1978), 131–44.

[39] Rev. R. S. Devane SJ, 'The Plight of Religion in the Patriarchate of Lisbon', *Irish Ecclesiastical Record* (1937), 40.

[40] Ibid. 39.

[41] Cf. Matos Ferreira, 'La Peninsula Iberique', 403.

[42] T. C. Bruneau, 'Church and State', 477.

[43] Devane, 'The Plight of Religion', 40.

identification with church interests. Thus in 1935 he declared that 'the Catholic Church had nothing to do with my entering government, and they did not influence my political decisions'.[44] Another five years were to elapse before a concordat was signed which regulated relations between the Holy See, the Portuguese Church, and the State. It was only agreed after protracted negotiations between the various parties. Salazar drove such a hard bargain that the papal nuncio was moved to describe him as 'the living incarnation of the devil' in an outburst to Portugal's negotiator.[45] Negotiations almost fell through and it was only a last-minute ultimatum to Rome requesting that government terms be accepted or the concordat would be shelved, which caused it to be promulgated on 7 May 1940.[46]

Under the 1940 Concordat the Church was recognized as a privileged institution with a very large role in society but Church and State remained separate and some basic laws from Republican days were not overturned: religious teaching in schools remained voluntary, civil marriage and civil divorce were retained, and Church property seized after 1910 by the State remained sequestrated. Article 10 stipulated that the Holy See must, before nominating a bishop, communicate the name to the Portuguese government in order to determine whether there was any objection of a political nature.[47] By way of a contrast, churches and seminaries were to be exempt from taxation and the State was prepared to finance partly the building of churches. But given Salazar's Catholic formation many were surprised that the 1940 settlement was not more favourable to the Church.

The Concordat was promulgated in May 1940 amidst celebrations marking the 800th anniversary of the formation of Portugal and the tercentenary of its deliverance from sixty years of Spanish captivity. Since much of the rest of continental Europe was embroiled in war as Portugal celebrated the normalization of relations with Rome and two of the formative events in her history, the May 1940 celebrations acquired a special symbolism which marked the high-water mark of the Salazar regime. As Portugal avoided becoming involved in the European conflict, thanks undoubtedly to Salazar's skilful conduct of foreign policy, much of the Catholic faithful came to view this as a miracle stemming not just from God's protection but from the intercession of Our Lady of Fátima.[48]

Cardinal Cerejeira took a pro-Allied position, influenced in part by the Nazi seizure of Catholic Poland and subsequent religious persecution there.[49] Portugal's ability to remain neutral in the world conflict, its distance from the main theatres of land warfare, and the fact that it was bordered on three sides by Spain, which possessed an analagous regime of authoritarian conservatism under General Franco, meant that it was one of the few parts of Europe to emerge relatively unchanged from the war years. But Salazar's place in the pantheon of conservative heroes was not as

---

[44] Braga da Cruz, *As orígens da democracia cristã*, 366.

[45] A. F. Nogueira, *Salazar*, iii (Coimbra, 1978), 263.

[46] Id., *História de Portugal, 1933–1974* (Oporto, 1981), 184.

[47] Bruneau, *Church and State*, 471.   [48] Matos Ferreira, 'La Peninsula Iberique', 409.

[49] Public Records Office (hereafter PRO), Foreign Office (hereafter FO), 371, 34844: Report from British embassy in Lisbon, 4 Aug. 1943.

secure as it had been in the late 1930s when Portugal was a place of intellectual pilgrimage for European conservatives impressed by the way in which Salazar had produced order from chaos apparently within a Christian political and social framework. As he obstinately refused to adapt his regime to changing times, he began to appear as an anachronistic and compromised figure for Catholics involved in public life elsewhere who were keen to find applicable models for the reconstruction of Europe but along Christian democratic lines. By the 1950s the verdict of many of Salazar's European Catholic peers on his New State was that it had been a formula which might have suited a disturbed period in European politics but which new conditions had rendered obsolete.

However, for those Catholics who possessed a Cold War mentality, especially in North America, Salazar's Christian order remained a beacon of inspiration. The Marian cult centred on Fátima was the main point of contact between the Portuguese Church and Catholics from the rest of Europe and from overseas, conservative-minded exponents of their faith who may have reinforced the traditionalism of the Portuguese Church. The content of the Fátima message was interpreted in strongly anti-communist terms, Pope Pius XII in 1946 having crowned Our Lady of Fátima queen of the world.[50] Suitably enough, it was also in 1946 that Opus Dei spread to Portugal: given the Portuguese terrain, its traditionalism, stress on individualistic piety, and theology of political conservatism were bound to acquire a growing niche, despite its Spanish origins.

Nearly all Portuguese Catholics who had growing qualms about the ethical basis of the Salazar regime shrank from going into public opposition. Their Church leaders sanctioned obedience to what they regarded as legitimate authority and the Portuguese opposition, still dominated by Republican anticlericals as well as a growing Communist presence, remained unattractive to most Catholics. But one exception was Francisco Veloso, one of Salazar's most steadfast colleagues in the CADC at Coimbra (described by Cerejeira as the true editor of its paper *Imparçial* 'in its first and most brilliant year of existence'),[51] who in 1945 embraced a Christian democratic position. He joined the opposition Movimiento Democrático Unido (United Democratic Movement: MUD) which was the first body allowed to stand against the National Union when elections for the National Assembly were held in November 1945. The opposition won no seats (nor would it in any of the decorative elections regularly held over the next thirty years). But censorship was briefly lifted during the weeks of campaigning which enabled Veloso to mount the first public critique of the regime by a representative Catholic figure. Veloso argued that dictatorship should only be a temporary expedient required in times of emergency and must not be turned into a permanent system of government; his charge that the younger generation was being given no opportunity to play a role in a government which had grown remote from the people through operating behind firmly closed doors was one that would be repeated even by regime insiders in the years to come.[52]

[50] Matos Ferreira, 'La Peninsula Iberique', 413. [51] Cerejeira, *Vinte Anos de Coimbra*, 215.
[52] Nogueira, *Salazar*, iv. 29–30.

No other dissenting voices emerged from Catholic circles at this time. Christian democracy was still to prove itself as a governing philosophy in Italy and Germany. Disenchantment among those Catholics who were well placed to see that the benefits of the regime were distributed very selectively, was outweighed by a fear of communism. Despite the oblique language he used in his public addresses, Salazar left few in any doubt about his abhorrence of democracy as a governing system or of his belief that the Portuguese were temperamentally unsuited to applying it in their own affairs. Even cautious liberalization would, he felt, only place the fruits of his regime of peace and order at risk but as he grew older he offered no clues about his thinking on who or what would succeed him.

Younger generations of Catholics, and those who felt that the problems of post-war Portugal required solutions different from those imposed in 1926, had no channels through which they could bring their views to bear within the system. The dissolution of the CCP and the relegation of the CADC to a memorialist body which commemorated the spirited days of combating atheistic liberalism, had left a vacuum. Salazar may have disposed of the bodies which had provided him with his political formation to allay fears of a Catholic dictatorship; however, he was also aware that his autocratic political system was particularly vulnerable to criticism from Catholics who felt that he had renounced the truths contained in the encyclicals of Pope Leo XIII merely in order to install a dictatorship of the privileged. Signs that the lay apostolate were moving beyond conceiving their role as one of piety and good works emerged in the post-war years. A series of congresses were held between 1948 and 1953 at which the various branches of Catholic Action discussed social and religious questions, moving beyond the abstract and relating them to contemporary Portugal. Thousands attended what were inaugural conferences for Catholic primary teachers and Catholic men while delegates had the chance to share experiences and views at Catholic conferences abroad where they found that in order to maintain links with the poor and the marginalized, injustices were being exposed and challenged by their Catholic colleagues.[53] Any possibility that religious life would become the basis for social criticism and social action was effectively dashed in the early 1950s. Against the background of growing disquiet within the regime about incipient trends within the Church, full control was reasserted over Catholic Action in 1953 and its relevance as a force in the lives of even the most traditional Catholics declined steadily thereafter.

Those groups ready to involve the Church in contemporary national debates needed backing from people high up in the ecclesiastical hierarchy in order to create the space in which to realize their aims. But such well-placed allies ready to act as mediators between the Church's advanced groups and the State were not to be found. In its public statements the Catholic hierarchy betrayed no apprehension about whether it was in the Church's long-term interests to be so closely identified with a regime increasingly revealed to be a personal dictatorship whose future only

53 Matos Ferreira, 'La Peninsula Iberique', 410; J. Canico SJ, *The Church in Portugal* (Brussels, 1981), 12.

seemed certain as long as Salazar possessed the will and the stamina to plot its course. In a pastoral letter issued in November 1945, Cardinal Cerejeira repeated the existing formula that 'the Church is above and outside the concrete policies of specific regimes . . . as long as these respect the liberty of the Church and the fundamental principles of the moral order'.[54] But there was no official ceremony in Portugal—the opening of a new public building, the completion of a dam, or the opening of a new session of the National Assembly—without the presence of a bishop or, very often, the Cardinal himself. However, in the post-war years the previous close co-operation between church and state would fade somewhat. By the 1940s Salazar was no longer able to draw upon former CADC colleagues to fill cabinet posts. No less than ten of his eighty-seven ministers came from this small association, but by the 1940s it was technicians from a Catholic background who were emerging to replace them as Salazar's CADC colleagues along with other founders of the regime opted for more lucrative positions in industry and the professions.[55]

A limited degree of opposition was permitted in carefully policed elections for the presidency and the National Assembly. But the aura of calm and continuity which had become synonymous with the New State was shattered in the campaign for the 1958 presidential election when General Humberto Delgado, an air-force officer who had held a series of important state appointments, announced his decision to challenge the official nominee. His nationwide election campaign was greeted by highly enthusiastic crowds even in parts of the northern countryside where the regime had been thought to enjoy a real degree of popular acceptance. Seeing that this populist officer had tapped a genuine vein of discontent, the liberal Republican and Communist wings of the opposition rallied around him as the sole opposition challenger. Delgado received just under a quarter of the vote amidst widespread claims that the poll had been rigged by state officials to stave off certain defeat.[56] One source has claimed that in Braga the authorities obliged priests in every electoral ward to identify parishioners liable to support the opposition challenger so that they could be removed from the voting lists.[57] Since it was not unknown for parish priests in country towns and villages to act as dispensers of official propaganda and agents of social conformity and political vigilance, it is not surprising if local officials felt that they could rely on politically minded clergy in this way.

Dr Franco Nogueira, Salazar's former foreign minister, has admitted that 'many Catholics supported Delgado with their votes if not by public word or action'.[58] In his influential life of Salazar, he went on to concede that a split had opened up in the Church between traditionalists and a minority progressive wing.[59] Salazar had been

---

[54] Nogueira, *Salazar*, iv. 30.

[55] T. Gallagher, 'Os 87 Ministros de Salazar', *História* (Lisbon), 28 (Feb. 1981), 11–12.

[56] The British consul in Oporto, A. D. Francis, reported that 'the general feeling is that on a free vote the opposition would have won in this area'. PRO FO 371 136534: Sir C. N. Stirling to Selwyn Lloyd, 14 June 1958.

[57] S. Cerqueira, 'L'Église catholique et la dictature corporatiste portugaise', *Revue Française de Science Politique*, 23 (1975), 496.

[58] A. F. Nogueira, *Salazar*, v (Oporto, 1984), 18.   [59] Ibid. iv. 494.

informed earlier in 1958 that a meeting in Fátima of leaders of the Catholic Student's Movement (JUC) had given rise to a welter of criticism of the choice made by the institutional Church and the precepts which had shaped Portuguese Catholicism for the previous generation. The new progressive thinking had found its way into other branches of the lay apostolate, such as the Catholic Workers Movement, the League of Catholic Men, and the Catholic Information Centre. Catholic newspapers like *Novidades* and *O Trabalhador* were affected and the new questioning mood had even taken hold among members of the diocesan clergy.[60]

The bishops were thought to be unaffected until Antonio Ferreira Gomes, bishop of Oporto since 1952, caused a major political upheaval by writing a long letter of twenty-four pages to Salazar in July 1958, critical of his stewardship of the country, which soon became public knowledge. He wrote of a deepening gulf between the country and the New State and warned that while it was necessary to defend Portugal, closing ranks behind the New State was not the only means of salvation.[61] He criticized restrictions on human rights in Portugal and the neglect and suffering experienced by much of the population in the overseas territories, depicted corporativism as a way of depriving workers of their natural right to association, and drew attention to the harshness of Portugal's poverty, especially in the countryside. Turning to the Church, he insisted that it 'is not free to teach its social doctrine' and related that even in rural areas of northern Portugal, supposed to be strong in their support of Salazar, the men walked out of church in indignation when the priests referred in their sermons to the elections.[62]

Outwardly Ferreira Gomes had appeared to be just another of the conformist bishops from a devout northern small farming background who had shaped the Portuguese Church into a pious and conventional force. However, his first episcopal appointment had been in the Alentejan diocese of Portalegre from 1949 to 1952 where he had been much affected by the neglect of education and the misery experienced by landless labourers. A study of his homilies and pastoral letters, as well as contributions he made to the local press, reveals that Church–State relations, the dangers of totalitarianism, and the importance of liberty were recurring themes.[63]

The events of 1958 revealed simmering discontent within two national institutions, the Church and the military, which had hitherto acted as the chief pillars of the regime. Their loyalty and co-operation had enabled Salazar to grant them a certain degree of autonomy in an otherwise highly regulated political system. However, in the uncertain years immediately after 1958, such political immunity was lifted. Delgado was dismissed from the air force and forced to flee abroad where he plotted against the regime until his assassination by the secret police in 1965. On returning from a holiday abroad in July 1959, the Bishop of Oporto was prevented from

---

[60] Ibid. [61] Ibid. 512.

[62] Kay, *Salazar*, 360; G. Grohs, 'The Church in Portugal after the Coup of 1974', *Journal of Iberian Studies*, 5/1 (1976), 36.

[63] A. Praça, 'D. António Ferreira Gomes: O bispo que recusou a "Pax Augusta" de Salazar', *O Jornal* (Lisbon), 26 Feb. 1982.

re-entering Portugal. When the Vatican declined to act upon the government's wish that a new bishop be appointed, an apostolic administrator was chosen to run the diocese in the absence of Ferreira Gomes; the bishop found himself in exile for the next ten years, during which time he remained under close watch from the secret police as his voluminous file in their archives makes clear.[64]

The Ferreira Gomes affair was a grievous blow to the standing of an authoritarian regime which was far more vulnerable to the withdrawal of official Church backing than was Franco's in Spain. Much of its legitimacy derived from being seen as a governing system which had tried to implement Catholic doctrines through its public policy. The Bishop of Oporto had repudiated that claim as Salazar's regime faced unprecedented opposition. If his critique had been endorsed by others among Portugal's forty-nine bishops, it might have given the Church vital detachment which would have enabled it to keep its options open as the regime began a slow but inexorable decline which culminated in it being removed by force in 1974.

But the Ferreira Gomes affair proved not to be the turning-point that would recast Church–State relations. None of the other bishops in mainland Portugal echoed his views, nor is there evidence that any tried to intercede with Salazar to get his expulsion lifted. *A Voz*, the conservative Catholic daily, provided a platform for Catholic traditionalists to denounce the bishop for using 'subversive communist terminology' and for 'defending the class struggle as the motor of history'.[65] But in a 1959 dispatch to London, the British ambassador reported that in talking to a journalist on the Lisbon archdiocese's own daily paper, *Novidades*, one of his staff had been left with the impression that many in the Church 'felt that the Bishop of Oporto's strictures on the Government and the Church in Portugal were justified'. The view was also conveyed from this *Novidades* source that the Cardinal, through his longstanding friendship with Dr Salazar, was allowing the Church to be used as an instrument of what was termed the 'situation' (i.e. the regime). He maintained that 'there was an abyss between the ordinary people and the Church whose present state could be likened to that of the Church of England in Victorian days.'[66]

When the furore over the Bishop of Oporto's letter had been at its height, Salazar had delivered a stern speech in which he hinted strongly that the consequences for the Church could be painful if a threatened breach with the government was not avoided in time. Given its importance, the speech, delivered to the executive committee of the National Union on 6 December 1958 is worth quoting at some length:

Certain Catholics actually boast of having broken the front of national unity and have gone to such lengths that they have won the applause not only of the Liberals with whom they have allied themselves, but of the Communists . . . I consider this fact of the utmost gravity, not because of the individual elements which are lost to the National Front, but because of the disturbance which it causes in the consciences of many . . . I shall not address myself to the

[64] Bishop António Ferreira Gomes dossiers, 2878/58 SR and 3953-CI, PIDE/DGS (Portuguese secret police) archive, Fortress prison, Caxias, Portugal. The bishop's dossier consists of two bulky files and the PIDE had a concise list of his pastorals, homilies, conference addresses, etc. from 1950 onwards. His private mail was being opened until the end of 1973.   [65] A. Praça, Afonso, 'Gomes'.

[66] PRO FO 371, 144851 1781, 'Religion in Portugal': Sir C. N. Stirling to J. M. Addis, 5 Feb. 1959.

question today; it contains such serious implications with respect to the Concordat and even to the future relations between the State and the Church, that I have thought it right to maintain complete silence about it in public . . .

I who have contributed something to religious pacification and to the liberty of the Church in Portugal, as well as to the position of affection and prestige in which it has been placed in the last thirty years, should find it extremely painful if I were forced to register complaints.[67]

Salazar's speech was a warning that Church–State relations and even the 1940 Concordat might be imperilled if the dissidents were not called to order. In response, a pastoral letter issued by the bishops on 18 January 1959 noted that the Church had been accused by some of having become a vassal of the political system while being attacked by others for having failed in moments of crisis to use its authority on behalf of the system. Both these accusations stemmed from the same misconception of ascribing to the Church a political mission, the statement went on to say. The Church's task was to preach the gospel and the State had an obligation to build its institutions on the basis of a Christian social programme. But the statement did not mention whether the bishops felt that the government had been fulfilling that obligation and what the role of those Catholics should be who in their own spheres of existence had clear evidence that it was not. However, members of Catholic Action were reminded that the constitution of the Portuguese branch provided that it should operate outside and above all political movements and that members were required to exercise discipline and show all due obedience to ecclesiastical authority. Perhaps the most comforting part of the bishop's message for the government was the declaration that obedience to legitimate authority was always necessary as it was only in a climate of order and peace that true progress could be achieved.[68]

The bishops, in their statement, had placed on record their special concern for the humblest classes in society but in a meeting with the British minister to the Vatican a day after it had been issued, Cardinal Cerejeira talked frankly about 'the innate political ineptitude of the Portuguese people'. Their flaws 'made stable government in Portugal so difficult and were shared by all Latin peoples', remarks which suggested that there was little to choose between his highly restricted political outlook and that of Salazar.[69]

As long as Cerejeira remained the leading churchman in Portugal, the chances of the Church distancing itself from the regime were extremely remote. Yet, less than two months after the bishop's statement, there was unmistakable evidence that important Catholic figures, mainly drawn from the laity, had concluded that the main arena for securing meaningful change in Portugal was no longer within the ranks of the Church.

At the last minute, the secret police discovered a revolutionary attempt due to have taken place on 11–12 March 1959, known as 'the Cathedral plot'. In the words

---

[67] PRO FO 371 136569, 'Relations between the Roman Catholic Church and the Government': C. N. Stirling to Selwyn Lloyd, 13 Dec. 1958.

[68] PRO FO 371 144851, 'Catholics in Portugal': Sir C. N. Stirling to London, 9 Jan. 1959.

[69] PRO FO 371 144851, 'Catholics in Portugal': Marcus Cheke to Sir C. N. Stirling, 23 Jan. 1959.

of the Socialist leader and subsequent president of Portugal, Mário Soares, it was a conspiracy which 'had nothing to do with the old "putschist" movements of former times . . . Neither by its basic inspiration nor by the people who participated in it, in responsible positions'.[70] One of the key organizers was Manuel Serra, a senior Catholic Youth leader. He was in charge of some 300 armed civilians, many of whom were young activists whose formation had been in the Juventude Operaria Catolica (JOC: Catholic Workers Youth) and Juventude Universitaria Catolica (JUC: Catholic Student Youth).[71] Several of the junior officers involved had a background of Catholic activism and the crypt of Lisbon Cathedral was a storehouse for weapons. Fr João Perestrello de Vasconcelos, chaplain to the merchant navy, was arrested carrying weapons in what turned out to be the most elaborate conspiracy mounted against the Salazar regime for many years.

JUC members were to the fore in the university conflicts of the early 1960s which bore eloquent testimony to the regime's complete estrangement from educated young people, something that even Salazar acknowledged as a reality.[72] While some Catholic activists remained committed to revolutionary activity, others chose to follow more moderate and legalistic paths and worked in close alliance with liberals and socialists.[73] Opposition tendencies within the Church were reinforced by the Second Vatican Council (1962–5) which set in motion a process of open discussion and radical change that was to profoundly alter the character of the Church. The emphasis on collegiality rather than hierarchy and the willingness to allow the laity to play a role as full participants in the work of the Church encouraged progressives while Salazar viewed the process as deeply subversive of the kind of church he had sought to foster. The encyclical *Pacem in Terris* (Peace on Earth) issued by John XXIII in 1963, which dealt with human rights and the relation of the individual to the State, was censored in Portugal and the overseas territories.[73] Portuguese bishops attended the Council but their role was secondary since they had clearly been on the periphery of the theological and pastoral movement which in other parts of Europe had paved the way for this crucial convocation of the Church. Official encouragement was lacking for the spread and penetration of conciliar ideas among both laity and clergy through discussion, publications, and study weeks, etc. Instead, according to a Portuguese Jesuit writing in the late 1970s, 'the hierarchy adopted . . . the role of surveillance and acted as a break on whatever was attempted'.[74]

When Pope Paul VI visited India in 1964 the government of Salazar regarded it as an insult because a few years earlier, India had annexed the Portuguese territory of Goa. The media was forbidden from mentioning the visit, Salazar having become ultra-sensitive to threats posed against Portugal's African territories where since 1961 an armed struggle against colonial rule had begun to be mounted by Black and

[70] M. Soares, *Portugal Amordacado*, 272–6, quoted in D. L. Raby, *Fascism and Resistance in Portugal: Communists, Liberals and Military Dissidents in the Opposition to Salazar* (Manchester, 1988), 201.

[71] Ibid.

[72] PRO FO 371 153100, 'Internal Political Situation': Frank K. Roberts to Sir C. Stirling, 25 Jan. 1960.

[73] Raby, *Fascism and Resistance*, 293. [74] J. Canico SJ, *The Church in Portugal* (Brussels, 1981).

mixed-race liberation movements.[75] Tensions between Church and State had manifested themselves in the colonies over a lengthy period. As early as 1941 M. Alves
Correia, vicar-general of the Luanda diocese, had been accused by the governor-
general of Angola of engaging in political action which threatened to separate the
territory of Angola from mainland Portugal. Tensions had grown from the willingness of this churchman, who had the backing of his bishop, to defend African interests by applying Catholic social teaching and to take initial steps to foster a native
clergy.[76] Sebastião Resende, Bishop of Beira in Mozambique from 1943 to 1967, had
been a stern critic of forced labour in the Portuguese territories but had been
marginalized by nationalist sectors of the Church. His successor, Manuel Vieira
Pinto, would declare towards the end of the long authoritarian era that 'we prefer a
Church that is persecuted but alive to a Church that is generously subsidised but at
the price of damaging connivance at the behaviour of the temporal powers'.[77]

The Vatican's growing criticism of colonialism was the issue which increasingly
overshadowed relations with the Portuguese government as its determination to
remain in Africa showed no let-up during the 1960s in the face of disengagement by
other European powers. A brief thaw was evident in 1967 when Pope Paul VI visited
Portugal on a pilgrimage to Fátima. But in 1970 he deeply angered the Portuguese
authorities by granting a private audience to the leaders of liberation movements in
the Portuguese African territories.

By the middle of the 1960s it was becoming clear that the existing strands of
opposition to dictatorship, represented by the Republicans and the different wings of
the left, had been joined by a third current emanating from within Portuguese
Catholicism. The progressive lead given by the Second Vatican Council and the intransigence of the New State in the face of cries for liberalization at home and self-
determination in the colonies, produced a new generation of liberal Catholic activists
ready to test the limits of the regime's tolerance.

Dissatisfaction among lower clergy was revealed in 1963 when two priests in
Oporto were arrested upon refusing to serve a tour of duty as military chaplains in
Africa. In the same year a new monthly magazine, *O Tempo e o Modo*, was launched
which for the remainder of the 1960s was to be an important vehicle of expression for
the progressive intelligentsia.[78] The majority of its editorial board and contributors
were Catholic intellectuals. Non-Catholic liberals and Marxists contributed to its
pages and collaborated with Catholics in various opposition initiatives. Old-style
Republicans were forced to reassess their attitude towards Catholics when in 1963 an
important conference of Catholic economists could discuss such sensitive issues as
nationalization of industries and agrarian reform. Later in 1965, Catholic intellectuals were instrumental in forming a cultural co-operative called *Pragma* which
held public meetings, published policy analyses, and offered educational courses.[79]

---

[75] J. Baptista, *Caminhos para uma Revolução*, (Lisbon, 1975), 31.
[76] Matos Ferreira, 'La Peninsula Iberique', 417.
[77] E. Keefe, *Area Handbook for Portugal* (Washington, 1977), 16.
[78] Raby, *Fascism and Resistance*, 234.   [79] Ibid. 235.

Such initiatives proved effective in taking the heat out of what remained of the anti-clerical cause and ensured that religion would not return to be a contentious issue when democracy was eventually restored in the 1970s. In the face of hostility from an inward-looking institutional Church, they also turned Catholic intellectuals and student activists towards Marxism. Attempts to synthesize Marxist and Catholic teaching in order to develop blueprints for a just moral order were made by small groups who saw their goals being realized by political revolution. When Portugal experienced an authentic if short-lived revolution in 1974–5 as a result of the military overthrow of the dictatorship, such knots of activists would briefly come into their own.

Politicized Catholics grew increasingly bold in their pronouncements as the wars in Africa intensified against a background of political paralysis at home. In 1965 the manifesto of the newly launched Christian Movement of Democratic Action stated that 'the Portuguese social situation is anti-Christian . . . Personal power which surpasses the occasional necessary need for it is by definition anti-Christian . . . A totalitarian state of a conservative type is the most anti-Christian social situation . . . Christ can never be on the side of shock police, suffocation of thought, violation of law.'[80]

Over one hundred Catholic laymen identified with this manifesto and in a public statement condemned Salazar's authoritarian state and expressed support for the right of self-determination in Africa's colonies. Three days later over one hundred conservative Catholics issued a counter-statement reaffirming their faith in the policies of the government; the most outspoken Church traditionalist was Francisco Mária de Silva, the Archbishop of Braga, for whom Salazar was 'the bold and tenacious man at the helm who restored the nation's unity around the sacred symbol of the redeeming Cross'.[81]

The African situation and the uncertainty about who and what would succeed Salazar who celebrated his seventy-fifth birthday in 1964, heightened the intransigence of Catholic traditionalists linked to the regime. The malaise which gripped the institutional Church in turn encouraged Catholic liberals to channel their energies into overtly political activities even in the confined space tolerated by the regime. An ageing hierarchy was unable and unwilling to strike a balance between the Catholic intelligentsia of the cities and traditionalists in the north. Indeed a public breach occurred between Catholic progressives and the vast majority of the hierarchy in the second half of the 1960s. The founding of the Study Group for the Inter-change of Documents, Information and Experience (GEDOC) by priests and laity revealed the extent of the polarization. Letters and documents were addressed to the hierarchy concerning their failure to heed encyclicals such as *Mater et Magistra* (1961), *Pacem in Terris* (1963), and *Populorum Progressio* (1967). Seventy-eight priests signed a letter to Cardinal Cerejeira in December 1968 which pointed out that 'little positive activity was taking place in the archdiocese and the malaise of the clergy was great'.

The hierarchy reacted harshly to critics who had written about 'an infection weakening all the ecclesiastical body like a leukemia'. GEDOC disappeared following

---

[80] Robinson, *Contemporary Portugal*, 79.   [81] Ibid. 64.

a statement by Cerejeira in February 1969 which amounted to a virtual inter-diction.[82] The priests aligned with GEDOC had expressed their determination to 'fight from within the church so that she . . . becomes involved in the difficult but re-warding process of renovation',[83] but between 1969 and 1974 there was little debate and no innovation and many of the Church's most dynamic elements simply left or retreated into isolation. In the slightly freer conditions which existed under Marcelo Caetano, who became prime minister in October 1968, following the collapse of Salazar's health, *Broteria*, the leading Jesuit publication, carried an article in 1972 which acknowledged the parlous state of the Church:

Nobody can argue that there exists . . . a dialogue or a taking of a position at the diocesan or na-tional level which mobilises laymen, priests and bishops to take up the renovation of our Catholicism in confrontation with the problems of our country as is taking place, for example, in neighbouring Spain . . . The conditions for a post-Conciliar Roman Catholicism among us have not been created.[84]

In Spain, the emergence of a Church with a strong progressive wing prepared to con-tribute actively to securing a democratic transition from Francoism had been encouraged by the Vatican and its papal nuncio on the spot. But even during the papacies of John XXIII and Paul VI the nuncios sent to Lisbon proved to be conservative figures who failed to assist the progressives trying to implement the encyclicals of the Second Vatican Council.[85]

The biographical parallelism between the leaders of Church and State finally ended in 1969 when the Cardinal primate retired a few months after Salazar had ceased to perform his prime ministerial functions. Cerejeira's successor, António de Ribeiro, was not yet 40 but he was prepared to operate within existing parameters. This was shown by the incident which occurred in the Largo do Rato chapel, Lisbon in the last day of 1972 when a group of Catholics tried to commemorate the Pope's Day of Peace. The wars in Africa were discussed and a statement was issued ques-tioning the motivations behind Portuguese policy. This was a signal for the police to arrest all the participants, some being sent to prison while those employed by the State lost their jobs.

Cardinal Ribeiro kept a judicious silence, neither condemning the gathering nor supporting those arrested.[86] Earlier, the Church had been accorded some additional concessions by the Caetano regime which included permission to found a private university (the New University of Lisbon) and to launch a radio station, *Radio Renascenca*. But Caetano, like Salazar before him, showed every sign that in return for State preferment, he expected a compliant Church prepared to bestow legitimacy upon the government even though its foolhardy policies in Africa had left it steadily more isolated and discredited even among former well-wishers.

[82] For this episode, see Bruneau, 'Church and State', 478–9.
[83] Cadernos de GEDOC (Feb. 1969), 3, quoted ibid. 478.
[84] B. Domingues, 'Dez Anos de Conçílio em Portugal', in *Broteria*, 95 (1972), quoted ibid. 473.
[85] Ibid. 485.   [86] Ibid.

   The failure of the dictatorship to mount even limited resistance to the coup of 25 April 1974 mounted by junior officers, showed how moribund the political system devised by Salazar forty years before, had become. Thrust into the vacant seat of government were officers and civilians who espoused different forms of political radicalism. But the Church was largely ignored perhaps because to Portugal's exultant revolutionaries, it seemed archaic and irrelevant. In the face of a tidal wave of change, the Church leadership was as disorientated as its predecessor had been in 1910 but in the summer of 1975 many priests used the pulpit to urge popular resistance against what seemed like an authentic Bolshevik revolution threatening to tear asunder the Christian character of the country.[87]

   In mid-1975 the Church joined an increasingly powerful coalition that included the democratic left which campaigned to save newly acquired liberties from being extinguished by pro-Communists. Local priests in northern districts blessed crowds which attacked Communist offices and drove out their occupants. By the end of 1975 political gradualists had snatched the reins of power from the divided and incoherent forces of the far left, among whom not a few radical Catholics were to be found.

   The Church could draw some comfort from the findings of an exhaustive sociological study of the role of religion in Portuguese society, published in 1980, which showed that 95 per cent of Portuguese declared themselves to be Roman Catholic and 90 per cent had been baptized in Church.[88] But the low weekly attendance figure of 29 per cent for mass was more indicative of the relevance of the Church in the lives of citizens. Moreover, the ability of the Church to fulfil its customary role was being undermined by the shortage of priests which, in some southern areas, was acute. Between 1957 and 1977 candidates for the priesthood attending senior seminary declined from 1,263 to 348. In terms of religious behaviour, the country remained divided along North–South lines. Mass attendance in the two main northern cities of Oporto and Braga was 35.1 per cent and 50.2 per cent respectively compared with 11.5 per cent in Lisbon. Civil marriages, while only 2.6 per cent of the total in Braga and 8.3 per cent in Oporto, were 43.8 per cent in Lisbon and 58.3 per cent in Setubal.[89]

   A number of factors bound up with the dramatic social and economic changes witnessed in Portugal from the 1960s onwards, have weakened the ability of the Church to shape public attitudes and behaviour patterns even in those areas of the country where its deep implantation had enabled it to withstand persecution. The drift to the cities, the growing influence of foreign ideas and lifestyles popularized by returning emigrants, the decline of a family-based economy, and Portugal's absorption into a consumer-based international economy, have eroded the traditional values which enabled the Church to function as an important national institution. If its loss of

---

[87] Gallagher, 'Peasant Conservatism', 63; id., *Portugal: A Twentieth Century Interpretation*, 219. A description of the lengths which the Archbishop of Braga was prepared to go to in order to unseat the revolutionary order is contained in G. Walraff, *A descoberta de uma conspiração* (Lisbon, 1976).

[88] *Expresso* (24 Dec. 1980).

[89] M. Ferreira and A. J. Cadavez, 'A Hierarquia passou a fornecer a imagem de marca do cristianismo português', *Expresso*, 22 Dec. 1979.

influence and respect has been steeper than in comparable countries such as Spain and Italy, then some of the reasons for this can be found in the compliant role it played in public affairs for most of this century. Catholics were only encouraged to play an innovative role in politics after 1910 when the Church's survival as a viable institution was briefly threatened. Thereafter, the Church fell into the role of being a compliant vassal of an authoritarian regime whose claim to embody Christian values in its governing practice was met by increasing scepticism as its tenure of power lengthened. By the 1950s large numbers of Catholics were coming to realize that the Church was being badly damaged through its close association with a regime notorious for its tolerance of gross inequalities and appetite for repression. But voices which proclaimed that Catholic ascendancy in public affairs had been obtained at the cost of the respect and affection of the most vital elements in society, were stilled by those who could have harnessed their energy in a way that would have strengthened the prestige of the Church. The institutional Church was disinclined to act as a mediator between an isolated, autocratic regime and the popular forces that eventually would overwhelm it. Those in positions of religious authority thought that the New State, with or without Salazar at the helm, was the context in which they would function for the indefinite future. Only the Bishop of Oporto seems to have realized that the Church would have to prepare for more challenging times. If democracy's chance had come in the late 1950s or early 1960s, rather than in 1974, Catholics could have played an important role in defining the shape of the new politics. The Church and its lay offshoots had many public-spirited individuals within its ranks at that time whose dedication to the cause of political and economic justice was shaped by profound religious convictions. But most of them would subsequently channel their energies in other directions as the space in which to express political and social concerns within the church became increasingly circumscribed. The impact of Vatican II was surprisingly muted and even orthodox churchmen keen to see the Church influencing national affairs could see no validity in Portugal following the path of Italy where political Catholicism became a central force following the overthrow of Mussolini.

The verdict of future historians may yet be that fate was more cruel to the Portuguese Church during the deceptively secure Salazar era than in the more challenging times of the secular republic when the entry of Catholic laymen into politics opened up a route followed by Catholics in other European countries but one which had reached a dead end in Portugal before the era of Christian democracy in Europe had properly got under way.

5

Germany

KARL-EGON LÖNNE*

1. The Historical Background

In Germany Catholicism is not simply a religious phenomenon: it has also been a historically significant political force. In strictly numerical terms the importance of Catholicism in Germany since unification in 1870 is clearly illustrated by the following figures: 35 per cent of the population of the Empire (not including Alsace) in 1871 were Catholics, as were 32.4 per cent of the population of the Weimar Republic in 1925, and 44.6 per cent of the population of West Germany in 1970.[1] Numbers are, however, only part of the story. During the later nineteenth century a relatively cohesive political and indeed party-political Catholic movement developed—especially in areas with large Catholic populations in the Rhineland and Westphalia, in Bavaria, and in parts of Franconia and Upper Silesia. In 1870 the establishment of the overwhelmingly Catholic Centre Party (Zentrumspartei) gave this political Catholicism the form which it was to retain until 1933.[2]

German Catholics also formed a broad network of organizations and associations which formed very close links with the Church and the Centre Party and which kept alive an extensive Catholic subculture. Through these organizations German Catholics involved themselves with the wider society. For instance, they responded to endemic social problems through the Kolping-Vereine (Kolping Societies) established in 1851 and the Caritas-Verband (Charity Association) founded in 1897, and worked successfully for socio-political influence with the Catholic Workers' Associations (after 1894), the Christian trade unions, and especially with the People's Union for Catholic Germany (Volksverein für das Katholische Deutschland) founded in 1890. From 1848 annual Katholikentage ('Catholic Day' rallies) provided such organizations and associations with a forum which increasingly involved Centre Party politicians as well as Church leaders.

These institutions arose, in part, in response to a series of challenges to their religious and social status that German Catholics faced in the course of the nineteenth

---

* Translated by Cyprian Blamires.

[1] On the relevant figures see e.g. H. Maier, *Katholizismus und Demokratie* (Freiburg, 1983), 271–86; on East Germany see below.

[2] For further bibliographical material see K.-E. Lönne, *Politischer Katholizismus im 19. und 20. Jahrhundert. Deutschland, Frankreich, Italien* (Frankfurt am Main, 1986), 327–33.

century. The secularization laws of 1803 resulted in the dissolution of the monasteries and the loss of many Catholic educational establishments, deepening a sense of disadvantage amongst Catholics within German society and forcing them to look increasingly to Rome for support and leadership. German unification in 1870, under the auspices of the predominantly Protestant state of Prussia, cut Catholics off from Catholic Austria and increased their alienation. Finally, in the 1870s Imperial Chancellor Bismarck launched his *Kulturkampf* (cultural struggle) against German Catholicism, identifying the Church as a potential focus of opposition to the new state. The *Kulturkampf* met with stiff resistance from the Catholic minority, and was abandoned in the late 1870s, not least because Bismarck began to need the Centre Party's support in the Reichstag.[3] However, the aspersions that he had cast on the national loyalty of German Catholics had a profound impact on their identity well into the twentieth century.

One unexpected result of the *Kulturkampf* was that the Centre Party, to a large extent, became politically representative of German Catholics. Already in the second Reichstag election in 1874 the party had gained 27.9 per cent of the votes and, with 91 deputies, a quarter of the total seats. In the 1870s the party could count on up to 83 per cent of the Catholic vote.[4] Electoral support for the Centre Party thus became an almost plebiscitary expression of the growing sense of solidarity which German Catholics felt with the Church in its battle against the effects of the *Kulturkampf*.

There were always two aspects to the Centre Party: the confessional and the political. As a political party it was open in principle to Protestants as well as Catholics. One result of the *Kulturkampf* was, however, to accentuate the specifically Catholic basis of the party; it was this that became the focal point of party unity and, as such, it created the popular image of the party.[5] This identification of party and religious confession speeded up the consolidation of the Centre Party's support and enabled the party to integrate voters from all points in the very broad Catholic socio-economic spectrum. In this manner it acted as a kind of political brace holding together widely divergent interest groups in its religious and ideological grip.

Yet, though Catholicism was a powerful unifying factor for the party, this also had problematic consequences. Excessive importance, for instance, was attributed to clerics and to the ecclesiastical and papal hierarchy in the formation of the party's demands and policies. In the longer term, the Centre Party became too identified with Catholicism's generally hostile reaction to secularizing trends in society. Ideological rivals such as the Liberals or the Socialists, with whom pragmatic political collaboration was perfectly possible, were increasingly objects of suspicion; and in the case of

---

[3] On the *Kulturkampf* see L. Gall, *Bismarck* (Boston, 1986), ii, 12–39.

[4] R. Morsey, 'Der Kulturkampf', in A. Rauscher (ed.), *Der soziale und politische Katholizismus*, i (Munich, 1981), 126.

[5] On the pre-1914 Centre Party see M. L. Anderson, *Windthorst: A Political Biography* (Oxford, 1981); D. Blackbourn, *Class, Religion and Local Politics in Wilhelmine Germany: The Centre Party in Württemberg before 1914* (New Haven, 1980); R. J. Ross, *Beleaguered Tower: The Dilemma of Political Catholicism in Wilhelmine Germany* (Notre Dame, 1976); E. L. Evans, *The Center Party 1870–1933: A Study in Political Catholicism* (Carbondale, Ill., 1981).

the Communists this developed into outright hatred. In contrast, Fascists and National Socialists often came to seem quite acceptable as allies.

With the end of the *Kulturkampf* the Centre Party was increasingly integrated into the political system of the Empire. On many occasions it was involved in the formation of pro-government majorities in the Reichstag, without, however, ever reaching the point of being able to mount a serious challenge to the leadership claims of Conservatives or Liberals. Instead, the Centre Party was to be persistently drawn towards strengthening the dominance of the Conservatives both in the Empire and in the individual German states. Consequently, the party proved unable to take any decisive step towards overcoming the political exclusion of the Social Democrats (SPD), which became the largest single party in the Reichstag with 110 deputies elected in 1912.

At the outbreak of the First World War, German Catholics fell as much under the spell of the prevailing mood of nationalistic zeal as did their compatriots of other political persuasions and their fellow-Catholics in enemy countries.[6] A Peace Resolution put forward in the Reichstag by one of the Centre Party's leaders, Matthias Erzberger, advocated a negotiated peace and was broadly supported by his party, but its impact was quickly marginalized by political and military developments. The war had a particular appeal to German Catholics in that it offered them an opportunity to prove beyond doubt their loyalty to the nation. In the first waves of war fever, divisions among Catholics were forgotten. In particular, the long-running tension within the Centre Party between the minority of aristocrats and middle classes who had previously monopolized the leadership and those white-collar employees, peasants, and workers who were striving for recognition and influence was temporarily submerged.

This national solidarity soon began to crumble as the anticipated rapid victory failed to materialize and the sheer extent of the sacrifices the population were having to make began to dawn on them. As a result of the unfair distribution of the material burdens of war between the middle and working classes, German society began to polarize rapidly. This proved to be the case even within the Centre Party. The fact that the workers had interests in common diminished the distance between Social Democrats and Christian workers' organizations to such an extent that their involvement in common protests seemed to threaten the independence of the Christian organizations. It was not until the last War Cabinet meeting at the beginning of October 1918 that the political reform process reached a point where the Centre Party together with the Social Democrats and left Liberals could take up the role of a responsible party of government. It exercised this role just long enough for the military élite and politicians of the right to be able to blame it (with some appearance of plausibility) for Germany's final military capitulation in the war. The fact that their leader Erzberger had had the task of signing the Armistice on Germany's behalf at Compiègne in November 1918 made it easier to portray the Centre Party as traitors.

---

[6] H.-J. Scheidgen, *Deutsche Bischöfe im Ersten Weltkrieg* (Cologne, 1991).

Ironically, therefore, the Centre Party reached the apogee of its importance as the un-questioned political voice of German Catholicism in the Hohenzollern Empire just at the moment when that Empire was on the verge of collapse. The party's new posi-tion of apparent strength was thus no more than a cruel illusion.

2. Catholics in Weimar the Republic

The fall of the Hohenzollern Empire was profoundly traumatic for the German na-tion, and for German Catholicism in particular. In the case of political Catholicism, an indication of the depth of this trauma may be found in the fact that its representat-ives initially made no contribution to the political debate concerning the nature of a post-Imperial Germany.[7] The first phase of the Revolution of 1918–19 was almost exclusively inspired by the Independent Social Democrats (USPD) and the Major-ity Social Democrats (MSPD). Initially Centre Party politicians holding high office in the regime simply carried on with the roles which they had filled under the mon-archy. As interior minister, for instance, the Centre Party leader Erzberger fought on single-mindedly to end the war through a negotiated peace. Only in the states of Baden, Württemberg, and Hesse did the leaders of the Centre Party take an active part in the first revolutionary regimes.

Within the party this brief period of inactivity was followed by one of uncertainty. Proposals were put forward in Cologne and Berlin for it to be given a stronger demo-cratic and social character. In Cologne the 'Free German People's Party' was added to the old party title, while in Berlin the party's name was changed to 'Christian Democrat People's Party'. On the other hand, individual conservative Centre Party politicians pressed for it to be transformed into a Christian-Conservative party. On both wings there were proposals to go beyond the former, almost exclusively Cath-olic, character of the party and to set up instead a supra-denominational Christian party. In the case of the Bavarian branch of the Centre Party an earlier trend in favour of regional independence was reinforced and led to its transformation into a separate Bavarian People's Party, dominated by conservative and monarchical elements.

It was crucial for the subsequent development of political Catholicism in Germany that the leadership of the Centre Party finally decided to preserve the party unchanged. They thereby both affirmed their unconditional acceptance of the new constitutional arrangements created by the Revolution and, at the same time, pre-pared to be a part of the new state whose constitution was to be created by a national assembly chosen by universal suffrage. The Centre Party deliberately avoided making a clear-cut stand for or against the monarchy, as such a move would certainly have forced the party's internal divisions out into the open.

These decisions provided the Centre Party with a basis for pursuing its pragmatic policies, encompassing both Erzberger's collaboration with the new authorities as well as the instances of Centre Party participation in individual revolutionary regimes. The decision to remain loyal to the traditional approach of the Centre Party

---

[7] R. Morsey, *Die deutsche Zentrumspartei 1917–1923* (Düsseldorf, 1966).

also meant the abandonment of more expansionist policies, such as the plans (whether under a social-democratic or a national-conservative banner) to widen the party's confessional base.

As far as the leadership were concerned, such radical departures appeared either superfluous or far too ambitious. In Prussia, in particular, the revolutionary socialist regime's hostility to the traditional position of the religious denominations in state and education was forcing political Catholicism to adopt a resolutely defensive posture. This threat encouraged the Centre Party to resort to the tried and trusted appeal to confessional interests. As before, the Centre Party saw its chief task as the best possible defence of the Church's interests in politics and culture. But, though the party remained loyal to its confessional origins, it also made clear its commitment to bringing about a wide-ranging social and political settlement. This would make it possible for the middle classes to collaborate equally with the revolutionary workers represented above all by the SPD and USPD. Such collaboration would also reduce the potential for conflict between proletariat and property-owners, while a policy promoting a strong Germany would be combined with efforts to come to terms with the reality of the defeat in war.

It is clear that the Centre Party's double strategy of preserving denominational interests while seeking to maintain a balance between opposing ideological and social positions also meant that the Centre Party was able to respond effectively to the need to reconcile the very broad range of social and political outlooks represented within its own ranks. The party, therefore, unquestionably played a crucial role in the laborious process of bringing stability to the Weimar Republic. But this stability depended more on bridging over conflicts—or simply ignoring them—than it did on the elaboration of constructive plans that could have prompted the emergence of a new democratic mentality. No truly creative or dynamic power emerged in the party, yet this would have been an essential prerequisite for any powerful impulse to be given to the process of building the Republic.

While the Revolution was a shattering experience for Germany, the origins of the Centre Party's 'balancing act' may, in fact, already be glimpsed in the policies followed by the party during the last years of the war. As early as 1917 the Centre Party had collaborated with the majority SPD and the left-wing liberal Progress Party on an interparty committee. In the 1919 Weimar Assembly the party was quick to cooperate with the MSPD and the newly established left-wing liberal German Democratic Party (DDP) in the so-called Weimar Coalition, in which the Centre Party emerged as one of the leading participants in the discussions about the content of the new constitution.

Bourgeois liberal principles predominated in the Weimar Constitution but the ideas of the Social Democrats also found expression and the latter recognized in the Republic the basis for democratic development in the direction of socialist objectives. The Centre Party therefore performed the considerable service of managing to extract compromises from the opposing parties, as well as making concessions itself. With its help the Weimar state became a parliamentary republic. The Reichstag, chosen by proportional representation, had considerable power within it, and only the political parties were in a position to form majorities on the strength of which chancellors, chosen by the Reich President, were appointed to office.

The Centre Party achieved important confessional objectives in the constitutional discussions on the establishment of equal rights for the religious denominations and on issues of freedom of belief and conscience. It prevented a rigid separation of Church and State which was quite unacceptable to Catholics. Instead, the churches were recognized in public law as corporate institutions enjoying full control over their internal affairs. Church property and State payments to the Church—for example, as compensation for confiscations in the course of secularization—were placed under constitutional guarantee. The right of the churches to raise money and to receive financial support from the State was guaranteed, as were provision for the care of souls in public institutions like the army and hospitals. Religious orders were granted complete and unlimited freedom in respect of their establishment and operations. However, although the Constitution foresaw the provision of a law to give a legal role to parents and guardians in the organization of confessional schools, and this was strongly supported by the Centre Party, proposals for such a law in the Reichstag failed in 1925 and 1927. Nor, in spite of several initiatives, was any concordat established between the Weimar Republic and the Papacy, as the future Pope Pius XII, Eugenio Pacelli, Papal Nuncio in Bavaria and to the Reich government between 1917 and 1929, would have liked. The Papacy managed to conclude concordats only with Bavaria (1924), Prussia (1929), and Baden (1932).

Overall, despite these unfulfilled hopes, the founding of the Weimar Republic brought clear improvements for Catholics on confessional issues. None the less, Catholics did not develop any close bond with the Republic. What occurred instead was a weakening of the influence within the Catholic community of the Centre Party, which now had to content itself with a much-reduced proportion of the Catholic vote. Even the introduction of votes for women did not counter this trend, despite the fact that the party's female supporters outnumbered the men at the polls by 3 to 2. In 1920 the Centre Party still attracted only 13.6 per cent of the votes (19.7 per cent when combined with the votes of the Bavarian People's Party) and in 1932 (the last free Reichstag elections) it received 11.9 per cent.

This decline in Catholic support was not the only factor behind the decline of the Centre Party. Its claim to be the sole political mouthpiece for German Catholics was further brought into question, first by the secession of its Bavarian state association as the more right-wing Bavarian People's Party (BVP); secondly because of the existence of a grouping of conservative Catholics within the German National People's Party (DNVP), which was attracting the support of 6–8 per cent of Catholic voters; and finally on account of the emergence of the Christian Social Party under Vitus Heller—though this was in fact minimally successful.[8]

It is, therefore, only with some reservations that we can equate the Centre Party with political Catholicism in the Weimar Republic. Even so, the Centre Party turned

[8] W. Fritsch, 'Christlich-soziale Reichspartei', in D. Fricke *et al.*, *Lexikon*, i (Leipzig, 1983), 440 ff.

political Catholicism into a major force. Its considerable influence is illustrated by the fact that out of the twenty cabinets of the Weimar period up to the appointment of Hitler as Chancellor on 30 January 1933 ten were led by Centre Party politicians. These cabinets had a variety of different political configurations, ranging from the 'Weimar Coalition' of SPD, DDP, and Centre, through coalitions of the right, to presidential cabinets (backed by emergency decree of the Reich President). Furthermore, the Centre Party—or at least individual Centre Party politicians—were involved in every single cabinet with the exception of those led by von Papen (from June to December 1932), von Schleicher (from December 1932 to January 1933), and that of Hitler established in January 1933.[9]

Thus under the Weimar Republic the Centre Party represented an extremely important force for political integration. But the widely differing configurations of the cabinets in which it participated ensured that, while it could offer political stability, it was unable to provide clear political leadership. Instead, the strength of the Centre Party lay much more in its ability to hold opposites in equilibrium and to build bridges between them. This was particularly important in the area of economic policy. Under the influence of Christian trade-unionist and Centre Party politician Adam Stegerwald, the Central Labour Association for the organization of a new collaboration between employers and workers came into being. Moreover, the Centre Party deputy Heinrich Braun, one of the most important spokesmen for the socio-political policies of the People's Union for Catholic Germany,[10] held the position of minister of labour without a break through twelve cabinets between 1920 and 1928. During his period in office he was responsible for the most important socio-political achievement of the Weimar Republic—unemployment insurance—even though this played only a limited role in attenuating the ensuing economic crisis.

The open and pluralistic Weimar regime supported by the Centre Party was increasingly under threat from the right. After their success in the election of September 1930, the National Socialists (NSDAP) subjected the Centre Party first of all to verbal threats and then to actual violence. But the party lacked sufficient resolution to make common cause against this violence with any other political forces. Its vulnerability was cruelly exposed as it was forced to accept increasingly artificial restrictions on fundamental democratic freedoms within the presidential system. These concessions were an inevitable consequence of its reluctance to look for allies on the left to help to defend democracy, or to countenance the state-imposed dissolution of the Nazi Party.

As the right grew more powerful so the centre of gravity of political Catholicism shifted increasingly in that direction. Coalitions with the DNVP in 1925 and 1927 had already presaged a rightward shift. In addition, after the election of Prelate Kaas

---

[9] K. Ruppert, *Im Dienst am Staat von Weimar* (Düsseldorf, 1992); U. von Hehl, *Wilhelm Marx 1863–1946* (Mainz, 1987). On Weimar political developments see e.g. E. Kolb, *The Weimar Republic* (Boston, 1988), 1–126.

[10] The People's Union was a mass organization with more than 100,000 members which provided organization and training for local Catholic officials and trade-unionists.

as party chairman in 1928, instead of either Stegerwald (as representative of the German Trades Union Congress) or Josef Joos (as spokesman for the Catholic Workers' Associations), important social interests remained without a voice. With the election of Kaas, who as a cleric stood above social conflicts, a much more successful attempt was made to strengthen the confessional coherence of the Centre Party and to gloss over complex social problems instead of addressing them. As it shifted to the right the Centre Party now fitted even more comfortably than before into the general system of the Weimar Republic. It had less reason than ever to take account of the point of view of its working-class electorate and the features of the Centre Party which might have blocked any further rightward shift in the Weimar Republic's political and ideological focus were all eliminated in advance.

The Centre Party's character as a confessional party necessarily led it to be more alienated by the pluralist atmosphere of the Weimar Republic than would have been the case if it had become a party focused on immediate social and economic concerns. The latter approach would have prompted the Centre Party to opt for some form of collaboration with the Social Democrats. Instead, its justified anxieties about its own inner cohesiveness and future ability to manœuvre, as well as its growing alarm about social trends (most notably the spread of secularization) were all factors which acted as very unfortunate influences on the way the Centre Party operated in the final crisis phase of the Weimar Republic.

These difficulties prompted a number of demands for the adoption of alternative political strategies. As early as 1918 Adam Stegerwald argued very strongly for a broader-based Centre Party boosted by an appeal to Protestants, something which had in theory been envisaged since the party's foundation. As a representative of Christian trade unions and a member of the Centre Party, Stegerwald played a crucial role in the establishment of the German Trades Union Congress (Deutsche Gewerkschaftsbund) and was its chairman for many years. This was a Christian and national bourgeois worker and white-collar organization which emerged as a competitor to the Social Democratic trade unions in the Weimar period.

In November 1920 Stegerwald used his trade-union position to press for the creation of a single moderate Christian party that would be German, Christian, democratic, and social.[11] He based his argument on the existence of a gulf between the Centre Party's task of acting as mediator in the party system and its actual sociopolitical composition which, he argued, made it quite inadequate to perform such a role. Stegerwald considered it essential that there be a moderate party with the power to hold opposites in equilibrium while at the same time providing a source of political and social creativity.

Stegerwald believed that the moderate party he was endorsing would appeal not only to all levels in the Centre Party but also to the liberal bourgeois and the conservative parties close to it, the DVP and the DNVP, as well as the diverse membership of the Deutsche Gewerkschaftsbund; the hope was that such a moderate party would attract them to the centre of the party political spectrum and hold them there.

[11] A. Stegerwald, *Deutsche Lebensfragen* (Berlin, 1921).

This was not to be simply an enlarged and strengthened Centre Party. Social and economic cooperation between all groups in society with the rejection of both social-ist and capitalist claims to hegemony was to be presented as an alternative to social democracy. In order to achieve this co-operation, Stegerwald emphasized the re-sponsibility of the national state to encourage social integration and to provide leadership.

In making his proposal Stegerwald took account of the fact that the Centre Party was simply overstretched by the role it needed to perform in the parliamentary Republic. But it seems very doubtful whether the non-socialist middle-class ele-ments Stegerwald considered essential to the new party would have accepted the stabilizing and positive role he had planned for them in the new state. In 1920 the hardening of bourgeois parties against social democracy was a theme which still made a powerful impact in German bourgeois circles. It would, anyway, hardly have been able permanently to neutralize the hostility to the Republic endemic in the bourgeoisie, given the emotionally charged response of the whole nation—including Catholics—to the Versailles Treaty. From this point of view an appeal to a supra-confessional Christianity was not likely to make much headway, for the Protestants were more ready to console themselves for the fall of the monarchy by resorting to a new assertive nationalist consciousness. It has also rightly been pointed out that Stegerwald cherished visions of a hierarchical state which were not in the least likely to win the middle classes over to the democratic republic. On the contrary they were calculated to induce entirely contrary sentiments.[12] Although a failure in its own time, the emergence of the Christian Union parties (CDU and CSU) immediately after the Second World War demonstrates the prophetic quality of Stegerwald's vision of a pan-confessional Christian party.

Stegerwald was not the only figure looking for a more powerful and creative altern-ative to the Centre Party's policy of pragmatism and compromise. A broadly similar democratic and republican tone was set by Joseph Wirth, who was associated with South German Catholicism and liberal traditions. He wanted to go beyond the atti-tude of resigned acceptance of the Weimar Republic and hoped to attract new voters to the party by a marked democratic and republican reorientation in its policies. In 1922 when he was chancellor of the Reich Wirth saw all too clearly the damage being done to the Republic by its enemies on the nationalistic right. A prime example was the murder of his Jewish Foreign Minister Walter Rathenau. In mounting his counter-attack, however, Wirth set his sights way beyond the circle of those directly responsible for the murder; he took as his target the nationalistic anti-republican and anti-democratic forces that had recently developed both in the DNVP and in the DVP. But his strategy also brought him into confrontation with certain elements within German Catholicism and the German episcopate. It was, after all, quite nat-ural that Catholics, discredited in the *Kulturkampf* as enemies of the Reich, should wholeheartedly associate themselves with national protest movements of the time;

[12] H. Lutz, *Demokratie im Zwielicht: Der Weg der deutschen Katholiken aus dem Kaiserreich in die Republik 1914–25* (Munich, 1963), 100.

and that in doing so they should quite often have adopted strongly nationalistic, revisionist, and anti-Republican postures.[13]

Nevertheless, Wirth repeatedly rejected all collaboration with the DNVP and called vociferously for a full-blooded alliance with all the forces of the moderate left. This approach met with little favour either in German Catholicism or in his own party, and frequently aroused bitter repudiation. For many years he enjoyed the support of the Catholic Workers' Associations but he did not succeed in developing a reliable power base in them for himself and his policies. Wirth was supported by the *Rhein-Mainische Volkszeitung*, a paper belonging to Friedrich Dessauer.[14] Dessauer combined a successful career as physicist and industrialist with an intense political commitment to the Centre Party group in the Reichstag. He gathered around him at his paper a dedicated team of young journalists and fully supported their aim of giving a definite social and republican character to the Centre Party. His regional paper developed into a national daily with a wide readership among young Catholic intellectuals, following Wirth's political line even after Wirth had discredited himself through numerous stubborn and clumsily fought battles with his party. This circle also argued that the Centre Party should weaken its confessional dimension. The party's emphasis on questions relating to ideology and ecclesiastical politics meant that general problems about socio-political and economic development were pushed into the background, and there was certainly no attempt by them to make such issues the driving-force of party-political activity, as the circle around Dessauer had wished.

In fact, the Republic and the parliamentary democratic system were widely taken for granted. The Centre Party took its stand on the new reality that had resulted from the revolution but generally made no effort at any serious debate about the actual historical legitimacy of the process. German Catholicism, therefore, missed a precious opportunity to identify with the ideals and practical political potential of the new democratic state and hence to make a complete emotional commitment to the creation of the Weimar Republic. A further obstacle was the Papacy's ambivalent attitude towards democracy.[15] Indeed, it was all too clear that, although the Weimar Republic could certainly expect help from the Papacy in its confrontation with the threat of communism and revolution, Rome's willingness to identify with it would be limited to a cool recognition of its *de facto* existence.[16]

German political Catholicism could not even derive much comfort or encouragement from the general state of contemporary Catholicism either at home or in the wider world. An important trend in German Catholicism in the 1920s was an emerging mood of spiritual renewal which diminished the importance of political and social issues and had a tendency to discriminate against democratic politics. A significant example of this is Quickborn and the newspaper he created, *Die Schildgenossen*

---

[13] For convincing examples see ibid.

[14] H. Blankenberg, *Politischer Katholizismus in Frankfurt a. M. 1918–1933* (Mainz, 1981).

[15] H. Lutz, *Katholizismus und Faschismus* (Düsseldorf, 1970); K.-E. Lönne, 'Heinrich Lutz und Franz Schnabel: Zwei Historiker unter den Eindruch der deutschen Katastrophe', in *Die Einheit der Neuzeit: Zum historischen Werk von Heinrich Lutz* (Vienna, 1988), 18–47.

[16] E. Fattorini, *Germania e santa sede* (Bologna, 1992).

(Companions of the Shield). Quickborn was one of the leaders of the Catholic youth movement who had come under the influence of Romano Guardini and who had stimulated a mood of religious and liturgical renewal in many local Catholic groups. This had exercised considerable influence over Catholic élites. In political terms Quickborn weakened the democratic tendency in Catholicism and instead the journal favoured an authoritarian and élitist view of the State.[17] This journal believed it possessed the means to lift itself above sordid and mundane party-political interests and to create a new form of state governed by the common good. Along with contempt for conflicts of social interests went veneration for a glorified state authority. An ecclesiastical community and a society impregnated with Christian values stood at the forefront of their concerns.

This new spiritual enthusiasm also affected the attitudes of many Catholics towards the numerous Catholic associations and organizations, which had hitherto been seen as instruments of their socio-political mobilization and influence. These now looked to many Catholics to be no more than a vehicle for the protection of their vested interests. The People's Union for Catholic Germany—hitherto an inspirational and educative influence on the leadership of the Workers' Associations, Christian trade unions, and societies—was not unaffected by this new climate of hostility to the associations and organizations and managed thereby to undermine its own influence.[18]

The young Republic received benevolent support from papal diplomacy in numerous moments of foreign-policy crisis in the post-war era. But in the long term this support had less influence on Catholics than decisions taken by the Papacy concerning matters of ecclesiastical organization, even though the effects of the latter on politics were only indirect. Thus, the general intention behind the creation of Catholic Action in the 1920s was a reinvigoration of religious energies and a concentration of all Catholic initiatives and organizations in parish communities. On the recommendation of the Pope, Catholic Action was transplanted to Germany after having developed on an entirely different basis in Italy. Although the ideals of Catholic Action were not widely or systematically established in Germany, it did help to distance Catholic associations from socio-political problems. By concentrating on the religious as the principal sphere of activity, Catholic Action strengthened tendencies already present that were antagonistic to a broad politicization of Catholics.

When the socio-political system of the Weimar Republic entered a new crisis in the late 1920s, the nature of the Centre Party as a constitutional party offered no obstacle to the actions of the Centre Party Chancellor Heinrich Brüning. He employed an excessive extension of the Reich President's emergency powers in order to bring in creeping changes to the constitution which resulted in a crucial strengthening of

[17] H. Lutz, *Politischer Katholizismus*, 110–17. Confirmation may be found in A.-B. Gerl, *Romano Guardini 1885–1968* (Mainz, 1985), 199–204; from the wider perspective of Guardini's later development L. Wetzal (*Das Politische bei Romano Guardini* (Percha, 1987), 158) comes to the conclusion that in his handling of democracy Guardini simply ignored the reality of it.
[18] H. Hürten, *Deutsche Katholiken 1918–1945* (Paderborn, 1992).

the State and the executive. Brüning's policy, and the support he received from the Centre Party, made it clear that a large proportion of Catholics (as was the case—even more strikingly—with the majority of their Protestant fellow-citizens) were not defending the Republic unreservedly, but saw it rather as open to change in fundamental areas of its constitution.

A further indication of the uncertain attitude of German Catholics towards the parliamentary democratic Republic was the attitude of German political Catholicism to the rise of Italian Fascism. The German Catholic press had, initially, warmly welcomed the foundation of the Italian People's Party (PPI) and criticized Fascist attacks on it in the early 1920s. However, the Fascist regime's willingness to make concessions to Church interests, and especially the Lateran Treaty, cast it in a favourable light in comparison with the Weimar regime. By the time that some Catholics began to realize that a similar fate awaited their party as had already befallen the PPI, it was already too late.

In conclusion, it can be stated that under the Weimar Republic, although the Centre Party continued to see itself as the voice of political Catholicism, it failed to create any clear political image for itself, and lost much of its former political dynamism. The party wasted significant opportunities to develop a definite new political orientation. It thereby retained its solid confessional foundation while remaining in thrall to the tradition of a party integrated on confessional lines, a tradition that was gradually losing its appeal.

3. Political Catholicism and National Socialism

At the elections of September 1930 the National Socialist German Workers' Party (NSDAP) grew from being a splinter group with 2.6 per cent of the votes into the second largest body in the Reichstag with 18.3 per cent of the votes and 107 deputies. It had overtaken not only the Centre Party with its 68 deputies but even the Centre Party and BVP combined with their total of 87 seats in the Reichstag—although by this stage the BVP cannot really be considered alongside the Centre Party as it had moved markedly further to the right. Neither the Centre Party nor the BVP was directly affected by this political earthquake since both maintained their share of the vote more or less unchanged. But the preferred centre-right coalition partners of the Centre Party, the DDP and the DVP, as well as the SPD—the left-wing coalition partner of the early years of the Weimar Republic as well as between 1928 and 1930, and of the important Prussian coalition regime—had all suffered substantial losses. The erstwhile right bourgeois partner of the Centre Party, the DNVP, was reduced to less than half of its previous share of the vote.

The self-destructive indecision and disunity of their political rivals gave the Nazis evermore opportunity to mock and discredit the existing order. Intractable opponents like the Communists and Social Democrats were provoked and wherever possible were deliberately humiliated and intimidated. Enthusiastically provoking a situation close to civil war, while unemployment climbed above 6 million by 1932, the National Socialists presented themselves to the upper and lower middle classes as a new force for order that was ready and able to help Germany regain domestic peace, revive the economy, rid herself of the consequences of the war, and recover the respect of the international community. To many supporters of other parties—to the Communists for example with regard to the Social Democrats, the hope of seeing opponents defeated by the National Socialists was stronger than any fear of danger to themselves resulting from the latter's growing power.[19]

There can be no doubt as to the atmosphere of mutual hostility which existed between the Centre Party–BVP and the NSDAP. While the Nazis denounced the Centre Party as belonging amongst the 'November traitors', their own violence and demagogy appalled the Centre Party. The strategy adopted by them in response was to attempt to neutralize the threat until the disappearance of the Nazis, which was assumed to be only a matter of time, by taming them, where possible, through temporary collaboration. Centre Party politicians took comfort from their long experience of dealing with difficult coalition partners. This view received some confirmation from the fact that the combination of traditional party-political attachment and Church hostility to National Socialism enabled the Centre Party and the BVP to retain their traditional support in the teeth of the apparently irresistible rise of the National Socialists. But, like all the other political forces, the Catholics underestimated the threat from these new rivals. In spite of the temporary consolidation of its vote, political Catholicism would not be able to maintain a strong identity in the face of the rapidly growing Nazi threat without reliable allies. This consideration ought to have led the Centre Party to consider at least a tactical alliance with the SPD. There was a precedent for such an alliance in the existing cooperative arrangement with the SPD in Prussia, which also involved a remnant of the left-liberal bourgeoisie in the shape of the DDP.[20] The *Rhein-Mainische Volkszeitung* and especially its contributor Walter Dirks gave vigorous support and backing to the idea of a close collaboration between the Centre Party and the SPD with the tactical goal of blocking the National Socialists. Dirks advocated these ideas in numerous other newspapers without, however, winning over a majority of Catholic opinion. The distinctive feature of Dirks' opposition to Nazism was that he recognized more clearly than anybody else that Catholic middle-class opinion was also susceptible to Nazi ideology—even though Nazism was, as events would demonstrate, hostile to Catholic interests.

Starting with an analysis of contemporary society, Dirks outlined an ideal of a 'sozialen Volksstaates' (social people's state) in which the negative political and social consequences of capitalism, which he believed underlay the widespread trend towards fascism, could be overcome.

The only socio-political ideal that can positively counterbalance the ideal of fascism is that of socialism—at least in its pure form, cleansed of the impurities accumulated in the course of party [i.e. the SPD's] development. What is needed if the spectre of fascism is to be banished

[19] K.-E. Lönne, *Faschismus als Herausforderung: Die Auseinandersetzung von 'Roter Fahne' und 'Vorwärts' mit dem italienischen Faschismus* (Cologne, 1981).

[20] H. Hömig, *Das Preussische Zentrum in der Weimarer Republik* (Mainz, 1979).

is an alliance between the ideal of this pure form of socialism and the power of the faith of Christendom. Catholicism, as the only possible focus for the mobilization of the religious powers of Christendom in the great arena of politics, is particularly called to bring about such an alliance.[21]

The critical attitude of the Centre Party and the BVP was echoed and strengthened by the widespread rejection of National Socialism within the Church. The episcopal authorities in Mainz even went so far as to exclude enrolled members of the NSDAP from the sacrament. Its decision was grounded in the anti-Christian character of National Socialism, which the episcopal authorities noted, for example, in Nazi racial ideas as formulated in the NSDAP programme:

The Christian moral law is founded on love for our neighbour. National Socialist writers do not accept this commandment in the sense taught by Christ; they preach too much respect for the Germanic race and too little respect for foreign races. For many what begins as mere lack of respect ends up as full-blown hatred of foreign races and it is unchristian and uncatholic. Moreover the Christian moral law is universal and valid for all times and races: so there is a gross error in requiring that the Christian faith be suited to the moral sentiments of the Germanic race.[22]

The same message was set out in a declaration by the Bavarian bishops. This also included criticism of National Socialism's hostility to the Concordat, its preference for non-denominational schooling, and its excessively nationalistic thinking; these were condemned as traits strongly reminiscent of the *Kulturkampf*. Any possibility of debate with the political ideals of National Socialism was expressly ruled out. In retrospect however it must said that even in this document the rejection of National Socialism was worded somewhat cautiously, and that room was left for the possibility of compromise, a possibility that Hitler was able to exploit after his seizure of power.[23]

In general in the early 1930s the Centre Party overlooked, or at least underestimated, the special characteristics of National Socialism and overestimated the strength of its own position in relation to it. The party believed that it could control National Socialism with the tried and tested methods of coalition politics. The Church's condemnation of National Socialism did not stand in the way of such a policy as it was fundamentally directed against the religious and moral errors of the National Socialists and went hand in hand with an awareness that the latter shared the Church's hostility to Marxism. The Church's points of dispute could be toned down in a pragmatic coalition policy such as had previously been allowed to the Centre Party by the Church in respect of other parties. In fact no such coalition ever developed, and Hitler succeeded instead in his quest for the post of Reich chancellor by forming a coalition with the conservative DNVP. Against its will and in spite of earlier negotiations the Centre Party was excluded from the new coalition regime, so it was never able to put its ideas about taming National Socialism to the test.

21 W. Dirks, *Gegen die faschistische Koalition: Politische Publizistik 1930–1933* (Zürich, 1990).
22 H. Müller (ed.), *Katholische Kirche und Nationalsozialismus* (Munich, 1965), 170.
23 K. Scholder, *Die Kirchen und das Dritte Reich*, ĩ (Frankfurt, 1977).

When in March 1933 the Reich President allowed the Nazi-led minority cabinet to seek a majority at the polls, Hitler seized the opportunity to influence the result in favour of the National Socialists by trickery and violence. Even so, the proportion of the vote won by the Centre Party and the BVP was only very slightly reduced, and the Centre Party was even able to win additional votes. It was only by combining the 43.9 per cent of National Socialist votes with the 8 per cent of votes gained by the DNVP that Hitler's regime was able to obtain an absolute majority in the Reichstag.

It was only because the regime sought dictatorial plenary powers by means of an Enabling Law that the Centre Party re-emerged in a key position, as its votes were necessary for the two-thirds majority required for passing it. In negotiations the Centre Party put forward a catalogue of demands that Hitler promised to fulfil, publicly confirming his promise in his speech proposing the Enabling Law. These demands had both a cultural content—a guarantee of continuing Christian influence in schools and education, respect for the state concordats with the Papacy and for the rights of the Christian confessions—and a constitutional and public law content— the preservation of the position of Reich President, retention of the Reichstag and the Reichsrat, a guarantee of continued existence for the states and of the independence of the judiciary. The Centre Party would have achieved an unquestionable success if Hitler's public statements had been trustworthy. This was precisely what a minority of Centre Party deputies doubted, passionately opposing acceptance of the measure and abandoning their opposition only for the sake of the unity of their political grouping.

It was no accident that in the published version of Hitler's speech on the occasion of the introduction of the Enabling Law, a sentence of great importance for Catholics was left out of the text: 'The national government will encourage and entrench the influence properly exercised by the Christian confessions in schooling and education.'[24] This omission was a sign that even as the concessions to the Centre Party were being made, discussions were under way on how to restrict their scope as far as possible.

In considering the arguments for the ultimate acceptance by the Centre Party and BVP of the Enabling Law, the atmosphere of tyranny and terror in which the National Socialist regime was operating must be taken into account. Centre Party deputies were subjected to intimidation. The temporary home of the Reichstag, the Kroll Opera House, was surrounded by armed SA and SS troops, and after the Communist deputies had been illegally arrested no one knew whether these forces would respect the immunity of the Assembly. Centre Party deputies were worried about rejecting the Enabling Law to the extent that such a rejection would be interpreted as a declaration of war against National Socialist domination, with the likely consequence that Hitler would simply pursue his goals by force without legal powers. Among the members of the Centre Party the sight of public officials being dismissed from their jobs and arrested had given rise to widespread anxiety and fear.

---

[24] H. Müller (ed.), *Katholische Kirche*, 84.

Thus, in accepting the Enabling Law, the Centre Party was bowing to enormously strong political and psychological pressure. The result showed political Catholicism, represented by the deputies who had been chosen in a hard-fought electoral battle with National Socialism, co-operating in an apparently legal extension of the powers of the Hitler regime. While this regime thereby gained additional means of power and prestige there remained no real possibility of subjecting it to constitutional restraints. The consequent general feeling of despair within Centre Party ranks eventually drove some individuals and groups to move closer to the Nazi regime or even simply to go over to National Socialism.

The disintegration of the Centre Party was accelerated by a fresh episcopal statement on National Socialism which has subsequently provoked a wide range of reactions ranging from astonishment to emphatic condemnation. After the passing of the Enabling Law on 23 March, the Fulda Bishops' Conference issued a declaration on 28 March that redefined the Church's relationship to National Socialism. In contrast to the earlier rejection of National Socialism by the Church this declaration signalled an abrupt change of position, acknowledging the new facts of power relations in Germany and making the support and preservation of this regime a matter of duty for Catholics.[25] Acceptance of this new relationship was imposed on Catholics out of a blinkered preoccupation with the protection of the interests and cultural concerns of the Church, while the warning against 'illegal or subversive behaviour' offered no hope for opposing the destruction of the legal order of the Weimar Republic.

Although no direct connection between the Bishops' Declaration and the plans for a concordat made a little later has so far been proved, there cannot be any real doubt that the new attitude of the German bishops made the Concordat negotiations a great deal easier. These began in Rome at the beginning of April 1933 and continued with various interruptions until 8 July (three days after the dissolution of the Centre Party) when an agreement was signed by the Papacy and the Nazi regime, opening the way for a potential understanding between National Socialists and Catholicism.

With its general veto on any clergy participation in political activities the Concordat finally confirmed the already *de facto* marginalization of political Catholicism. The clergy had played an important role in the Centre Party and the BVP in the late 1920s and early 1930s, and the active collaboration which had developed between the party and the parish priests had been its greatest strength.

---

25 Ibid. 88 ff.: 'It must now be recognized that solemn public declarations have been made by the highest representative of the Reich government, who is at the same time the authoritative leader of this movement, guaranteeing the Church's right to teach the Catholic faith as well as her right to carry out her other tasks. In addition, the full validity of treaties made by individual German states with the Church has been expressly affirmed by the Reich government. Without going back on the condemnation of specific moral and religious errors contained in our earlier declarations the episcopate is therefore satisfied that the aforesaid general prohibitions and warnings do not need to be repeated. There is no need at the present juncture to make any special exhortation to Catholic Christians, for whom the voice of the Church is holy, to be loyal to their legally established sovereign and to carry out their civil duties conscientiously, eschewing absolutely any illegal or subversive behaviour.' See also E. C. Helmreich, *The German Churches under Hitler: Background, Struggle, Epilogue* (Detroit, 1979), 237–240.

The question of how to assess the value of the Concordat for the position of Catholicism under the Third Reich has been a matter of intense scholarly debate.[26] On the positive side it needs to be remembered that the Concordat accorded the Church the freedom to pursue its spiritual activities while at the same time providing it with a legal basis for the defence of Church associations and publications. However, the Concordat associated the Church with a regime which had already shown that it had not the least respect for right or law. The Nazis clearly intended to exploit the prestige of the Catholic Church for their own purposes,[27] and, at the same time, to limit the independence of Catholic citizens as much as possible.

This objection is still valid even if one accepts that for the National Socialists the Concordat agreement was primarily intended to undermine political Catholicism and that, strictly speaking, Hitler gained nothing from it since political Catholicism had already collapsed before the signing of the Treaty.[28] The mere knowledge that such negotiations were taking place was sufficient to undermine German political Catholicism. In this sense Hitler was rewarded in advance for the Concordat.

Nor were the freedoms which the Concordat granted to German Catholics for the propagation of their faith of any great significance. These legal guarantees only retained their value as long as the Nazis felt obliged by the pressures of the domestic and international situation to honour them. Moreover, the very doubtful value of these advantages has to be balanced against the fact that the conclusion of the treaty gave added legitimacy at home and abroad to the Nazi regime. As a contemporary witness later commented:

German Catholics—and the whole Catholic world—were in the position that they had a kind of moral obligation to believe that a compromise would be possible with National Socialism at least in the future. They had to hope that the (still evolving) movement was ultimately on the way to improvement.[29]

The Concordat strengthened the illusions of right-wing Catholics such as the all-party 'the Cross and the Eagle' movement.[30] Although patronage of this movement was taken over by the then vice-chancellor Franz von Papen, its hope of influencing the Third Reich in the direction of conservative Christian and authoritarian hierarchical values remained unfulfilled. The dissolution of the movement in the autumn of 1934 set the seal on the failure of an initiative based on the false assumption that there existed a readiness for co-operation on the part of the National Socialists.

---

[26] Scholder, *Die Kirche und das Dritte Reich*; see also id., *Die Kirchen zwischen Republik und Gewaltherrschaft* (Berlin, 1988); K. Repgen, *Von der Reformation zur Gegenwart* (Paderborn, 1988). E. C. Helmreich, *German Churches*, 240–273.

[27] For Hitler's attitude towards the Lateran Treaties see Scholder, *Die Kirche und das Dritte Reich*, 488 ff.

[28] On the internal and external collapse of the Centre see R. Morsey, *Der Untergang des politischen Katholizismus: Die Zentrumspartei zwischen christlichem Selbstverständnis und nationaler Erhebung 1932/3* (Stuttgart, 1977), 207.

[29] F. Muckermann, *Im Kampf zwischen zwei Epochen* (Mainz, 1973), 584.

[30] K. Breuning, *Die Vision des Reiches* (Munich, 1969).

With the benefit of hindsight, the Bishops' Declaration, the conclusion of the Concordat, and the quest for a working relationship with the regime must be seen as a product of the state of mind of German Catholicism which arose from its distinctive historical experience.[31] Three factors were of particular importance: first a sense of alienation from the modern state and society together with a tendency (strengthened by the experience of the *Kulturkampf*) for the Church to withdraw into its own religious sphere; secondly, a preoccupation with the defence of religion, church, and school as the crucial arbiters of political policy; and finally a deeply rooted antiliberalism, which sealed off Catholic thinking from the developing movement towards parliamentary-democratic models of government. This antiliberalism seemed to make the authoritarian defeat of modern individualism in state and society desirable and therefore gave Catholicism an affinity with authoritarian regimes.

Something of this kind of attitude was apparent in the conduct of the leading clerical representatives of German Catholicism in helping, objectively if not intentionally, to stabilize National Socialist hegemony in the decisive phase of its development after March 1933. This meant that as soon as the inevitable conflicts and controversies arose between the Church and the regime, they were limited almost exclusively to the defence of the ecclesiastical and institutional positions of the Church rather than to any broader political and moral principles. Nor should it be forgotten that National Socialism had its supporters even among Catholics at home and abroad, including both the laity and priests.[32]

From the point of view of the Papacy the development of the Church and of Catholicism in society was to be secured independently of that society through the conclusion of a concordat between the Church and the State. As far as the Papacy was concerned, the National Socialist state was viewed as a legal sovereign rather than as an apparatus for the oppression of the socio-political forces opposed to it. The capacity of Church and Catholicism to be an active force in society was progressively paralysed by the increasing number of measures taken against the activities of Church associations, against the Catholic press, and against confessional schools. Moreover, by means of constant supervision they also attempted to prevent the clergy from uttering any word of criticism of the regime, as well as to seal them off as much as possible from the faithful in order to minimize their influence.

At the same time the fundamentals of Catholic teaching were attacked through the propagation of a racist substitute religion as expounded in Alfred Rosenberg's *Mythus des 20. Jahrhunderts* (Myth of the Twentieth Century). In addition, a propaganda campaign against the religious orders was mounted with a view to discrediting the clergy and thereby undermining the inner cohesion of the Church.[33] During the war new measures were introduced for the confiscation of monastic and Church property. Not even in the midst of war was there any let-up in the oppressive strategy

[31] E.-W. Böckenförde, *Der Deutsche Katholizismus im Jahre 1933: Mit einem historiographischen Rückblick von K.-E. Lönne* (Freiburg, 1988).

[32] See the numerous examples in Muckermann, *Im Kampf*.

[33] H.-G. Hockerts, *Die Sittlichkeitsprozesse gegen katholische Ordensangehörige und Priester 1936/7* (Mainz, 1971).

and indeed the high tide of anti-Church measures had not yet been reached, as was indicated by the annihilation methods employed during the war against other unwanted groups such as Jews and the mentally handicapped.

Catholics were still able to carry on a war of ideas against Rosenberg's anti-Christian campaign in the pages of an assortment of Catholic publications.[34] But the Church never found any effective means of coping with the torrent of oppressive government measures. Together with the Vatican, the German episcopate, and especially the President of the Fulda Bishops' Conference, Cardinal Bertram, exploited the legal rights guaranteed by the Concordat to make numerous futile written protests against the encroachments on Church privileges. In 1937 the papal encyclical *Mit brennender Sorge*, brought to the attention of the faithful by public readings from church pulpits, was the occasion for a stirring protest against anti-Church policies and the whole totalitarian system of National Socialism; but it had no power to stem the tide of Nazi aggression.

This encyclical did, however, make an important contribution to the growing awareness of Catholics. It helped them to evade the totalitarian claims of National Socialism, at least in the essential sphere of their Christian faith, for, along with its complaints about the oppression of the Church, it contained a detailed defence of the content of the Catholic religion.[35] Catholicism's spirit of independence was always at least potentially subversive of National Socialist domination. This emerges clearly from reports by the state authorities on the situation of the Church in Bavaria.[36] But the bishops limited themselves to written complaints and their public silence amounted to an abandonment of any real attempt to mobilize the heightened awareness of Catholics against the regime or even against any of its individual measures. On the other hand, the sermons of the Bishop of Münster, Clemens August Graf von Galen, did make a considerable impact with their condemnation of the euthanasia policy launched by the Nazi regime in 1942. Copies of the text of the sermons were passed secretly from hand to hand and precipitated a partial cessation of the programme.

However, even within the episcopate, the desire for a more energetic opposition was thwarted and none of the proposed comprehensive condemnations of the regime ever saw the light of day. The episcopal sense of solidarity meant that no individual bishop was prepared to speak out on his own account against the numerous appalling crimes perpetrated by the regime. Indeed, with total inappropriateness, the President of the Fulda Bishops' Conference, Cardinal Bertram, actually sent birthday greetings to Hitler. How could individual Catholics find the strength for refusal, for public dissent, or protest against the crimes of the National Socialists or indeed

[34] R. Baumgärtner, *Weltanschauungskampf im Dritten Reich* (Mainz, 1977).

[35] For the text see D. Albrecht (ed.), *Der Notenwechsel zwischen dem Heiligen Stuhl und der Deutschen Reichsregierung*, i (Mainz, 1965), 404–43.

[36] 'Die kirchliche Lage in Bayern nach den Regierungspräsidentenberichten 1933–1943', *Veröffentlichungen der Kommission für Zeitgeschichte bei der katholischen Akademie in Bayern*, Reihe A: Quellen: Bde 3, 8, 14, 16, 24, 31, 32. On popular Catholic attitudes to Nazism in Bavaria see also I. Kershaw, *Popular Opinion and Political Dissent in the Third Reich: Bavaria 1933–1945* (Oxford, 1983).

ultimately for martyrdom, if individual bishops and indeed the majority of the episcopate never once felt able to follow their consciences instead of sticking passively to
a policy of solidarity with their colleagues?

In spite of this silence it is undeniable that the Church and Catholicism did achieve
something of importance in asserting their independence in the face of the totalitarian claims of the National Socialist regime. To a large extent, they closed themselves off from the influence of the philosophy of National Socialism. This is a valid
point even though it must be admitted that many individual Catholics contributed to
the functioning of the National Socialist regime and that many did therefore incur
real guilt, albeit with differing degrees of a bad conscience and on the basis of more
or less worthy motives. For most Catholics this spirit of independence amounted to
nothing more than the type of inner refusal which occasionally took the form of an
outburst of intense religiosity. Moreover, it would be unrealistic or inappropriate to
have expected a more heroic or outspoken attitude on the part of ordinary Catholics.
In this perspective, the behaviour of the bishops may appear more explicable, especially in so far as they knew that the individual clerics or laymen appointed as their
representatives were in effect potential hostages to the regime. But ultimately it must
be stressed that their faith gave many lay Catholics and priests support in their resistance, even if such resistance only rarely went beyond a spirit of independence and
even more rarely involved taking a stand against the National Socialist regime in all
its facets.

The real influence of Catholicism during the Nazi years was not political but ethical and religious. Its independence of mind did have a considerable political effect,
to the extent that it set limits to the potential for the infinite manipulation of the citizen which the regime coveted. No one could predict when this inner hostility might
find expression. In general, the National Socialist state was faced with a typical kind
of Catholic stoicism, a stoicism that discouraged Catholics from committing themselves to actions in the social sphere while encouraging them to restrict themselves
for as long as possible to a defence of their own spiritual and religious existence, or at
best to a defence of the existence of the Church and her institutions.[37]

A clear indication of the independence adopted by elements of the Catholic population towards the Nazi regime was the involvement of influential Catholics in the
Kreisauer Circle.[38] This circle was Protestant in inspiration and remained so in sub-
stance. It did, however, involve Catholics and especially Jesuits in its decision-
making and had links with Catholic as well as with Lutheran bishops. The circle did
not believe itself to be called upon to defeat National Socialism but rather to prepare
the new order that would be established after the much-anticipated fall of the regime.

The papers that survive from the work of the circle clearly show a strong Christian
component.[39] The greatest importance was attributed to the Christian heritage,
whose various confessions and Church institutions were expected to be key factors

---

[37] On the obstacles to Catholic resistance created by the Concordat see Muckermann, *Im Kampf*, 584 ff.

[38] On this problem see K.-E. Lönne in Böckenförde, *Der Deutsche Katholizismus*, 127 ff.

[39] G. van Roon, *Neuordnung im Widerstand* (Munich, 1967).

in the establishment of a new order. Although Catholic Christianity was only one component within the Kreisauer Circle and its goals, its discussions always clearly showed what a major role commitment to the Christian confessions played in bolstering the opposition to the National Socialist regime. The notes made by the Jesuit Alfred Delp during his imprisonment and before his execution also serve as an impressive testimony to the religious inspirations which could support Catholic resistance in enormously distressing situations.[40]

In conclusion, therefore, though the preservation of a distinctive religious outlook in a substantial sector of the population during the Nazi period constituted a significant achievement on the part of Catholicism, the underlying weakness in the way in which Catholics responded to the Third Reich related to the wider framework of the tension between Catholicism and modern society. While it is true that Catholic resistance to the Nazis in the closing stages of the Weimar Republic and the initial period of the Third Reich was significant, with political parties, episcopate, and large portions of the electorate each making their own contribution, it nevertheless remained limited to the defence of Catholic interests. The wider interests of the State and of a legitimate socio-political order were almost entirely neglected.

This exclusive focus on the Church and its interests grew more and more prevalent with the increasing dominance of the National Socialist regime and became endemic with the Concordat negotiations. By contrast Catholics failed to respond to the provocation of the regime's violent and arbitrary treatment of Communists and Jews and its brutal disregard for the law. The Catholic resistance also paid too little attention to the protection of those physically threatened or attacked by the Nazi regime. This is not intended to belittle the dedication of individuals and institutions such as Dean Lichtenberg of Berlin Cathedral or the Aid Committee for Catholic Non-Aryans, whose heroic actions only served to throw the general lack of such initiative into an even more cruel relief.[41]

German political Catholicism as represented by the Centre Party and the BVP collapsed with unexpected rapidity in 1933, but in spite of relentless persecution by National Socialism the Catholic Church and its structures remained in existence. On the other hand Catholic community life was more and more restricted, despite the provisions of the Concordat. Thus, as a force for religious integration, the Church grew stronger through its experience of defending itself against persistent aggression and of suffering both wartime deprivations and the even greater hardships of the immediate post-war years. This prepared the way for the resurgence of Catholicism as a political force in the years following the collapse of the Third Reich.

4. Political Catholicism in the Post-War New Order

As the war ended, the Catholic Church enjoyed an enhanced reputation, chiefly as a consequence of its independence of mind *vis-à-vis* National Socialism.[42]

[40] A. Delp, *Gesammelte Schriften IV: Aus dem Gefängnis* (Frankfurt, 1984).

[41] L.-E. Reutter, *Katholische Kirche als Fluchthelfer im Dritten Reich* (Recklinghausen, 1971).

[42] T. M. Gauly, *Katholiken, Machtanspruch und Machtverlust* (Bonn, 1991).

Expectations were high within the German episcopate of a renewed Christianization of society after the fall of a regime which was seen to symbolize the moral bankruptcy of a secularized society.[43] The bishops were encouraged in these views by the Church's increased power over the Catholic community and even more by the renewed devotion shown by some of the faithful in the first years after the war. For many, too, the Church provided vital moral support in the hardships of the post-war era, when hunger, homelessness, and displacement were everyday experiences.

Following the unconditional German surrender of May 1945 Germany was divided into American, British, French, and Soviet Occupation Zones. Limited by this factor, political life developed in different forms and at a different pace in the various zones. Political structures had to be rebuilt completely, and in the light of all that had taken place this could only take the form of an uncompromising rejection of National Socialism and its criminal regime. The traditional political forces of the Weimar Republic played roles of varying importance in this phase of political reconstruction. With their history of consistent hostility to the National Socialist regime, the KPD and the SPD were free to embark on their own task of reconstruction without delay. More problematic was the position of the supporters of the former Liberal and Conservative parties, which had shown considerable weakness towards National Socialism.

As far as political Catholicism was concerned, the impulse to a new order emanated predominantly from former supporters of the Centre Party. But a watershed was reached when the decision was taken that no straightforward revival of the old Centre Party should be attempted. Any such revival would in any case have been compromised from the start by ghosts from the past such as the (with hindsight highly problematic) vote for the Enabling Law, the rapid collapse and unopposed dissolution of the parties, and the absence of any significant resistance activity by Centre Party politicians either within Germany or abroad. In the main party centres, Berlin and Cologne, as well as in numerous other places, moves were none the less afoot to reactivate the Centre Party as a much more broadly based supraconfessional Christian party—recalling what Stegerwald in particular had tried to do in the Weimar era—and to give it a shape more suitable for the new social conditions. In the resistance movement against National Socialism a new relationship between the Christian confessions had begun to develop, in which a new attitude of co-operation and collaboration had replaced the long-established tendencies to separation and confrontation. This new conception of political Catholicism implied the launch of an entirely new enterprise that would of necessity transform the political activity of Catholics very profoundly. One consequence of this important change in Catholic attitudes was to encourage lay Catholics to become more independent of their own Church and spiritual leaders, and this impulse was to be greatly reinforced from the early 1960s onwards as a result of the controversies over the attitude adopted by the Catholic bishops to National Socialism.

[43] K. Gotto, 'Zum Selbstverständnis der katholischen Kirche im Jahr 1945', in *Politik und Konfession: Festschrift für K. Repgen* (Berlin, 1983), 465–81.

The reasons for the abandonment of the old Centre Party lay in the changed political situation of Catholics compared with the era when the party had been founded.
They were no longer faced by a strong Protestant State in alliance with a State
Church as in the days of the Empire, and Catholics now represented almost 45 per
cent of the West German population. Moreover, although the Centre Party had
always claimed it could achieve a fundamental integration of Christian forces extending beyond just Catholics it had never managed to fulfil this promise. With its
image as a confessional Catholic Party it could not realistically hope to do so even
after the collapse of the National Socialist regime.

Among the advocates of a single all-embracing Christian party in Berlin were
Andreas Hermes and Jacob Kaiser. In 1933 Kaiser had been involved in an attempt
to bring together Christian and non-Christian trade unions into one single union.[44]
In common with others who participated in this Berlin initiative, he had been in contact with the conspirators in the bomb plot against Hitler of 20 July 1944. Thus,
in June 1945 they issued a call for a rallying of all Christian and Democratic forces,
having a few days previously founded the German Christian-Democratic Union
(CDUD), initially only within the Soviet Occupation Zone. Together with fierce
criticism of the defeated National Socialist regime, the programmatic *Appeal to the
German People* contained a demand for the nationalization of the coal and other key
industries and for the appropriation of the large landed estates for the creation of new
housing. It did not reject private property but wanted to see it limited to a modest
size, and called for an end to the manipulation of the State by economic interest
groups. In addition, social demands were voiced on behalf of deprived and disadvantaged groups such as the war-wounded and working women.

Although the Berlin initiative preceded all other attempts to found a more broadly
based Christian party, it had little immediate impact. The main reason for this was
that the Soviet occupying power exercised a very strong influence over the new party
and forced it to collaborate with the Socialist Unity Party (SED). The Soviets prevented the party leaders from having contact with the organizers of similar initiatives
in the western zones of Germany, although in doing so they actually assisted the West
German groupings in remaining free from the influence of the Berlin party leadership.

With Kaiser at the helm the CDUD followed a domestic reform strategy that
could be called Christian socialist. It stressed German unity and aimed at keeping
Germany free from subservience to the great powers currently in control of the
different Occupation Zones, attributing to Germany a bridging role between East
and West. In 1948 the CDUD, however, fell completely under the political dominance of the SED while an exiled remnant merged with the western CDU. The
CDUD in the east could only continue to exist as a bloc party in enforced alliance
with the SED. For the CDUD this meant a substantial loss of its identity. Thus, in

---

[44] U. Schmidt, 'Christlich-Democratische Union Deutschlands', in V. R. Stoss (ed.), *Parteienhandbuch* (Opladen, 1983), 490–661. On the CDUD see M. McCauley, *The German Democratic Republic since
1945* (London, 1983), 6–41.

the Soviet Occupation Zone and later in the German Democratic Republic (the DDR) political Catholicism was no longer able to find any significant way of expressing itself, while in the newly established West Germany (the FDR) the CDU–CSU offered it a much wider scope for action. With Catholics forming only 7 per cent of the population of East Germany the CDUD lacked the strong support of a Catholic population which was to be a crucial factor in the development of the CDU–CSU in West Germany. The Catholic Church in the east sought to withdraw into the spheres of religious and charitable action, but—especially after the division of Germany—it endured severe repression.

The most significant initiatives for a new political organization of Catholicism after 1945 were launched in the Rhineland and especially in Cologne.[45] As in Berlin the impulse came from former Centre Party politicians. The first point they agreed on was to found a new party open to Protestants rather than to reactivate the old Centre Party. In this way, former Conservatives and Liberals were to be drawn in, and Lutheran leaders could be brought into policy discussions from the start. These discussions led to the publication of the Cologne Principles in July 1945. The establishment of the party then ensued in Cologne, under the name 'Christian Democratic Party'. It was not until the end of the year that the name 'Christian Democratic Union' (CDU) was adopted at a conference of the Christian Democrats in Godesberg. In 1947 the Baden Christian Social People's Party (BCSV) joined the CDU and took its name, while in Bavaria the Christian Social Union (CSU) retained its independence while collaborating very closely with the CDU.

The Cologne Principles were the product of several round-table discussions held in the Dominican House at Walberberg. The foundations of the programme had already been laid during the National Socialist era in conversations between the Dominicans Laurentius Siemer and Eberhard Welty and various Catholic lay figures in Cologne. The heavy stress laid on Christian Socialism which came particularly from Siemer was not followed up in subsequent negotiations and in particular found no expression in the name of the new party. Even so, the Principles still contained a demand for a 'true Christian socialism', which was given a basis in Christian natural law. In addition to political demands for the rule of law and freedom of expression, the Principles also contained wide-ranging social demands, including calls for a 'social wage policy, a just equalization of wealth', and nationalization in the interest of the common good.

In later years, however, Christian solidarism as developed by the Jesuits, rather than Christian socialism, exercised a greater influence on the programme and actions of the CDU–CSU.[46] In the conception of solidarism, elaborated by Heinrich Pesch and further developed by Gustav Gundlach and Oswald von Nell-Breuning, the interests of the community did not play such a dominant role as in the Christian socialism of the Dominicans. Much more emphasis was placed on the individual and

---

[45] H. G. Wieck, *Die Entstehung der CDU und die Wiedergründung des Zentrums im Jahre 1945* (Düsseldorf, 1953); U. Schmidt, *Zentrum oder CDU* (Opladen, 1987).

[46] R. Uertz, *Christentum und Sozialismus in der frühen CDU* (Stuttgart, 1981).

his or her development, even though the individual's bond with society and obligation to serve the common good was always stressed. Solidarism was flexible enough
on the one hand to be able to exploit and develop capitalist economic methods, while
on the other hand highlighting the requirements of the community and the solidarity of the whole of society. State action to resolve particular social problems was
permitted, but regulatory socialist or statist tendencies were rejected as opening the
way to an unhealthy collectivism. Equally, however, liberal economic management
without reference to the common good found no acceptance. It was to the solidaristic
school in Catholic social teaching that the strong social component in the policy
of the CDU–CSU generally owed its ideological foundation and its consistent
vitality.[47]

Unlike in the Weimar Republic, the collaboration of the former Centre Party with
Conservative and Liberal forces in the CDU and CSU offered an opportunity for the
development of new alliances. The new party was to unite Catholics and Protestants
in practical cooperation, and as a result of the shared struggle of the Christian denominations against National Socialism there was considerable enthusiasm for this
enterprise on all sides.

Against the background of this determination that the confessions should work
together in the CDU and the CSU a tension developed between the social reformist
elements among the Catholics and those Protestants who came to the CDU chiefly
from the more right-wing parties of the Weimar Republic. This was soon evident in
the formulation of the Cologne Principles, influenced by the involvement of a Protestant group in Wuppertal[48] and also in the success of Konrad Adenauer's efforts to
restrict the social reformist movement within the CDU in favour of a system of limited capitalism. In these efforts he was able to rely on the support of the Protestant
constituency.

Despite the existence of so many factors militating against any re-establishment of
the Centre Party, a small group of former members remained faithful to their old
party. But, although they did found the German Centre Party (DZP) in October
1945, it was never powerful enough to be able to offer any serious competition to the
rapidly evolving CDU. Its biggest problem was that the episcopate was quickly won
over to the CDU and CSU and was very anxious to avoid any disastrous split in the
Catholic vote. Until 1949 a substantial element of the Centre Party's vote continued
to pass over to the CDU and by 1953 membership of the DZP had dwindled to the
point where it was only by virtue of an electoral pact with the CDU that the party
gained any seats in the Bundestag. Centre parties established in Hessen (1947/8) and
Baden (1951) also failed to meet with any lasting success.

Relations between the Catholic Church and the CDU and CSU were not always
easy. Education policy was one point of conflict. The plan put forward by Schwering,
initiator of the Cologne discussions on the founding of the CDU, was criticized by

---

[47] O. von Nell-Breuning, 'Der Beitrag des Katholizismus zur Sozialpolitik der Nachkriegszeit', in
A. Rauscher (ed.), *Kirche und Staat in der Bundesrepublik 1949–1963* (Paderborn, 1979), 109–21.
[48] Wieck, *Die Entstehung*.

the Church 'for aiming to reorganize the entire education system on the pattern of the Christian non-denominational school, with provision for obligatory religious instruction'.[49] Catholic authorities sought instead the re-establishment of the confessional Catholic school system. In a second version of the Cologne Principles issued in September–October 1945 a return to a confessional basis for education was called for—mainly with an eye to the tradition of the Centre Party and the wishes of the bishops—but this suggestion never had any prospect of success. Even Catholic politicians had finally to accept that confessional schools were an unattainable demand. In the course of the 1950s this issue, however, lost much of its former importance, especially since confessional religious instruction in non-Catholic schools was guaranteed in the constitution.

The abandonment by the CDU of Schwering's original concept of a deconfessional school system made it easier for the episcopate to take a positive attitude towards the new party. In general the Catholic Church came to enjoy a close relationship with the CDU–CSU and the newly established Federal Republic.[50] In addition, the CDU was also approved by the Lutheran Church, confirming the Christian foundations of the new united party.

Pressure from Adenauer meant that concerns for the common good and the ideas of Christian socialism put forward in the Cologne Principles were increasingly excluded. The efforts of the CDU's founders in Frankfurt and of the *Frankfurter Heft*, a monthly journal established in 1946 and edited by Walter Dirks and Eugen Kogon, proved insufficient to block this tendency. Dirks argued—as he had in the *Rhein-Mainische Volkszeitung* under the Weimar Republic—for a socialism based on Christian responsibility and for a Christian political system embodying Marxist ideals. He uttered 'a dire warning to the Christian Democrats as a political party not to discredit Christianity by allowing its message to be mixed up with a bourgeois ideology'.[51] With this warning Dirks set himself in opposition to the intentions of a large majority of the founders of the CDU, who did in fact see a party based on Christian principles as a focus for bourgeois defenders of law and order. In fact, the CDU never fully became such a party, and some disgruntled elements moved away to establish the more right-wing but secular Free Democratic Party (FDP).

The social reformists had their opportunity to express their views at the CDU's national assembly held at Bad Godesberg in late 1945. The result was a resolution affirming that 'socialism based on Christian responsibility' was officially recognized as a key element in CDU thinking. It seemed that the influence of the social reformist wing of the party was getting stronger, especially as the eastern zone CDUD made Christian socialism central to its programme, and such ideas were propagated in the west through Jacob Kaiser. But an opposite direction was adopted in a draft programme for the CDU in the British occupation zone as presented by Adenauer at

[49] H. Schwering, *Vorgeschichte und Entstehung der CDU* (Cologne, 1952).

[50] R. Morsey, 'Katholizismus und Unionsparteien in der Ära Adenauer', in A. Langner (ed.), *Katholizismus im politischen System der Bundesrepublik 1949–1963* (Paderborn, 1978), 33–59.

[51] F. Focke, *Sozialismus aus christlicher Verantwortung* (Wuppertal, 1981), 204.

Neheim-Hüsten. This indefinitely postponed the implementation of plans for the nationalization of the primary industries and the state regulation of banks and insurance companies. It derived all social demands from the idea of personalism, which, it was claimed, involved a recognition of employers' and employees' rights and responsibilities. What distinguished personalism was that it could be used to justify actions by employers which only indirectly could be regarded as concerned with the common good, whereas, for the social reformers, a concern for the common good had always remained the central consideration.

The social reformist tendency in the CDU finally found expression in the Ahlen Programme of the British zone CDU.[52] This programme was prefaced by a preamble in which the inadequacy of the capitalist economic system was affirmed and a fundamentally new order called for, but it showed signs of inner contradiction; for, while it argued that an economic order based on the common good would ensure peace at home and abroad, it also gave a generally strong endorsement to the freedom of the individual in the political and economic spheres. The impulse to a new order was not sought in an economy run for the benefit of the community but in the development of the individual, even though the concentration of economic power was expressly condemned.

Beginning with a detailed critique of the industrial economy of the past the Programme formulated principles for the creation of an economic structure that would be defined neither by the 'unlimited domination of private capitalism' nor by some alternative 'state capitalism'. It expressed hostility to capitalism and socialism alike and sought a third way between them. Excessive economic concentrations of power were to be combated through restrictions on corporations, cartels, and shareholdings. The coal and steel industries were to be nationalized. Co-operatives and small and medium-sized businesses were to be encouraged. The position of the employee was to be strengthened by guaranteed consultation and the creation of factory councils.

While the Ahlen Programme contained proposals for substantial intervention in the process of reconstruction of the economic system, subsequent developments pushed fundamental reform measures into the background. In the social market economy of the first two decades of the Federal Republic—mainly the work of Ludwig Erhard—the capitalist market economy had a major part in the programme and policies of the CDU, although it was admittedly subject to regulation in accordance with state economic and social policies aimed at securing the common good and favouring socially disadvantaged groups and individuals. The economic policy guidelines of the CDU, the so-called Düsseldorf Principles, included the following definition: 'The "social market economy" means that the market is regulated by the needs of society—i.e. the activity of free and competent agents is directed to the highest possible degree towards the economic benefit and social justice of all.'[53]

---

[52] For the text see O. K. Flechtheim (ed.), *Dokumente zur parteipolitischen Entwicklung in Deutschland seit 1945*, ii (Berlin, 1963), 53–8. On the social market economy see A. J. Nicholls, *Freedom with Responsibility: The Social Market Economy in Germany, 1918–1963* (Oxford, 1994).

[53] Flechtheim (ed.), *Dokumente*, ii. 53–8.

Within the party the Düsseldorf Principles were taken to be a market-economy extension of the Ahlen Programme, but in reality they represented a marked and final shift in CDU thinking away from a policy of socio-economic reform and towards a capitalistic market policy where society's needs were secondary and had to compete for resources with vested interests of economic groups and forces.

In the Hamburg Programme of 1953 the CDU put forward a comprehensive list of their aims and policies. This programme cited a range of demands for political rights including a guarantee of full freedom and independence for the churches in their official public functions, while opposition was expressed to any revival of confessional hostilities. The programme also contained a substantial treatment of social and economic problems. A key factor in the success of the CDU at the polls in 1957, when they won an absolute majority, was their introduction of index-linked old-age pensions.[54] The party's general self-confidence and the breadth of its agenda as embodied in the Hamburg Programme undoubtedly created the basis for the party's remarkable electoral success.

When the social market economy was further developed into a 'planned society' under the leadership of Ludwig Erhard during the 1960s, this led to a shift of emphasis from a recognition of the importance of a multiplicity of social forces to the State's role as the regulator of society. At the same time, there was a strong desire on the part of the people for a greater role in political and economic decision-making. The SPD and the FDP proved able to channel this sentiment and the result was that the reign of the CDU which had lasted almost twenty years finally came to an end and the party was driven into opposition in 1969.

Though, at least in West Germany the development of the CDU–CSU has more or less reflected the development of political Catholicism, there has been a gradual decline—especially since the late 1950s—in Catholic alienation from social democracy. Even the most dedicated of Catholics increasingly claim and practise freedom of choice in their socio-political ideas and their voting behaviour; some have even opted for movements such as Christians for Socialism.[55] Since the late 1960s the Bensberg Group, an informal association of Catholics, has sought to discuss important current issues from the perspective of Christian responsibility, in detachment from the influence of one-sided party-political considerations, with the aim of promoting such debate in the public arena.[56] The most notable action taken by this group was shortly before the treaty agreements between West Germany and the Soviet Union and Poland, when it called for steps to be taken on moral grounds towards reconciliation and peace with Poland.

A more serious element of tension within German political Catholicism since the immediate post-war period has been the Bavarian CSU. The party was created at the same time as the CDU and arose out of a similar political impulse. But it had to operate in a distinct regional political culture forged by long historical traditions. As a result the main characteristic of the CSU has been an intense and frequently

---

[54] H. G. Hockerts, *Sozialpolitische Entscheidungen im Nachkriegsdeutschland* (Stuttgart, 1980).
[55] Gauly, *Katholiken*.   [56] H. Misalla, *Der Bensberger Kreis* (Düsseldorf, 1973).

excessive spirit of independence. Indeed, in contrast to other regional parties which have all eventually been integrated into the CDU, the CSU has maintained its independence. It has been able to exercise a dual role as a Bavarian party and a party of the Federal Republic, at once a leading political force in Bavaria and an independent factor in the politics of the FDR.[57]

The decision of political Catholicism to opt for the founding of the CDU–CSU in 1945 has thus proved crucially important for its development. Not only were former Centre Party politicians leading participants in the groups that sprang up spontaneously in many places to found the new united Christian party, but the support of Catholic votes was a key element in its growing success. It began to obtain increasing support from the electorate in Protestant communities too, though a resurgent confessionalism in Protestant ranks in the 1950s counterbalanced its influence, as did the feeling that the CDU and CSU were too closely tied to influence of the Catholic Church. The continued disproportionality of the commitment of Catholics to the CDU can be observed over a long period during which the party experienced marked fluctuations in its fortunes. The Catholic element in its support was 25.2 per cent (+CSU 31 per cent) in 1949, 36.4 per cent (+CSU 45.2 per cent) in 1953, 39.0 per cent (+CSU 50.2 per cent) in 1957, and 35.8 per cent (+CSU 45.4 per cent) in 1961, while at the point of its departure from government in 1969 the proportion was 36.6 per cent (+CSU 46.1 per cent). Up to 1969 between 60 and 62 per cent of Catholics voted for the CDU–CSU.[58] Thus there is much to suggest that at least until the 1960s the CDU and CSU were to be regarded as a clear expression of political Catholicism, though of a political Catholicism that made significant concessions to its Protestant partners—especially as regards its leading personnel. At the same time, its secular and liberal concessions to its bourgeois coalition partners (notably the Free Democrats) left much room for conflict with its Protestant allies. Catholic influence within the CDU was mitigated both by the influence of Protestant circles, which were able to draw on a considerable potential electorate, as well as by those conservative and liberal forces which were absorbed into the Christian unity party. These influences were increased through the actions of the CDU's liberal bourgeois coalition partners with whom the CDU was obliged to work in order to ensure a majority in parliament. These included the FDP (with whom the CDU worked almost continuously up until 1966), as well as more intermittently the more right-wing German Party (DP), and the Association for Exiles and the Dispossessed (BHE), the rapid growth of which was followed by an equally rapid decline. The leaders of the CDU and CSU have also been at pains to distance themselves from an exclusively Catholic image of their parties. Despite the large-scale involvement of the Catholic population with the CDU–CSU, the leaders have asserted ever more strongly their inter-confessional nature.

[57] A. Mintzel, 'Die Christlich-soziale Union in Bayern' in Stoss (ed.), *Parteienhandbuch*, 661–718.

[58] For a fuller analysis of the voting behaviour of Catholics see K. Gotto, 'Die deutschen Katholiken und die Wahlen in der Adenauer-Ära', in Langner (ed.), *Katholizismus im Politischen System*, 7–32. For a general account of the CDU and CSU in post-war Germany, see G. Pridham, *Christian Democracy in Western Germany: The CDU and CSU in Government and Opposition, 1945–1976* (London, 1977).

From the start the commitment of Catholics to the CDU and CSU was assisted by the satisfactory position accorded to the Church in the West German Constitution. The framework for the relationship between Church and State was incorporated from the Weimar Constitution as the fundamental laws of the Federal Republic. The right to freedom of religion was guaranteed in the fundamental articles. Moreover, the validity of existing concordats was recognized, including eventually the one made in 1933. Rights of participation and consultation in the operation of public institutions were accorded both to the Lutheran and Catholic Churches. Institutions such as kindergartens, youth organizations, and hospitals were entrusted to the administration of the Church while being largely financed by the State, and they proved to be one of the key elements of the Catholic Church's presence in society. Thus, although the Church's advantageous position did not depend entirely on the influence of the CDU and CSU, they played a central role in establishing it. Moreover, in return they enjoyed the support of the Catholic hierarchy, as was clearly expressed in the Church's electoral exhortations to the Catholic faithful.

Since the late 1960s the relationship between the Catholic Church and the CDU and CSU has become increasingly more difficult. There are a number of reasons for this: their growth into genuine 'People's Parties' as a result of greater participation by Protestants, the gradual *rapprochement* of some Catholics with social democracy, and the general modernization brought about by the Second Vatican Council, which opened up new political perspectives.[59] Secularization has of course also increasingly affected the Christian parties. With Catholic voters this has found expression in a tendency (though somewhat limited in scope) towards political pluralism, expressed notably in an attraction to the SPD, though the wider gulf between Catholics and the FDP has persisted.

While in power (until 1963) Adenauer pursued an economic policy that favoured a social market economy, combining this with a foreign policy which looked especially towards the Western nations, the USA, Great Britain, and France. While Kaiser and the CDUD in the Soviet occupation zone tried to prevent the establishment of close ties between the individual German occupation zones and their occupying powers in hopes of maintaining German unity, Adenauer opted for a close dependence on the Western powers.

It remains to be seen how far religious affiliation to Catholicism and its inspiration for political activity will continue to be of significance. If political Catholicism is to survive there must at the very least be no abandonment of religious values and Christian virtues as controls on the actions of the Christian parties. Catholic teachings must also serve to a certain degree as the doctrine of the CDU and CSU, but not to the extent that political Catholicism's every aim and policy has to be judged according to the very highest standards. On the contrary, it has to be in perpetual debate with these religious values. Political Catholicism cannot claim for itself a heightened insight and a special capacity to resolve problems on the basis of its

---

[59] G. Lindgens, *Katholische Kirche und moderner Pluralismus* (Stuttgart, 1980).

connection with a religious world-view, but must rather display an increased readiness to think in terms of the needs and the future of the whole of humankind. How it goes about doing this will be more important for its future opportunities than any insistence on guaranteed rights for the Church and the Catholic faith, if their presence and their influence in society continue to diminish at the rate they are currently doing in the early 1990s.[60]

[60] See Gauly, *Katholiken*, and M. Klöcker, *Katholisch-von der Wiege bis zur Bahre* (Munich, 1991).

6

Belgium

MARTIN CONWAY

Belgium has been a heartland of Catholic Europe during the twentieth century. As foreign visitors to the country were often quick to remark, in no other European state from the First World War to the 1960s did Catholicism consistently enjoy such a preponderant influence over religious, social, and political life as in Belgium.[1] High levels of religious practice (though with marked regional and social variations) were combined with a formidable network of social, cultural, and educational institutions which enveloped the lives of the faithful from childhood to old age. The power of the Church and its myriad affiliated organizations was guaranteed by the dominant position occupied in Belgian politics by the Catholic Party. As Fig. 6.1 illustrates, its share of the national vote only once fell below 30 per cent (in 1936) and, with a peak of 47.7 per cent in the election of 1950, the party usually formed the largest grouping

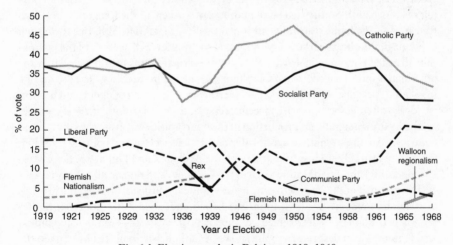

Fig. 6.1. Election results in Belgium, 1919–1968.

---

[1] See e.g. H. Somerville, *Studies in the Catholic Social Movement* (London, 1933); D. Woodruff, 'Recovery in the Low Countries (II): Belgian Catholics and Belgian Politics', *Tablet*, 24 Nov. 1945, pp. 244–5.

in the Belgian parliament. This electoral success was reflected in the control which the party exercised over government. Although, with the exception of the years 1950–4, it never possessed an overall majority in parliament, the Catholic Party in its successive manifestations formed an indispensable element of the many coalition governments which ruled Belgium. Sharing power with either the Socialists or the predominantly centre-right Liberals (or, on occasions, with both of its major rivals simultaneously), the Catholic Party enjoyed a quasi-permanent presence in government. Apart from the hiatus imposed by the German Occupation of 1940 to 1944 and brief periods of opposition from 1945 to 1947 and again from 1954 to 1958, politicians representing Catholic parties have formed part of every government coalition in Belgium since 1884. Of the thirty-six governments which ruled Belgium from 1918 to 1968, no fewer than twenty-seven were headed by a Catholic prime minister.[2]

Superficially, the power exercised by the Catholic Party reflected the powerful position occupied by the Catholic Church in Belgian life. With the exception of small Jewish and Protestant minorities, some 98–9 per cent of the population was nominally Catholic.[3] The immigrant groups, notably from Italy, which settled in Belgium during the inter-war years did nothing to undermine the ascendancy of Catholicism and only since the 1960s with the arrival of new immigrant populations from Turkey and North Africa has religious pluralism become a significant feature of Belgian society. The appearance of a uniformly Catholic population did, however, mask significant differences in levels of religious practice between different regions and social classes. The rapid industrial growth and urbanization experienced by Belgium during the nineteenth century led large numbers of workers in the francophone industrial areas of Wallonia to abandon all contact with the Catholic faith. In a town such as Seraing in the heart of the Liège industrial basin as few as 8 per cent of the population attended church regularly by 1920 and the situation was broadly similar in the other major industrial centres of Charleroi and the Borinage. Elsewhere the decline in religious practice was less marked. Nevertheless, the spread of liberal and positivist ideas (often associated with Freemasonry and organizations of *libre-penseurs*) gradually drew a significant proportion of the bourgeoisie away from the Church and contributed to the strength of a rationalist and anticlerical Liberal political tradition. Only in the rural bastions of the francophone Ardennes and Dutch-speaking West Flanders and Limburg did adherence to the Catholic faith remain all but universal.[4]

The first half of the twentieth century saw, however, little further decline in levels of religious practice. Secularization was halted and, though Catholic hopes of a rechristianization of society remained unrealistic, there was—even in some industrial regions—a modest return to the rituals of Catholicism indicated by a rise in the numbers of religious baptisms, marriages, and burials. More significantly, for many

[2] R. De Smet, R. Evalenko, and W. Fraeys, *Atlas des élections belges 1919–1954* (Brussels, 1958) annexe statistique, 10; E. Witte and J. Craeybeckx, *La Belgique politique de 1830 à nos jours* (Brussels, 1987), 264 and 590–2.   [3] R. Aubert, *150 ans de vie des églises* (Brussels, [1980]), 47–9.

[4] Ibid. 48–52; L. de Saint-Moulin, 'Contribution à l'histoire de la déchristianisation: La Pratique religieuse à Seraing depuis 1830', *Annuaire d'histoire liégeoise*, 10 (1967), 33–126; H. Hasquin (ed.), *Histoire de la laïcité principalement en Belgique et en France* (Brussels, 1979).

of those who were already practising Catholics, their religious faith acquired a greater centrality in their lives. During the early 1930s and again in the later 1940s a mood of spiritual renewal was evident within Belgian Catholicism. A surge in religious vocations, enthusiastic participation in pilgrimages and religious retreats, and the mass membership of lay movements such as the Association Catholique de la Jeunesse Belge (Catholic Association of Belgian Youth) and the Legion of Mary all bore witness to the vitality of a Catholic faith which went beyond the rituals of conventional observance.[5]

Catholicism in Belgium was, thus, for much of the twentieth century not a religion in decline. In 1950 there was one priest for every 600 inhabitants (compared, for example, with figures of one for 751 inhabitants in Italy and one for 970 inhabitants in Spain) and a major survey of religious practice carried out in the same year discovered that some 42 per cent of the adult population attended mass regularly. The long-established regional and social variations remained. In Brussels and the province of Hainaut (which included the industrial cities of Charleroi and La Louvière as well as the mining region of the Borinage) attendance fell below 30 per cent, while in predominantly rural provinces such as Luxembourg, West Flanders, and Limburg the average was over 60 per cent. The accuracy of these figures, based on returns compiled by parish priests, is open to question and sociological research consistently demonstrated an imbalance in religious practice towards women, the young, and those living in smaller communities.[6] Nevertheless, it is clear that, assisted by a centralized ecclesiastical hierarchy based on the archbishopric of Mechelen (Malines), the Belgian Catholic Church retained a strong hold over much of the population. Only from the 1960s onwards would the rapid economic modernization of Flanders and the consequent social and cultural changes provoke a further marked fall in religious practice.

The strength of the Catholic faith did not, however, in itself guarantee the political success enjoyed by the Catholic Party. Catholicism was a bond which united Belgians from a wide variety of backgrounds but the faithful shared little else in common and throughout the twentieth century the Catholic Party was forced to confront divisions within its ranks fostered by differences of political ideology, regional identity, and social class. In part, these divisions were the consequence of the dominant position enjoyed by Catholicism within Belgium. Simply because the vast majority of the population was in a nominal sense Catholic and because the Catholic Party exercised such a decisive influence within the political process, the need to maintain Catholic political unity at all costs was less evident. Unlike, for example, in the

[5] Aubert, *150 ans*, 47–65; G. Hoyois, *Aux origines de l'Action Catholique: Monseigneur Picard* (Brussels, 1960); J. Art, 'De evolutie van het aantal mannelijke roepingen in België tussen 1830 en 1975: Basisgegevens en richtingen voor verder onderzoek', *Belgisch tijdschrift voor nieuwste geschiedenis*, 10 (1979), 281–370; A. Tihon, 'Les Religieuses en Belgique du XVIIIe siècle au XXe siècle: Approche statistique', *Revue belge d'histoire contemporaine*, 7 (1976), 1–54; Cardinal Suenens, *Memories and Hopes* (Dublin, 1992), 45–8.

[6] Aubert, *150 ans*, 55; E. Collard, 'Commentaire de la carte de la pratique dominicale en Belgique', *Lumen vitae*, 7 (1952), 644–52; J. Remy and L. Dingemans, *Charleroi et son agglomération: Aspects sociologiques de la pratique religieuse* (Brussels, 1962), 112–176 and 399.

neighbouring states of Germany and the Netherlands, the Catholics of Belgium never formed a distinct minority mindful of the need to protect their particular interests against those of a Protestant majority. But the challenges posed to Catholic political unity also reflected the wider problem of the unity of the Belgian state. Despite Belgium's origins in a diplomatic compromise in 1830, the rulers of the new state succeeded in inculcating a sense of nationalism into their new citizens which was made manifest in the patriotic commitment with which almost all Belgians responded to the German invasion of August 1914. During the subsequent fifty years, however, a process of social and regional dislocation gradually gathered pace which in the 1960s led to the emergence of substantial regionalist movements in both Dutch-speaking Flanders and francophone Wallonia. The institutions of the Belgian state—its monarchy, army, and parliament—still existed but their hold over the loyalties of the population could no longer be taken for granted and Belgium's political leaders began the complex process of transition to a new federal political system.[7]

The history of political Catholicism in Belgium from the First World War to the 1960s is, thus, largely the story of the efforts to maintain a unitary Catholic Party in an increasingly diverse, even fragmented, society. If much of the electoral base of the party was composed of the Dutch-speaking peasantry and *petite bourgeoisie* of Flanders, it also enjoyed considerable support from the francophone farmers and middle classes of Wallonia and Brussels. Divisions of social class reinforced regional tensions. The gradual emancipation of the working classes gave rise to a predominantly Flemish Christian Democrat movement which challenged the more conservative stance of the party's largely francophone and bourgeois leadership. Encouraged by the Church hierarchy, the different components of the Catholic Party maintained a unity based on a shared hostility to their Socialist and Liberal opponents, but this integrated Catholic pillar could not survive indefinitely the process of regional and social fragmentation. Finally, in the 1960s the pillar shattered. The francophone and Flemish wings of the party split into separate groupings while the exhaustion of old clerical–anticlerical antagonisms and the theological changes initiated by the Second Vatican Council created a new political climate in which the former close connection between religious practice and political allegiance declined. Many Catholics no longer saw any necessary connection between their religious beliefs and their political actions, while others preferred to pursue new forms of Catholic-inspired political engagement outside distinctively Catholic political structures.

The resilience with which the party resisted for so long this process of fragmentation owed much to the strong tradition of Catholic political action inherited from the nineteenth century. Indeed, Belgium has good claim to have been the birthplace of modern forms of political Catholicism. Immediately after the achievement of independence from the Netherlands in 1830, Catholic politicians and the Church

---

[7] There is no satisfactory modern history of Belgium in English. E. H. Kossmann, *The Low Countries 1780–1940* (Oxford, 1978) provides an introductory synthesis, albeit one written from a Dutch perspective. A much more comprehensive and stimulating account is given by Witte and Craeybeckx, *Belgique politique*.

hierarchy had participated actively in the structures of the new Belgian state. The Constitution of 1831 guaranteed the position of the Catholic Church and was reinforced by subsequent laws which granted the Church considerable influence over education. Opposition to the Church was a rallying-point for Liberal politicians and during the 1860s and 1870s the power of the Catholic Church became the dominant issue in Belgian political life. Rival Catholic and Liberal electoral associations were formed and, stimulated by the anticlerical actions of the Liberal government after 1878, the newly constituted Catholic Party won a decisive victory in the elections of 1884. A system of plural male suffrage was introduced in 1893 which granted every adult male the vote while ensuring the supremacy of bourgeois interests. But this limited concession to working-class pressure did little to undermine Catholic power. The Catholic Party gained an overall majority of parliamentary seats in every election from 1884 until the First World War and enjoyed a monopoly over political power. These successive Catholic governments worked to protect the material interests of the Catholic electorate while also ensuring that the Church, and in particular its rapidly expanding network of educational institutions, retained its privileged position in Belgian society.[8]

This uninterrupted thirty-year period of Catholic government was unique in pre-1914 Europe and, not surprisingly, the Belgian Catholic Party became a model which Catholics elsewhere in Europe sought to emulate. It was not, however, a unified organization. No central structure existed and, though the party retained its unity in the face of determined opposition from the Liberals and, subsequently, the Socialist Parti Ouvrier Belge (Belgian Workers' Party), it remained an informal coalition of parliamentary deputies, local electoral associations and social organizations.[9] The greatest challenge to its unity came from the Catholic workers' movement. From the 1880s onwards, Catholic trade unions and social insurance organizations developed rapidly and they soon demanded representation for the interests of Catholic workers in parliament. In 1891 a Catholic Ligue démocratique belge (Belgian Democratic League) was formed and throughout the 1890s a Flemish priest, Adolf Daens, sought to build an alliance of Catholic workers and agricultural labourers in East Flanders. The goal of an autonomous Catholic workers' party was, however, consistently opposed by the leaders of the Catholic Party and by the ecclesiastical hierarchy which expelled Daens and finally obtained a papal condemnation of 'Daenisme' in 1905.[10]

Nevertheless, Catholic workers' organizations continued to expand and a national confederation of Catholic trade unions was created in 1912. By then, the nascent Christian democrat movement had been drawn firmly within the fold of the governing Catholic Party. In 1905 the bishops officially recognised Catholic workers'

---

[8] R. Aubert, 'L'Église et l'état en Belgique au XIXᵉ siècle', *Res Publica*, 10 (1968), 9–31; *Algemene Geschiedenis der Nederlanden* (Bussum, 1978) xiii. 178–85 and 395–429; P. Gérin, 'L'Église et la politique en Belgique avant 1914', *Res Publica*, 27 (1985), 523–31; A. Simon, 'Le Cardinal Mercier et la politique', *Res Publica*, 6 (1964), 112–16.

[9] A. Simon, *Le Parti catholique belge 1830–1945* (Brussels, 1958), 85–9 and 111–15; E. Gerard, *De Katholieke Partij in crisis* (Leuven, 1985), 49.

[10] L. Wils, *Het Daenisme* (Leuven, 1969); Witte and Craeybeckx, *Belgique politique*, 112–16.

organizations as one of the constituent groupings of the Catholic Party and a number of deputies were elected to parliament who expressed the concerns of Catholic workers. In many respects, these concessions were of little real significance. The party remained opposed to simple manhood suffrage and continued to give priority to the defence of the interests of the middle classes and of the rural population. But it guaranteed the principle of a single Catholic Party and ensured that, amidst the often stormy electoral politics of the 1900s, the party retained its unity and its control of governmental power.[11]

The Catholic Party's long ascendancy ensured that, almost uniquely in Europe, there was no tradition of Catholic alienation from the parliamentary regime. In marked contrast to Third Republic France or post-Unification Italy, Catholics in Belgium readily identified with the system of liberal parliamentarism established by the Constitution of 1831. Together with the monarchy, the constitution—and the regime of controlled bourgeois parliamentary politics which it incarnated—came to form a central symbol of the new Belgian nation. Thus, although the Catholic bishops frequently railed against other modern evils, the parliamentary regime was exempted from their strictures. Their electoral success as well as the absence of any historical antipathy to the political system led the bishops and the Catholic political élite to regard the liberal regime, if not as a truly Catholic political order, at least as one which favoured their material and spiritual interests. In contrast to the travails experienced by Catholics elsewhere in Europe, Belgium in the pre-1914 years appeared almost as a Catholic paradise in which control of political power combined with a strong Church and a flourishing network of schools and social organizations protected the faithful from the twin horrors of atheistic liberalism and Marxist socialism.[12]

The First World War reinforced the identification of the Catholic Party with the established political order. The German violation of Belgian neutrality in August 1914 and the subsequent harsh occupation of the country provided a rallying-point for Belgian patriotism as well as bringing together the leaders of the Catholic, Liberal, and Socialist parties in a wartime coalition of national unity. While Belgian troops under the personal leadership of King Albert I continued the military struggle against the German armies on the Yser front in West Flanders, the tripartite government in exile at Le Havre acted as the custodian of the political interests of the nation. Within the occupied country, the Catholic primate of Belgium, Cardinal Mercier, emerged as the principal spokesman for the population, denouncing in a series of outspoken pastoral letters the sufferings inflicted on Belgium by the German authorities.[13]

---

[11] Witte and Craeybeckx, *Belgique politique*, 116–17; J. Neuville, *Une génération syndicale* (n.p., 1959), 75–123; L. Van Molle, *Katholieken en Landbouw: Landbouwpolitiek in België 1884–1914* (Leuven, 1987).

[12] A. Simon, 'Le Cardinal Mercier et la politique', *Res Publica*, 6 (1964), 112–16; M. Claeys-Van Haegendoren, 'L'Église et l'État au xxᵉ siècle', *Courrier hebdomadaire du CRISP*, 542–3 (1971), 3–5; J. Remy, 'Le Défi de la modernité: La Stratégie de la hiérarchie catholique aux xixᵉ et xxᵉ siècles et l'idée de chrétienté', *Social Compass*, 34 (1987), 153–61.

[13] H. Haag, 'Le Cardinal Mercier devant la guerre et la paix', *Revue d'histoire ecclésiastique*, 79 (1984), 709–83.

With the abrupt German withdrawal from Belgium in November 1918 and the subsequent triumphant return of the King, the Catholic Party appeared well placed to resume its dominant role in Belgian political life. In fact, the liberation of 1918 marked the beginning of a period of unprecedented crisis for the party during which it struggled to retain its unity against a combination of social, ideological, and regional divisions. The reasons for this crisis were both external and internal to the Catholic Party. In the months following the liberation, King Albert initiated a series of constitutional reforms intended to placate the demands made before and during the war by Socialist and Flemish groups. Their effect was to bring about a democratization of the political system. Most importantly, simple manhood suffrage was introduced, thereby destroying almost at a stroke the Catholic Party's monopoly over political power. Though it won 37.02 per cent of the vote in the elections of 1919 (compared with the Liberals' 17.64 per cent and the Socialists' 36.67 per cent), the party could no longer hope to enjoy an overall majority of seats in parliament and throughout the inter-war years it was obliged to share power in coalition with one or both of its historic adversaries.[14] In addition, the events of the First World War and the consequent mood of democratization in the country caused a marked shift of power within the Catholic Party away from its predominantly francophone and bourgeois leadership towards Flemish and working-class or 'Christian democrat' elements. No longer were these groupings content to accept a subsidiary role within the party and in the elections of 1919 independent Catholic worker candidates contested a number of Flemish electoral districts.[15]

Confronted by this democratic breakthrough within Belgian politics, the need for reform of the Catholic Party's structures was evident. The informal arrangements of the pre-1914 era would no longer suffice and in 1921 a new party organization was introduced. The Union Catholique Belge/Katholiek Verbond van België (Belgian Catholic Union), as it was titled, was composed of four groupings of farmers, workers, the middle classes, and the Fédération des Cercles (Federation of Circles, the pre-1914 political associations), each of which had an equal part in the selection of candidates and elaboration of policy.[16] In practice, this new structure did little to resolve the party's difficulties. The central problem was the socio-linguistic division between the predominantly francophone bourgeois figures who controlled the Fédération des Cercles and the largely Flemish Christian democrat wing of the party represented by the Algemeen Christelijk Werkersverbond/Ligue Nationale des Travailleurs Chrétiens (National Christian Workers' Union, ACW/LNTC). This was established as an umbrella organization for Catholic worker organizations in 1923 and it worked closely with a grouping of Flemish Catholic Party deputies in parliament, the Katholieke Vlaamse Kamergroep (Flemish Catholic Parliamentary Group) led by Frans Van Cauwelaert. Differences of temperament and ideology

[14] Witte and Craeybeckx, *Belgique politique*, 151–7.

[15] E. Gerard, 'Ontplooiing van de christelijke arbeidersbeweging (1904–1921)', in id. (ed.), *De christelijke arbeidersbeweging in België* (Leuven, 1991) i. 151–71.

[16] Id., *Documents relatifs à l'organisation du Parti Catholique Belge (1920–1922, 1931–1933)* (Cahiers du Centre interuniversitaire d'histoire contemporaine, 91; Louvain, 1981).

between these two camps ran deep and reached a climax after the elections of 1925 when the Christian democrat wing of the party led by Prosper Poullet chose to enter government with the Parti Ouvrier Belge of Emile Vandervelde. This unprecedented coalition of Marxist Socialists and Christian democrat Catholics aroused fierce opposition from both business interests and conservative Catholic politicians and, although the government was forced to resign in 1926, its legacy of bitterness and recrimination endured within the Catholic Party throughout the later 1920s and early 1930s.[17]

That the Catholic Party did not disintegrate into its heterogeneous components during the difficult years after the First World War owed much to the forces which still worked to preserve the unity of Catholic political organization. One such factor was the discreet but effective role played by the ecclesiastical hierarchy. In 1926 the wartime primate of Belgium, Cardinal Mercier, who had opposed the introduction of simple manhood suffrage and had also taken a firm stand against Flemish demands, died and he was replaced by the less charismatic but more cautious figure of Cardinal Van Roey. The son of a Flemish peasant family, Van Roey remained archbishop of Mechelen (Malines) and primate of Belgium for thirty-five years until his death in 1961 and he undoubtedly did more than any other individual to determine the course of Catholic politics from the 1920s to the 1960s. Van Roey's attitudes were highly traditional. Although Flemish in origin, he was distrustful of Flemish nationalism and possessed a deep-rooted antipathy to the atheistic, corrupting influences of modern culture. All forms of innovation—be they doctrinal, political, or social— were in Van Roey's eyes suspect and his aim throughout his long primacy was to protect the Catholic faithful against the evil spirit of the modern age. He sought to achieve this goal by two means. On the one hand, he encouraged the further expansion of Catholic social and educational institutions in order to surround the faithful with a comprehensive network of distinctly Catholic organizations; while, on the other hand, he consistently supported the Catholic Party as the sole authorized Catholic political grouping. Only by maintaining their political unity, Van Roey believed, could the Catholics ensure effective representation of their interests while also providing a rampart against the malevolent anticlericalism of the Liberal and Socialist parties.[18]

Van Roey had no hesitation in making public his support for the Catholic Party. His pastoral letters and other public pronouncements made clear to the faithful their duty to vote for the party's candidates, declaring, for example, in a speech in 1931 that 'C'est notre parti catholique traditionnel seul qui prend et assure sur le terrain politique la défense de nos intérêts suprêmes: sans lui, nous aurions à redouter

---

[17] E. Gerard, *De Katholieke Partij in crisis*, 219–43; id., 'Aanpassing in crisistijd (1921–1944)', in id. (ed.), *De christelijke arbeidersbeweging in België*, i. 178–86; C.-H. Höjer, *Le Régime parlementaire belge de 1918 à 1940* (Uppsala, 1946), 145–63; H. Haag, *Le Comte Charles De Broqueville, ministre d'état, et les luttes pour le pouvoir (1910–1940)* (Louvain-la-Neuve, 1990), ii. 727.

[18] A. Simon, 'L'Influence de l'église sur la vie politique dans l'entre-deux-guerres', *Res Publica*, 4 (1962), 393–4; R. Aubert, 'Le Cardinal Van Roey', *Revue Nouvelle*, 34 (Sept. 1961), 113–30; W. S. Plavsic, *Le Cardinal Van Roey* (Brussels, 1974); Cardinal Suenens, *Memories and Hopes*, 53–5.

comme en d'autres pays où l'organisation politique des catholiques fait défaut, les pires catastrophes.'[19] Reinforced by the advice offered by many local priests, such instructions did much to bolster electoral support for the Catholic Party and were complemented by the influential role which Van Roey and his fellow bishops played within the Catholic Party. Relations between the Church hierarchy and the Catholic political élite were always close and, in addition to ensuring that Catholic ministers were responsive to the Church's interests on matters such as education policy, the bishops intervened regularly in disputes between the party's different groupings in order to preserve the overall unity of the Catholic cause.

That unity was also reinforced by broader political and socio-economic factors. Compared with the polarised politics of the pre-1914 era, conflicts between the three main parties during the 1920s and 1930s were relatively muted. Despite their allegiance to different philosophies, little divided Catholics, Socialists, and Liberals on many practical issues while the absence of an overall parliamentary majority for any one party obliged them to work together in the continually shifting but essentially immobile coalition politics of the era.[20] Such cohabitation did little, however, to blur the distinctions between the three major parties. Indeed, it served to reinforce the compartmentalization of Belgian society into distinct Catholic, Socialist, and Liberal socio-cultural communities. This phenomenon of the pillarization of Belgian political and social life has frequently been remarked upon by historians and political scientists. Initially derived from the comparable example of the Netherlands,[21] it highlights the process whereby the political fault-lines derived from the nineteenth century gradually brought about a political segregation of Belgian society. Separate educational systems, youth movements, trade unions, insurance leagues, women's organizations, and even football teams and pensioners' groups, all served to reinforce this division into three largely separate Catholic, Socialist, and Liberal worlds in which an individual's allegiance to one or other political tradition was continually reinforced by the patterns of his or her daily life.[22]

Expressed in abstract terms, such an analysis can provide a misleading caricature of Belgian society. In reality, the increasing sophistication of a more technologically advanced, mobile, and urbanized society made any complete compartmentalization of social and cultural life impossible. Moreover, this emphasis on vertical pillarization should not be allowed to disguise the horizontal divisions of social class which, especially in times of crisis, transcended these socio-cultural divisions.[23] Nevertheless, especially during the fifty years from the First World War to the 1960s, most Belgians did identify with one of the three socio-cultural groupings. These loyalties

---

[19] Claeys-Van Haegendoren, 'L'Église et l'État au xxᵉ siècle', 7.

[20] A good general account of inter-war Belgian politics is provided in Höjer, *Le Régime parlementaire belge de 1918 à 1940*.

[21] See A. Lijphart, *The Politics of Accommodation: Pluralism and Democracy in the Netherlands* (Berkeley and Los Angeles, 1968). [22] Witte and Craeybeckx, *Belgique politique*, 292–304.

[23] See e.g. J. Billiet, 'Verzuiling en politiek: Theoretische beschouwingen over België na 1945', and P. Gérin, 'A propos de la "pilarisation" en Wallonie', *Belgisch tijdschrift voor nieuwste geschiedenis / Revue belge d'histoire contemporaine*, 13 (1982), 83–118 and 163–76.

worked to reinforce the immobility of the political landscape and also helped to preserve the unity of the Catholic Party. To cast one's vote for the party was the expression of an identification which for many Belgian Catholics had determined the pattern of their lives since childhood. In these circumstances, the opportunities for dissident movements were limited. The Catholic Party alone possessed the mantle of the authentic representative of the Catholic community while breakaway movements were deprived of access to the unofficial sources of influence and patronage which the network of Catholic religious, social, and economic organizations provided.

Nor for most Belgian Catholics did such dissident movements seem desirable or necessary. The compartmentalization of Belgian social life fostered a strong sense of a homogeneous Catholic identity which transcended internal regional or social divisions. Despite all the disputes within the Catholic Party during the 1920s and 1930s, most Catholics still retained a sense of their fundamental differentness from those of their compatriots who did not practise their faith. Continually reinforced by the teachings of the Church, the rhetoric of the Catholic press, and the prejudices expressed in private conversations, this hidden frontier between Catholic and non-Catholic was a durable reality which helps to explain the superficially illogical coexistence of different linguistic, ideological, and social groups within a common Catholic political organization.

That unitary Catholic political structure never appeared so vulnerable as it did in the early 1930s when three distinct but closely connected crises threatened the Catholic Party with disintegration. The first of these arose from the continuing tensions between the party's Christian democrat groupings and its predominantly conservative leadership. The demise of the Poullet–Vandervelde government in 1926 was the starting-point of a concerted attempt by the party's parliamentary leaders, aided by Van Roey and his fellow bishops, to impose a greater conformity within Catholic political ranks. The Christian democrat organizations grouped in the Algemeen Christelijk Werkersverbond/Ligue Nationale des Travailleurs Chrétiens (ACW/LNTC) were repeatedly accused by the Fédération des Cercles of bringing a spirit of class struggle into Catholic politics while the bishops ensured that lay religious organizations such as the highly successful Jeunesse Ouvrière Chrétienne (Christian Workers' Youth) founded in 1925 by the abbé Cardijn were kept apart from Christian democrat political activities.[24]

The various Catholic worker groups were, however, not easily intimidated. Membership of Catholic workers' organizations, such as insurance leagues and cooperatives, grew rapidly during the 1920s and, under the leadership of Henri Pauwels, the Catholic trade-union confederation, the Algemeen Christelijk Vakverbond/ Confédération des Syndicats Chrétiens (Union of Christian Trade Unions, ACV/ CSC) expanded from 133,156 members in 1925 to 304,010 by 1933. All these groupings were predominantly Flemish in composition. For example, 74.4 per cent of the membership of the ACV/CSC in 1940 was located in Flanders, 7.4 per cent in

---

[24] Gerard, *De Katholieke Partij in crisis*, 245–82; id., 'Cardijn, arbeidersbeweging en Katholieke Actie', in *Cardijn, un homme, un mouvement, een mens, een beweging* (Leuven, 1983), 119–47.

Brussels and only 18.3 per cent in the industrial heartlands of Wallonia.[25] In part, this was a consequence of the Socialist hegemony in the heavy industries of francophone Belgium, but it also reflected the close connection between the Catholic workers' movement and the development of a Flemish consciousness. Flemish grievances against the power exercised by the political and economic élite of Brussels as well as by a francophone bourgeoisie within Flanders had gained strength after the First World War. Demands for equal rights for the Dutch language in education and public administration went hand in hand with resentment at the prosecution by the Belgian judicial authorities of the small number of Flemish intellectuals who had chosen to work with the German administrators of Belgium during the First World War. Catholic workers' organizations could not remain immune from this upsurge in Flemish aspirations. In the 1920s the ACW was to the fore in Flemish campaigns and, though much of Flemish nationalism moved towards the political right during the 1930s, the Flemish and Christian democrat causes remained inextricably intertwined.[26]

Conversely, the association between the Flemish and Christian democrat movements strengthened the resolve of the largely francophone élite of the Catholic Party to counter the challenge represented by those whom they termed the 'démocrates flamands'. This tension became more marked as the world economic depression of the early 1930s made itself felt within Belgium. The Liberal–Catholic coalition government headed by the Catholic prime minister Charles De Broqueville implemented a policy of orthodox deflation which increased unemployment and imposed reductions in public expenditure. The depression threw the Catholic trade unions and the ACW/LNTC on the defensive. While seeking to minimize the reductions in welfare programmes, the Christian democrat groups were obliged to support the policies of a Catholic-led government, the consequences of which were keenly felt by their own supporters.[27] The strains which this created were evident throughout the Catholic Party but it was in the francophone industrial city of Charleroi that they found their clearest expression. Already during the 1920s the local Catholic Party had become polarized between its conservative leaders and Christian democrat groups led by an energetic young lawyer, Jean Bodart. Polemics in the local press and rivalries over control of Catholic social organizations sustained the conflict which took on a national dimension when Bodart was elected to parliament in 1932. His election had been preceded by attempts by the local Fédération des Cercles to insist that Bodart express his willingness to accept party discipline but in 1933 he resigned from parliament rather than support the policies of the De Broqueville government.

[25] Neuville, *Une génération syndicale*, 151; E. Gerard, 'Aanpassing in crisistijd', 234–8; J. Van Bouchaute, 'Het algemeen christelijk werkersverbond en de coöperaties (1924–1935)', *Belgisch tijdschrift voor nieuwste geschiedenis*, 22 (1991), 129–85.

[26] J. Billiet and E. Gerard, 'Église et politique: Les Relations difficiles entre les organisations catholiques et leur parti politique avant 1940', *Recherches sociologiques*, 16/3 (1985), 94.

[27] Haag, *Charles De Broqueville*, ii. 769–71, 773–8, 808–13, and 815–27; J. Neuville, *Adieu à la démocratie chrétienne? Elie Baussart et le mouvement ouvrier* (Brussels, 1973), 78–84; P. Wynants, 'La Jeunesse Ouvrière Chrétienne face au chômage des jeunes (1931–1936)', *Revue belge d'histoire contemporaine*, 10 (1979), 461–82.

At the subsequent general election in 1936, the local LNTC ran an independent electoral list against the Catholic Party and two of its candidates, including Bodart, were elected to parliament.[28]

The emergence of rival Catholic camps in Charleroi was, however, exceptional. Elsewhere, Christian democrat groups stopped short of breaking with the Catholic Party and the national congress of the ACW/LNTC in 1933 reluctantly expressed its support for government policies. Similarly, the ACW/LNTC rejected approaches from the Socialist Parti Ouvrier Belge to join its campaign for a plan for national recovery and the formation of a new tripartite Catholic–Socialist–Liberal government in 1935 led by a Catholic economist, Paul Van Zeeland, which devalued the Belgian franc and began a policy of modest reflation, made it easier for the Christian democrat groups to give their full support to the party's leadership.[29] This caution illustrated the self-imposed limits within which the leaders of the ACW/LNTC operated. Though eager to acquire a powerful position within the Catholic Party, most Catholic worker organizations were reluctant to contemplate forming their own party or forging alliances with those outside the Catholic community. Their ambitions remained rooted within the traditional mentalities of the Catholic world and, though they were Christian democrat in the sense that they claimed a Catholic inspiration for their desire for social, economic, and political reforms, their ideology stopped short of acceptance of participation in a pluralist politics and secular society which the term 'Christian democracy' would come to acquire by the 1960s.

The second challenge faced by the Catholic Party in the 1930s was the support shown by much of its Flemish electorate for demands for greater rights for Flanders. As early as 1919, Flemish grievances had led to the creation of a nationalist Front-partij (Front Party) and, though only a small minority supported independence, there was considerable support for an enhanced status for Flanders within the Belgian state. Reluctance on the part of the government to concede to their demands fed Flemish resentments and in a by-election in Antwerp in 1928 the Frontpartij candidate, Auguste Borms, one of those figures who had worked with the Germans during the Occupation of 1914–18 and who had been sentenced to death after the Liberation, was elected to parliament. This result was exceptional but in 1933 a new nationalist political grouping, the Vlaams Nationaal Verbond (Flemish National Union, VNV), was founded which in the 1936 elections won 13.56 per cent of the vote in Flanders and gained sixteen seats in parliament.[30] Initially an amalgam of pacifist, Socialist, and Catholic ideas, Flemish nationalism had become by the 1930s a largely Catholic-inspired movement which, in opposition to the parliamentary

---

[28] E. Gerard, 'Tussen apostolat en emancipatie: De christelijke arbeidersbeweging en de strijd om de sociale werken 1925–1933', in id. and J. Mampuys (eds.), *Voor Kerk en Werk* (Leuven, 1986), 203–56; P. Wynants, 'La Controverse Cardijn-Valschaerts (mars–avril 1931)', *Revue belge d'histoire contemporaine*, 15 (1984), 103–36; Neuville, *Adieu à la démocratie chrétienne*, 77–8, 85–97, and 103–5.

[29] Gerard 'Aanpassing in crisistijd', 198–213; Claeys-Van Haegendoren 'L'Église et l'État au xxᵉ siècle', 10–11.

[30] A. W. Willemsen *De Vlaamse Beweging* (Hasselt, 1975), ii. 80–353; De Smet, Evalenko, and Fraeys, *Atlas des élections belges 1919–1954*, annexe statistique, 294.

Belgian regime, gravitated towards the authoritarian right of the political spectrum. The association between the Flemish movement and Christian democrat groups continued but it was increasingly overshadowed by the emergence of nationalist groupings of the extreme right. Rather as in Croatia and Slovakia, Flemish nationalism of the inter-war years acquired a particular religious and political character which was reflected in the symbolism of the Yser Tower, inaugurated in 1930 to commemorate the Flemish dead of the First World War, with its unambiguous inscription: 'Alles voor Vlaanderen, Vlaanderen voor Kristus' (All for Flanders, Flanders for Christ).[31]

The policies of incremental reform practised by Van Cauwelaert's Katholieke Vlaamse Kamergroep in parliament no longer satisfied Flemish aspirations and new, more radical, forms of action were demanded. It was from the young that this pressure was strongest. The Catholic student organization in Flanders, the Algemeen Katholiek Vlaams Studentenverbond (Flemish Catholic Student Union), was disowned by the bishops because of its outspoken support for Flemish nationalist aspirations and in 1934 an influential periodical, *Nieuw Vlaanderen* (New Flanders), was launched which became the rallying-point for a new generation of Flemish Catholic politicians. Though it stopped short of support for an independent Flanders, *Nieuw Vlaanderen* called for wide-ranging political reforms and advocated an alliance with Flemish nationalist groups.[32]

Combined with the support for Flemish demands long voiced by Christian democrat groupings, this pressure obliged the Catholic political leaders to respond to Flemish aspirations. Support for the Catholic Party in Flanders fell from 47.22 per cent in 1932 to 37.32 per cent in the elections of 1936, largely at the expense of the nationalists of the VNV and in December 1936 the newly created Catholic Party organization in Flanders, the Katholieke Vlaamse Volkspartij (Flemish Catholic People's Party, KVV), signed a limited agreement with the VNV. Though it had few immediate consequences, this accord expressed the willingness of the two parties to work together to advance Flemish interests and led to some local collaboration between the KVV and the VNV. The *rapprochement* between the Catholic Party and Flemish nationalist groups helped to limit the losses suffered by the party in Flanders. In the 1939 elections, both the KVV and the VNV gained votes and, though the continued absence of major political reforms led some Flemish Catholics to opt for the integral nationalism represented by the VNV, others—such as the editor of *Nieuw Vlaanderen* and future Catholic prime minister, Gaston Eyskens— chose to remain within the Catholic fold.[33]

---

[31] J. Stengers 'Belgium', in H. Rogger and E. Weber (eds.), *The European Right: A Historical Profile* (London, 1965), 153–5; G. Van Hamer, *Onmacht der verdeelden: Katholieken in Vlaanderen tussen democratie en fascisme 1929–1940* (Berchem, 1983); L. Vos, 'De ideologische orientering van de katholieke studerende jeugd in Vlaanderen (1930–1940): Een voorlopige balans', *Belgisch tijdschrift voor nieuwste geschiedenis*, 8 (1977), 207–35; Witte and Craeybeckx, *Belgique politique*, 189–90.

[32] Gerard, *De Katholieke Partij in crisis*, 413–18; Billiet and Gerard, 'Église et politique', 99.

[33] Gerard, 'Aanpassing in crisistijd', 219–21; De Smet, Evalenko, and Fraeys, *Atlas des élections belges 1919–1954*, annexe statistique, 10.

The third source of division in Catholic political ranks came from a very different quarter. While the Christian democrat and Flemish nationalist groups posed the major challenge to Catholic unity in Flanders, in francophone Belgium it was an amalgam of bourgeois and rural discontents which threatened the position of the Catholic Party. In Brussels and Wallonia, the Socialist party was the dominant force among the working class and the Catholic Party drew its support largely from the Catholic elements of the bourgeoisie and the rural populations of southern Wallonia. Both these groups had strong grievances. For the francophone bourgeoisie, the democratic reforms introduced after the First World War had destroyed their former political ascendancy while the economic upheavals of the inter-war years created unprecedented difficulties for many members of the middle classes. The rural communities of areas such as southern Namur and the Ardennes were similarly adversely affected by economic trends. The fall in world agricultural prices was felt particularly severely by the small-scale farmers of these upland regions who struggled to maintain their living standards in the face of strong competition from cheaper imports.

Francophone Catholic discontent first surfaced immediately after the First World War in the modest success enjoyed by periodicals such as *L'Autorité* (Authority) and the nationalist league, the Jeunesses Nationales (National Youth), established by the Catholic writer and politician Pierre Nothomb.[34] It was, however, during the 1920s that this dissatisfaction gathered strength. A vogue for authoritarian figures such as Mussolini and the Action Française movement of Charles Maurras was evident among Catholic university students and many senior Catholic figures who found in such foreign examples an expression of their own discontent towards a parliamentary regime which no longer seemed responsive to their interests. The largely conservative political organization within the Catholic Party, the Fédération des Cercles, was strongly influenced by these ideas as were periodicals such as the influential *Revue catholique des idées et des faits* (Catholic Review of Ideas and Events) which maintained a steady attack on the alleged failings of the democratic political system.[35] Not all francophone Catholic discontent was, however, merely reactionary in nature. It also drew much of its strength from the enthusiasm evident among many younger Catholics during the 1920s for a more assertive Catholic faith. This generational revolt against what the young perceived to be the spiritual complacency of their elders formed part of a more general upsurge in Catholic radicalism throughout Europe. As in other predominantly Catholic countries such as Portugal and Austria, young Catholic intellectuals—encouraged by the encyclicals of Pius XI—advocated a more

---

[34] J. Serruys, *Sous le signe de l'autorité* (Brussels, 1935); L. Schepens, 'Fascists and Nationalists in Belgium 1919–40', in S. V. Larsen, B. Hagtvet, and J. P. Myklebust (eds.), *Who were the Fascists* (Bergen, 1980), 504–5.

[35] E. Defoort, 'Le Courant réactionnaire dans le catholicisme francophone belge, 1918–1926', *Revue belge d'histoire contemporaine*, 8 (1977), 81–149; F. Balace, 'Fascisme et catholicisme politique dans la Belgique francophone de l'entre-deux-guerres', *Handelingen van het XXXIIᵉ Vlaams filologencongres* (Leuven, 1979), 146–64; *Revue catholique des idées et des faits*, 24–31 May 1929, p. 1, and 13 Oct. 1933, p. 1, 'La Semaine'.

heroic and confrontational Catholicism which sought to reverse the ascendancy of modern liberal values in Belgium.

The principal manifestation of this spiritual resurgence was the rapid growth of the Association Catholique de la Jeunesse Belge (ACJB) which was founded only in 1921 but which ten years later held a congress of 100,000 young supporters in Brussels.[36] The immediate impact of the success of the ACJB was to draw many young francophone Catholics away from conventional political activities. The youth groups of the Catholic Party shrank into insignificance while the ACJB, with its rhetoric of spiritual purity and Catholic reconquest, led much of Catholic youth to look on the inevitable compromises and coalitions of parliamentary politics with distaste.[37] By the early 1930s, however, the pressure of events both within and outside Belgium caused some of these Catholic radicals to seek a political expression for their ideal of a more militant Catholicism. The impact of the economic depression combined with events such as the rise of 'pagan' Nazism in Germany and the murder of the Austrian Catholic leader Dollfuss in 1934 created a mood of urgency in which the ACJB's goal of a gradual reconversion of Belgium to the Catholic faith no longer seemed sufficient. Instead, periodicals such as *La Cité chrétienne* (The Christian City) and *L'Esprit nouveau* (New Spirit) called for a Catholic-inspired New Order in Belgium inspired by papal doctrines and modelled on the analogous examples of Salazar in Portugal and Dollfuss's regime in Austria.[38]

This quest for a Catholic third way between liberal parliamentarism and the statist authoritarianism of Mussolini and Hitler gave rise to the most significant Catholic dissident grouping in inter-war Belgium: the Rexist movement led by Léon Degrelle. Rex derived its name from a publishing house, Christus Rex (Christ the King), owned by the ACJB in the Catholic university town of Louvain (Leuven). Its title was in itself significant. The cult of Christ the King reigning in majesty over the world was central to the imagery of the ACJB and Degrelle and the other Rexists, as they soon became known, were young students who had been enthused by the mood of Catholic spiritual renewal in Louvain during the 1920s. Degrelle was from the outset the dominant figure within Rex. He was a charismatic and ebullient figure who, after his appointment as the director of the publishing house, used his journalistic and commercial talents to launch a series of mass-circulation periodicals which combined Catholic piety with a shrewd grasp of popular tastes. His father was a provincial Catholic politician in the Luxembourg but the young Degrelle soon became dissatisfied with the cautious conservatism of the Catholic Party. His ambitions broadened in scope and during 1934 he began to hold public meetings at which he used his considerable rhetorical powers to heap scorn on the

[36] G. Hoyois, *Gestes de jeunes* (Louvain, n.d.) and id., *Aux origines de l'Action Catholique*.

[37] J. Streel, *Les Jeunes Gens et la politique* (Louvain, 1932); R. Verlaine, *Sans haine et sans gloire* (Liège, 1944), 65–70.

[38] M. Conway, 'Building the Christian City: Catholics and Politics in Inter-War Francophone Belgium', *Past and Present*, 128 (1990), 139–40; id., 'Du catholicisme à la collaboration: Le Cas de José Streel', in *Belgique 1940: Une société en crise, un pays en guerre* (Brussels, 1993), 310–15.

political élite and to call for a new political and social order inspired by Catholic ideals.[39]

In the difficult circumstances of the early 1930s, Degrelle's simplistic message enjoyed considerable appeal and Rexist groups of young Catholic militants gradually appeared throughout francophone Belgium. Finally, in November 1935 Degrelle chose to challenge the leaders of the Catholic Party directly. Together with a group of young supporters, he stormed into a meeting of the national leadership of the Fédération des Cercles at Kortrijk (Courtrai) and delivered a passionate denunciation of their personal and political failings.[40] Whether Degrelle intended to launch his own political movement or simply to bring about a transformation within the Catholic Party was unclear but this *coup de Courtrai* led both the Church and the Catholic political leadership to distance themselves publicly from Rex. Degrelle, carried away by his own success and by the enthusiasm of his supporters, responded by announcing that Rex would contest the forthcoming elections in May 1936 as an independent political force. After a turbulent and improvised election campaign, during which Degrelle combined Poujadist denunciations of the political élite with vague promises of wide-ranging political and socio-economic reforms, his movement won 11.49 per cent of the vote and twenty-one of its candidates were elected to parliament.[41]

This remarkable success was based principally on the Catholic electorate of francophone Belgium. In Flanders, Rex gained only 7.01 per cent of the vote while in the francophone rural provinces of Namur and the Luxembourg it won 20.35 and 29.06 per cent respectively. All the major parties lost votes to Rex but it was the Catholic Party which was the principal victim of Degrelle's appeal. The party slumped from 38.55 per cent of the vote in 1932 to 27.67 per cent in 1936—its lowest electoral score until 1981.[42] Degrelle's demagogic talents had capitalized upon the political and socio-economic grievances of the bourgeois and rural electorate of the francophone Catholic Party. Peasant anger at the problems of the agricultural economy combined with student radicalism and bourgeois discontents to create a heterogeneous coalition of the Catholic discontented. It did not, however, prove to be a durable basis upon which to build a mass party. During the summer and autumn of 1936 Degrelle and his colleagues tried to capitalize upon their electoral success but, faced with the resolve of the Van Zeeland government to oppose the new movement, the Rexist leaders were forced to adopt ever more desperate tactics. A Mussolinian 'March on Brussels' in October 1936 was a fiasco and in April 1937 Rex sought to recover the political initiative by instigating a by-election in Brussels in which Degrelle stood against a single candidate representing the Catholic, Liberal, and Socialist parties, the prime minister Paul Van Zeeland.[43]

---

[39] J.-M. Etienne, *Le Mouvement rexiste jusqu'en 1940* (Paris, 1968), 14–26.

[40] Ibid. 28–9.   [41] Ibid. 43–9 and 53–63.

[42] De Smet, Evalenko, and Fraeys *Atlas des élections belges 1919–1954*, 27–9, and annexe statistique, 10, 247, and 273.

[43] J. Stengers, 'Belgium', in Rogger and Weber (eds.), *European Right*, 157–61; Etienne, *Mouvement*, 117–26 and 133–40.

The outcome of this unequal contest was probably never in doubt but a few days before the election Degrelle unwisely sought to claim at a public rally that his party enjoyed the unspoken support of the primate of Belgium, Cardinal Van Roey. The Archbishop of Mechelen's attitude towards Rex had always been very circumspect. Although he had repeatedly made clear that Rex was in no sense an official Catholic organization, he had avoided making any categorical condemnation of the new movement and had long hoped that a reconciliation between Degrelle and the Catholic Party would prove possible. The Rexist leader's attempt to claim episcopal backing for his campaign against Van Zeeland did, however, force Van Roey to abandon his former caution. Pressed by the leaders of the Catholic Party to declare his support for the prime minister, the Cardinal duly issued a public statement denouncing Rex as 'un danger pour le pays et pour l'Église'.[44] This intervention consolidated Degrelle's already inevitable defeat and when the results of the election on 11 April were announced the Rexist leader had won only 19 per cent of the popular vote. The defeat hastened the process of internal disintegration of Rex which from the summer of 1937 entered into a rapid decline. Having broken with his initial Catholic inspiration, Degrelle drifted towards an emulation of Nazi and Italian Fascist models and in the subsequent general elections in 1939 Rex gained the support of only 4.43 per cent of the electorate while most of its erstwhile supporters returned to the Catholic Party.[45]

Probably the only chance for Rex to have established a permanent place in Belgian political life was if conservative francophone elements in the Catholic Party had opted to ally themselves with it. There certainly were prominent Catholic figures who privately advocated such an alliance during the winter of 1936–7 but they finally chose to remain loyal to the Van Zeeland coalition government of Catholics, Socialists, and Liberals.[46] The maintenance of Catholic political unity was greatly assisted by the energetic leadership of the new president of the Catholic Party, Hubert Pierlot. A former Catholic minister of the interior from the Luxembourg, Pierlot was well aware of the seriousness of the Rexist challenge and he seized on the electoral defeat of May 1936 to accomplish wide-ranging reforms of the party's internal structure. The unwieldy system of power-sharing between different groups introduced in 1921 was abandoned and a new structure implemented which combined a system of individual membership with devolution of power to the francophone and Flemish wings of the party, each of which acquired its own identity and its own name: the Parti Chrétien Social (Social Christian Party) in francophone Belgium and the Katholieke Vlaamse Volkspartij (Flemish Christian People's Party) in Flanders. The new structure was not without its problems, and antipathies between the Fédération des Cercles and the LNTC ensured that it never came fully into operation in

[44] A. Dantoing, *La 'Collaboration' du Cardinal* (Brussels, 1991), 208–11; E. Gerard, 'La Responsabilité du monde catholique dans la naissance et l'essor du rexisme', *Revue Nouvelle* (Jan. 1987), 72–5.

[45] Etienne, *Mouvement*, 141–67.

[46] Gerard, 'La Responsabilité du monde catholique', 74; M.-H. Jaspar, *Souvenirs sans retouche* (Paris, 1968), 204–7.

francophone Belgium.[47] Nevertheless, the changes introduced by Pierlot did mark a major step towards the creation of a modern political party and, combined with a modest economic recovery and the political reforms introduced by Van Zeeland, they ensured that the Catholic Party of the immediate pre-war years recovered some of the unity of purpose and organisation which had been so absent for much of the inter-war years.

As war approached, the Catholic Party once again stood at the centre of attempts to organize national defence. Pierlot himself became prime minister in February 1939 and during the subsequent summer and winter his coalition government sought to preserve Belgium's neutrality. On 10 May 1940, however, the German forces attacked and Pierlot and his fellow ministers joined King Léopold III in leading the struggle against the Nazi invaders. The superiority of the German military machine was, however, soon evident and on 28 May 1940 the King, as commander of the Belgian armed forces, was obliged to conclude an armistice with the Nazi authorities.

In military terms, the logic of the armistice was unavoidable but its political consequences were considerable. The Nazi invasion had brought to a head the long-standing tensions between the political élite and the young king, who had come to the throne on the death of his father Albert in February 1934. Léopold was a firm supporter of the diplomatic independence of Belgium and he regarded the armistice as having marked the conclusion of his country's involvement in the war. Pierlot and his principal ministers disagreed and, while Léopold chose to remain in Belgium and was taken prisoner by the German armies, the ministers retreated to France intending to continue the military struggle alongside the Western Allies. Compromise between the King and the government proved impossible and the Belgian ministers in France issued a decree on 28 May stating that, by virtue of his imprisonment, the King was unable to exercise his responsibilities and that the government had temporarily assumed his powers. For his part, the King refused to accept the legitimacy of the government's actions and during the remainder of 1940 he tried to reach some form of accommodation with the Nazi authorities, culminating in an inconclusive meeting with Hitler at Berchtesgaden on 19 November 1940. After the defeat of France in June 1940, the Pierlot government sought to enter into negotiations with the King and the Nazi authorities but their approaches were rebuffed and in the autumn Pierlot and his Foreign Minister, Paul-Henri Spaak, escaped from France via Spain to London where they established a government in exile in December 1940. This was recognized by the Western Allies but not by Léopold III who remained a mute but influential figure within German-Occupied Belgium until his deportation to Germany in 1944.[48]

The conflict between the King and the government was to overshadow much of Belgium's post-war history but in the immediate aftermath of the defeat attention

---

[47] J.-C. Ricquier, 'Auguste De Schryver: Souvenirs politiques et autres', *Revue générale* (May 1982), 21; Gerard, *De Katholieke Partij in crisis*, 485–506; Simon, *Le Parti catholique belge*, 116–17.

[48] J. Stengers, *Léopold III et le gouvernement: Les Deux Politiques belges de 1940* (Paris, 1980).

was focused instead on the need to adapt to the German military victory. In the summer of 1940 almost all Belgians accepted that Germany had achieved a definitive hegemony over continental Europe and they supported the King's efforts to preserve some form of unified Belgian state. Catholics shared in this national consensus. Cardinal Van Roey and the majority of his fellow bishops gave Léopold their full support while many ordinary Catholics participated in the process of national reconstruction.[49] For those Catholic militants who before 1940 had opposed the parliamentary regime, the military defeat had, however, a wider significance. It appeared to vindicate their pre-war views and in the summer of 1940 a number of Catholic-inspired groups emerged which—as in Vichy France—advocated a new political and social structure based on Catholic principles.[50]

Such enthusiasms were on the whole short-lived. As it became apparent that the war was not in fact over and that the Nazi authorities were unwilling to support the emergence of a new regime within Belgium, so the prospects of wide-ranging political reform receded. Nevertheless, some Catholic elements remained committed to a vision of an authoritarian and corporatist Belgium and chose to adopt a policy of collaboration with the Third Reich. The two principal collaborationist movements in wartime Belgium were the Flemish nationalist VNV and the Rexist movement led by Léon Degrelle. Both were, at least in part, dissident Catholic groups in origin and, though they had already evolved before the war towards a quasi-fascist political stance, much of their ideology and social composition continued to reflect their Catholic background. The VNV rapidly emerged as the foremost partners of the German military administrators of Belgium and several thousand members of the VNV served in German military and paramilitary units both within Belgium and in Russia. The predominantly francophone Rexist movement followed an even more extreme course. Though initially shunned by the Nazis, Degrelle opted unambivalently for the German cause. Rexist soldiers—including Degrelle—fought on the Eastern Front while in francophone areas of Belgium Rexist militants were appointed by the German authorities to positions of influence in local and provincial government. As German military fortunes waned, so the VNV gradually sought to withdraw from wholehearted collaboration but the Rexists remained loyal to the Nazi cause. Degrelle forged an alliance with Himmler's SS and during the latter years of the war the erstwhile advocate of a Catholic spiritual revolution became an unlikely hero of the Nazi propaganda machine.[51]

Though spectacular, the evolution of the VNV and Rex was atypical of majority Catholic opinion. The oppressive policies of the German authorities served to discredit anti-democratic political ideas and, as the war progressed, there was a substantial evolution in Catholic political attitudes away from the authoritarian projects

[49] Dantoing, *La 'Collaboration' du Cardinal*, 111–45.

[50] e.g. J. Gérard-Libois and J. Gotovitch, *L'An 40* (Brussels, 1971), 467–73.

[51] B. De Wever, *Greep naar de macht: Vlaams nationalisme en nieuwe orde. Het VNV, 1933–1945* (Tielt, 1994); M. Conway, *Collaboration in Belgium: Léon Degrelle and the Rexist Movement 1940–1944* (New Haven, 1993); Gérard-Libois and Gotovitch, *L'An 40*, 298–305; A. Dantoing, 'Du fascisme occidental à la politique de présence: Robert Poulet', in *Belgique 1940: Une société en crise, un pays en guerre*, 337–43.

of the 1930s and towards a vision of a new, more democratic, political and social order.[52] As during the first German Occupation of 1914–18, the Church emerged as a prominent institution in wartime Belgium. The cautious Van Roey was ill-suited to assume the role of national spokesman adopted by his predecessor Cardinal Mercier but his pastoral letters criticizing German policies had a considerable impact, while at a local level it was often Catholic priests who from the relative freedom of the pulpit acted as a voice for patriotic sentiments.[53] Some Catholics also became involved in active resistance to the German forces. Catholic militants were prominent in both the substantial clandestine press and in the intelligence networks which supplied military information to London as well as in the escape networks created for Allied airmen. Others joined the patriotic, army officer-led Armée Secrète (Secret Army) which emerged as a clandestine military force within Belgium while some Christian democrat figures, notably in Wallonia, joined the coalition of left-wing Resistance groups which constituted the Front de l'Indépendance (Independence Front).[54]

With the Allied liberation of Belgium in September 1944, the question of Catholic political organization once again came to the fore. At first sight, the events of the war years appeared to have rendered obsolete any unitary Catholic grouping. Distrust of the pre-war parties and the political conflicts which they represented was widespread and amidst the euphoria of Liberation there was—as in much of Europe—an expectation that the divisions of the past would give way to a more democratic and egalitarian society. The Catholic Party was too rooted in the pre-war system to participate in this new world and there were many Catholic intellectuals who, through their wartime experiences in Resistance organizations and study groups, had come to regard the ghetto mentality fostered by distinctly Catholic forms of political organization as outmoded.[55] Nor was it merely intellectuals who shared this outlook. The sufferings and disruptions of the war years had done much to break down the divisions within Belgian society. By throwing together Catholic and non-Catholic, the Nazi Occupation had undermined the mutual distrust fostered by the pillarization of Belgian social institutions while stimulating a new mood of national common purpose.

In other respects, however, the war years had consolidated Catholic unity. The suspension of political activity imposed by the German invasion had silenced the factional squabbles within the Catholic political elite while the decision of the Rexist movement and the VNV to collaborate with the Nazi authorities had discredited the two major dissident groupings within the Catholic world. The experience of Occupation also worked in other ways to restore a sense of a distinctive Catholic

---

[52] J. Willequet, *La Belgique sous la botte: Résistances et collaborations 1940–1945* (Paris, 1986), 117–18 and 127–33; P. Struye, *L'Évolution du sentiment public en Belgique sous l'occupation allemande* (Brussels, 1945), 63–4, 94–8 and 123–5.

[53] A. Dantoing, 'La Hiérarchie catholique et la Belgique sous l'occupation allemande', *Revue du Nord*, 60 (1978), 315–24.

[54] H. Bernard, *La Résistance 1940–1945* (Brussels, 1969), 37, 60–1, 63–4, and 104–11; J. Gotovitch, *Du rouge au tricolore: Les Communistes belges de 1939 à 1944* (Brussels, 1992), 382–3.

[55] 'Entretiens avec un homme libre: Marcel Grégoire (III)', *Revue générale* (Nov. 1985), 5–7.

identity. The prominent role played by the Church during the war reinforced the power of the ecclesiastical hierarchy and had also helped to stimulate a mood of spiritual renewal. Attendance at mass rose markedly amidst the uncertainties and dangers of war and Catholic social and youth groups—as well as the Catholic-sponsored charitable organization Secours d'hiver/Winterhulp (Winter Help)—had galvanized the energies and idealism of the Catholic laity.[56]

Thus, though all were agreed on the need to avoid a return to the Catholic Party of the inter-war years, Belgian Catholics emerged from the war with a renewed sense of their common purpose and a heightened optimism that the values of Catholicism did indeed offer a distinctive solution to the problems of a modern democratic society. The ecclesiastical hierarchy encouraged this attitude. Van Roey feared that a post-war secular coalition of Liberals, Socialists, and Communists would attack the power of the Catholic Church and he regarded the resuscitation of a Catholic political grouping to be an urgent priority.[57] Aided by the return of Pierlot and other Catholic political leaders from London, Van Roey encouraged the efforts of a predominantly younger generation of politicians to create a new Catholic Party which, while rejecting the ghetto mentality of its predecessor, would act as a spokesman for distinctively Catholic values and interests. The result was the Parti Social Chrétien/Christelijke Volkspartij (Christian Social Party/Christian People's Party, PSC/CVP). Already in December 1944, a preliminary basis for the new party's programme had been defined and in May 1945 a more detailed programme was published. In the summer of 1945 the liberation of Léopold III from detention in Austria provoked a crisis within the government of national unity and the Catholic ministers resigned. Their departure from government hastened the creation of the new party. An inaugural congress was held in August at which Auguste De Schryver was elected as the PSC/CVP's first president and a series of commissions were established which defined its stance on a wide variety of social and political issues. These formed the basis of the PSC/CVP's manifesto in the first post-war elections held in February 1946. Supported strenuously by Van Roey and his fellow bishops, the party won a remarkable 42.66 per cent of the vote—the highest score achieved by any Catholic political grouping since the First World War.[58]

The success of the PSC/CVP was all the more striking because it was achieved despite the challenge posed by a rival Catholic political grouping, the Union Démocratique Belge (Belgian Democratic Union, UDB). This had been created in the immediate aftermath of the liberation by a group of predominantly francophone Catholic intellectuals who intended that it should be a non-confessional progressive party based on the example of the British Labour party. The party made much of its Resistance credentials and advocated wide-ranging social reforms as well as an end to

[56] A. Dantoing, 'La Vie religieuse sous l'occupation allemande', in *1940–1945: La vie quotidienne en Belgique* (Brussels, 1984), 169–75.

[57] R. Aubert, 'L'Église catholique et la vie politique en Belgique depuis la seconde guerre mondiale', *Res Publica*, 15 (1973), 187–8.

[58] M. Van den Wijngaert, *Onstaan en stichting van de CVP–PSC: De lange weg naar het kerstprogramma* (Brussels, 1976).

the confessional divisions in Belgian social and political life. It enjoyed the support of a new newspaper, *La Cité nouvelle* (New City), and the first congress of the party was held in Brussels in June 1945. When the Catholic ministers resigned from the government in the summer, supporters of the UDB took their place and the party's principal spokesman, Marcel Grégoire, became minister of justice. The success of the new party did, however, prove to be transient. Its main strength was in the city of Liège and it possessed little by way of national organization. Moreover, the UDB was, despite its claims to be a workers' party, predominantly a middle-class organization and most Catholic trade-unionists even in Wallonia chose to remain aloof from it. Most importantly, the UDB encountered the implacable opposition of the ecclesiastical hierarchy. In October 1945 Van Roey received De Schryver, the president of the PSC/CVP, and the Cardinal subsequently called on all Catholics to unite behind the new 'official' Catholic Party. Crushed between the rise of the PSC/CVP and the ascendancy of the Socialist and Communist parties among the francophone industrial working class, the UDB could appeal only to a small predominantly middle-class electorate and in the 1946 elections it won a mere 2.19 per cent of the vote. Soon afterwards, the party's leadership resigned and the UDB disappeared as a political grouping.[59]

The demise of the UDB symbolized the immobilism of the post-war Belgian political landscape. Despite the rise of the Communist Party, the three historical parties—the Catholics, Socialists, and Liberals—remained the dominant political forces and continued to enjoy the support of a large majority of the electorate.[60] These traditional divisions acted as a weight on the new PSC/CVP forcing it almost despite itself to adopt the attitudes and mentality of the pre-war Catholic Party. There is no doubt, however, that the founders of the party intended that it should be a genuinely new political force. 'Un parti nouveau, une doctrine neuve, des équipes jeunes, voilà ce qu'est le PSC', declared its manifesto and three-quarters of its deputies elected to parliament in 1946 were indeed new figures who had not held office before 1940.[61] The structures of the party were also consciously intended to be a break with the pre-war Catholic Party. Building on the reforms introduced by Pierlot in the late 1930s, the PSC/CVP was composed of individual members and separate regional bureaucracies were established to direct the party in Flanders and francophone Belgium. The Fédération des Cercles was abolished while the Christian democrat groups were obliged to surrender their formal power in favour of an indirect if nevertheless substantial influence from outside the structures of the party.[62]

[59] J. C. Williame, 'L'Union Démocratique Belge', *Courrier hebdomadaire du CRISP* 743–4 (1976); 'Entretiens avec un homme libre: Marcel Grégoire (III)', *Revue générale* (Nov. 1985), 7–9 and 14; Plavsic, *Cardinal Van Roey*, 142–4.

[60] E. Witte, 'Tussen restauratie en vernieuwing: Een introductie op de Belgische politieke evolutie tussen 1944 en 1950', in id., J. Burgelman, and P. Stouthuysen, *Tussen restauratie en vernieuwing* (Brussels, 1990), 13–56; Aubert 'L'Église catholique et la vie politique', 188.

[61] *Principes et tendances du Parti Social Chrétien* (Brussels, [1946]), 9; J.-C. Ricquier, 'Auguste De Schryver (II)', *Revue générale* (June–July 1982), 26–28.

[62] Gerard, *De Katholieke Partij in crisis*, 507–9; J. Smits, 'De afbouw van de autonome politieke actie van het ACW en de oprichting van de CVP', in Gerard and Mampuys (eds.), *Voor Kerk en Werk*, 313–53.

The most important change in the post-war PSC/CVP was, however, in its ideology. Rather than merely acting as the defender of the interests of the Catholic Church and faithful, the new party was—its propagandists insisted—committed to a new form of society which would provide a 'third way' between liberal capitalism and Marxist totalitarianism:

Nous voulons avant tout sauver l'homme. Aujourd'hui celui-ci est asservi. Ou bien il est dominé par les puissances d'argent, ou bien il est guetté par le césarisme administratif d'un État totalitaire. Nous voulons restaurer la liberté. En centrant toute sa doctrine et toute sà politique sur la notion de la personne humaine épanouie dans ses sociétés naturelles saines, le PSC s'oppose absolument aussi bien à la théorie capitaliste libérale qu'à la philosophie marxiste.[63]

'Personalism' was the key word in their ideology. Like the MRP in post-war France, the PSC/CVP derived many of its ideas from Catholic philosophers such as Jacques Maritain and Emmanuel Mounier whose calls for the liberation of the individual from the twin perils of the totalitarian state and the anomie of liberal society permeated its rhetoric. Though it was inspired by these Catholic values, the PSC/CVP was eager to insist that it was not confessional in character. The replacement of the word 'Catholic' by the more conciliatory term 'Christian' in the party's title was one indication of this change in outlook and its leaders insisted that the PSC/CVP was open to all Belgians who supported their programme of political and socio-economic reforms. This programme was a genuinely new departure. In contrast to Catholic infatuation with authoritarian models in the 1930s, the PSC/CVP stressed its commitment to a more open and democratic parliamentary regime, albeit reinforced by a strong executive capable of assuring the supremacy of the national interest. Similarly, the party rejected pre-war Catholic dreams of a corporatist socio-economic structure, advocating instead substantial social reforms including improved welfare provision, industrial democracy, and a more egalitarian distribution of wealth.[64]

The bold ambitions of the founders of the PSC/CVP were, however, contradicted by the realities of the political situation. In 1947 the party formed a coalition government with the Socialists but few elements of their programme of reforms were put into operation. The priorities of economic reconstruction and the diplomatic and ideological integration of Belgium into the Cold War West European alliance cast disfavour on ideas of political or economic reform while pressure from Cardinal Van Roey ensured that the party remained closely tied to the defence of traditional Catholic interests.[65] Similar pressures were felt by Catholic parties elsewhere in Europe but it was above all the controversy surrounding King Léopold III which undermined the efforts of the PSC/CVP to emerge as a truly non-confessional party

---

[63] *Principes et tendances du Parti Social Chrétien*, 11.

[64] Ibid.; Van den Wijngaert, *Onstaan en stichting van de CVP–PSC*, 29–35 and 47–9; Witte, 'Tussen restauratie en vernieuwing', 19–20.

[65] J. Gérard-Libois and R. Lewin, *La Belgique entre dans la guerre froide et l'Europe (1947–1953)* (Brussels, 1992), 199–203; J. Smits, 'De afbouw van de autonome politieke actie van het ACW', in Gerard and Mampuys (eds.), *Voor Kerk en Werk*, 344–351; Aubert 'L'Église catholique et la vie politique', 191–4.

in Belgium. At the Liberation, Léopold's brother, Prince Charles, had been appointed as regent but in 1945 the King was released from detention in Austria and declared his intention of recovering his throne. Negotiations between Léopold III and the government failed, however, to reach an agreement on the conditions for such a return and Léopold reluctantly went into exile in Switzerland. Within Belgium, the future of the King soon became the dominant political issue. The Liberal, Socialist, and Communist parties all opposed the King's return, accusing him of having sought to collaborate with the Germans during the Occupation and of wishing to undermine the democratic constitution. In response, the Catholic Church emerged as the principal defender of the King. Van Roey was convinced of the rectitude of Léopold's wartime actions. He visited the King in exile in Switzerland and in a pastoral letter issued in 1951 bitterly denounced the accusations levelled at the King as 'une campagne effrénée de calomnie et de diffamation'.[66]

The 'question royale', as it was termed, confronted the Catholic political leaders with an awkward dilemma. On the one hand, the majority of them instinctively supported the King, and the Catholic ministers had resigned from the government in 1945 in protest at Léopold's exclusion from Belgium.[67] On the other hand, to support the campaign for the King's return would be to encourage the very polarization of politics on clerical–anticlerical lines which it had been the intention of the PSC/CVP to avoid. Their initial response was to take refuge in advocating that the issue should be resolved by a national referendum and the Socialist–Catholic coalition government formed in 1947 tacitly agreed not to confront the problem. The royal issue refused, however, to disappear. The country became ever more clearly divided into pro-and anti-Léopoldist camps while from exile the King led a determined campaign to clear his name and regain the throne. There still were Catholic leaders—especially Christian democrats in Wallonia—who avoided giving their support to Léopold but in general the struggle became one between a 'progressive' coalition of Socialists and Liberals and a rival 'clerico-royalist' coalition of Catholics and right-wing Resistance groups. Regional differences added to the bitterness of the conflict. In Brussels and Wallonia, support for the King was muted while in Flanders the Léopoldist cause also became a struggle to assert the Flemish Catholic identity against the liberal and secular influences of francophone Belgium.[68]

Support for the King worked to the electoral advantage of the PSC/CVP. In 1948 women had finally been accorded the vote in parliamentary elections and in the subsequent elections in 1949 a female Catholic vote and the party's status as the principal standard-bearer for the Léopoldist cause enabled it to win 43.56 per cent of the vote and brought it within one seat of capturing an overall majority in the Chamber

---

[66] J. Gérard-Libois and J. Gotovitch, 'Léopold III: Le Non-retour', *Courrier hebdomadaire du CRISP*, 1010 (1983); Plavsic, *Cardinal Van Roey*, 123 and 132–6; Claeys-Van Haegendoren, 'L'Église et l'État au xxᵉ siècle', 23.

[67] P. Theunissen, *1950: Le Dénouement de la question royale* (Brussels, 1986), 15.

[68] J. Duvieusart, *La Question royale, crise et dénouement: Juin, juillet, août 1950* (Brussels, 1976), 47–52; P. Pasture, 'Herstel en expansie (1945–1960)' in Gerard (ed.), *De christelijke arbeidersbeweging in België*, i. 255–6.

of Deputies. The new Catholic–Liberal coalition government led by the Flemish Catholic prime minister Gaston Eyskens pressed ahead with organizing a national referendum on the King's future. The referendum held on 12 March 1950, far from resolving the royal question, merely served, however, to demonstrate the depth of the divisions within the country. The pro-Léopold cause won a narrow majority of 57.68 per cent of the national vote but only 42 per cent of the voters in Wallonia had supported the King while in Flanders he had gained 72 per cent of the vote.[69] Unable to agree on how to proceed, the government resigned and fresh elections were held on 4 June 1950. Once again, the PSC/CVP benefited from its support for the King winning 47.68 per cent of the vote and for the first and only time since the First World War it gained an overall majority in the Chamber of Deputies. A government composed solely of PSC/CVP ministers was formed under the leadership of Jean Duvieusart and in July Léopold finally returned from exile to his palace in Brussels.

The determination of the PSC/CVP to use its narrow parliamentary majority to restore the King to power was, however, opposed by the anti-Léopoldist forces. In a confrontation with gendarmes at Grâce-Berleur near Liège three anti-Léopold demonstrators were shot dead and a general strike was launched by the Socialist trade unions in Wallonia. There was talk of a march on Brussels by groups opposed to the King and, amidst a quasi-insurrectionary atmosphere, the Duvieusart government desperately sought a solution to the crisis. Some of its members remained adamant in their support for the King but a majority of the government finally chose to support a compromise proposal (which also enjoyed Socialist and Liberal support) whereby Léopold would delegate all powers to his son Baudouin and formally abdicate in his favour when Baudouin came of age in 1951. During a tense night of negotiations from 31 July to 1 August the King initially appeared to accept this proposal and then rejected it and flirted with forming a new government composed of his supporters before finally backing down and accepting the compromise solution.[70]

National conflict had been narrowly avoided but the repercussions of the denouement of the royal crisis within the PSC/CVP were substantial. Despite its overall majority, the party had failed to impose its views and the party's right wing led by Paul Vanden Boeynants angrily denounced those Catholic ministers—principally Flemish Christian democrats—whom they accused of having betrayed the King and the party. Both the prime minister, Jean Duvieusart, and the president of the party, Baron van der Straten-Waillet, resigned and a mood of bitter recrimination dominated the special congress of the PSC/CVP held in September 1950. The royal crisis had sapped the morale of the new party and, although it retained power until 1954, it enacted little legislation of consequence. Membership of the party declined markedly and in the subsequent elections in 1954 the PSC/CVP lost its overall majority of seats and left office.[71]

The disunity in Catholic ranks was, however, rapidly restored by the actions of the

[69] Duvieusart, *Question royale*, 52–3.   [70] Ibid. 71–162; Theunissen, *1950*, 33–187.
[71] J. Gérard-Libois, '1950: L'Effacement de Léopold III, tempête au PSC–CVP', *Courrier hebdomadaire du CRISP*, 1169–70 (1987); Pasture, 'Herstel en expansie', 283.

new Liberal–Socialist government of Achille Van Acker. This alliance of Socialists and centre-right Liberals had its origins in their common struggle against Léopold's return but it possessed little rationale other than a shared antipathy to the PSC/CVP. Divisions over economic issues were inevitable and the members of the government chose to concentrate on the one goal on which they could unambivalently agree: education reform. Although their proposals to modernize the state system of schooling were in many respects no more than an overdue reform of an archaic structure, they were inevitably perceived by the Catholic Church as an attempt to undermine its own substantial network of schools. Van Roey had always made defence of this separate Catholic educational system a central element of his strategy for the protection of the faithful and he promptly voiced his categorical opposition to the proposed legislation.[72]

More surprisingly perhaps, the PSC/CVP under the leadership of its new president Théo Lefevre also threw itself enthusiastically into what rapidly became known as the *guerre scolaire*. Still recovering from the trauma of the royal crisis and for once out of government, the various factions of the PSC/CVP found in opposition to the education reforms a means of restoring their sense of purpose and identity. A Comité pour la défense des libertés démocratiques/Nationaal Comité voor Vrijheid en Democratie (Committee for the Defence of Democratic Freedoms) was founded to lead the campaign against the reforms and, although its petitions and mass rallies could not prevent the proposals from becoming law, they did demonstrate the ability of the Catholic community to unite against the 'atheist' menace. As a collective pastoral letter issued by the bishops declared with undisguised relief in 1955:

Nous voyons avec une grande satisfaction que l'union de toutes les forces catholiques sans exception s'est fait solide et ferme sur le terrain de l'enseignement et de l'éducation, parce qu'il touche au domaine de la conscience et de la religion. Depuis des mois, cette union s'est forgée partout avec enthousiasme.[73]

In many respects, the politics of the 1950s appeared to mark an anachronistic return to the battle-lines of the 1880s and 1890s. Liberals and Socialists—the *gauches* of the nineteenth century—had come together in support of their old rallying-call of secular education while the Catholics had united in defence of their Church, schools, and faith. This appearance was, however, largely illusory. The Socialist–Liberal alliance was no more than transitory and after the 1958 elections was replaced by a more orthodox Catholic–Liberal government headed by Gaston Eyskens. It introduced compromise legislation enabling the public education system to expand while guaranteeing state funding of Catholic schools and effectively brought the *guerre scolaire* to a close.[74] More significantly, the common defence of Catholic schooling could not postpone indefinitely the factors working to undermine Catholic political unity. These were a combination of the old and the new. Prominent among them was the

---

[72] Claeys-Van Haegendoren 'L'Église et l'État au xxᵉ siècle', 31–4; Aubert 'Le Cardinal Van Roey', *Revue Nouvelle*, 34 (Sept. 1961), 121–2.

[73] Plavsic *Cardinal Van Roey*, 175–82; Pasture, 'Herstel en expansie', 290–2.

[74] Claeys-Van Haegendoren, 'L'Église et L'État', 34.

unresolved nature of the relationship between the PSC/CVP and the Catholic trade unions and other worker organizations. The new structure of the PSC/CVP introduced after the war had deprived the Christian democrat federation, the Algemeen Christelijk Werkersverbond/Mouvement Ouvrier Chrétien (as the Ligue Nationale des Travailleurs Chrétiens was renamed in francophone Belgium), of any official status within the party. Nevertheless, especially in Flanders, the ACW remained a major force in Catholic politics. It was an important financier of the PSC–CVP and also enjoyed considerable influence over the selection of party candidates. Its power was reinforced by the continuing rapid expansion of Catholic worker organizations. Membership of the Catholic trade-union federation, the ACV/CSC, for example, rose from 342,099 in 1945 to 731,281 in 1959 and for the first time exceeded that of the rival Socialist grouping, the Fédération Générale du Travail de Belgique (General Federation of Belgian Workers, FGTB).[75]

Despite this growth, a mood of dissatisfaction was evident within Christian democrat ranks. The events of the war years had reinforced the divisions between the largely Flemish leadership of the ACW/MOC which retained a traditional vision of the movement operating within a Catholic political and socio-economic pillar and its groups in Wallonia where many militants had been attracted by the short-lived UDB and by the social and apostolic radicalism of a lay Catholic spiritual movement, the Mouvement Populaire des Familles (People's Family Movement, MPF). The bishops suppressed the MPF and in October 1946 the Mouvement Ouvrier Chrétien (Christian Workers' Movement, MOC) was established as the new official Christian democrat organization in francophone Belgium. This subordination to the Church hierarchy and to the Flemish majority of the ACW was not, however, acceptable to all francophone Christian democrat militants, some of whom remained aloof from the MOC or became active in the Walloon regionalist movement.[76] Nor was such discontent limited to Wallonia. In Flanders too, many members of the ACW were frustrated by the absence of substantial political or socio-economic reforms. The events of the Cold War and the *question royale* had enabled more conservative elements in the PSC/CVP to stifle much of the initial radicalism of the new party. The Socialist–Catholic coalition government of 1947–9 and the Catholic government of 1950–4 enacted few major reforms and, especially among the Flemish rank and file of the ACW, there was bitterness that their numerical strength had still not enabled them to exercise decisive influence over the policies of the PSC/CVP.[77]

As in the 1930s, Flemish aspirations for greater political and cultural autonomy constituted another challenge to Catholic political unity. No significant devolution of power from Brussels occurred after the liberation and Flemish nationalism suffered during the immediate post-war years from the discredit cast upon it by the VNV's wartime collaboration with the Nazi authorities. Gradually, however, Flemish

[75] Pasture, 'Herstel en expansie', 262–9; J. Fitzmaurice, *The Politics of Belgium* (London, 1983), 200–1.
[76] Pasture, 'Herstel en expansie', 250–5 and 260–2; Neuville, *Adieu à la démocratie chrétienne*, 129–48; J. Remy, 'Le Défi de la modernité', *Social Compass*, 34 (1987), 165; J. Lothe, 'Le Mouvement wallon: Divisions, fluctuations et prélude à la mutation', in H. Hasquin (ed.), *La Wallonie: Le Pays et les hommes* (Brussels, 1980), ii. 326–31.   [77] Pasture, 'Herstel en expansie', 283–97.

grievances resurfaced. A new Flemish nationalist grouping, the Christelijke Vlaamse Volksunie (Flemish Christian People's Union), contested the elections of 1954 and, although it subsequently abandoned its Christian label, this party once again drew its strength from Flemish Catholic discontent at francophone political and economic dominance. Similar sentiments were felt by many within the CVP and, especially among its Flemish youth groups, the aspiration for a more just society had become inseparable from substantial constitutional reform. Radical figures—such as the president of the Flemish Catholic Students' Association and future prime minister Wilfried Martens—openly called for a federalization of the Belgian state while the leaders of the CVP and the ACW established a Vlaamse Werkgroep (Flemish Working Group) in 1955 which advocated in more moderate terms a substantial redistribution of economic wealth and political power in favour of Flanders.[78]

A third factor working to undermine Catholic political unity was the emergence of a more educated and self-confident Catholic laity reluctant to accept uncritically the guidance of the ecclesiastical hierarchy. Much of the strength both of the pre-war Catholic Party and of the PSC/CVP had always rested on the willingness of the Catholic faithful to obey the exhortations from the clergy and bishops to remain united behind a single political party. Throughout the 1940s and 1950s, the bishops continued to issue instructions to the laity to vote, as Van Roey expressed it, for 'des hommes qui respectent l'Église catholique, ses droits et ses représentants, plutôt que des gens qui la considèrent comme une institution ennemie et dangereuse, qu'il faut brimer sournoisement, si pas ouvertement combattre'.[79] The effectiveness of such interventions did, however, steadily decline. If most Catholics were willing to mobilize in defence of their educational system during the *guerre scolaire* of the 1950s, they no longer shared the octogenarian Van Roey's apocalyptic view of the world. Social and economic changes had created a more integrated and fluid society in which the isolation of the Catholic community no longer seemed to many Catholics to be either feasible or desirable. Periodicals such as the francophone *La Revue Nouvelle* (New Review) and the Flemish *De Maand* (The Month) reflected the opinions of a new Catholic middle class, confident in its beliefs and open both to the new theological ideas being expounded by figures such as the Louvain professor Gustave Thils and to contact with those beyond Catholic ranks who shared their views. The mentality of the ghetto had begun to disappear and, although the combined influence of Pius XII and of Cardinal Van Roey ensured that heretical voices within the Belgian Church were marginalized, the aspiration for a more democratic and open community of the Catholic faithful made itself felt with ever greater insistence during the 1950s.[80]

It was during the subsequent often tumultuous decade of the 1960s that these various forces finally destroyed Catholic political unity. In Belgium, as in much of

---

[78] L. Bosman, 'De Vlaamse Beweging na 1945', in Witte, Burgelman, and Stouthuysen (eds.), *Tussen restauratie en vernieuwing*, 225–61; Pasture, 'Herstel en expansie', 277–82; H. De Ridder, *Le Cas Martens* (Paris, 1991), 14–39.

[79] W. S. Plavsic, 'L'Église et la politique en Belgique', *Res Publica*, 10 (1968), 230 and 234–40.

[80] Remy, 'Le Défi de la modernité', 164; Suenens, *Memories and Hopes*, 38–40 and 54–5; G. Thils, *L'Église et les Églises* (Louvain, 1967).

western Europe, the 1960s formed, in the words of the Belgian sociologist Karel Dobbelaere, 'un moment décisif de rupture culturelle'.[81] A combination of generational, material, and ideological conflicts overwhelmed traditional boundaries of segregation and obedience and, in the case of Belgium, also came close to destroying the structures of the unitary state.[82] In no area of Belgian life were these upheavals more dramatic than within Catholicism. In August 1961 Van Roey died aged 87 and his successor Cardinal Suenens, who played a prominent role at the Second Vatican Council, did not seek to impose the same political or spiritual uniformity on the faithful. New ecumenical and spiritual initiatives were launched while the clergy no longer advised the faithful on how to cast their vote.[83] Stimulated above all by the rapid pace of socio-economic change in Flanders, attendance at church fell markedly. After 1968 the level of religious practice fell by an average of 1.9 per cent per year and by 1981 only 26 per cent of the population regularly attended mass. This remarkably rapid transition to a largely secular society was also reflected in a fall in recruitment to the clergy and, though membership of Catholic social organizations such as trade unions and the numbers attending Catholic schools both continued to rise, these institutions increasingly took on a deconfessional and pluralist character.[84]

In the political sphere, the most significant change was a surge in support for Walloon and Flemish autonomy. Pressure for constitutional reform developed rapidly during the 1960s among both the francophone and Flemish populations of Belgium. In Wallonia, the stimulus was provided by the bitter general strike during the winter of 1960–1 against the economic austerity measures implemented by the Catholic–Liberal government of Gaston Eyskens. The strike was initiated by the Socialist trade-union federation, the FGTB, but many Catholic trade-unionists of the CSC also became involved and, although the national leadership of the CSC/ACV avoided giving its approval to a strike against a Catholic-led government, it expressed its general support for the aims of the strikers. Rarely had internal Catholic political unity been so visibly challenged and, in response, Cardinal Van Roey issued a statement denouncing 'les grèves désordonnées et déraisonnables auxquelles nous assistons à présent' and calling on the strikers to return to work.[85] The time for such magisterial dictates had, however, passed. The CSC leaders were furious at Van Roey's intervention and, though the strike eventually petered out amidst violence and mutual recrimination, it acted as a catalyst for the emergence of Walloon regionalism as a major political force. Support for a distinct Walloon identity had for the first time acquired a mass audience and in March 1961 the Socialist trade-union leader André Renard launched his Mouvement Populaire Wallon (Popular Walloon

---

[81] K. Dobbelaere, 'La Dominante Catholique', *Recherches sociologiques*, 16/3 (1985), 213.

[82] A. Méan, *La Belgique de Papa* (Brussels, 1989), 57–172.

[83] Suenens, *Memories and Hopes*, 56–9; Plavsic, 'L'Église et la politique', 243; Aubert, 'L'Église catholique et la vie politique', 200–2.

[84] K. Dobbelaere, *Dominante catholique*, 194; L. Voyé, 'Aspects de l'évolution récente du "monde catholique" ', *Courrier hebdomadaire du CRISP*, 925–6 (1981).

[85] J. Neuville and J. Yerna, *Le Choc de l'hiver 1960–1961* (Brussels, 1990), 63–95.

Movement). Isolated Catholic figures had long been active in Walloon regionalist groups but after the strike they too acquired a significant following. The Catholic-inspired regionalist movement Rénovation Wallonne (Walloon Renovation) gained considerable support among Christian democrat militants of the Mouvement Ouvrier Chrétien and formed an important element of the new Walloon regionalist political grouping, the Rassemblement Wallon (Walloon Alliance), which in the elections of 1968 won 10.6 per cent of the vote in Wallonia.[86]

The rise in regionalist sentiments also eroded support for the Flemish wing of the PSC/CVP. A series of political controversies in the early 1960s concerning the linguistic frontier between Flemish and francophone areas and the status of the largely francophone city of Brussels within Flanders aggravated long-standing Flemish grievances at what they perceived to be the inferior status of Flanders within the Belgian state. The CVP sought as far as possible to act as a mouthpiece for Flemish discontents but it was out of step with the radical mood of many younger Flemish militants who organized a series of marches on Brussels and who swelled the ranks of the nationalist Volksunie. In the 1968 elections, the Volksunie won 16.9 per cent of the vote in Flanders, largely at the expense of the CVP which saw its share of the vote in Flanders fall from 56.5 per cent in 1958 to 39 per cent in 1968.[87]

It was above all the controversy surrounding the University of Louvain or Leuven which symbolized the linguistic divisions within the Catholic community. This historic central institution of Belgian Catholic life was increasingly paralysed in the 1960s by conflicts between its francophone and Flemish students. The Flemish demanded that, as it was located in Flanders, the university should become a Dutch-language institution but in a pastoral letter issued in 1966 the bishops categorically opposed any change in its bilingual national character. This provoked an angry response from many Flemish Catholics and their campaign of 'Walen buiten' (Walloons Out) forced the Catholic–Liberal coalition government headed by the francophone Catholic Paul Vanden Boeynants to intervene. The government refused to support the immediate transfer of the francophone students from Louvain and, in response, the Flemish CVP ministers unilaterally resigned from the government in February 1968. At the subsequent elections in March, the PSC and CVP presented for the first time separate party programmes and, although they maintained a common national president until 1972, they rapidly became—and have remained—separate regional parties committed to independent policies.[88]

The divorce within the unitary Catholic Party brought about by the symbolic but highly emotive issue of the University of Louvain marked the end of a certain form of political Catholicism in Belgium. A party which straddled the division between the francophone and Flemish populations was no longer viable and, in common with

---

[86] Ibid. 171–4; Hasquin, 'Naissance de la Wallonie', 343–53; P. Pasture, 'In de welvaarstaat', in Gerard (ed.), *De christelijke arbeidersbeweging in België*, i. 307–13; Witte and Craeybeckx, *Belgique politique*, 267.

[87] Witte and Craeybeckx, *Belgique politique*, 267; J. Billiet and K. Dobbelaere, 'Vers une désinstitutionnalisation du pilier chrétien?', *Recherches sociologiques*, 16/3 (1985), 128; 'L'Évolution récente de la "Volksunie" ', *Courrier hebdomadaire du CRISP*, 604 and 606 (1973).

[88] Méan *Belgique de Papa*, 84–92; J. Fitzmaurice, *Politics of Belgium*, 144–54.

the Socialist and Liberal parties, the Catholics were forced to accept the pre-eminence of the linguistic division. It was not, however, merely regional tensions which had undermined Catholic unity. The concept of a fundamental division of outlook between Catholic and non-Catholic held so dear by Cardinal Van Roey and reinforced by the social and cultural pillarization of Belgian life no longer reflected the reality of a modern pluralist society. As the emergence of non-confessional regional parties in Flanders and Wallonia had demonstrated, it was possible for Catholics and non-Catholics to collaborate on many issues and, with the resolution of the *guerre scolaire*, clerical–anticlerical disputes appeared finally to have become part of history. The Liberal and Socialist parties were both quick to recognize this change. In 1961 the Liberal Party had relaunched itself as the Parti pour la Liberté et le Progrès/Partij voor Vrijheid en Vooruitgang (Party for Liberty and Progress, PLP/PVV) which explicitly rejected its anticlerical heritage and sought to win middle-class Catholic votes. Similarly, in his May Day message of 1969 the president of the Socialist party, Léo Collard, declared the clerical–anticlerical division to be a relic of the past and called on all progressive forces to unite on a non-confessional basis.[89]

Neither the Liberal nor Socialist initiatives brought them immediate success but, combined with the growth of the Rassemblement Wallon and the Volksunie, they contributed to the erosion of the electoral base of the PSC and CVP. In 1958 the unified PSC/CVP had won 46.5 per cent of the vote; by 1971 the combined vote of the now separate CVP and PSC was only 30 per cent.[90] The main change was, however, less one of numbers than of mentality. No longer did it seem natural to Catholics and non-Catholics alike that the Catholic community should remain unified behind a single party. Though opinion polls showed that most Catholics who attended mass regularly continued to support the PSC and CVP, the 'invisible frontier' between Catholic and non-Catholic had been substantially eroded. Catholics participated in a variety of political formations while the PSC and CVP began hesitantly to develop new identities deprived of the quasi-automatic loyalty of the faithful.[91]

Viewed with the often misleading benefit of hindsight, the maintenance of Catholic political unity in Belgium during much of the twentieth century must inevitably appear to have been a largely artificial enterprise. Composed of militants united by the all too slender thread of religion and tied to a unitary nation-state which itself was increasingly threatened by divisions between its francophone and Flemish populations, it is tempting to dismiss the Catholic Party and the PSC/CVP as historical anachronisms inherited from the nineteenth century. However, as this chapter has sought to indicate, the political unity of Belgian Catholics was not merely part of the

---

[89] Witte and Craeybeckx, *Belgique politique*, 534 and 554–6.

[90] Billiet and Dobbelaere, 'Vers une désinstitutionnalisation', 128.

[91] A.-P. Frognier, 'Vote, classe sociale et religion/pratique religieuse', *Res Publica*, 17 (1975), 479–90; M. Van Haegendoren and L. Vandenhove, 'Le Monde catholique flamand (I)', *Courrier hebdomadaire du CRISP*, 1070 (1985); F. Houtart, 'Nouvelles formes d'engagements socio-politiques des chrétiens', *Recherches sociologiques*, 16/3 (1985), 175–90.

baggage of past history. The consistent electoral success of the Catholic Party from the 1880s to the 1960s reflected the real sense of community which existed among most Belgian Catholics. Amidst the relatively placid landscape of Belgian society, the division between Catholic and non-Catholic was one deeply rooted in the patterns of family and social life. Catholics felt themselves to be distinct from their religiously indifferent or atheist compatriots and this sense of differentness was continually reinforced by their participation in the extensive network of Catholic social, educational and cultural institutions.

Support for the Catholic Party was the expression of that reality and, though divisions of region or social class often worked to undermine Catholic unity, they did not destroy the conviction that Catholicism represented a distinct political ideology. Alongside the other dominant forces of liberalism and socialism, Catholicism did seem to possess a coherent political agenda derived both from papal teachings and a Catholic intellectual heritage. Over time the content of that ideology underwent significant changes, veering in the 1930s toward some variant of corporatist authoritarianism before emerging after the Second World War as a personalist ideology of social liberation. But the conviction that a core of Catholic ideas existed survived these various changes. Only with the broader social and political transformations during the post-war years did the basis of Catholic unity begin to disappear. The notion of a distinctive Catholic community no longer matched a more educated, more mobile, and more urbanized society while ideological changes both within and beyond Catholicism eroded the sense of a separate Catholic value structure. In the 1960s the centrifugal forces of social, regional, and ideological diversity at last outweighed the centripetal forces of religious solidarity. A unitary Catholic political structure was no longer possible and in its place there emerged a variety of forms of Catholic political engagement which reflected the plural character of Belgian Catholicism.

7

*The Netherlands**

PAUL LUYKX

During the half-century between 1917 and 1967, Dutch Catholics formed a strong social bloc and a significant political force. The granting of universal male suffrage in 1917 confirmed the emergence of Catholicism as a major force in Dutch politics. This remained the case until the political and social changes of the 1960s—notably the electoral defeat suffered by the Catholic Party in 1967. This combination of political and social strength was, however, in marked contrast to the position of Catholics in earlier centuries. During the era of the Dutch Republic from the sixteenth to the eighteenth centuries, the Catholic minority had suffered severe discrimination. The public exercise of their religion was forbidden and they were barred from occupying any public office. Although the Republic—which had come into existence through opposition to the Catholic Habsburg Empire—recognized no official state religion, it was Calvinism which formed the dominant faith. Long into the twentieth century there remained a belief among Protestants that the wars of the sixteenth century had been exclusively religious in nature and that the Netherlands was therefore essentially a Protestant nation. However, in 1795 the arrival of the French revolutionary armies and the consequent Batavian revolution brought about the end of the Republic and established a strict division of Church and State, as well as the legal equality of the Catholic community. Indeed for a short time the Catholics came to form a majority of the population in the new Dutch monarchy which was created by the conservative powers at the Congress of Vienna in 1815. This state was intended to serve as a bastion against a potentially revolutionary and warlike France, and it therefore incorporated the former southern Habsburg Netherlands, which were exclusively Catholic in composition. In 1830, however, these territories broke away from northern rule to form the new Belgian state and the frontiers of the Netherlands have subsequently remained almost unchanged to the present day. The Catholics have formed a significant minority within this state, comprising approximately 35 per cent of the population, of whom half live in the homogenous Catholic areas in the south of the country and the remainder in the centre and west.[1]

It was only in 1853 that the Catholics once again obtained their own episcopal

* The author is most grateful to Mrs J. Moonen and Dr M. Conway for the considerable assistance which they have so generously given to the translation of this chapter.

[1] A general account of Dutch history in the 19th and 20th cents. is provided in E. H. Kossmann, *The Low Countries 1780–1940* (Oxford, 1978).

hierarchy. This stimulated a fierce anti-Papist reaction among some Protestants known as the 'April Movement', but this movement proved to have little relevance for the development of relations between Catholics and Protestants. By 1888 relations between Catholic and Protestant politicians had improved so markedly that they were able to form their first confessional coalition government. In the late nineteenth and early twentieth centuries the modernization of Dutch society and the democratization of the State gained momentum. With the exception of the increasingly marginalized Liberals, it was above all Socialism, orthodox Protestantism, and Catholicism which came to the fore in political life and which contributed to the shaping of the modern Dutch state. Until 1939 the Socialists did so, however, exclusively from the ranks of the parliamentary opposition.

The Catholics have therefore played a permanent role in government from 1918 to the present day and their parliamentary party has almost invariably been the largest grouping represented in parliament. Their political organization, the Rooms Katholieke Staats Partij (Roman Catholic State Party) or RKSP, which was established in its definitive form in 1926 and remodelled as the Katholieke Volks Partij (Catholic People's Party) or KVP in 1945, has collaborated in all forms of parliamentary coalitions, working with the Protestants as well as with the Socialists and the Liberals. Although until the Second World War political leadership lay with the Protestants, after the war this role moved more and more to the Catholics, to such an extent that the era from the 1950s to 1967 can be regarded as marking the high point in the political power of the Dutch Catholics. The decline of the KVP since 1967 was one of the reasons for the creation of an interconfessional Christian unity party, the Christen-Democratisch Appèl (Christian Democratic Party) formed out of the former Catholic and Protestant parties. The CDA participated in national elections for the first time in 1977 and has subsequently proved able to prevent the further decline of the confessional parties.

The 1960s thus formed a turning-point in the development of political Catholicism, and indeed of Catholicism as a whole. The German occupation from 1940 to 1945 and a short period of post-war uncertainty and instability from 1944 to 1946 had already clearly demonstrated the decline in the internal cohesion of the Catholics, while the unity of the pre-1940 era had also been on occasions more apparent than real. Attempts by various parties and groups in the post-war era to challenge the established confessional party-system were nevertheless entirely unsuccessful and the Catholic politicians and the Church leadership were therefore able to re-establish—at least in their external forms—the former structures of Catholic organizational life. When, however, in the 1950s and the early 1960s a second wave of industrialization and modernization gathered momentum, the unity of the Catholic world came under renewed substantial pressure. Secularization has subsequently advanced remorselessly and the organizational unity of Catholicism, both politically and socially, has been repeatedly undermined. Even in the mid-1990s, the ultimate outcome of these radical changes is still not evident.

This contribution focuses, however, on the period of the full emergence of

Catholicism as a powerful force in Dutch political life, and will attempt to shed light on certain of the underlying reasons and distinctive features which have characterized this process. Through an examination of the phenomenon of 'pillarization' (in Sect. 1) and of the influence of the Catholic Church (in Sect. 2), the reasons for the growth in Catholic power can be clearly identified. The problem which then arises was what Catholics chose to do with their political power? Did they use it to impose their own alternatives in the process of the construction of a modern state and society? In this respect, it is necessary to investigate their support for corporatism (Sect. 3) and family policy (Sect. 4) as the main motives of Catholic political action. Catholic politicians also, however, had to assume responsibility for national tasks and issues, and this aspect of Catholic policy is considered in Sect. 5 of this chapter. In the conclusion, some more general remarks and conclusions will be attempted.

1. Political Catholicism and Pillarization

In this section, a brief analysis will be attempted first of the concepts of pillars and pillarization. Then, a number of explanations of the historical reasons for this phenomenon will be presented, with special attention paid to the factors which clarify the relationship between the Catholic pillar and Catholic politics.[2]

The classic quotation from the Dutch historian L. J. Rogier will perhaps provide a useful starting-point:

A Dutch Catholic, at least one who has lived in [the majority Protestant areas of] 'Holland' was, as it were, aware every day of the fact that he was not a Protestant. He did his best to ensure that he decorated his home in such a way that a visitor on entering the house could judge from the wall decorations, crucifixes, saints, and sometimes even devotional candles that he was entering Roman Catholic territory. Not only did he pray differently from most of his neighbours, he voted differently, read a different paper and different books, listened to his own radio programmes, watched his own television channel, travelled, swam, cycled, played tennis, billiards, and football and even insured his life in a Roman Catholic fashion. Moreover, he was considered to have denied his faith from a false sense of shame if he wore his wedding ring on his right hand (which no self-respecting Catholic would ever do) or if he wished people a 'Happy' New Year rather than a 'Blissful' New Year or if he used the Protestant spellings of Biblical names such as Isiah, Solomon, Samson, and Nebuchadnezzar or spelt Christ as 'Jezus' and not 'Jesus'.[3]

[2] A general account of social science theories and of the historiography on pillarization is provided in a number of articles. See e.g. W. ten Have, 'De geschiedschrijving over crisis en verzuiling', in W. Mijnhardt (ed.), *Kantelend geschiedbeeld: Nederlandse historiografie sinds 1945* (Utrecht, 1983), 256–88; J. C. H. Blom, 'Onderzoek naar verzuiling in Nederland. Status quaestionis en wenselijke ontwikkeling', in J. C. H. Blom and C. J. Misset (eds.), *'Broeders sluit U aan': Aspecten van verzuiling in zeven Hollandse gemeenten* (n.p., 1985), 10–29; J. A. Righart, *De katholieke zuil in Europa: Een vergelijkend onderzoek naar het ontstaan van verzuiling onder katholieken in Oostenrijk, Zwitserland, België en Nederland* (Meppel, 1986), 189–95; T. Duffhues, 'Staat "De wankele zuil" nog overeind? Een verkenning van de recente literatuur over verzuiling en ontzuiling', *Jaarboek Katholiek Documentatie Centrum*, 17 (1987), 134–62; J. Ramakers and H. Righart, 'Het katholicisme', in P. Luykx and N. Bootsma (eds.), *De laatste tijd: Geschiedschrijving over Nederland in de 20e eeuw* (Utrecht, 1987), 99–134. A classic account of the phenomenon of pillarization in English is A. Lijphart, *The Politics of Accommodation: Pluralism and Democracy in the Netherlands* (Berkeley and Los Angeles, 1968).   [3] L. J. Rogier, *Vandaag en morgen* (Bilthoven, 1974), 10.

To describe the phenomenon that Rogier depicts so aptly, the word 'pillar' has firmly taken hold in Dutch sociology and social history. This term has been applied not only to the Catholics but also to the orthodox Protestants and Socialists, and even by some to the middle-class liberals not included in the former categories. The use of the term 'pillarization' is intended to indicate that Dutch politics, society, and culture have been systematically and profoundly affected by this phenomenon, notably through the actions of the major political parties, all of which were closely tied to their respective pillars. In addition, both words have now entered into common usage to describe societies elsewhere in the world.

In their original meaning, these terms—as they were used from the late 1930s to approximately 1950—had a positive connotation. The different sections of the population were seen as distinct pillars, all of which supported the common national 'roof' and possessed a shared loyalty to national values, traditions, and institutions. In spite of these independent groups or pillars, there did indeed exist—so the initial theorists of the concept of pillarization declared—a sense of national solidarity. Hence, a subsidiary discussion soon developed as to whether the Socialists could really be considered to form a pillar. Given that they continued to adopt a political stance inspired by Marxist principles and proclaimed their commitment to class struggle and revolution, they could hardly be regarded as constituting one of the props of the existing order.

Principally among Socialists but also in liberal Protestant circles, and to a lesser degree among Catholics, there was dissatisfaction with the system of confessional pillarization. In the case of orthodox Protestantism and of Catholicism, some found the fusion of religion and politics in the form of separate confessional parties highly objectionable. Moreover, the Socialist Party, which after the Second World War was transformed into the Labour Party (Partij van de Arbeid), directly experienced in its election results and membership the consequences of this system of confessional pillarization. It was believed, not without reason, by the Socialists that the stagnation in their growth was due to the fact that significant sections of the working class remained loyal to the Protestant or Catholic parties, rather than rallying to their cause. Nevertheless, the efforts to bring about a remoulding of the existing party structure after 1945 were a complete failure, principally as a consequence of the comprehensive restoration of the Catholic organizational institutions and the reorganization of the Catholic Party (KVP). Because many workers were from Catholic backgrounds and remained strongly attached to the Catholic pillar, the Partij van de Arbeid entertained high hopes of bringing about the disintegration of the Catholic pillar. Frustration at this failure gave the terminology of confessional pillarization a highly negative connotation in left-wing circles. Moreover, as during subsequent decades the concept of natural confessional party-political divisions also disappeared among Protestants and Catholics, so too among these groups the word took on a critical connotation.

As, however, the term was introduced into scholarly discourse, first in the social sciences and then also in historiography, so it gradually lost its critical-normative character and became a generally accepted technical concept. It is therefore, for example, possible nowadays to describe in neutral terms the Catholic pillar as a comprehensive organizational complex, ranging from the Catholic Party to the much-maligned Catholic goatbreeders club, all held together and integrated by a common religious belief and loyalty to the Church. This pillarization created a society of vertical pluralism, cutting across horizontal divisions of social class and extending into all sectors of society. In this manner, the social system was characterized by a cementing of the different pillars, with as the consequence a marked segmentation of society.

In the Netherlands pillarization firmly established itself in the late nineteenth and early twentieth centuries, after the Protestants and Catholics had begun the struggle earlier in the nineteenth century to achieve state-financing of their separate confessional educational systems. This demand was finally satisfied in 1917. But pillarization continued and reached its high point around 1950. At the same time it became evident that the need for a linkage between religious beliefs and politico-social organizations was evident to fewer and fewer people. Since the 1960s this deconfessionalization has led to a partial erosion of the organizational structures of Protestants and Catholics, often described by the term 'depillarization'.

It is generally accepted that this process of pillarization was most marked among the Catholic population. Some figures serve to illustrate this point. If one combines the number of organizations active in eight areas of social life (social work, education, youth groups, the press, sport, health care, culture, and trade unions), it emerges that the percentage of broad-based non-pillarized social organizations fell between 1914 and 1956 from 56 per cent to 47 per cent, while at the same time the share of distinctly Catholic organizations rose from 13 per cent to 21 per cent. The participation rate of Catholics in these specifically Catholic institutions is even more striking. Thus, in 1959 about 90 per cent of Catholic parents sent their children to a Catholic elementary school and approximately 95 per cent of Catholic farmers belonged to Catholic farmers' unions, while some 79 per cent of Catholic newspaper readers read a Catholic newspaper.[4] As far as the political party was concerned, between 1920 and the 1960s 80–90 per cent of the Catholic electorate always voted for the Catholic Party (RKSP/KVP).[5]

The explanations which have been advanced for this phenomenon of pillarization have been highly varied and have laid emphasis on a number of different factors.[6] As far as the leaders of the Catholic community have been concerned, they have always sought to justify pillarization as part of a process of emancipation. For Catholics, organizational isolation was a necessary consequence of the backwardness imposed on the Catholic community by the discrimination which they had experienced during the Republic and which remained evident during the nineteenth century. This explanation receives little support from historians today. Around 1900 the traditional

---

[4] J. P. Kruijt and W. Goddijn OFM, 'Verzuiling en ontzuiling als sociologisch proces', in A. N. J. den Hollander *et al.* (eds.), *Drift en koers: Een halve eeuw sociale verandering in Nederland* (3rd edn.) (Assen, 1968), 227–263, esp. 244 and 242.

[5] H. Bakvis, *Catholic Power in the Netherlands* (Kingston, 1981), 1–9.

[6] P. Luykx, 'Versäulung in den Niederlanden: Eine kritische Betrachtung der neueren Historiographie', *Jahrbuch des Zentrums für Niederlande-Studien*, 2 (1991), 39–51, esp. 40–3.

discrimination against Catholics by Protestants was limited exclusively to the higher middle classes, notably concerning posts and offices in government, the universities and education, the legal system, and other professions. It would therefore not seem possible to explain—or indeed to provide any evidence of—how the mass of Catholic farmers and workers were discriminated against at this time because of their religion. Thus, their willingness to form Catholic organizations cannot be explained solely on the basis of supposed religious discrimination.

The two explanations of pillarization most frequently advanced by scholars are excellently summarized in the title of a recent collection of essays. According to its Belgian editor, the motives for pillarization were *Between Protection and Conquest*, namely they were both defensive and offensive in nature.[7] It is, however, the defensive, protectionist motive which has been most frequently emphasized in the research of the last twenty years. Thus, according to this interpretation, the purpose of Catholic organizations was the defence of the interests of the Church and faith which in the course of the nineteenth century were increasingly threatened by the remorseless secularization of State and society while, at the same time, protecting the faithful from the dangers and risks which threatened them in a modernizing society and culture. Several different variants of this interpretation have been given. According to one version, in order to ensure that this protective structure was able to call on wide social support, Catholic leaders were sometimes willing to make concessions to modern developments and adapted their traditions to the realities of modern life. 'Protection by Adaptation' would be the most concise summary of this interpretation.[8] An example from the political sphere, the so-called householders' suffrage, serves to illustrate this case. Though ideologically entirely in accordance with the patriarchal traditions current in religious circles, the application of this measure would in fact lead to a substantial expansion of the suffrage which would almost amount to the universal male suffrage demanded by the Socialists. Another, more radical, variant of this protectionist theory is the neo-Marxist and feminist-inspired interpretation which sees pillarization as directly connected to the need to respond to the challenge posed by socialism and feminism, which threatened to alienate Catholic workers and women from their Church and faith.[9] Despite their differences, all these variants are agreed in the emphasis which they place on negative motives as the dominant influence behind the process of pillarization, and in this respect this interpretation concurs with a much older liberal interpretation which saw pillarization as 'a contemporary form of social control'.[10]

On the other hand, a number of researchers whose work has come to prominence in recent years have preferred to see pillarization as merely the organizational basis for a broader social movement seeking to construct an alternative to a liberal and

---

[7] J. Billiet (ed.), *Tussen bescherming en verovering: Sociologen en historici over zuilvorming* (Leuven, 1988). [8] J. A. Righart, *De katholieke zuil in Europa*.

[9] S. Stuurman, *Verzuiling, kapitalisme en patriarchaat: Aspecten van de ontwikkeling van de moderne staat in Nederland* (Nijmegen, 1983).

[10] J. A. A. van Doorn, 'Verzuiling, een eigentijds systeem van sociale controle', *Sociologische Gids*, 3 (1956), 41–9.

capitalist version of modernity. This was particularly pronounced in the case of Catholicism.[11] The pillarized social institutions contributed to this social movement not only in the negative sense of assisting in the struggle against liberalism and capitalism, but also in the positive role of helping to bring about a viable alternative to these dominant ideologies. Moreover, these different social movements, each possessed of their own vision of the ideal social order, came inevitably into conflict provoking what could be termed a 'Struggle for Modernity'. This last phrase is the title of a book which provides the best presentation of this interpretation and which has developed it as a general theory for four countries, considering in each case both the Socialist and Catholic movements.[12] Given that political power is an essential condition for bringing about an alternative social order, it is natural that the advocates of this interpretation should place greater emphasis than others have done on the role played by the political party. This does not mean, however, that politics or the political party are regarded as the central focus of the explanation of pillarization. On the contrary, pillarization is seen as the organizational manifestation of a much wider movement, the origins of which lie in a nineteenth-century Catholic religious revival. This emphasis on religious motives, which preceded the creation of the Catholic movement and thus also the Catholic pillarization which it helped to bring about, is an essential element of this interpretation.

In these two interpretations of pillarization, both that which stresses its defensive, protectionist role and that which looks instead to an offensive, creative purpose, the Church and religion emerge as the central forces. It is important that this should be stressed at the beginning of an essay on political Catholicism. The only author to have taken the opposite approach and to have sought the origins of political Catholicism in politics, R. Steininger, has received no support from historians.[13] Steininger, who by no coincidence happened to be a political scientist, simply could not conceive that religion and the Church could have had a major influence and therefore concluded, without much empirical research, that politicians must therefore have played a central role. In his opinion, pillarization was a permanent mobilization of the electorate designed to serve party-political ends. In fact, the development in the Netherlands of political Catholicism was on the contrary an extremely slow and complex process which finally led to the creation of a political party only in the 1920s. Thus, it is the creation of the political party which needs to be explained, rather than using that party to explain the process of pillarization.

This applies not merely to the creation of the Catholic Party but also to its subsequent operation. In the course of the years between 1920 and 1960 a wide variety

[11] See e.g. A. T. M. Duffhues, *Generaties en patronen: De katholieke beweging te Arnhem in de 19e en 20ste eeuw* (Baarn, 1991). For a contribution from this perspective in English, see T. Duffhues and A. Felling, 'The Development, Change and Decline of the Dutch Catholic Movement', *International Social Movement Research*, 2 (1989), 95–114.

[12] S. Hellemans, *Strijd om de moderniteit: Sociale bewegingen en verzuiling in Europa sinds 1800* (Leuven, 1990).

[13] R. Steininger, *Polarisierung und Integration: Eine vergleichende Untersuchung der strukturellen Versäulung der Gesellschaft in den Niederlanden und in Österreich* (Meisenheim-am-Glan, 1975).

of Catholic pillar organizations assisted 'their' party in many ways. Thus, the impact of the permanent support of the Catholic press and radio can hardly be overestimated. Still more important for its success was the continuous support which the party received from Catholic social organizations, especially those of farmers and workers. Many instances of such support, notably during the crises of the 1930s, could be provided. It was precisely the fact that the Catholic Party was embedded in what can variously be described as the Catholic pillar or the Catholic social movement which made its operation possible and which contributed substantially to its success.

2. Political Catholicism and the Church

If political Catholicism did indeed form part of a more general Catholic religious revival, it is to be expected that the ecclesiastical hierarchy played an important role. In the Netherlands, the foundations of the Catholic Party were laid during the 1880s and 1890s by a priest, Herman Schaepman (who died in 1903), and during the two decades after 1910 it was again a priest, Willem Nolens, who was the political leader of the Catholics. But it was especially the overt support for a unified Catholic Party by the Dutch Catholic bishops and their condemnation of other political and social groupings which sought to win the support of the Catholic electorate that greatly strengthened the power of the Catholic Party between 1920 and 1960. This section will consider the various aspects which this support took.[14]

A first remark might appear somewhat surprising. During Schaepman's efforts to found a Catholic party, the bishops did nothing to assist him. On the contrary, some of them sought wholeheartedly to frustrate his work. This was especially true of the bishop of Haarlem, Mgr. C. Bottemanne, a strongly conservative prelate, who in many respects managed to dominate his fellow bishops. On controversial political issues such as suffrage reform and compulsory education he followed traditional conservative opinion in opposing both policies, while the more progressive Schaepman supported an extension of the suffrage and the introduction of compulsory education. The conflict between the two men reached its climax in 1894 when the bishop imposed a temporary ban on Schaepman speaking in his diocese. The archbishop of Utrecht then followed his example. Although the relationship between the bishops and Schaepman was not always as bad as at that time and showed some improvement in the early years of the twentieth century, the difference in their attitude from that which they were to adopt after 1918 was very marked.[15]

---

[14] H. Bakvis, *Catholic Power in the Netherlands*. See also two recent articles on this subject: J. A. Bornewasser, 'Beraad tegen wil en dank: Het Nederlandse episcopaat en de politiek', in G. A. Ackermans, A. Davids, and P. J. A. Nissen (eds.), *Kerk in beraad. Opstellen aangeboden aan prof. dr. J. C. P. A. van Laarhoven* (Nijmegen, 1991), 279–300, and P. Luykx, ' "Van de dorpspastorie naar het torentje": Kerken en de macht der confessionele partijen', in P. Luykx and H. Righart (eds.), *Van de pastorie naar het torentje: Een eeuw confessionele politiek* (The Hague, 1991), pp. 35–71.

[15] J. A. Bornewasser, 'De "open" katholiciteit van Paus Leo XIII en zijn "Bisschop in politicis" Schaepman', in W. Frijhoff and M. Hiemstra (eds.), *Bewogen en bewegen: De historicus in het spanningsveld tussen economie en cultuur* (Tilburg, 1986), 378–92; J. A. Bornewasser, 'Curiale appreciaties van de priester-

The bishops' attitude is not difficult to explain. The religious climate during these years was highly conservative. The openness and progressive character of the pontificate of Leo XIII must certainly not be exaggerated, as the encyclical *Graves de communi re* indicated. Christian democracy, so it declared, should take the form of a social movement for the benefit of the working class and must not take on the character of a political party. Moreover, the manner in which during the era of Pius X anti-modernism in the form of religious integralism temporarily gained a dominant influence within the Church is well known. Ecclesiastical conservatives set themselves against any form of Catholic Party whatsoever, insisting that parties were an integral element of the modern, democratic state and therefore could bring no benefit to the Catholic cause. The Dutch episcopate felt very much at home in a traditional society and they opposed the progressive Schaepman, who, in order to achieve his goals, was willing to make the necessary concessions and who was even willing to participate in coalition cabinets with the Protestants (in the eyes of the bishops the hereditary enemies of Dutch Catholics). In the bishops' opinion, a purely religious grouping of parliamentary deputies who could defend the general cause of religious freedom and more particularly the religious interests of the Church was quite sufficient. Hence, they were more inclined to rely on the substantial group of Catholic conservative deputies in parliament, than on the more modern approach of Schaepman and his few supporters.[16]

However, as the modernization of state and society progressed during the twentieth century, so the willingness of the bishops and politicians to adapt to modern realities increased. Thus, there gradually emerged an alliance of the Church and of political Catholicism. In the years after 1917, this process gained momentum as a consequence of three factors. First, in that year the most important goal of political Catholicism up until then, the complete financial parity of the Catholic education system with the state system, was achieved. In order to ensure that, deprived of the unifying bond of the educational issue, the Catholic Party (RKSP) was not seriously weakened, its need for the support of the Church authorities was all the greater. Secondly, also in 1917, universal suffrage for men was introduced, followed in 1919 by universal suffrage for women. As at the same time voting was made compulsory, the issue arose as to whether all these new Catholic votes would rally behind the Catholic Party (RKSP) and more especially whether they would instead be captured by the Socialist Party. This formed a further common concern of both Catholic politicians and the Church. Lastly, at the beginning of the 1920s, Catholic political unity began to be seriously threatened. Small Catholic dissident parties of the right and left were established and there also emerged a substantial grouping of progressives, the so-called Michaelists, who threatened to break away from the single party. The leadership of the party was naturally anxious to forestall these defections, but

politicus Schaepman', *Mededelingen der Koninklijke Nederlandse Akademie van Wetenschappen (Afdeling Letterkunde)*, 49/7 (1986), 211–48.

[16] J. van Miert, 'Conservatisme onder katholieken in een biografisch perspectief: Mr. J. B. van Son (1804–1875)', *Bijdragen en Mededelingen betreffende de Geschiedenis der Nederlanden*, 104 (1989), 393–413.

the bishops also wished to prevent internal Catholic political disputes from leading to serious discord among the faithful.

This combination of factors led the bishops from 1918 to participate actively in Catholic politics. They recognized the political monopoly of the Catholic Party (RKSP) as well as forbidding all other Catholic organizations from becoming involved in politics and until the 1950s they consistently intervened to support the unitary Catholic Party. Indeed, in 1922 their support led to uproar in parliament and the government had to respond to questions about the pressure being exerted by the Church hierarchy on the Catholic faithful. This did not make much impact on the bishops and it became commonplace during national elections for them to impress on the faithful from the pulpit which party they must support. To vote for the Catholic Party was felt to be and was presented as a natural duty of conscience, as is clearly evident from an internal memorandum written by one of the bishops in 1918. When a Catholic does not vote for the Catholic Party, it declared, he 'betrays himself; he denies his Catholic principles; he does harm to the Church; and he undermines Catholic education, thereby harming the souls of our children'.[17] That the Catholic Party could not and did not wish to resist this intermingling of religion and politics was clearly evident from the phrasing of its General Programme of 1936 in which the party in reciprocation for the support of the Church undertook to act 'as the shield and protection for the Catholic Church in the Netherlands'.[18] After 1945 the episcopate still acted in a similar manner on a number of occasions, for the last time in 1954, two years after the party had lost a substantial number of votes to a right splinter party as well as to the Labour Party.

The Church did not merely advance the interests of the Catholic Party by these direct forms of support. Clerical attacks on those movements which could be considered to be competitors of the party were also indirectly of great advantage to political Catholicism. The greatest danger was, in the opinion of the bishops, posed by the Socialist Party. Indeed, some historians have even argued that clerical and Catholic anti-socialism formed the most important cause of pillarization. Two interconnected motives lay behind their anti-socialist obsession. On the one hand, in terms of ideology, they feared above all that ideas of atheism, materialism, and class struggle might infect Catholic workers. But, on the other hand, the Catholic leaders were also aware that the working class formed a particularly large group within the Catholic community and that the unity and power of the Catholic bloc would therefore be seriously undermined by Socialist success. Hence a tradition of anti-socialism within Catholicism can be traced back into the latter decades of the nineteenth century when especially at a local level there was an intense struggle for the loyalty of the Catholic worker. Significantly, nowhere else within society were so many priests deployed as in this sector. Of special significance was the role played within Catholic workers' organizations by priests who, though formally restricted to a narrow advisory role, in

---

[17] Cited in J. A. Bornewasser, 'De katholieken van Nederland en hun politieke partij. Verschuivingen in de argumenten pro', *Archief voor de Geschiedenis van de Katholieke Kerk in Nederland*, 32 (1990), 183–215, esp. 201.　　　　　　　　　　　　　　　　　　　　　　　　　　　[18] Ibid. 203.

practice intervened in all possible social and political matters.[19] From 1918 the bishops regularly rejected any Catholic support for Socialism and spoke out against any form of collaboration between the 'Romans' and the 'Reds'. They directed their energies strenuously against the pre-war Social Democratic Party, threatening the heavy sanction of refusal of the sacraments to any Catholics who became involved with the party. In contrast, membership of the post-war Labour Party was denounced in their declaration of 1954 'only' as irresponsible.

The Nationaal Socialistische Beweging was also condemned by the bishops. This extreme-right movement which took much of its inspiration from the model of German Nazism, remained on the whole relatively insignificant and Catholics played only a very limited role among its leadership and membership. This was partly a consequence of the stance adopted by the bishops. In 1934 participation in the movement or support for it had been forbidden only to certain categories of the faithful, but after the NSB had won almost 8 per cent of the vote in 1935 the bishops acted in the following year to forbid any significant form of Catholic support for the party and supplemented this ban with the threat of refusal of the sacraments to those who ignored their order. Though it is clear that in this case the ideological incompatibility between Catholicism and National Socialism also played a role in determining the attitude of the bishops, structural considerations should also not be forgotten, for the NSB was also perceived as a threat to Catholic unity.

The consequences of these various clerical interventions for the successful operation of the Catholic Party was, as stressed earlier, highly important. It must be emphasized, however, that it is not possible to measure precisely their impact. Only occasionally can the effect of clerical intervention be conclusively demonstrated. In 1954, for example, the total membership of the party had fallen to 269,000, but the year after it rose to 430,000. This can only be attributed to the impact of the bishops' message of 1954. The Canadian political scientist H. Bakvis, in his study of the structures of power within Catholic circles, has spoken in general terms of the 'overwhelming importance of the Church in determining all aspects of Catholic political life'[20] and, even though this may be something of an exaggeration, it is nevertheless impossible to doubt the importance of the actions of the bishops.

In conclusion, two further remarks need to be made. The action of the clerical authorities and of the élites of Catholic pillar organizations in favour of the Catholic Party had a depoliticizing effect on the Catholic rank and file whose political passivity was thus greatly reinforced. This had adverse consequences for the development of a democratic spirit within Catholic ranks, as it hindered or at least delayed the emergence of independent political opinions. This was, however, only one side of the coin. The strength of a pillarized political Catholicism also served to reinforce the political stability of the Netherlands when, as during the era of National Socialist and Communist totalitarian ideologies in the 1930s, it was threatened by extremism of the left and right. And since, as one Dutch politician once remarked, 'political

---

[19] G. J. M. Wentholt, *Een arbeidersbeweging en haar priesters* (Nijmegen, 1984).
[20] Bakvis, *Catholic Power in the Netherlands*, 95.

stability is not something to be despised',[21] this positive consequence of Catholic pillarization should not be neglected.

Finally, it should be noted that, though there exists no extensive study into the precise relationship between the episcopacy and the Catholic political leadership,[22] it is clear that here too there were two sides to the coin. While it is clear that the alliance of Church and party offered advantages for both sides, there is also evidence to suggest that the leaders of the Catholic political party soon began to distance themselves from some of the consequences of the Catholic revival, preferring to adopt instead a more modern attitude towards the autonomy of political action and the individual responsibility of politicians. One example serves to illustrate this point. The episcopal ban on co-operation between the Catholics and the Social Democrats issued in 1921 was weakened by the politicians in the following year by the addition of a single word which made co-operation '*exclusively* between Catholics and Social Democrats' impossible, thereby leaving open the option that such co-operation might be possible if a third party was included. Some years later in 1925, moreover, a further significant step was taken when it was decided that in circumstances of the utmost necessity ('de uiterste noodzaak') collaboration was possible, thereby opening up the possibility of all sorts of casuistry. Shortly afterwards, the parliamentary faction of the Catholic Party (RKSP) decided that it and not the episcopacy should have the final say on such matters.[23]

In addition, it is clear that not all bishops in every circumstance believed that it was right to interfere in political matters. This was especially so after the Second World War. Thus, it is striking that during the restoration of the Catholic pillar in the years 1944–1946 the bishops regularly advocated the reconstruction of the Catholic social organizations, but that they made no such statement regarding the Catholic political party. Moreover, it is known that during the preparation of the last episcopal letter on political matters in 1954 the college of bishops was severely divided internally.[24] However, it would not be until 1967 that one of the bishops finally announced publicly that a Catholic could vote freely for a party other than the Catholic Party and thereby brought to an end a tradition which had lasted half a century.

3. The Corporatist Alternative

The intransigent ideology of the Catholic revival was clearly apparent in the goals of the Catholic Party but here too the impact of modernization had an effect on the ideology of the party and eventually caused a process of adaptation to modernity to

---

[21] Comment of the Dutch politician J. F. Glastra van Loon cited in D. F. J. Bosscher, 'Confessionele partijen en politieke stabiliteit', in P. Luykx and H. Righart (eds.), *Van de pastorie naar het torentje*, 93–103, esp. 102.

[22] See, however, the recent article by Bornewasser, 'Beraad tegen wil en dank'.

[23] R. A. Koole, 'Uiterste noodzaak en partijpolitieke eenwording: Over het belang van interne partijverhoudingen bij coalitievorming', *Jaarboek Documentatiecentrum Nederlandse Politieke Partijen* (1986), 99–117, esp. 105.

[24] A. F. Manning, 'Uit de voorgeschiedenis van het mandement van 1954', *Jaarboek Katholiek Documentatie Centrum*, 1 (1971), 138–48.

prevail. In order to examine this process, it is the attitude adopted by political Catholicism towards liberalism and capitalism which will form the focus of this section.[25]

Even in the nineteenth century, however backward and untouched by modern ideas they might have been, there were among some Dutch Catholics traces of an enlightened and liberal Catholicism. Thus, for example, around 1848 a group of Catholic politicians (who became known as 'papothorbeckians') co-operated with the Liberal leader Thorbecke in devising a constitution for the country. Similarly, in the political disputes over education, Catholic parliamentary deputies regularly supported the cause of public schooling, although this was directly opposed to the stance adopted by the bishops. It was only in the 1860s and the 1870s that under the pressure of the Catholic religious revival they developed into conservatives. In 1892 one of them declared 'I hold the democratic doctrine to be a gross and most unfortunate error'[26] and his comment was highly representative of the opinions of Catholic deputies at the time. This was even true of Schaepman and his small band of supporters, for the founder of the Catholic Party was no more a believer in democracy than were his conservative opponents. He too completely rejected, in accordance with Catholic teachings at the time, the principle of the sovereignty of the people and the democratic system based on it, and his political stance can only be described at best as progressive rather than truly democratic.[27]

In the years around 1900, alongside attacks on liberalism and democracy, a vision of a Catholic alternative gradually began to take shape around the concept of corporatism. This term had two meanings. It was used by some to define an alternative political organization of the State; while for others, it indicated a different structure for society. The first of these options, political corporatism, remained for a long time a minority current within the party and it was only in the 1930s that it emerged as a distinctive trend. Around 1935, it began to be advocated by a number of party commissions which helped to devise a new programme for the party.[28] According to the party chairman, Goseling, corporatism should serve to strengthen and restore the health of the democratic system. Thus, any form of dictatorship, at least in the Dutch situation, was explicitly rejected by the Catholic Party and the support of quite a few commission members for a corporative parliamentary chamber should therefore be

[25] Re this subject, see P. Luykx, 'Die Niederländischen Konfessionellen und das Verhältnis zwischen Staat und Gesellschaft im 20 Jahrhundert', in J. P. Nautz and J. F. E. Bläsing (eds.), *Staatliche Intervention und Gesellschaftliche Freiheit: Staat und Gesellschaft in den Niederlanden und Deutschland im 20 Jahrhundert* (Melsungen, 1987), 73–96; P. Luykx, 'De Nederlandse katholieken en de moderne maatschappij', *Kleio*, 33/4 (1992), 3–9; P. Luykx 'Niederländische Katholiken und die Demokratie 1900–1960', in J.-C. Kaiser *et al.* (eds.), *Christentum und Demokratie im 20 Jahrhundert* (Stuttgart, 1992), 89–110.

[26] Cited in J. van de Giessen, *De opkomst van het woord democratie als leuze in Nederland* (The Hague, 1948), 232.

[27] A. F. Manning, 'Mag men spreken van christen-democraten in de vorige eeuw?', in A. F. Manning, *Scenes uit het katholiek leven in de negentiende en twintigste eeuw* (Baarn, 1990), 267–86.

[28] S. Vaessen, 'Democratie-kritiek in de RKSP: Staatkundige beginselen, corporatieve denkbeelden en het streven naar hervorming van het Nederlandse staatsbestel, 1931–1940', *Jaarboek Katholiek Documentatie Centrum*, 17 (1987), 86–111.

seen as supplementing rather than replacing the existing democratically elected chambers. Catholic politicians also proposed controls on the legal authorization of political parties, advocating that when any party expressed morally inadmissible opinions it should be outlawed. This was a proposal which was aimed especially at the Communist Party and, on the same basis, they also advocated limitations on the rights of association and assembly.

The party never went beyond these limited proposals and it cannot therefore be argued that the Catholic Party as a whole was committed to a wide-ranging revision of the constitution of the state. Nevertheless, individual Catholic politicians were on occasions willing to make much more radical proposals. The best known of these was C. Romme who until shortly after the Second World War continued to defend radical corporatist political ideas.[29] In his opinion, both the existing parliamentary chambers should be replaced by a corporatist chamber (rather than merely supplemented by such an institution) and he was similarly explicit on the conditions for the granting of legal status to political parties. They must, he insisted, acknowledge both the existence of God and the right to private property and he believed that similar conditions should also be extended to appointments to public offices. In addition, Romme sought a reduction in the powers of parliament and a strengthening of the responsibilities of the executive. These radical views did, however, distinguish Romme from other Catholic politicians and the number of actual initiatives and reforms remained limited. In 1938, in order to counter political extremism, Goseling (who in the mean time had become a minister) introduced legislation to parliament which limited freedom of association and assembly. Similarly, as a consequence of Catholic political initiatives, the Netherlands also experienced some limited measures of censorship of radio and film. The radio measures were intended above all to control the broadcasts of the Socialist broadcasting organization while the restrictions on film were aimed principally at the protection of children. Given their minority position, the Catholic Party (RKSP) had, however, only a partial responsibility for all such measures.

Nevertheless, as can be imagined, many non-Catholic Dutch found Catholic support for such views and ideas surprising. This was also true of the sympathetic attitude adopted by some in Catholic circles towards authoritarian regimes in Europe which were based on Catholic corporatist principles, such as those of Dollfuss in Austria and Salazar in Portugal. The greatest stir was caused by Catholic support for Franco's Nationalist forces during the uprising of 1936 and the subsequent Spanish Civil War. In the context of Dutch politics, this was an extraordinary stance and their support for Franco was shared only by Mussert's extreme-right National Socialists.[30]

Outside the mainstream of the unitary Catholic party, however, other elements within Dutch Catholicism were at the same time advocating extremist anti-democratic and Catholic authoritarian ideas. These were predominantly small groups

[29] J. Bosmans, *Romme: Biografie 1896–1946* (Utrecht, 1991), pts VI.3, VIII.3 and 6, and IX.4.
[30] M. Braams *et al.* (eds.), *Nederland en de Spaanse burgeroorlog* (Utrechtse Historische Cahiers, 1; Utrecht, 1982).

of students and intellectuals, who gathered around certain journals which attacked the democratic system together with the Catholic Party which operated within it as well as advocating radical Catholic integralist and fascist views. In addition, these young self-styled Catholic revolutionaries denounced the mentality of small-minded complacency and indolence which they perceived in Dutch Catholic circles. For them, capitalism and socialism were both equal enemies, and there was sometimes an unmistakable flavour of anti-Semitism to their rhetoric. The actions of these small groups and individuals have tended to attract a degree of attention from historians which is out of proportion to the limited scale of their activities.[31] Nevertheless, in certain cases, they did succeed in creating some form of political organization. This was true in the case of the Zwart Front (later renamed the Nationaal Front) which contested national elections without ever winning a parliamentary seat. Subsequently, during the German Occupation, the Nationaal Front collaborated closely with the Nazi authorities. The influence which these radicals had on the stance of the Catholic Party (RKSP) was on the whole insignificant and it is clear that in general the Catholic Party did not devote a great deal of attention to the construction of a Catholic alternative to the modern, liberal democratic state.

Nevertheless, the legacy of these ideas was evident in the political behaviour of some Dutch Catholics during the German Occupation of the country from 1940 to 1945. The Nazi regime attacked the Netherlands on 10 May 1940 and won a rapid military victory. The Queen fled to exile in London but within the country there were many Dutch who felt that it was necessary to reach some form of accommodation with the Nazi authorities. This led to the establishment of contact between the Dutch and German authorities over issues relating to the economy and public administration. It also, however, led a number of political figures to develop plans for the introduction of a new political system, modelled in part on the Nazi model. Though these ideas were advocated by political figures from many political backgrounds, Catholics were not absent from these discussions. As elsewhere in Europe, Dutch Catholics during the early months of the Occupation were torn between loyalty to the political status quo and the attractions of political reform.

The most important political initiative at this time was the Nederlandse Unie (Dutch Union) which was established shortly after the German invasion of 1940 and which hoped, somewhat naïvely, to carry through a corporatist reform of the political system in collaboration with the German occupation authorities.[32] The Catholics were prominent in their support for this initiative but at the end of 1941 the Unie was outlawed by the German authorities. Moreover, it must also be borne in mind that the Nederlandse Unie served as a safety-valve for the expression of patriotic and anti-German sentiments, and that it perhaps owed its success principally to this

---

[31] See e.g. L. M. H. Joosten, *Katholieken en fascisme in Nederland 1920–1940* (Hilversum, 1964).

[32] On the Nederlandse Unie see e.g. two English-language articles: G. Hirschfeld, 'Collaboration and Attentism in the Netherlands 1940–41', *Journal of Contemporary History*, 16 (1981), 467–86; M. L. Smith, 'Neither Resistance nor Collaboration: Historians and the Problem of the *Nederlandse Unie*', *History*, 72 (1987), 251–78.

aspect of its activities. With the collapse of the Unie, it was the Nationaal Socialist-ische Beweging led by Anton Mussert which emerged as the advocate of unlimited collaboration with the Nazi authorities. As has already been indicated, however, the NSB had been strenuously denounced by the Dutch Catholic bishops during the 1930s and few Catholics were active in this movement. Instead, the Catholic popula-tion, in common with most of their compatriots, were gradually drawn towards a stance of resistance to German oppression.

The corporatist initiatives during the 1930s and the years of the Second World War merely serve to highlight the ambivalence and vagueness which often character-ized Catholic attitudes. However, they also raise the question as to how political Catholicism came gradually to move towards a full acceptance of the democratic sys-tem. In explaining this evolution, four factors need to be stressed. First, both the ec-clesiastical and secular Catholic élites from the nineteenth century onwards were inevitably obliged to appreciate that their own emancipation as well as the interests of the Church had been favoured by the acquisition of various democratic rights and freedoms. Thus, it may be assumed, that they evolved from a purely instrumental attitude to democracy to a more principled appreciation of its benefits. Secondly, their participation and integration in the democratic system had a substantial effect. From 1919 onwards no cabinet was formed without the co-operation of the Catholic Party, and this participation in the democratic exercise of power has deeply influ-enced their attitude towards the system as a whole. Thirdly, their experience of Na-tional Socialism, and of the German Occupation of their country during the Second World War served to make the Catholics aware of the fundamental virtues of demo-cracy. Finally, the Second Vatican Council confirmed all these positive experiences by breaking with traditional Catholic political and social teachings and indicating that the Church did not possess a monopoly over truth. In this respect, the constitu-tion *Gaudium et Spes* was of especial significance.

If one turns from political corporatism to social corporatism, then a similar com-bination of factors is evident, with the distinction that in this case Catholic social organizations, working in co-operation with Catholic politicians, made a much greater effort to construct an alternative to capitalism. This had already begun dir-ectly after the First World War. Between 1919 and 1921 an experimental system of joint industrial councils was established on a private basis among Catholics, in the hope that they would prove so popular that they would lead to the establishment of a public system of such councils. Catholic employers and employees worked together in these councils as a demonstration of their resolve to replace capitalism by a better social system. Judging from the sixty-four councils which were established quite rapidly, this experiment was a success, but already in the course of 1920 the first dif-ficulties began to emerge. Reluctance on the part of the employers as well as the radicalism of the initiator of the councils, Veraart, who wanted them to assume immediate responsibility for many economic matters, led eventually to the failure of this experiment.[33]

[33] W. Tomassen, *Het R.K. Bedrijfsradenstelsel (1919–1922)* (Leiden, 1974).

Some ten or fifteen years later, during the economic crisis of the 1930s, the Catholics once again played an active part in the sometimes seemingly endless debates in the Netherlands about a restructuring of society. It was the Catholic workers' movement which was to the fore in these debates, bringing intense pressure to bear on the Catholic Party to enact essential social reforms. Through a vast campaign entitled 'Towards the New Community' ('Naar de Nieuwe Gemeenschap') they sought to mobilize the entire Catholic population to ensure that this was the last time that a capitalist crisis would cause such suffering to the working population. From within the ranks of the political party, their efforts were supported by, among others, the radical figure Max van Poll. He sought to 'break the power of capital' by advocating that even the banks should be subjected to the authority of a system of economic councils. The German wartime Occupation merely imposed a pause on these efforts to create a corporatist reorganization of society which were pursued after 1945 in collaboration with the Labour Party and resulted finally in 1950 in a parliamentary Act on Public Industrial Organization which was unanimously welcomed by the Catholic population. It was intended that this legislation would provide the legal framework for an anti-capitalist reorganization of society along the lines laid down in the papal encyclical *Quadragesimo Anno*, in which the corporatist industrial councils would take on wide-ranging public responsibilities.[34]

Nevertheless, although the former Catholic workers' leader, De Bruyn, was appointed as the new Minister for Public Industrial Organization, this law proved to be a failure. This was the consequence of various factors, including the lack of determination on the part of the Catholic Party (KVP), the obstruction which the law encountered from employers, and the absence of firm support from the Protestant parties, which had always been much less enthusiastic towards the project. By far the most important factor was, however, the enormous rise in prosperity and the remarkable levels of economic growth which were achieved during the 1950s and 1960s, with the consequent benefits for large sections of the population. It is noticeable that the ideal of a corporatist economic system attracted widespread support principally in times of economic hardship, such as the years after the First World War, the economic recession of the 1930s and the years of economic reconstruction after 1945. Conversely, as soon as capitalism recovered and began to bring higher levels of prosperity, so the appeal of the corporatist alternative faded. When during the 1950s one wage increase succeeded another and cars, televisions, and refrigerators came within the reach of almost everybody, it seemed possible to dispense with a fundamental reorganization of the very capitalist system which was responsible for all these benefits. Thus, it is clear that the defeat of a social corporatist model of society was essentially a product of the success of modern capitalism.

This does not, however, mean that the Catholic pursuit of a corporatist alternative

---

[34] P. de Rooy, 'Het zoeken naar de moederwetenschap. Ordening in de jaren dertig', in R. A. Koole (ed.), *Van Bastille tot Binnenhof: De Franse Revolutie en haar invloed op de Nederlandse politieke partijen* (Houten, 1989), 66–88; H. de Liagre Böhl, 'De confessionelen en het corporatisme in Nederland', in P. Luykx and H. Righart (eds.), *Van de pastorie naar het torentje*, 104–23.

had no consequences for the existing socio-economic system. Its influence must be sought instead in the emergence, principally after 1918, of a substantial network of governmental institutions and advisory councils in which employers, employees, and the government consulted with each other and discussed matters of common concern. Thus, for example, the Socio-Economic Council, which was provided for in the law of 1950, has subsequently become the most important advisory organization to the government. Moreover, in two other significant respects, Catholic corporatism has had an effect. First, in no other country in the world was a system of collective wage bargaining—this 'truce in the class struggle', as it has been termed[35]— developed as rapidly and applied so widely as in the Netherlands. Secondly, among many Catholic moral theologians and politicians, the right of workers to resort to industrial action was resolutely rejected. Dutch strike figures rank among the lowest in Europe, and the right to strike has never been firmly established in law. Whether a strike was legal or not was left to the judges who acted on the basis of jurisprudence. Only with the establishment of the European Social Charter has the government recently been obliged to accept the legal recognition of strikes.[36]

Thus, although it must be accepted that the ideals of social corporatism have indeed been rendered redundant by modern developments, they nevertheless made a substantial impact on the nature of the socio-economic system. And, in this respect, the influence exercised by social corporatism differed markedly from that exercised by concepts of political corporatism which finally failed to leave any trace on the structures of the Dutch political system.

4. Family Policy

In a recent article, it was pointed out that the Catholic revival of the nineteenth century contained a strong disciplinary and moralizing component.[37] By means of its separate educational system, clerical poor relief, and various new religious associations, the secular and ecclesiastical Catholic élites sought to keep the Catholic working class under social and moral control. Visits to homes by the clergy and by members of organizations such as the associations of St Vincent de Paul were a commonly used means of supervision while the campaigns for the strengthening of marriage and family ties and against alcoholism, promiscuity, indolence, prostitution, and neo-Malthusianism all featured prominently. Thus, it is not surprising that political Catholicism as a part of the wider Catholic movement should have also sought to contribute to these goals.

[35] W. Albeda and W. J. Dercksen, *Arbeidsverhoudingen in Nederland* (4th edn., Alphen aan den Rijn, 1989), 127.

[36] W. S. P. Fortuyn, *Stakingsrecht in Nederland: Theorie en praktijk 1872–1986* (Weesp, 1985), 41–4 and 126–7. On Catholicism and strikes in the Netherlands, see pt. II of P. Luykx, 'A Century of Dutch Catholicism and *Rerum Novarum*', in P. Furlong and D. Curtis (eds.), *The Church faces the Modern World: Rerum Novarum and its Impact* (Scunthorpe, 1994).

[37] H. Righart, 'Moraliseringsoffensief in Nederland in de periode 1850–1880', in H. Peters *et al.* (eds.), *Vijf eeuwen gezinsleven: Liefde, huwelijk en opvoeding in Nederland* (Nijmegen, 1988), 194–207. See also n. 25, above.

The family as the basis and central unit of society had long been a central article of Catholic belief but it was one which took on a particular importance during the nineteenth century. The reasons for this lay primarily in the perception of 'the family as an anti-revolutionary project under clerical supervision'.[38] The Church's fear of riots and revolution was shared by much of the nineteenth-century bourgeoisie and this common concern formed an important opportunity for collaboration between the two. A close-knit family life would, they hoped, provide a rampart against the recurrence of revolution and chaos and would ensure the eventual creation of a contented and hard-working population. The Church's concern for the family, however, also arose from the fact that the Church relied on the family, along with the education system and the new Catholic associationism, as a means of clerical recruitment and religious socialization. Moreover, the Church's desire to bring about a full emancipation of the Catholic population within Dutch society also played a role in fostering the Church's concern for the family, for, by reinforcing family bonds, the Church hoped to strengthen numerically the place of the Catholic minority in society. Thus, these various considerations combined to ensure that the Catholics used all available means—including political ones—to strengthen the family and to reinforce the bonds between marriage, procreation, and the family in the face of modern trends towards their dissolution. In collaboration with the Protestant parties and with broad support from the Liberals and the Socialists, political Catholicism was temporarily able to achieve much needed successes in this field.

The immorality laws of 1911, which were prepared and brought into force by a Catholic minister, marked a break with the former liberal-inspired legislation of the nineteenth century. This had been limited to excluding immorality from the public sphere in order that the citizen would not be confronted 'despite himself' with such immorality. The laws of 1911, on the other hand, sought to establish a supra-personal moral order, which would govern the behaviour and relationships of citizens. Thus, the State assumed a new role as the moral arbiter of society. For example, a new regulation was introduced which protected adolescents against homosexual temptation and for the first time since 1811 homosexuality became a punishable offence. A further indication of the new mentality was the strengthening of the regulations against pornography. Whereas formerly the law had limited itself to protecting the citizen against accidental contact with pornographic materials, the production and trade in pornography was now forbidden and made an offence. This was also true of the sale and distribution of contraceptive and abortion devices, which were similarly banned. By means of all these measures, the minister sought, so he declared, to build a dam against 'the great threat which immorality in its continually changing forms poses to the life of society'.[39]

In the course of the following decades, Catholic politicians made life difficult for movements aimed at sexual emancipation such as the Neo–Malthusian Federation

---

[38] T. van Eupen, 'Kerk en gezin in Nederland', in G. A. Kooy (ed.), *Gezinsgeschiedenis: Vier eeuwen gezin in Nederland* (Assen, 1985), 7–30, esp. 20–1.

[39] Cited in T. Schalken, *Pornografie en strafrecht* (Arnhem, 1972), 138.

and the homosexual association, the COC, which were refused a corporate legal character and were therefore seriously hampered in their public activities. As late as 1950, the Centrum voor Staatkundige Vorming (the Centre for Political Education) which was affiliated to the Catholic Party (KVP), proposed that homosexuality between consenting adults should also be forbidden and that convicted homosexuals should be committed to hospital for medical treatment. These far-reaching proposals were not, however, adopted by the party.[40]

In Catholic tradition, marriage had always been considered to be an indissoluble bond. But the Protestant influence on Dutch legislation had ensured that serious grounds for divorce such as desertion or adultery were acknowledged and laid down in law. Divorce on the grounds of mutual agreement by the partners concerned was not, however, permitted. But when in 1883 a judge decreed that the admission of adultery by one of the partners was sufficient proof of adultery an increasing number of couples used this possibility—regardless of whether adultery had actually taken place—to bring about a dissolution of their marriage. This procedure rapidly became known as 'the big lie' as there was apparently often reason to doubt the admissions, mostly by husbands, of their supposed adultery. In the course of the first half of the twentieth century, numerous Catholic committees, party politicians, and ministers tried to end this practice by bringing about a reversal of the 1883 decision in order to ensure that an admission of adultery would no longer be sufficient and positive proof would instead be required. The Catholics were, however, always opposed by a majority of the other political parties and on this point the efforts of the Catholic politicians, though highly revealing of the nature of their ambitions, brought no reward. At the end of the 1960s divorce legislation was changed but finally only in the opposite, more permissive direction.

Catholic family policy also sought to keep women out of the public and political spheres and to maintain them within the home. This was evident, for example, in the campaign to ensure that female civil servants and teachers were dismissed from public service when they married. This goal was achieved in 1924 and the Catholic minister Romme even proposed in 1937 that married women should be forbidden from working in factories.[41] Several factors underlay this proposal, including the wish to diminish mass unemployment during the depression, but it was also indicative of a patriarchal ideology which believed that a woman ought to devote herself to her family and home. The opposition aroused by his suggestion was, however, so substantial that the minister was forced to retreat and chose to withdraw his proposal. Moreover, in 1957 some Protestant and female Catholic deputies voted with the opposition to force the government (of which the Catholic Party—KVP—was a member) to withdraw the 1924 legislation which discriminated against married female civil servants and teachers.

---

[40] H. Oosterhuis, *Homoseksualiteit in katholiek Nederland: Een sociale geschiedenis 1900–1970* (Amsterdam, 1992), 101–2.

[41] A. Schoot Uiterkamp, 'Terug naar het paradijs? Acties tegen de beperking van vrouwenarbeid in de jaren dertig', *Jaarboek voor de geschiedenis van socialisme en arbeidersbeweging in Nederland* (1978), 182–244.

Catholic politicians have also striven to create a strong material foundation for family life in which its self-reliance and independence would be guaranteed and strengthened. One element of this policy was, for example, the idea of a family wage, which was directly inspired by the encyclical *Rerum Novarum* and which meant that the wages of a husband and father should be sufficient to support a family. Housing policy was similarly influenced by these goals in so far as the provision of sufficient housing for large families was always kept in mind and, more especially perhaps, because private home ownership was always strongly favoured. The same was also true of children's allowances. The first extensive provision of such allowances in 1939 was the product of an initiative by the Catholic Party (RKSP), and in the subsequent decades the Catholics and the Social Democrats were their strongest advocates. Various elements of Catholic family policy have thus come to form an integral element of Dutch social legislation.

If one was to try to assess how successful the Catholic attempts were to impose their views concerning the family, then the answer must be rather similar to that already provided concerning their corporatist policies. The moral offensive by the Catholic movement, via the influence of the Catholic Party, working with orthodox Protestantism and supported by other groups, did indeed temporarily exert an incontrovertible influence on Dutch legislation and thereby on the behaviour of the Dutch population. This impact was, however, only temporary for between 1969 and 1981 legislation with regard to contraception, homosexuality, pornography, abortion, and divorce was again changed, this time in a liberal direction. These were the years in which 'the permissive society' was created. At the same time, moreover, the under-representation of women in public offices and the professional world was slowly but surely overcome. If some financial elements of Catholic family policies have remained in force, this is because they have become instruments of social or welfare policy, and not because they are generally regarded as serving moral purposes.

The conclusions of demographic analyses of Dutch society also demonstrate the influence which Catholic teachings exerted during the first half of the twentieth century. In comparison with other countries, the Netherlands experienced a much slower decline in marital fertility (as part of the wider demographic revolution) and a marked fall in the total number of extra-marital births as well as low divorce and abortion rates. The historical demographer E. W. Hofstee has no hesitation in attributing these trends to what he terms 'the organized confessionalism' that has left a strong mark on Dutch society, whereby 'a concern for family, marriage and procreation and for the relationship between the sexes in general [was] central, especially for the Catholic population'. A characteristic feature of Dutch society in the first half of the twentieth century was, he concludes, 'a far-reaching control of sexual behaviour which by comparison with other countries appears sometimes unreal'.[42]

On the other hand, as a number of recent publications have stressed, the modernization of fertility patterns and of sexual behaviour did, nevertheless, steadily

[42] E. W. Hofstee, *Korte demografische geschiedenis van Nederland van 1800 tot heden* (Haarlem, 1981), 59–60.

progress in the Netherlands during these years.[43] This was also true of the Catholic population, the rates of marital fertility among whom, though higher than the Dutch average, did nevertheless show a steady fall. Moreover, it seems that this somewhat higher figure was much more a product of economic wishes or necessities than of the pressure of Catholic teachings. For the Catholic population as a whole it was, thus, certainly not true that the Catholic revival and the moral offensive was sufficient to prevent them from sharing all modern opinions and forms of behaviour.

This last point appears very strikingly from a recent study of the practice of rhythm methods of contraception in Catholic circles during the 1930s.[44] Until the decision of Pius XII in 1951, the question as to whether this method of contraception was permitted or not remained unclear. In the Netherlands most moral theologians favoured a restrictive interpretation and argued that the method could only be permitted in exceptional circumstances. Nevertheless, it appears from this study that a significant number of Catholic couples who were in no sense exceptional regularly used the rhythm method under the guidance of Catholic doctors and with the knowledge of the parish priest. Although it was an unreliable form of contraception, the rhythm method was nevertheless clearly a system of birth control and it is therefore scarcely surprising that among many Catholics the practice of this method was only a transitional stage towards the adoption of other more modern forms of contraception. In addition, a number of recent studies have drawn attention to the more general imbalance between the enormous volume of verbal denunciations levelled by Catholic groups at neo-Malthusian ideas and 'other forms of immorality' and, on the other hand, the gradual but remorseless process of adaptation which characterized the behaviour of the Catholic population. In the light of this analysis, the conventional perception of the Dutch as a somewhat prudish nation becomes no more than a misleading cliché.[45] This may be something of an exaggerated revision of the traditional interpretation but it is nevertheless clear that the co-operation of the Church and the Catholic Party in the moral offensive during the first half of the century proved unable to halt the modernization of marital and family life.

5. National Policy

As has been outlined in the earlier sections of this chapter, participation in the democratic system gave political Catholicism the opportunity to advance its own ideals. It could attempt to give shape to its alternatives to the modern liberal and capitalist structures as well as striving to reinforce both the family and personal morality. However, this participation in both parliament and government also involved Catholic

---

[43] See the various publications of T. L. M. Engelen and J. H. A. Hillebrand, esp. 'De daling van de vruchtbaarheid in de negentiende en twintigste eeuw: Een historiografisch overzicht met bijzondere aandacht voor Nederland', *Bijdragen en Mededelingen betreffende de Geschiedenis der Nederlanden*, 105/3 (1990), 354–67.

[44] H. Westhoff, *Natuurlijk geboortenregelen in de twintigste eeuw* (Baarn, 1986).

[45] H. Q. Röling, 'Permanente seksuele revolutie in Nederland?', *Spiegel Historiael*, 26/9 (1991), 376–80.

politicians in other tasks and responsibilities at a national level which had little to do with Catholic doctrines, but which drew on national traditions and even on sentiments of loyalty and devotion to the Dutch nation. A comprehensive analysis of the connection between Catholic and national politics is not possible here, and this section of the chapter will therefore concentrate on an investigation of two questions which serve to illustrate this more general theme. First, what stance did the political arm of Catholicism adopt towards defence policy and imperialism and colonialism? And, secondly, how monarchist were the Catholics? In both cases, the analysis will highlight Catholic traditions and ideals and seek to examine how far these conflicted with national ideals, just as in the other fields already examined, Catholic teachings on occasions came into conflict with modern ideas.[46]

Until the Netherlands became part of NATO after 1945, its defence policy was a source of continual problems. Catholic politicians, moreover, did little to assist in the resolution of these problems. Their relative lack of attention to defence issues was due to a number of widely differing motives which had their origins in the nineteenth century. Thus, at that time, it was rare to encounter a Catholic officer in the army or navy, and, as far as the higher officer corps was concerned, this remained the case during the first half of the twentieth century. Unintentionally, the military hierarchy therefore acquired a Liberal and Protestant character which reflected the traditional backwardness of the Catholics as a minority group in society. Secondly, there was the problem of universal military conscription, which was only finally introduced in 1898. In their long-standing and determined opposition to this democratic reform during much of the nineteenth century, two considerations were of importance to the Catholics. On the one hand, their oft-expressed objections to the coarseness of barracks life was, of course, a product of their religious convictions and would indeed continue to be expressed regularly until long into the twentieth century. But, on the other hand, conservative Catholic politicians also wished to maintain the undemocratic and discriminatory replacement system which enabled an individual to avoid military conscription by paying for it to be undertaken by somebody else. Apparently, moral dangers were more threatening to the rich than to the poor. . . .

The malaise in national defence policy during the inter-war period was due not only to the pursuit of disarmament by the Liberals and Social Democrats but also to the hesitations and reluctance shown by the confessional groups, above all the Catholics.[47] This was most clearly apparent in the failure of the Navy Act of 1923.[48] Within the Catholic parliamentary group, ten dissidents voted against this measure and thereby obstructed the enlargement and strengthening of the Dutch navy. Similarly, until the second half of the 1930s, many in Catholic circles remained opposed to essential reforms of the army. From 1917 onwards, these Catholics could derive

[46] This section is based partly on P. Luykx, 'Nederlandse katholieken en de natie 1900–1960: Enkele verkenningen', *Ex Tempore: Historisch Tijdschrift KU Nijmegen*, 11/3 (1992), 203–15.

[47] J. A. M. M. Janssen, 'Kerk, coalitie en defensie in het Interbellum', in G. Teitler (ed.), *Tussen crisis en oorlog: Maatschappij en krijgsmacht in de jaren '30* (Dieren, 1984), 42–62.

[48] H. J. G. Beunders, *'Weg met de vlootwet!' De maritieme bewapeningspolitiek van het kabinet Ruys de Beerenbrouck en het succesvolle verzet daartegen in 1923* (Amsterdam, 1984), 118–28.

new justifications from the peace initiatives of Pope Benedict XV. Though it is true that these proposals had stressed arbitration and mutual disarmament, some Catholics believed that in order to reach this goal it was necessary to begin with unilateral national disarmament. Like the German Dominican, Stratmann, some also questioned the validity of the Church's teachings on the concept of a just war and in the ranks of the Catholic Youth Peace Action (Katholieke Jongeren Vredes Actie) any form of conscription was rejected in favour of a professional army. A very different but highly important motive behind the hesitant behaviour of the Catholic Party was the pressure exercised on its parliamentary group by deputies from the Catholic workers' movement. Because of its heterogeneous social composition, the party was continually faced with the dilemma of deciding whether to give priority in the budget to expenditure on social policy (favoured by the Catholic workers' movement) or on national defence.

Certainly, as far as the navy was concerned, the Catholics always displayed little interest. Its main purpose was to defend the Dutch East Indies and the Catholics felt little sympathy with the colonial world. They did not play a significant role either in the economy or the administration of the East Indies and on matters of colonial policy the Catholic Party was content to follow the lead of its Protestant coalition partner. Catholic enthusiasm for the colony was only aroused where the issue of missionary activity was concerned. With the number of missionaries that Catholic Holland produced, they easily dominated the foreign Catholic missionaries and it was therefore all the more galling for them that the constitution of the Dutch East Indies proved to be far more favourable to Protestant missionaries than to the Catholics. The colonial policy of the Catholic Party (RKSP) during the inter-war period, thus amounted to little more than continual efforts to bring about a reform of the constitution of the East Indies on this matter. However, despite heavy pressure from their supporters, the leaders of the Catholic Party were never willing to put their alliance with their Protestant coalition partners at stake over the issue. A similar pragmatism—some preferred to call it opportunism—was displayed by the party towards a number of Catholic intellectuals, youth figures, and politicians from within their own ranks who, on the basis of their Catholic beliefs, expressed support for the nationalist independence struggle in the colony and thereby sought to bring Catholic doctrine in line with a principled anti-colonialism. On an ideological level, the leaders of the Catholic Party were unable to counter these arguments, but in practice they always preferred to ignore the demands of the East Indian nationalists.[49]

Thus, the stance of the Catholics on defence and colonial matters could be criticized on a number of grounds and it is not surprising that their ideological and political opponents should have accused them of being too weak in their defence of the national interests of the country. That such criticisms were often mixed with old Protestant prejudices about the unpatriotic character of the Catholics should not be allowed to undermine these arguments. Nevertheless, the extent of Catholic hesitation should not be exaggerated. Under pressure from the German threat, the

[49] J. Bank, *Katholieken en de Indonesische Revolutie* (Baarn, 1983), 15–71.

Catholic Party (RKSP) in the second half of the 1930s did make strenuous efforts to rectify the military situation. And when after 1945 Catholic politicians came to play the leading role in the process of decolonization from the Dutch East Indies, they defended Dutch national interests (or what they took them to be) as consistently and determinedly as possible, including the repeated use of military means in order to break the nationalist resistance. Thus, as regards both of the issues analysed briefly here, the stance of political Catholicism in effect lay somewhere between Catholic and national traditions, interests and opinions.

The impression of a somewhat ambivalent attitude on the part of the Catholics towards Dutch national interests was reinforced by the extensive cult of the Papacy which was current in Catholic circles. This orientation towards Rome, which had already been evident among the Catholic minority during the era of the Republic, increased considerably during the nineteenth century as a consequence of the anti-revolutionary triumphalism of the Papacy. The manner in which Dutch Catholic loyalties were focused especially strongly on Rome and the Pope was evident from two factors: the already mentioned missionary movement and the Zouave movement of the 1860s. This consisted of volunteers who assisted the papal army in their defence of the Papal State against the Italian nationalists and cost quite a number of young Catholic men their Dutch nationality or even their lives. In comparison with other countries, the number of Dutch participants was in both cases exceptionally high while other evidence, such as, for example, the representation and mythologization of the Popes in the Catholic press and the growth in organized pilgrimages to Rome also points towards a highly developed identification with the Papacy as the centre of the universal Church. Where else, for example, did Catholics build a small-scale replica of St Peter's in Rome, as the Dutch Catholic architect Cuypers did at Oudenbosch? And where else could an ode to the Pope—the famous *To You, O King of Ages* (*Aan U, o Koning der Eeuwen*) composed by Schaepman—become the favourite song of Catholics?

Thus, Dutch Catholics and their political party regularly came into conflict with their non-Catholic fellow citizens over policy towards the Papacy. The best known example of such conflict was provided by the long-drawn-out question of the Dutch diplomatic representation at the Vatican, which was removed as the result of a Liberal initiative in 1872 but restored as a diplomatic listening-post during the First World War. Shortly after the war, the Liberals, Socialists, and Protestants refused to confirm its re-establishment, provoking a serious political crisis in relations with the Catholic Party (RKSP), and the embassy was only definitively re-established in 1943. Problems also, however, arose at other times, notably, for example, on the occasion of the Borromaeus encyclical of 1910. In this text, the Pope referred to the sixteenth-century religious reformers as 'haughty and rebellious people', who suited, among others, 'the first and most corrupted monarch or nation'.[50] Public protests and a debate in parliament ensued, leading the Catholic Party leadership to take

---

[50] Cited in J. P. Gribling, *Willem Hubert Nolens 1860–1931: Uit het leven van een Priester-Staatsman* (Assen, 1978), 163–5.

action and draw up an apology on the part of the Pope. His words, so it was insisted, could not be taken as a reference either to the Dutch royal family of Orange–Nassau or to the Dutch Protestants.

Over this issue, the Catholic cult of the Papacy came directly into conflict with the pre-eminent symbol of Dutch nationalism, the royal family. And it is this which provided one of the roots of the Catholic glorification of the Dutch royal family. What better way for the Catholics to refute allegations regarding their extra-national ultramontane loyalties than by a glorification of the Dutch monarchy? However, there was also a second reason for their royalist devotion. One of the major motives for the establishment and development of the Catholic pillar by the clerical and secular Catholic leaders had, after all, been their not unfounded fear that the power of attraction exercised by the Socialists might draw the Catholic workers away from the Church and the Catholic faith. Moreover, until the 1930s the Socialists retained a strong anti-monarchist tradition.[51] In the 1880s their leader had spent some time in jail on a charge of *lèse-majesté* and they referred to William III as William the Last. For a long time, the Socialist Party remained committed in principle to republicanism and its deputies refused to attend the annual speech from the throne by the head of state. It was no wonder then that one of the songs popular among the bourgeoisie which began 'Up, Up, Up, Hang the Socialists Up' concluded equally naturally 'Up with Orange, Long Live Queen Wilhelmina'. Catholic leaders seized upon this socialist anti-monarchism by seeking to give their own monarchism a marked anti-socialist bias. This was evident, for example, at the inauguration of Queen Wilhelmina in 1898. The Socialists absented themselves from this ceremony, but the R. K. Volksbond (Roman Catholic People's Union), which relied on the support of workers and the middle class, was prominently represented and took the opportunity to send an Address to Her Majesty, in which the Catholic workers declared themselves to be 'faithful subjects, devoted to the House of Orange'.[52] The climax of this strategy was the role which Catholic working-class organizations played, under the direction of Catholic politicians, during November 1918 when the spectre of a Socialist revolution briefly raised its head. Once the danger had passed, a substantial homage to the royal family took place in The Hague in which Catholic organizations played the major part.[53]

How closely Catholic loyalty towards the monarchy was linked to considerations of Catholic self-interest was clear from the attitude which for half a century Queen Wilhelmina adopted towards her Catholic subjects. She felt no sympathy whatsoever for them and barely tolerated Catholic ministers.[54] For the Catholic leaders, the

[51] N. Wilterdink, ' "Leve de Republiek!" Anti-monarchisme in Nederland', in K. Bruin and K. Verrips (eds.), *Door het volk gedragen: Koningschap en samenleving* (Groningen, 1989), 133–61.

[52] A. I. Wierdsma, 'Consensus en conflict rond een staatsceremonieel: De inhuldigingen (1814–1980) als ritueel van de publieke godsdienst in Nederland', *Sociologisch Tijdschrift*, 13/2 (1986–7), 288–316, esp. 302.

[53] J. Bank, 'Katholieken en de Nederlandse monarchie: Tussen staatsraison en populariteit', in C. Tamse (ed.), *De monarchie in Nederland* (Amsterdam, 1980), 195–208.

[54] A. F. Manning, 'Koningin Wilhelmina', in A. C. Tamse (ed.), *Nassau en Oranje in de Nederlandse geschiedenis* (Alphen aan den Rijn, 1979), 359–96, esp. 382.

unrequited nature of their love was, however, of no real significance. Their monarchism had its own particular motivations and, thus, even the loyalty shown by the Catholics to the House of Orange as a symbol of their national loyalty was not entirely devoid of ambivalence.

6. Conclusion

Rooted in the organizational pillarization of the Catholic world, and assured of the consistent support of the Church hierarchy, political Catholicism considerably influenced Dutch politics and society over a number of decades. Though it did not ultimately prove able to enact a distinctly Catholic alternative to the liberal, capitalist system and the national traditions of the Netherlands, its influence, nevertheless, remains noticeable today, even if since the 1960s the ideological impulses which lay behind Catholic political action have all but disappeared.

In conclusion, it is perhaps worthwhile to examine more closely the dates of 1917 and 1967 chosen at the outset of the chapter as the framework for this study. On the one hand, it is not difficult to argue in favour of the importance of both of these dates. As has already been described, the introduction of universal male suffrage in 1917 exacerbated the fears of the Church and of the Catholic leadership and therefore hastened their wish to create a clearly defined Catholic Party (the RKSP). In the elections held in the subsequent year, the party immediately won thirty of the hundred parliamentary seats and, despite some fluctuations, it maintained this position until 1967. In that year, however, as has also already been mentioned, one of the bishops openly stated that Catholics were free to vote for whichever party they wished. Consequently, in 1967, the party (KVP) experienced its first major defeat, and in the subsequent elections of 1971 and 1972 this dramatic decline continued. Though some 40 per cent of the Catholic population still supported the Catholic Party, this marked a radical change from the 80 or 90 per cent who had formerly habitually voted for it. The successful development of co-operation with the Protestant parties, from which would emerge a few years later the new Christian Democratic Party (Christen Democratisch Appèl) is inconceivable without the decline of the Catholic Party which began in 1967. On the other hand, the complex historical trends described in this chapter cannot be confined by neat end-dates. Thus, despite numerous divisions, political Catholicism was already a reality in the Netherlands in the decades around 1900 while the debate about the possibility and desirability of a distinctly Catholic form of politics did not suddenly emerge after 1967 but had gradually developed from 1945 onwards.

How far Catholic politicians were willing to go in their efforts to bring about an alternative form of Catholic political and social organization is very difficult to ascertain. In a recent provocative article, the German ecclesiastical historian C. Weber has proposed a sketch of an ideal type of what he terms 'ultramontane fundamentalism', a coherent, anti-modern, and fundamentalist range of objectives, incorporating not merely the strengthening of the central power of Rome and a cult of the Papacy, but also a complete programme of conservative, not to say reactionary, policies in such fields as politics, economics, sexual relationships, science, and religious faith.[55] If one seeks to compare Dutch political Catholicism with the political and social components of this ideal type, then the limited influence of such ultramontane objectives would inevitably become evident. Radical voices could certainly be heard among Dutch Catholics, and in preceding sections of this chapter some of these have been described. But they did not exert a dominant influence. Two factors would seem to be of importance in explaining this relative moderation. Catholics were always aware of their position as a minority group in society, and this prevented them in advance from pursuing far-reaching ambitions. But of even greater importance was the influence which distinctive Dutch traditions of freedom and tolerance, that were in marked opposition to ultramontane fundamentalism, gradually gained over Dutch Catholics. Thus, in many cases, the commitment of Dutch Catholics to a distinctly Catholic or ultramontane alternative was limited to no more than lip-service and verbal denunciations.

That the influence which such ultramontane ideas exercised over the Catholic rank-and-file should not be exaggerated can also be emphasized by one last remark. In seeking to explain the process of depillarization in Dutch society in recent decades, sociologists have generally stressed the internal religious-theological crisis provoked by trends such as the emergence of the New Theology movement and the Second Vatican Council and the consequences which this had for undermining old certainties among priests and the Catholic faithful. According to this explanation, this religious crisis then spread to the secular components of Catholicism, including political Catholicism, and eroded the identification of the Catholic community with their pillar. Not unreasonably, other sociologists have pointed to the role played by external factors, above all the rapid economic growth of the 1950s and 1960s which definitively transformed the Netherlands into a modern society, thereby posing an unprecedented challenge to religion and tradition and severely weakening the strength of confessional structures of power. These interpretations have an undoubted validity but the historian is more inclined to seek the origins of depillarization further back in history. On the basis of an increasing number of studies, it is clear that the process of pillarization among Dutch Catholics was not easily achieved.[56] On the contrary, it was from the outset a process which was dominated by serious differences of opinion and beset by conflicts and frictions. In the case of political Catholicism, this was always evident but it was also true of the development of the Catholic workers movement as well as of numerous other initiatives which were directed at binding widely divergent groups such as intellectuals, women and young people to the Catholic cause. Opposition and resistance to these initiatives by the Church and Catholic élites was commonplace and only the deployment of the power

[55] C. Weber, 'Ultramontanismus als katholischer Fundamentalismus', in W. Loth (ed.), *Deutscher Katholizismus im Umbruch zur Moderne* (Stuttgart, 1991), 20–45.

[56] This is the argument elaborated in P. Luykx, 'Andere katholieken 1920–1940', *Jaarboek Katholiek Documentatie Centrum*, 16 (1986), 52–84.

and authority of the Church enabled the Catholic pillar to be held together. The significance of these historical studies is that it was not merely the short-term developments highlighted by sociologists but also long-standing historical factors which explain the rapidity and intensity of the process of deconfessionalization and depillarization in the Netherlands during the 1960s and 1970s, as well as the retreat and subsequent disappearance of the phenomenon of political Catholicism.

8

*Great Britain**

TOM BUCHANAN

No account of the political and social impact of Catholicism in twentieth-century Britain can ignore the fact that Catholics have formed a minority of the population. Catholics may, at times, have dreamed of reversing the pernicious effects of the Reformation but, in reality, their priority was defending their position within British society rather than trying to reconvert Britain to Catholicism. Moreover, this defence was undertaken in the absence of the socio-political institutions commonplace in continental European Catholic countries (even where Catholics were also in a minority)—most significantly, Catholic political parties, trade unions, or universities. Social and political divisions within the Catholic community, the long-standing British antipathy to confessional political parties, and a lack of funds and ambition have all conspired to make political Catholicism almost invisible in the twentieth century. However, it would be wrong to conclude from this that there was no tradition of political Catholicism in Britain. Catholics believed that the social and political principles derived from their faith were wholly relevant to a British society scarred by the effects of capitalism and liberalism, and now threatened by socialism. Accordingly, during most of the period covered by this chapter sections of the laity organized themselves, supported on occasion by a conservative hierarchy, to advance a distinctively Catholic critique of (and an alternative to) British society as they found it. Indeed, while the term 'political Catholicism' was alien to British Catholics, the term 'social Catholicism' was certainly not. Although explicitly not party-political, it will be one of the main contentions of this chapter that the many social Catholic movements of this period played an undeniably political role, both defensively (teaching the laity to resist socialism) and offensively (projecting a Catholic vision of a better society).

The purpose of this chapter is to analyse the attempts to articulate this Catholic social and political vision and to explain their ultimate failure. It will be argued that it is helpful to identify two distinct tiers of Catholic political activity in Britain. The first is the defence of communal interests, which was successfully pursued, and which was possible through any political party or none. The second tier is that of distinctive Catholic political thought and action—necessarily above party—which was mainly concerned with providing the ideas and resources to ensure that Catholics

---

* The main emphasis of this chapter will be on England and Wales, with reference to Scottish developments where appropriate. Northern Ireland is considered below, in Sect. 1.

would not be simply absorbed into the political system once the immediate threats to communal interests were averted. A British version of political Catholicism did operate in this second tier for most of the years 1918–65, but for reasons which will be discussed below, proved unable to sustain itself even before the great changes effected through the Second Vatican Council.

1. The Context

Compared with the nineteenth century, and especially the years since 1850, British twentieth-century Catholicism has been strangely neglected by historians, as the dramatic achievements and charismatic personalities associated with Catholicism in the later nineteenth century gave way to an administrative blandness and greater insularity after 1900.[1] The advances made by Catholicism since 1900 are generally seen as simply refining the work of the Church leaders of the nineteenth century, in particular Cardinal Manning, who rebuilt the ecclesiastical structures of Catholicism in the face of fierce opposition. The restoration of the Catholic hierarchy in England and Wales in 1850 (1878 in Scotland) was a highly controversial undertaking. Catholic Emancipation had, after all, only been achieved in 1829, and anti-Catholicism was still a potent force in British politics. Moreover, many petty restrictions, not to say prejudices, remained in place against Catholics, emphasizing that toleration should not be equated with full integration into British society.[2] The leaders of the 'Second Spring' of English Catholicism (many of them converts and, hence, particularly exposed to personal criticism) were forced to act in a very hostile environment, and inevitably took on a heroic stature in the process. By contrast, anti-Catholicism has been a diminishing force in the twentieth century (though not to be underestimated, especially in Scotland and the North-West of England) and Catholics have had to contend with a secular, rather than an explicitly anti-Catholic, society.

It would be wrong, however, to overlook the achievements of Catholics in the twentieth century. In fact, by any criteria, there was spectacular growth in the years covered by this chapter. Estimated numbers of Catholics in England and Wales, listed in the yearly *Catholic Directory*, rose from 1,890,018 in 1918, to 2,392,983 in 1945, and 3,956,500 in 1965.[3] Although there was a steady stream of converts—

[1] One of the best sources for information on 20th-cent. Catholicism in England and Wales remains the official history ed. Bishop Beck, *The English Catholics, 1850–1950* (London, 1950), commissioned to celebrate the centenary of the restored hierarchy. Edward Norman's general history of English Catholicism also offers an excellent, if brief, introduction to the subject (E. R. Norman, *Roman Catholicism in England from the Elizabethan Settlement to the Second Vatican Council* (Oxford, 1985)). However, the title of the relevant ch.—'Twentieth Century Developments'—reinforces the view that the years after 1900 offered little inherently new. A. Hastings's *A History of English Christianity 1920–1990* (3rd edn., London 1991) devotes considerable space to Catholicism.

[2] See e.g. G. I. T. Machin, 'The Liberal Government and the Eucharistic Procession, 1908', *Journal of Ecclesiastical History*, 34/4 (Oct. 1983), 559–83.

[3] It should be noted that the figures for Catholic population were supplied by parish clergy who supplied an estimate of the number of Catholics 'known to live in their parish' (*Catholic Directory, 1965*, 769), and cannot be treated as anything more than a general indication of Catholic numbers.

746,000 spread fairly evenly over the years between 1900 and 1960—the bulk of this increase came as a result of Irish immigration. Growth in numbers was matched by the building of churches and other facilities. The number of registered churches and public chapels rose from 1,380 in 1918 to 1,883 in 1945 and 3,319 in 1965; overall numbers of priests in the same period rose from 3,952 to 7,808. School provision also grew rapidly. In 1918 there were 1,623 Catholic secondary and elementary schools with some 390,000 pupils; by 1945 there were over 426,000 pupils attending 1,990 schools, and an even larger number attended the schools of the much more complex system of the 1960s. Thus, in the years covered by this chapter the Catholic Church in England and Wales sustained rapid growth. The same applies to the Catholic presence in Scotland. Almost negligible in the early nineteenth century, a survey in the mid-1950s showed that there were 774,000 Catholics in Scotland (15.1 per cent of the population, and over 25 per cent of the population of Glasgow).[4]

The very source of much of this growth—successive waves of Irish immigration—was, however, the key to many of the problems associated with achieving united Catholic political action. Catholicism could not have been so firmly re-established in the nineteenth century without the great influx of Irish labourers and their families during and after the Industrial Revolution. There was a further migration in the mid-twentieth century, following the closing of the United States to immigrants. Two hundred and fifty thousand Irish came to Britain during the Second World War, with 100,000 more in the years 1945–50, and, while their ancestors had settled in the North of England, this generation made for the new industrial belts of the Midlands and the South-East—especially London.[5] Thus, the patterns of Irish immigrant settlement (and, accordingly, of much of the Catholic community) in Britain were highly responsive to the changing demands of the national economy.

Irish immigrants brought strength in numbers, but also made the Catholic community in Britain peculiarly resistant to easy social categorization—more than in any European country it was a hybrid creation, the result of mass Irish immigration grafting a numerical base on to the descendants of the English recusant tradition (the 'old Catholics'). Converts, the third pillar in the Catholic community, provided a leavening influence, disproportionately represented in culture and the arts. Nor were the Irish the only immigrants. After the Second World War, for instance, many thousands of Poles and other Eastern Europeans settled for what, for many, became a permanent exile in Britain. Hence, the Catholic Church offered an umbrella for otherwise disparate constituents, in which the unskilled labourer of Irish descent had little in common with the essentially Tory Catholic élite—represented by the *Tablet* newspaper and the Catholic peers of the realm—or the generally well-educated and middle-class converts.

Many historians have taken the ethnic divide as the most important in the Catholic community, using it as a short-hand for other divisions such as those of class and politics. 'Irish Catholics', for instance, are often seen as synonymous with working-class

---

[4] *Tablet*, 4 June 1955.
[5] J. Fitzsimons, 'The Irish', in D. Mathew (ed.), *Catholicisme anglais* (Paris, 1958), 61–2.

Catholics. Steven Fielding, in an important recent contribution, has used detailed research on Salford to argue that Irish Catholics formed a 'viable and distinct culture that was a compound of class and ethnic influences'. Cultural traditions were strong enough to ensure that second- and third-generation Irish Catholics would still feel part of a group which enjoyed a distinctively 'intermediate way of life'—neither Irish nor British—which was still a very real entity in the city as late as 1939.[6] This Irish Catholic culture was expressed most publicly in the religious processions—especially the annual Whit Walks which were a Manchester institution (both for Anglicans and Catholics) from the 1880s onwards.[7] Fielding stresses that Irish Catholics may ultimately have joined British political movements, but did not do so uncritically—the Anglo-Irish treaty of 1921 (which temporarily resolved the 'Irish Question') and the collapse of Irish Nationalist politics in Britain 'did not mean that the Irish had been politically assimilated into English politics and that ethnic influences had evaporated'.[8]

This approach, however, deserves qualification. 'Irish Catholics', for instance, is a very loose term because Irish immigration had been under way for so long, and there was a difference in identity between first-generation Irish immigrants and the descendants of those of the 1840s.[9] Despite the relative social and cultural cohesion of the immigrant Irish, there is no great evidence to show that, apart from during times of crisis such as 1916–22, Irish Catholics in Britain made Irish politics the centre of their political activities.[10] The Catholic press was likely to have a page on Irish news, but, after the Anglo-Irish Treaty of 1921, Irish organizations served a mainly cultural and social purpose. These comments do not apply to Scotland where, as Tom Gallagher has argued, the ethnic and religious identity of Catholics of Irish descent became fused in the minds of their opponents in the inter-war years when, after many years of relatively peaceful coexistence, they began to be seen as an alien threat to Scottish nationality.[11] In England, however, it is important to note that in addition to the determinants of class and ethnicity, which contributed to an Irish Catholic identity, it is also important not to forget the role of religion itself. One of the main achievements of the Catholic Church was to stand above ethnic and class distinctions, and to attach the descendants of Irish immigrants to a Catholicism that went beyond such divisions. Almost all the lay Catholic social movements, for

---

[6] S. Fielding, *Class and Ethnicity: Irish Catholics in England, 1880–1939* (Buckingham, 1993), 1 and 17. Despite its title, this book is based almost entirely on a study of Salford, Manchester. M. McDermott's excellent 'Irish Catholics and the British Labour Movement: A Study with Particular Reference to London, 1918 to 1970', M. A. thesis, University of Kent, 1978, is also based on the concept of Irish Catholics.

[7] S. Fielding, *Class and Ethnicity*, 72–8.   [8] Ibid. 104.

[9] As Fielding accepts, 'the term "Irish Catholic" "also embraces those who might have considered themselves more Catholic than Irish" ' (ibid. p. xiii).

[10] The main exception to this was the short-lived 'Friends of Ireland', set up after the Second World War in alliance with the Anti-Partition League in Ireland. This is described in B. Purdie, 'The Friends of Ireland: British Labour and Irish Nationalism, 1945–1949', in T. Gallagher and J. O'Connell (eds.), *Contemporary Irish Studies* (Manchester, 1983).

[11] T. Gallagher, *Glasgow, The Uneasy Peace: Religious Tension in Modern Scotland* (Manchester, 1987), 134–6.

instance, contained converts and English recusants as well as members of the Irish working class.

The Irish legacy was, however, undoubtedly highly significant in forming the Catholic urban communities.[12] Catholic immigrants in the nineteenth century were made to feel alien within British society on both religious and ethnic grounds, and this acted as a check on their assimilation into it.[13] Many of the priests also came from Ireland, and imposed a strict and unimaginative Catholicism on their flocks. The hallmark of this era was the building of schools and churches by public subscription (raising funds from a very poor community), and the main lay organizations that emerged were those connected with charity and community leadership—groups such as the Knights of St Columba, the Ancient Order of Hibernians, and the St Vincent de Paul Society. Despite the beginnings of upward social mobility, these characteristics apply also to the period 1918–65, when it was still possible to identify a distinctive urban Catholic subculture that was primarily introspective, and extremely proud of (and defensive towards) its own local achievements.

Within these communities the dominant force remained the parish[14] priest, who was particularly keen to maintain discipline in the areas of schooling and marriage— in both areas assisted by papal pronouncements. In the question of education, Pius XI's 1929 encyclical *Divini Illius Magistri* restated papal opposition to mixed schooling, while the 1907 decree *No Temere* consolidated the official position on 'valid' Catholic marriages.[15] The success was striking. Michael Hornsby-Smith has shown that in 1939 valid non-mixed weddings (i.e. those in which both parties were Catholics and which were solemnized by a priest) formed 68.5 per cent of Catholic marriages, compared with 5.6 per cent for the invalid non-mixed. These proportions remained remarkably constant until the 1960s, but by the 1970s the percentages stood at 30.2 and 33 respectively.[16] These figures are symptomatic of the immense social changes which overwhelmed the Catholic communities after 1945—including social mobility, greater university attendance, and the growing use of proscribed birth-control—and which overlapped the Second Vatican Council. By the late 1970s, Hornsby-Smith has concluded, the distinctive Catholic subculture was effectively dissolved.[17] The political consequences of this dramatic change will be explored below.

The social and political heterogeneity of the Catholic population reinforced the hierarchy's desire to avoid any party-political commitment. Recent research has emphasized the lack of political cohesion amongst nineteenth-century Catholics, as

[12] There is an immense literature on the Irish in Britain. The classic account is J. Denvir's *The Irish in Britain: From Earliest Times to the Fall of Parnell* (London, 1892). For a comprehensive recent bibliography on the subject see Fielding, *Class and Ethnicity*, 163–75.

[13] J. Hickey, *Urban Catholics: Urban Catholicism in England and Wales from 1829 to the Present Day* (London, 1967), develops a model for the development of Catholic communities based on a case study of Cardiff.

[14] The Catholic parishes were not formally restored until 1918. Until then their status had been as 'missions'.   [15] P. Coman, *Catholics and the Welfare State* (London, 1977), 18–20.

[16] M. Hornsby-Smith, *Roman Catholics in England: Studies in Social Structure Since the Second World War* (Oxford, 1987), p. 94.   [17] Ibid. 115.

upper-class Catholics tended to support the Conservatives, while the enfranchised working class either voted Liberal or took a lead from Irish leaders like Parnell.[18] In the twentieth century Catholic MPs have been found scattered amongst all the main parties, although the proportion of Catholics in Parliament was, of course, drastically reduced by the departure of the southern Irish MPs (formalized in the Anglo-Irish Treaty of 1921). Catholic politics have most effectively emerged around the common denominator of the defence of those institutions seen as central to Catholic life—especially the schools. Catholics were regularly mobilized, often very successfully, to defend denominational schooling or increase grants in aid to their schools. Indeed, until the 1960s there were few that doubted, despite the great expense, that this was the cornerstone of Catholic life. The most striking example was the Catholic Parents' and Electors' Associations (CPEAs) formed in order to campaign for a revision of the terms of the 1944 Education Act. Strictly controlled by the hierarchy, both in terms of their organizational basis and their political goals, the CPEAs acted in a classic pressure-group manner (for instance, by questioning MPs during the 1950 election) and significantly contributed to the more generous policy adopted by the government towards Catholic schools in the 1950s.[19] Earlier, Catholics had mobilized against the Labour government's 1930 (Trevelyan) Education Bill, which was effectively killed by the rebellion of the Catholic Labour MP John Scurr.[20]

Education was particularly important because a perceived threat to Catholic schools could spark a broader mobilization. For instance, the 1906 Birrell Education Bill led to the formation of the diocesan Catholic Federations (originating in Salford), which soon extended their interests beyond the strictly educational sphere to the attempted marshalling of Catholic forces against the 'rising tides of Freemasonry, Socialism and an anti-Christian Democracy'.[21] Similarly, the 1942 Trades Union Congress (TUC) vote in favour of secular education led directly to the foundation of the Association of Catholic Trades Unionists (ACTU). In practice, however, it was precisely the success of the Church's own negotiations with the British state on issues such as schooling which made irrelevant the question of 'why was there no Catholic political party in Britain?'

Inevitably, the Catholic hierarchy played a crucial role in the development of Catholic political engagement. Although the twentieth-century archbishops of Westminster have suffered by comparison with their predecessors Wiseman, Manning, and Vaughan, most carried out a difficult task with sensitivity and one, Hinsley (1935–43), attained a kind of greatness during the Second World War. According to the ecclesiastical structure created in 1850, Westminster was the sole metropolitan

[18] See esp. the work of D. A. Quinn, 'English Roman Catholics and Politics in the Second Half of the Nineteenth Century', D.Phil. thesis, Univ. of Oxford, 1985; and J. Supple, 'The Political Attitudes and Activities of Yorkshire Catholics, 1850–1900', *Northern History*, 22 (1986), 230–49.

[19] See Coman, *Catholics and the Welfare State*, 53–4.

[20] There is evidence of the damage that the Education Bill caused to the Labour party at by-elections during the period 1930–1 in A. Thorpe, *The British General Election of 1931* (Oxford, 1991), 23–4.

[21] *Federationist* (Nov. 1910), quoted in P. Doyle, 'The Catholic Federation, 1906–1929', in W. J. Sheils and D. Wood (eds.), *Studies in Church History, xxiii. Voluntary Religion* (London, 1986), 462.

disocese, with, initially, twelve suffragan bishops. In 1911 two new metropolitan provinces were created, at Birmingham and Liverpool, each with its own archbishop. In 1916 Wales, too, was made a province with an archbishop in Cardiff. The Scottish hierarchy, as restored in 1878, contained the province of St Andrews and Edinburgh, including an archepiscopal and four suffragan sees, and the archepisocopal see of Glasgow. In the English hierarchy, Westminster became, from 1911, the permanent president of the bishops' conference, although the archbishop's power was restricted by the requirement to follow other bishops' majority opinion. The hierarchy was characterized by its close links with Rome. Hinsley, a former rector of the English College in Rome, was the best example of a strong and enduring Roman influence. Ironically, it was during Hinsley's archepiscopacy that relations with Rome experienced their greatest period of strain. The Vatican's decision to send an apostolic delegate to England in 1938 was initially resisted by the hierarchy on the grounds that he might revive religious bigotry at a time when the press saw the Pope as a 'tool of Fascism'.[22] A second important feature was the hierarchy's conservative recusant composition. Few converts were to be found amongst the bishops, and, until Cardinal Heenan (1963–76), archbishops of Westminster were not drawn from the Catholics of Irish descent.

The religious orders played a disproportionately large role in all areas of Catholic life. As elsewhere in Europe at this time the orders, which had languished after the Reformation, staged a remarkable recovery in the hundred years following the restoration of the hierarchy. Where in 1850 there had been a mere 10 male orders, with some 275 priests, by 1950 there were 70 orders and 2,360 priests. During the same period the 14 female orders in 53 convents grew into over 140 orders in 1,075 convents.[23] Not only was there a massive increase in the long-established orders such as the Jesuits (whose English province grew from 200 to 1,000 members between 1850 and 1950), there was also an infusion of new orders, many of which, such as the Passionists and Oratorians, brought a flamboyant form of Italian piety. The role of the orders was paramount in the development of Catholic education, conversion, and of course charity. Moreover, their publications (such as the Jesuits' *Month*) contributed markedly to an already thriving Catholic intellectual culture at the level of reviews and journals. However, their work is also highly significant in the context of this chapter, for it was frequently the orders that were best placed to offer leadership to Catholic lay movements. Three Jesuits, for instance, underpinned the life of the Catholic Social Guild—Father Plater, who founded it; Father O'Hea, who for over thirty years ran the Guild and the Catholic Workers' College; and Father Crane, whose energy and political views had an ambiguous effect on the movement in its latter years. Similarly, the Dominican Father Vincent McNabb, a 'trenchant critic of

---

[22] T. Moloney, *Westminster, Whitehall and the Vatican: The Role of Cardinal Hinsley, 1935–1943* (London, 1985), 90–7. Hinsley also caused offence by his clumsy attempts to defend the Pope against critics who said that he should have condemned Mussolini's aggression against Abyssinia in 1935: 'Well, what can the Pope do to prevent this or any other war? He is a helpless old man with a small police force to guard himself' (J. C. Heenan, *Cardinal Hinsley* (London, 1944), 58).

[23] E. Cruise, 'Development of the Religious Orders', in Beck, *English Catholics*, 442.

modern industrial life',[24] played a central role in the evolution of the Distributist movement in the inter-war years.

Thus, the orders, more than any other part of the Church, played a crucial role in shaping Catholic lay movements. But it was the hierarchy that retained the power to make or break such movements. Bishops often chose not to support new initiatives even when they were backed by the Archbishop of Westminster. For instance, Hinsley's enthusiastic backing for the wartime 'Sword of the Spirit' movement, and Cardinal Griffin's support for the ACTU, failed to engender significant support. For many bishops, any such movement was suspicious on political (and sometimes theological) grounds, and they preferred either to negotiate directly with government or to work through such conservative representatives of the Catholic establishment as the Catholic Union.[25] Acutely conscious of their minority status, and feeling an increasing sense of isolation within a secular society, the dominant concern of Catholic bishops was one of defence, encapsulated by the use of the term 'leakage' to describe the dreaded attenuation of the Catholic community. Hence, protection of Catholic schools, and the innoculation of working-class Catholics against a creeping loss of religion, easily took precedence over lay movements designed to attempt anything bolder—unless such movements could be clearly proven to serve the hierarchy's interests. The power of the bishops should not, however, be overestimated. The cerebral, strongly anti-socialist Bishop Casartelli of Salford found his attempts to promote the lay Catholic Federation movement before the First World War generally frustrated by the opposition or apathy of his own parish priests.

A very different situation pertained to Catholics in the British province of Northern Ireland.[26] Here, in addition to forming a minority, Catholics also found themselves living in what many saw as a discriminatory and artificially created 'Protestant' mini-state. As a result of the partition of Ireland under the terms of the 1921 Anglo-Irish Treaty Catholics formed a permanent minority in Northern Ireland (six of the nine counties of Ulster). The demographic balance changed little over time: Catholics formed 33.5 per cent of the Northern Irish population in the first official census of 1926 and 35 per cent in 1961.[27] Moreover, under the terms of the 1920 Government of Ireland Act, the province was accorded a highly devolved form of government

[24] Ibid. 465.

[25] The Catholic Union of Great Britain is a cross-party lay body established in 1872. Its main interests concern legislation affecting Catholics, and there is a Parliamentary Subcommittee composed of Catholic members of both Houses.

[26] A great deal has been published on the problems of Northern Ireland, esp. on the period since 1969. For a general history see J. J. Lee, *Ireland, 1912–1985: Politics and Society* (Cambridge, 1989). For a review of religious aspects of the conflict see J. H. Whyte, *Interpreting Northern Ireland* (Oxford, 1990), 26–51. M. Farrell's *Northern Ireland: The Orange State* (London, 1976) is generally critical of the role of the Catholic Church. S. Wichert, *Northern Ireland since 1945* (Harlow, 1991), is a compact recent survey. F. O'Connor, *In Search of a State: Catholics in Northern Ireland* (Belfast, 1993) is based on interviews with Catholics and sheds light on the Catholic politics of Northern Ireland before 1969. See also G. McElroy, *The Catholic Church and the Northern Ireland Crisis, 1968–1986* (Dublin, 1991).

[27] F. S. L. Lyons, *Ireland Since the Famine* (London, 1973), 717 and 749.

(with its own Parliament and government) which the preponderantly Protestant Unionists dominated.[28] In the first elections to the new parliament at Stormont House in May 1921 the Unionists won forty seats, while Catholic votes were split between the constitutionalist Nationalists and the more radical Republicans of Sinn Féin, both of whom won six seats. The new state came into being against a background of intimidation directed at the Catholic minority. The Belfast 'Troubles' (1920–2) began with the violent expulsion of 5,000 Catholic workers from the shipyards, and continued with attacks on Catholic churches, church-goers, and their homes. The IRA (Irish Republican Army) responded in kind, but was defeated by the security forces controlled by the Northern Irish government.

The creation of Northern Ireland, and the tensions that continued to bedevil relations between Catholics and Protestants, inevitably gave an important political role to the Catholic Church as the main representative of the Nationalist Catholic population. However, as was also the case in the South of Ireland, the dominance of the national question over all other political issues militated against the development of an overt political Catholicism. This affected Catholic politics in two ways. First, the Catholic-Nationalist community was bitterly divided along lines that reflected those within the nationalist tradition in Ireland as a whole (especially over whether to reject the 1921 Treaty or to accept it as a pragmatic temporary settlement). Secondly, the peculiarity of the situation in Northern Ireland encouraged the Church to maintain a degree of direct control over Catholic-Nationalist politics in this period that was not encountered either in the Irish Free State or in mainland Britain. The role of the Church was complicated by the fact that the border created in 1921 did not take into account existing religious boundaries. Thus, the sees of Clogher, Derry, and the archdiocese of Armagh all straddled the border, while the sees of Dromore and of Connor and Down did not. Inevitably, such Northern bishops were unable to limit their attention merely to Northern Ireland.

The Catholic Church bitterly opposed the partition of Ireland, both on nationalist grounds and also because it feared that a Protestant-dominated Northern Ireland would be inimical to Catholic religious interests. Initially the Church refused to recognize the new state, and many Catholic chaplains (in Poor Houses and other institutions) lost their jobs through refusing to swear allegiance to it. The bishops' hopes were focused on the Boundary Commission which had been promised under the Treaty, in the confident expectation that it would allow Catholic-majority areas such as the city of Derry and the border-county of Fermanagh and South Tyrone to join the Irish Free State. The failure of the Commission in 1925 to recommend any changes created a new situation in which the Church had to address the question of how Catholic interests could be promoted, at least in the short term, within the borders of Northern Ireland.[29] Thus, the Church began to recommend that, on tactical grounds, the Nationalist Catholic MPs should end their policy of abstention from Stormont.

[28] On the governing arrangements in Northern Ireland see Lyons, 695–705.
[29] M. Harris, *The Catholic Church and the Foundation of the Northern Irish State* (Cork, 1993), 173.

Thereafter, the political role of the Church was preponderant as, for instance, in the mobilization of Catholics in the anti-partition National League, founded in May 1928. While committed to a united Ireland, the League was also concerned with justice for Catholics in Northern Ireland. It was, however, opposed by Republicans who argued that the creation of what they saw as a 'Catholic party' would never win the wider support needed to create a majority for Irish unity in the province.[30] Catholic Action was actively promoted in the late 1920s, with a wide range of lay organizations being established. In this case, the Catholic sense of isolation and the need for their own institutions served to reinforce support for a movement that was found throughout Catholic Europe. The hierarchy and clergy were again prominent in supporting and promoting the Anti-Partition League established in November 1945.

However, the political lead offered by the Catholic Church was somewhat equivocal. While never losing sight of the goal of national unity, the hierarchy was also quick to gain what institutional advantage it could for the Church within Northern Ireland. Lord Londonderry, the province's first education minister and an advocate of non-denominational schooling, was forced to give way to Protestant pressures for religious control over local authority schools, culminating in the 1930 Education Act. In return, however, Catholics were able to secure 50 per cent grants for building and equipment costs in their voluntary schools. In addition, their teachers' salaries were paid by the State, and the costs of training Catholic teachers would soon be state-subsidized. No further attempts were made to challenge the segregated schools system. Thus, despite the Catholic community's political weakness, the Catholic Church defended its institutional interests robustly, and successfully exploited the sectarian assumptions of its Unionist rivals. There was, however, a price to be paid. While Catholic interests were safeguarded when the Butler Education Act (1944) was applied to Northern Ireland in 1947, Catholic schools only received 65 per cent support for capital expenditure rather than the 100 per cent that had been demanded. Similarly, when the 1949 Public Health Act brought Northern Ireland into line with the rest of Britain in relation to the National Health Service, Catholics successfully lobbied for their Mater Hospital in Belfast not to be appropriated by the Local Health Authority. It was, however, deprived of public funds.

In the two decades after 1945 many Northern Catholics appeared less concerned with the national question, especially after the creation of the Irish Republic in 1948 and the consequent Ireland Act (1949) made a united Ireland appear an even more distant possibility. The new archbishop of Armagh, John D'Alton, appointed in 1945, adopted a more conciliatory posture towards the Northern Ireland authorities, and it has been argued that in the post-war era many Catholics may have come to accept their lot within the province.[31] The IRA guerrilla campaigns in 1956–62 attracted relatively little support in the province. However, the continuing discrimination against Catholics in housing and jobs, as well as the overt gerrymandering of the province's political boundaries, prevented any real resolution of underlying Catholic

[30] Ibid. 174–85.
[31] O. P. Rafferty, *Catholicism in Ulster, 1603–1983: An Interpretative History* (London, 1994), 246.

grievances. In the mid-1960s a new generation of Catholic activists, many with university education, began to campaign for civil rights. The violence of the Protestant response escalated the descent into a new bout of 'Troubles' which finally boiled over in 1969. British troops were sent to restore order and in 1972 'direct rule' from Westminster was imposed. One significant result of the volatile situation after 1969 was the creation of new Catholic-Nationalist political leaderships which acted independently of the Catholic Church. These crystallized primarily around the Provisional IRA and Sinn Féin in the Republican camp, while the Social Democratic and Labour Party (SDLP), created in August 1970 from a number of predominantly Catholic political parties, replaced the Nationalist Party as the main representative of constitutional nationalism. Thus, the new Troubles marked a significant erosion of the Church's traditional political domination of the Catholic minority, and the emergence for the first time—despite the close links between the Church and the SDLP—of more autonomous forms of Catholic political organization.

2. Catholic Political and Social Engagement, 1918–1965

The year 1918 represented a watershed for Catholic political engagement in Britain for three main reasons. First, the introduction of universal suffrage greatly increased the enfranchisement of Catholics, thus preparing the way for the mobilization of Catholic voters around domestic political issues. It is notable that the organization of Catholic women dates, in effect, from these years, as the hierarchy came to see them as a new bulwark against state-sponsored attacks on the family.[32] Secondly, wartime measures, and post-war reforms, had greatly extended the powers of the State. In some cases this was beneficial—for instance, the 1918 Scottish school settlement was often seen by Catholics as a potential model for the English system. However, centralizing reform of the welfare system and the creation, for the first time, of a ministry of health was greeted with immense suspicion by Catholics. Thirdly, the political changes following the war greatly affected Catholics. In particular, the decline of the Liberals and the 1921 Anglo-Irish Treaty left the way clear for working-class Catholics (many of whom had previously favoured the Liberals because of their stance on Irish Home Rule) to support the Labour party. Yet, by its 1918 Constitution Labour had specifically identified itself with socialism for the first time. Thus, the events of 1918 brought to a head the previously avoided question of Catholic involvement with the Labour party.

Cardinal Bourne's 1918 Lenten Pastoral letter on 'The Nation's Crisis' showed awareness of these changes, couched in the distinctive voice of Catholic social thought. He called for a 'New Order' after the war, although not one that would minimize the family and magnify the State. He recognized the change in political consciousness amongst soldiers, and the 'undisguised revolt' of workers against the capitalist system, the excesses of which would have been unthinkable in a Catholic-inspired social order. And he endeavoured to see in the contemporary working-class

---

[32] See M. Fletcher, *O, Call Back Yesterday* (Oxford, 1939), 169.

unrest: 'the true lineament of the christian spirit. Its passion for fair treatment and for liberty; its resentment at bureaucratic interferences with family life; its desire for self-realisation and opportunities of education; above all, its conviction that persons are of more value than property'.[33] Whatever his real political views (perhaps better expressed by his forthright opposition to the 1926 General Strike),[34] Bourne's language is striking, and underlines the many dilemmas which the Church faced in confronting a volatile political situation as the war drew to a close. In particular, one should note the fundamental lack of sympathy for capitalism, and a tolerance of working-class radicalism—so long as it did not conflict with Catholic teaching.

Catholics in Britain had responded surprisingly slowly to the challenge of industrialization and the consequent rise of socialism. There was considerable interest in social problems such as drink in the later nineteenth century, and Cardinal Manning's intervention on behalf of the striking London dockers in 1889 created an enduring image of solidarity with the working class which later Catholic prelates were to perpetuate.[35] Conversely, there was little formal response to *Rerum Novarum* at the time of its publication in 1891. By 1918, however, there was broad agreement amongst interested Catholics that what were termed 'Catholic social principles' must revolve around a number of points: a more equally distributed private property, defence of the family, support for a 'Just Wage' and a code of industrial relations which did not rule out strikes but made them unlikely, and advocacy of 'subsidiary function'—in other words the belief that social tasks were best carried out by the lowest and smallest appropriate groups.[36] This package of ideas survived until the 1950s, when they had to be modified in the light of the introduction of the Welfare State.

A particularly important element in British Catholic social thought was the influence of Hilaire Belloc, G. K. Chesterton (who converted in 1922), and 'Distributism', the political movement that they founded. Belloc's memorable attack on *The Servile State* (1912) did much to make opposition to state power, and to collectivism in general, the most distinctive feature of social Catholic thought. Belloc went on to foster the concept of Distributism, according to which the redistribution of property should be tied in with a general anti-modernism—for instance, a quasi-medieval glorification of crafts and guilds and a 'back to the land' enthusiasm. Although not a confessional movement, Distributism was still the closest approximation to a specifically political Catholic movement in twentieth-century Britain. The movement

---

[33] E. Oldmeadow, *Francis Cardinal Bourne, ii* (London, 1944), 137–41. J. M. Cleary notes the role of Fr Plater and other members of the Catholic Social Guild in the preparation of this pastoral (*Catholic Social Action in Britain, 1909–1959* (Hinckley, 1961), 52).

[34] S. Mews, 'The Churches', in M. Morris (ed.), *The General Strike* (Harmondsworth, 1976), 330–3. In his High Mass on 9 May 1926, Cardinal Bourne declared that there was 'no moral justification' for the General Strike, and that '[A]ll are bound to uphold and assist the Government, which is the lawfully constituted authority of the country and represents therefore *in its own appointed sphere* the authority of God Himself [*sic*]'.

[35] In 1936 Cardinal Hinsley told Sir Walter Citrine, General Secretary of the TUC, at the height of the row with the labour movement over the Spanish Civil War, that he 'should favour Labour being the son of a working man', T. Buchanan, *The Spanish Civil War and the British Labour Movement* (Cambridge, 1991), 183.   [36] P. Coman, *Catholics and the Welfare State*, 27.

revolved around the journal *GK's Weekly*, which was launched in 1925, and the Distributist League, founded to support it in September 1926. Belloc and Chesterton's journalism, brilliant, assertive, and opinionated, played an important role in drawing out a younger generation of anti-liberal Catholic journalists such as Douglas Jerrold, according to whom 'the Chesterbelloc [in George Bernard Shaw's famous phrase] brought Catholicism out of private and into public life'.[37] The movement began to disintegrate following Chesterton's death in 1936, and Belloc's increasing support for both Fascism and Nazism. The Distributist League was disbanded in 1940, though it enjoyed sporadic revivals after the war, even after Belloc's death in 1947.

Distributism enjoyed an influence far beyond the membership of the Distributist League. It is clear that some of its themes (such as the 'diffusion of property') were widely accepted within the Catholic social movement. However, despite Belloc and Chesterton's influence, it would be wrong to exaggerate their importance, and, indeed, their more extreme views, and those of their followers, were often criticized by both social Catholics and the Church hierarchy. In the mid-1920s a leading figure in the Catholic Social Guild, Henry Somerville, led an attack against the anti-industrialism of the Distributists, arguing that 'Catholic social reformers should be striving for industrial peace and industrial efficiency instead of announcing every new industrial development as the work of the devil'.[38] He was supported by Michael de la Bedoyere SJ who warned against Distributism coming to be seen as 'official' Catholic economics.[39] Moreover, overtly Distributist movements had limited practical impact. One such was the Catholic Land Federation which was set up in 1934 to establish training farms for the unemployed and ran a journal *The Cross and the Plough*, proclaiming subsistence farming for Britain and opposing all use of machinery. The movement effectively collapsed when it fell foul of both the government's own Land Settlement Agency and the hierarchy, which felt that all available funds should be channelled into building schools and churches in new housing areas.[40]

Thus, despite the flamboyance of their leaders, the Distributists should not be seen as part of the mainstream of social Catholicism. Here the central figure was undoubtedly the dynamic Jesuit Father Charles Plater (1875–1921) (latterly Master of Campion Hall in Oxford)[41] who devoted most of his short life to propagating knowledge of continental social Catholic thinking, and to raising the awareness of English Catholics about social problems. Plater's particular interest lay in workers' spiritual retreats, which he described with typical enthusiasm on a continental tour as a young man: 'I am quite mad on the subject of the Belgian retreats for working men. It is

---

[37] Quoted in J. P. Corrin, *G. K. Chesterton and Hilaire Belloc: The Battle Against Modernity* (Athens, Ohio, 1981), 208. Corrin's book is a the best survey of the political impact of Distributism, and offers a valuable listing of the voluminous literature which it produced.

[38] *Catholic Times*, 22 Apr. 1927.   [39] Ibid., 30 September 1927.

[40] R. H. Butterworth, 'The Structure and Organization of Some Catholic Lay Organizations in Australia and Great Britain: A Comparative Study with Special Reference to the Function of Organizations as Pressure Groups', D.Phil thesis, Oxford, 1959, pp. 258–60; chapter 5.

[41] *Tablet*, 29 Jan. 1921, obituary of Plater.

really unspeakable—the cure for all our troubles I am sure; the results are really miraculous.'[42] In the context of this chapter, however, Plater's major contribution was the formation of the Catholic Social Guild (CSG) in 1909. Plater's role was to galvanize the many strands within Catholicism which were now taking an interest in social issues. These included the Catholic Truth Society, which was promoting literature and lectures on this theme and acted as the parent body for the CSG; Mgr. Henry Parkinson, Rector of Oscott College in Birmingham, who had instructed his seminarians in social studies for a number of years and was the Guild's first president; and a number of individual members of the laity and religious orders. The CSG was very much a child of its times, given the vogue for social investigation—nor were comparisons with the Fabian society irrelevant, given the personal connections between some Fabians and members of the CSG. Surprisingly, however, the Guild soon developed away from its intellectual and middle-class origins to lay the basis, with the support of some parish priests, of a committed working-class following in the years before the First World War.

Unlike other Catholic lay organizations, the CSG managed to continue operating during the First World War. After the war branches existed in many parts of England, and an annual summer school was established in Oxford from 1920. Membership was never particularly large, climbing slowly to some 3,910 in 1939, but it was exceptionally committed. Local study circles, which became the crux of the Guild's activities, were widely established, and it was possible for members to take examinations in a range of political and social studies. In 1924 the examiner noted a tendency amongst candidates for rash generalizations—for instance, 'to denounce land-owners and capitalists as a body, to attribute to socialists as a body very extreme views, and to imply that Catholics alone are anxious for social reform'.[43] The reality of the CSG was somewhat less radical. Its hallmark was analysis and enquiry rather than political intervention (which was deliberately eschewed) and the Guild's first *Year Book* in 1910 called for a 'careful and systematic enquiry into modern social conditions'.[44] At points in the Guild's life this emphasis was challenged by those who felt that it would be more effective as a specifically Fabian-style organization, actually within one of the main political currents. In the late 1920s Henry Somerville argued that the CSG should campaign for concrete social reforms—advocating industrial arbitration, family allowances, and industrial councils as possible goals.[45] In the 1950s, however, it was precisely the Guild's leaders' espousal of a clearly political stance (in this case right-wing anti-socialism) which caused a severe split in its ranks.[46]

[42] Cruise, 'Development of the Religious Orders', 467. There is a useful summary of Plater's ideas (emphasizing his role as a synthesizer and communicator of European social Catholic thought) in P. Doyle, 'Charles Plater SJ and the Origins of the Catholic Social Guild', *Recusant History*, 21/3 (May 1993).

[43] *Tablet*, 10 May 1924.   [44] Catholic Social Guild, *1910 Yearbook*, 18.

[45] H. Somerville, 'Programme for the Catholic Social Guild', *Month* (Jan. 1928), quoted in P. Fitzpatrick, 'Education and Social Engagement: The Lessons of the Catholic Social Guild', *Month* (Apr. 1988), 651.

[46] The best history of the CSG is J. M. Cleary's *Catholic Social Action in Britain* (Hinckley, 1961), which, although an official history, is a mine of useful information and interesting comment.

Plater died prematurely in 1921, but, despite his death, two very important steps were soon taken. First, a monthly paper—the *Christian Democrat*—was established, and, secondly, a Catholic Workers' College (CWC) was set up in Oxford. The mission of both the CSG and the CWC was to educate Catholics in Catholic social principles and to create a cadre of leadership. The college was not meant to help elevate Catholic workers socially, but rather to return them to their work places with improved powers of leadership. However, funding was always precarious, and relied on regular benefactions (many scholarships were provided by branches of the CSG). The college expanded from its small beginnings in 1921, but numbers were always disappointing. Writing in the report for 1963–4 Principal Joe Kirwan was to lament that over forty-two years only 280 British students had studied at the college: 'so small a band spread over so long a time is not going to revolutionise the land'.[47]

As noted above, the early twentieth century also saw the development of Catholic women's organizations. The first of these was the Catholic Women's League (CWL) founded by Margaret Fletcher in 1906. Fletcher was acutely aware of the suspicion with which the CWL would be treated at a time of militant female suffragism and socialism, and of the need to be 'non-political and officially neutral on the question of the suffrage'.[48] The CWL concerned itself mainly with social conditions affecting women, and spawned what would become independent bodies such as the Union of Catholic Mothers and the Junior League. The position of the women's organizations was transformed in 1918. Overnight Margaret Fletcher was inundated with requests from priests for study circles for women to be established. Despite this new-found respectability, however, the ambit of women's organizations remained limited. In 1918 Isabel Willis of the Catholic Women's Suffrage Society urged women to use their newly won votes on the grounds that parliament would be legislating on questions such as sexual morality, the rights of children to religious education, the sanctity of marriage, and the rights of motherhood.[49] In 1920 Archbishop MacIntyre of Birmingham called for the parish organization of women voters to defend their interests, defined as 'the welfare of their homes and the Catholic education of their children'.[50] Catholic women continued to encounter a mixture of expectation and condescension from their male leaders throughout this period. In 1950, for instance, Cardinal Griffin told a rally of 5,000 CWL members that their natural sphere was in local rather than national politics, as 'it is difficult for women to be travelling backwards and forwards to Westminster'.[51]

A Catholic Women's Suffrage Society (CWSS) was set up in 1911 by Catholic women already active within the non-militant campaign for female suffrage. Unlike the CWL, the CWSS was not particularly concerned with winning hierarchical

---

[47] G. Scott, *The RCs: A Report on Roman Catholics in Britain Today* (London, 1967), 85–6. On the history of the College see J. Keating, 'The Making of the Catholic Labour Activist; The Catholic Social Guild and The Catholic Workers' College, 1909–1939', *Labour History Review*, 59/3 (Winter 1994), 49–51.

[48] Fletcher, *Call Back Yesterday*, 141. For the history of the CWL see *Yesterday Recalled: A Jubilee History of the Catholic Women's League, 1906–1981*, comp. M. Ryan (London, 1981).

[49] *Tablet*, 23 Nov. 1918.   [50] Ibid., 7 Aug. 1920.   [51] Ibid., 10 June 1950.

approval, and much more overtly feminist in its goals. In 1918, after the vote had been achieved, the CWSS committed itself to campaigning 'to establish the political, social and economic equality between men and women; and to further the work and usefulness of Catholic women as citizens'. The Society's approval of the new Ministry of Health, as beneficial to women, went counter to mainstream Catholic opinion, and increasing tension with the Catholic hierarchy over a number of issues led to its renaming as St Joan's Social and Political Alliance in 1923.[52] Thus, the Society was able to slip the noose of religious authority that was intended for it.

The early decades of the century were also marked by a prolonged debate over how the Catholic Church should respond to the emergence of the Labour party. There was no problem over Catholicism's opposition to socialism dating from *Rerum Novarum*; similarly little real opposition was placed in the way of Catholics joining their respective trade unions. The question for the hierarchy was always one of whether the Labour party was socialist or not? This question was not starkly posed before 1918. In 1912, for instance, the National Confederation of Catholic Trade Unionists (NCCTU), organized by Thomas F. Burns, was able to persuade Labour to abandon a commitment to secular education. The NCCTU continued to meet after this, but faded away at the end of the First World War in the face of hierarchical ambivalence.

In 1918, however, Labour's explicitly socialist constitution revived the controversy, revealing genuine splits within the hierarchy and the laity over how to respond. The leading lay opponent was T. F. Burns, now running the Manchester Branch of the so-called 'Centre Labour Party', who campaigned tirelessly for Catholic trade-unionists to vote against the political levy for the Labour party. In October 1919 the Bishop of Salford said that Catholics should not belong to the party, though remaining free to vote for it so long as no Catholic issues were at stake.[53] Others, however, urged caution. Archbishop Whiteside of Liverpool proclaimed that: 'When Rome speaks the question will be decided. We must wait till Rome speaks.'[54] With these comments he revealed that at the request of Cardinal Gasparri, Secretary of State at the Vatican, an inquiry was being conducted into the Labour party's political stance by Bishop Amigo of Southwark (no friend of socialism). Amigo's conclusion, in a letter to Gasparri of 25 November 1919, was that the Labour party would soon be in power, and that it would be a 'profound mistake' if it were condemned. Most Catholics, he wrote, 'look upon it simply as a political party willing and ready to help them with their difficulties'.[55]

Two years later Burns and his followers revived the controversy when they passed a resolution at the conference of the Catholic Confederation (heavily weighted with members of his own Salford Federation) which affirmed that, as Catholics could not

---

[52] See F. Mason, 'The Newer Eve; The Catholic Women's Suffrage Society in England, 1911–1923', *Catholic Historical Review*, 72/4 (Oct. 1986).

[53] *Tablet*, 18 Oct. 1919. [54] Cleary, *Catholic Social Action in Britain*, 73.

[55] M. Clifton, *Amigo: Friend of the Poor* (Southampton, 1987), 108–10. Clifton's book is an account of the life of one of the most important bishops of the period, and quotes extensively from Amigo's letters and papers.

be socialists, Catholic trade-unionists should not pay the political levy.[56] The *Christian Democrat* sought a way through this issue by arguing that the Labour party had not gone as far to call for the *total* nationalization of *all* means of production, distribution, and exchange concluding that 'whatever is correctly described as socialism is condemned by the church, and whatever is not condemned is not really socialism'.[57]

This debate was finally resolved by Cardinal Bourne's statements in 1924–5, which declared that the Labour party was not strictly socialist, and that Catholics could therefore join it on the same terms as any other party apart from the Communist party. In 1924 Cardinal Bourne offered the following observations to the Dutch paper *De Tijd*:

I assure you positively that our Labour Party's programme contains nothing which threatens religion. No doubt there are extremists among them, but the Party as such has nothing in common with the Socialists of the Continent . . . Mr [James Ramsay] MacDonald is neither a materialist nor a Marxist, and one can say the same of the principal 'Labour men'.

He added that the Labour party approximated to Catholic social thought 'without knowing it'. Thus, English Catholics were in the happy position of seeing good in all three major parties: the Conservative's respect for authority, the Liberals' individualism, and Labour's derivation of inspiration from 'some of the ideals of Pope Leo XIII'.[58] A few months later, at a New Year rally in the East End he qualified these remarks, adding that Catholics should never allow themselves to put party before religion, and had a duty to leave their party should its principles diverge from those of Catholicism.[59] Amusingly, by this stage the *Tablet* was challenging Catholic Labour politicians such as John Wheatley for daring to suggest that the Labour party *was* socialist![60]

Whatever the attitude of the hierarchy, however, the reality was that this accommodation had been forced on it by the mass of Catholic workers voluntarily aligning themselves with the Labour party. It is possible to see this movement as a sign of increasing Catholic working-class radicalism in the latter stages of the First World War. Thus, considerable attention has been paid by historians to the role of John Wheatley's Catholic Socialist Society which operated in the Glasgow area from its inception in November 1906. Once converted to socialism Wheatley, a former Irish Nationalist and Liberal supporter, fought ardently against the Catholic hierarchy for the right for Catholics to be Catholics and socialists (of the British rather than continental type) at the same time. Indeed, Wheatley enjoyed considerable support from local priests in his debates with the Belgian Father Puissant who called for a priest-led Catholic Christian democratic party to resist socialism. However, recent research suggests that the movement of Catholics into the Labour party after the First World War in Glasgow was much more due to the Labour party's (and especially the puritanical Independent Labour party's) compromise in abandoning its

---

[56] *Tablet*, 8 Oct. 1921.   [57] Ibid., 5 Nov. 1921.   [58] Ibid., 15 Nov. 1924.
[59] Ibid., 17 Jan. 1925.   [60] Ibid., 28 Mar. 1925.

anti-drink stance and its former opposition to denominational schooling—a case not of Catholics becoming more socialist, but of socialists becoming less rigid in their beliefs.[61]

Thus, while Catholics were now freely joining and voting for the Labour party, this support was contingent on Labour respecting the beliefs and values of working-class Catholics. There were many points of friction between Catholics and Labour in the inter-war years, for instance over the Spanish Civil War, birth control, and Communist 'front' activities, and on the local level there were cases of groups of Catholics breaking away from the Labour party.[62] However, given the predominant Anglicanism of the Conservatives and the decline of the Liberals there was no real political alternative, and the issue of Catholic Labour party membership was not seriously revived on a national level. Anti-socialism reappeared, instead, as a generalized anti-collectivism after 1945, especially within the CSG in the 1950s.

In the 1930s, as elsewhere in Europe, there was a considerable expansion of lay activity with the impulse for Catholic Action from the encyclical *Quadregesimo Anno* of 1931. This was very much targeted at specific groups. For instance, the *Catholic Worker* newspaper founded in 1935, inspired by the American movement of the same name, saw itself as challenging the Communist *Daily Worker* amongst the working class. Although founded by the middle-class intellectual Bernard Wall, editor of the *Colosseum* review, the editorship soon passed to Bob Walsh, the quintessential social Catholic working-class activist.[63] The paper ceased publication in 1959. The *Catholic Worker* was closely involved with the Young Christian Workers movement (YCW), which began properly in Wigan in the late-1930s and was inspired by the continental 'Jocist' movement. After the war the YCW went on to become one of the most successful of the lay movements of this period, and Bob Walsh estimated that by the mid-1950s some 60,000 young Catholics had passed through it. One of the earliest recruits, Patrick Keegan, went on to be president of the World Movement of Christian Workers, attending (and addressing) the Second Vatican Council as a lay auditor.[64]

There was also in the 1930s an attempt to set up Catholic Vocational Guilds within the trade unions. Catholic Guilds were set up in a range of industries and workforces, although they were only really successful in public transport—and even that had lapsed into largely social activity by the Second World War.[65] Catholic activists were quick to deny that these were in any sense political 'Minority Movements' (on the

[61] P. Morris, 'The Irish in the Glasgow Region and the Labour Movement, 1891–1922', M.Litt. thesis, Oxford, 1989, p. 170. For an introduction to the controversies surrounding Wheatley see S. Gilley, 'Catholics and Socialists in Scotland, 1900–30', in R. Swift and S. Gilley (eds.), *The Irish in Britain, 1815–1939* (London, 1989), 212–38.

[62] Buchanan, *The Spanish Civil War*, 175. Tensions within the Camberwell Labour party over the Spanish Civil War lead to a breakaway Catholic 'Constitutional Labour Party' winning some 4,000 votes in the local elections of Nov. 1937.

[63] B. Wall, 'The English *Catholic Worker*: Early Days', *Chesterton Review*, 10 (3 Aug. 1984), 275–93. I am grateful to Frank Loughlin for drawing this article to my attention.

[64] *Guardian*, 9 Mar. 1990 carried a brief obituary for Keegan. See also R. P. (Bob) Walsh, *The Rise of the Social Conscience* (London, 1955), 8–12.   [65] Ibid. 5.

Communist model) within the unions or potential future Catholic trade unions. Rather, they were intended to provide Catholic workers with the spiritual guidance which the unions were unable to deliver, and to monitor the activities of Communists within the unions. However, the Guilds were treated with deep suspicion by the left, and it has to be said that their protestations were somewhat disingenuous. For instance, by seeing the Spanish Civil War as a spiritual question they inevitably came into conflict with the union leaderships on issues such as fund-raising for the Republican side. Similarly, Bob Walsh quite openly claimed that the Catholic Guilds played a leading role in preventing the London tramwaymen joining the 1937 London bus strike and thus helped Ernest Bevin (leader of the Transport and General Workers' Union) to defeat his left-wing opponents.[66]

Another project inspired by *Quadregesimo Anno* was the establishment of a forum for Catholic employers, resulting in the first meeting in March 1938 of the Conference of Catholic Industrialists under the direction of the Jesuit Father Lewis Watt. Like other lay movements, the Conference owed much to the support of the CSG, as well as to the Catenian Association (for Catholic businessmen). Links were immediately forged with the strong associations of Catholic employers in Holland, Belgium, and France. The Conference continued to meet in Oxford on a regular basis during the war. The theme of the 1940 Conference was, appropriately, 'Experience of State Control'. After the war the group extended its interests to include meetings with selected Catholic trades unionists, but does not appear to have exerted any real influence on industrial relations.[67]

Thus, in the 1930s a vocal Catholic minority were putting across a coherent political message, largely derived from papal encyclicals. The late 1930s was arguably the period in which the most distinctive political Catholic movement emerged in Britain, advancing a positive case that was clearly marked off from the positions of right and left. Although neglected in standard works on the 'Red Decade', the *Catholic Worker*, with its woodcuttings and fashionable European devotions, was as characteristic in its own way as many of the better known icons of the era. The 1930s was the last period in which Catholicism genuinely could appear alien within British society, and some of the young Catholic intellectuals deliberately encouraged this with their sympathy for foreign Fascist movements, authoritarian regimes, and continental Catholic movements. This feeling of Catholic uniqueness is evident even in the writings of the convert novelist Graham Greene who came away from his visit to Mexico in 1938 with a heightened sense of the martyrdom of the Catholic church, and of the possibility of Catholic Action. Before entering Mexico from Texas Greene had witnessed a strike by Mexican pecan workers led by a Catholic priest: 'the first example I had come across of genuine Catholic Action on a social issue, a real attempt, led by the old, fiery, half-blind Archbishop, to put into force the papal encyclicals which have condemned capitalism quite as strongly as Communism'.[68] Such a scenario was

---

[66] Walsh, 5.　　　　　　　　　　　　[67] Cleary, *Catholic Social Action in Britain*, 148–50.

[68] Characteristically, Greene went on to note that: 'There was something a little pathetic about Catholic Action in San Antonio'; G. Greene, *The Lawless Roads* (Harmondsworth, 1947 edn.), 24. This

unlikely to be repeated in Britain. However, at a time of political stagnation and mass unemployment, combined with a sense of Catholic alienation and even persecution by the forces of socialism and secularism, there was some reason to suppose that the intellectuals would finally in the late 1930s strike a chord with the Catholic masses.

Catholicism in these years was evidently troubling to the political establishments of both left and right (although they made little attempt to understand it). In practice, however, the position of many working-class Catholic activists was a misleading one. Activists such as Bob Walsh were, in fact, naturally men of the left, but the peculiarities of 1930s politics, which did not allow for shades of grey, placed them on the right on issues such as the Spanish Civil War. This put them at odds with the Labourist tradition in the labour movement (which resented any independent action within its ranks) at a time when their objective (anti-fascist and anti-communist) interests were the same. In the post-war years this ambiguity was removed as, during the Cold War, Catholics and the labour movement leadership found it much easier to unite in anti-communism. With Fascism discredited there were fewer potential irritants to the relationship than had been the case in the 1930s. Instead, the social Catholic movement itself split over the question of how to respond to the Welfare State.

In the inter-war years Catholicism in Britain, as in Europe, enjoyed a controversial relationship with fascism. Indeed, by the later 1930s many on the left saw the Catholics as a potential fifth column for fascism. As Adrian Hastings has noted, Catholic claims to the contrary were not helped by the fact that reputable Catholic publishing houses were willing to publish books like J. K. Heydon's *Fascism and Providence*, which envisaged a fascist-monarchist-corporatist regime as the best chance to undo the damage caused by the Reformation (though even Heydon accepted that once in power fascism may well turn on Catholicism and persecute it).[69] During the 1920s the Catholic Church had allowed itself to be manipulated by the Fascists in the Italian immigrant communities—for instance, a Te Deum for Mussolini's survival of an assassination attempt was held in St Peter's, Liverpool.[70] However, it should also be noted that bitter debates raged in the Catholic press at the time of the rise of Mussolini, with Miss Barbara Barclay Carter a particularly strong supporter of the Catholic PPI against the Fascists (she would later look after the exiled PPI leader Don Sturzo in London), while certain English priests resident in Italy were enthusiastic apologists for Mussolini.[71] Sturzo played a central role in setting up the Christian democratic 'People and Freedom' group which maintained a critique of authoritarian governments of the right in the later 1930s.[72] Sympathy for Mussolini was, however, lingering. As late as 1944, in his panegyric for Hinsley, the future Cardinal

account of Greene's visit formed the basis for his famous novel *The Power and the Glory* (1940). For more on Greene's religious and political views see N. Sherry, *The Life of Graham Greene, i. 1904–1939* (London, 1989).

[69] A. Hastings, 'Some Reflections on the English Catholicism of the late 1930s', in id. (ed.), *Bishops and Writers: Aspects of the Evolution of Modern Catholicism* (Wheatampstead, 1977), 115. J. K. Heydon, *Fascism and Providence* (London, 1937).

[70] *Catholic Times*, 19 Nov. 1926.   [71] Ibid., 7 Jan. 1927 and ff.

[72] J. Keating, 'Christian Democrat Thought in 1930s Britain', unpub. conference paper, 1991, *passim*.

Heenan felt free to describe Italian Fascism as 'incomparably the best system of government ever to rule a United Italy'.[73]

Historians have laid different emphases on what fascism meant for British Catholics. Adrian Hastings has argued that the Catholic cultural 'renaissance' of the 1930s incorporated a blindness to the evils of fascism, and a sympathy for authoritarianism which owed much to the ideas of Belloc and Chesterton. However, this was mainly a phenomenon of the English Catholic upper class, and made little impression on the working class.[74] Similarly, E. R. Norman claims that fascism had little appeal, especially for working-class Catholics in England—'English Catholicism was too English in its social and political outlook'.[75] Thomas Moloney, however, has stressed the attractions of fascism for a new generation of socially mobile young Catholics, being educated in boys' grammar schools but still subject to discrimination and prejudice. He also points out that Oswald Mosley's British Union of Fascists was very willing to reach out to Catholics as potential allies, noting in its journal, for instance, that 'the philosophy of both is opposed to democracy'.[76] Indeed, Mosley was, apparently, known in Leeds as 'the Pope' due to the large number of Catholic BUF supporters.[77]

What is certainly true is that even those sections of the Catholic hierarchy which ultimately came out very strongly against Nazism in the Second World War persisted in refusing to share the left's blanket condemnation of authoritarian political regimes and movements of the right. The best example of this was the widespread support for Franco in the Catholic community which often went beyond mere revulsion at the anti-Catholic outrages of the early stages of the Civil War to support for the 'New Spain' that Franco was hoping to build. A few well-known Catholics (such as Eric Gill, the maverick convert sculptor) were willing to come out in support of the Republic. However, recent research has overturned the traditional assumption that the Catholic working class was likely to be pro-Republican, emphasizing instead the very real problems that Catholic discontent caused in local Labour party branches, trade unions, and the Co-operative movement. The Labour party agent in St Helens, for example, complained that: 'The issues of Spain have deeply disturbed large groups of our Roman Catholic supporters . . . It must be remembered that the Catholics of this and other towns are hearing from certain sources an incessant propaganda against the heroic defenders of Spanish democracy.'[78] However, this research also emphasizes the limitations of Catholic dissent. In the absence of another political home, and given the hierarchy's hostility to breakaway movements, Catholics ultimately had little choice but to remain and fight their corner within their own organizations.[79]

[73] J. C. Heenan, *Cardinal Hinsley* (London, 1944), 102.

[74] Hastings, 'English Catholicism of the late 1930s', 107–25.

[75] Norman, *Roman Catholicism in England*, 119.

[76] Moloney, *Westminster, Whitehall and the Vatican*, 55–60. Catholics continued to be associated with Mosley's movements—e.g. E. J. Hamm, Gen. Sec. of the Union Movement of the 1960s, as well as Mosley's private secretary, were both Catholics. Hamm claimed that 'in the Union Movement the social teachings of the church find their political expression' (letter to *Christian Democrat*, Nov. 1963).

[77] Fielding, *Class and Ethnicity*, 125.   [78] Buchanan, *Spanish Civil War*, 185.

[79] See ibid., ch. 5, and T. Gallagher, 'Scottish Catholics and the British Left, 1918–1939', *Innes Review*, 34/1 (Spring, 1983).

Even so, the lasting effects of the Civil War must be noted. Cardinal Hinsley was to keep a signed photograph of Franco on his desk during the Second World War at the same time as he was being placed on a Nazi death list—possibly because his Sword of the Spirit movement was mistaken for a kind of Home Guard![80] In the early 1950s Catholics led the campaign for full diplomatic relations to be restored with Franco's Spain. Reflecting in 1974 on his visit to Barcelona in 1952 for the Eucharistic conference Cardinal Heenan remarkably concluded that 'Franco's Spain is a dictatorship with a difference' due to the open criticism of the regime that he believed was permitted.[81] Hence, within the Catholic Church sympathy for Franco was widespread, and, especially during the Civil War, those progressive Catholics who were critical of Franco's crusade were made to feel like a beleaguered minority in the face of the 'corporate' outlook (in David Mathew's term) of the hierarchy and priesthood.[82]

For all these reasons historians have identified the early stages of the Second World War—especially the months following the fall of France—as a crucial phase in British Catholic history when the loyalties of Catholics could have been seriously eroded by the example of the 'Latin Bloc' of authoritarian pro-Catholic regimes in Spain, Italy, and Vichy France. Indeed, many of the Catholic newspapers were accused of defeatism in the days after Dunkirk.[83] Michael de la Bedoyere, editor of the *Catholic Herald*, was a leading advocate of the Latin Bloc, describing it as the 'specifically Catholic Christian work of Catholic statesmen like Salazar, de Valera or Pétain'. In February 1941 the same paper saw Pétain as standing for 'the spiritual, moral and cultural values of Christian Europe'.[84] Despite these and other examples of Catholic sympathy for the ideals of Vichy, Franco, and Mussolini, it is clear, however, that fears of Catholic disloyalty were grossly overexaggerated in the crisis months of mid-1940. Even so, there were clearly strong motives for Cardinal Hinsley's initiative in launching the Sword of the Spirit movement soon afterwards. It would educate Catholics in what the war was about and finally disperse the spectre of disloyalty to the war effort. More broadly, it filled a gap left by the Church of England in leading a campaign to establish the war as a spiritual crusade for a reconstructed Europe (the Anglican church being chastened by allegations of jingoism after the 1914–18 war and reluctant to give a lead again).

Sword of the Spirit (SoS), founded in August 1940, was a major success in this respect, uniting British people with the remnants of the French and Polish forces. Working under the presidency of Cardinal Hinsley, SoS united some of the leading

[80] Molony, *Westminster, Whitehall and the Vatican*, 71.

[81] J. C. Heenan, *A Crown of Thorns* (London, 1974), 47.

[82] D. Mathew, *Catholicism in England; The Portrait of a Minority; Its Culture and Tradition* (1936; 3rd edn., London, 1955), 271.

[83] S. Mews, 'The Sword of the Spirit: A Catholic Cultural Crusade of 1940', *Studies in Church History*, 20 (1983), 409–20.

[84] T. Greene, 'Vichy France and the Catholic Press in England: Contrasting Attitudes to a Moral Problem', *Recusant History*, 21/1 (May 1992), 118. Despite the *Catholic Herald*'s admiration for the 'Latin' dictators, an editorial of 11 July 1941 held up the more explicitly collaborationist Catholics such as the German Von Papen, the Slovak Tiso, and the Belgian Degrelle as men 'from whom we have nothing to learn except as a warning'.

progressive Catholic intellectuals of the day, such as Christopher Dawson, Barbara Ward, and A. C. F. Beales. In this way the 'Christian Democrats' of the 1930s were at last given a platform, and the pro-authoritarian intellectuals were marginalized— much to their own discomfort. SoS activities included public meetings and a series of publications, and its finest hour was probably the Stoll Theatre rally in May 1941, when Catholics, Free Churchmen, and Anglicans met under the chairmanship of the Archbishop of Canterbury (Cosmo Lang) to discuss 'A Christian Order for Britain'.[85] Tellingly, however, no Catholic bishops were present at the start of the meeting. Indeed, SoS was far from uniformly supported amongst the Catholic hierarchy, and fell foul of conservative theologians who protested against any moves to 'ecumenicalism'.[86] Thus, although a united front was created with the Church of England and the Free Churches, it ultimately proved impossible to draw up a joint statement on the question of religious liberty, because canon lawyers cavilled at the concept that there was 'a natural and civil right to religious freedom'.[87]

Moreover, the attempt to draw up a post-war social agenda through the SoS was far from successful, and the latent divisions were easily opened over questions such as birth-control once the immediate danger of German invasion had passed. In 1943 the Bishop of Salford cancelled a meeting of SoS branch secretaries after a non-Catholic speaker at an SoS public meeting had appeared to endorse divorce and birth-control.[88] Even so, by the time of his death in 1943 Hinsley, despite the divisions within his Church, had, through his radio broadcasts and campaigns, achieved a positive projection of British Catholicism unparalleled since the days of Cardinal Manning.

The same campaigning spirit that underpinned SoS was carried through into the post-war world, revolving around the issue of communism. Catholic opposition to communism was unflinching, especially given the strong pre-war links built up with Catholics in Poland, Czechoslovakia, and elsewhere in Eastern Europe, and was tempered only by the knowledge that the path from Communism to Catholicism (and vice versa) was a well-enough travelled one to preclude the complete demonization of the enemy.[89] Defecting Communists like Douglas Hyde and Hamish Fraser gave a particular lead to this work, although it was not always clear how their talents could best be used.[90]

In the 1940s all the new Catholic lay movements adopted a strongly anti-communist orientation. In Scotland, the Catholic Workers' Guild, an alternative to the CSG, criticized the alleged middle-class dominance of the CSG and the fact that

---

[85] M. Walsh, *From Sword to Ploughshare: Sword of the Spirit to Catholic Institute for International Relations, 1940–1980* (London, 1980).

[86] Id., 'Ecumenism in War-time Britain: The Sword of the Spirit and Religion and Life, 1940–1945', pts. 1 and 2, *Heythrop Journal*, 23/3 (July and Oct. 1982); Mews, 'The Sword of the Spirit'.

[87] Walsh, *From Sword to Ploughshare*.　　　　　　　　　　　　　　　　[88] Ibid. 11.

[89] Author's interview with Bob Walsh, Jan. 1985.

[90] Hyde was former news editor for the *Daily Worker*, Fraser had been a member of the International Brigades in Spain. See D. Hyde, *I Believed* (London, 1950) and *From Communism Towards Catholicism* (London, 1949); H. Fraser, *Fatal Star* (London, 1952).

many workers who went to the Catholic Workers' College returned less able to communicate with their workmates.[91] Founded in 1941 by Anthony Hepburn and James Darragh, it has been argued that the Guild should take some of the credit for the Communist party's relative failure on Clydeside in the war.[92] Importantly, the new guild was not diocesan but workplace based. In England, the Association of Catholic Trade Unionists (ACTU) was set up on a diocesan basis, initially to overturn the TUC's 1942 vote against denominational education, but increasingly to act as a weapon against communist infiltration of the unions, working closely with right-wing trade-union leaders and other anti-communist organizations such as IRIS and Common Cause.[93] However, despite strong backing from Cardinal Griffin, ACTU received only patchy support from the hierarchy, and the consistently inflated membership figures concealed a rapidly declining organization. Joan Keating's detailed research suggests that the mass movement of anti-communist Catholics (on the Australian model), which some leaders had envisaged, was always illusory.[94]

The main problem was that ACTU's pervasive anti-communism aroused (justified) fears that such a negative attitude would ultimately lead to failure. Bob Walsh, for instance, was keen for Catholic activists to spell out the positive, radical side to their own programme. The Communist was 'not an evil man to be exterminated . . . He shares my vision in which I see the end of a system that is worked for the benefit of a few . . . I tell employers that I am out to end capitalism. The Communist and I [only] part company in the method of attack on these evils and in the system that must replace capitalism.'[95] The truth of these warnings was borne out in the 1950s when the Communist peril faded after the death of Stalin, and when the Hungarian uprising weakened the Communist party in Britain. By the 1960s and 1970s Catholics were as likely to be interested in development issues in the Third World as in the defence of the 'free world' or rolling back communism. The evolution of the Sword of the Spirit into the Catholic Institute for International Relations (CIIR), which in 1974 led the criticism of Portuguese colonialism in Mozambique, was highly symbolic of this shift.[96]

By the late 1940s, however, the real issue for many Catholics was not the threat of communist subversion, but what they saw as the crypto-communist 'big government' of the post-war consensus. The Welfare State appeared abhorrent to traditional Catholic social thought with its emphasis on the powerful state (as against subsidiary function), and its centralizing of schools and medical services. The 1942 Beveridge report and 1944 Butler Education Act caused considerable Catholic apprehension at the end of the Second World War, softened only by the knowledge that working-class Catholics would stand to gain financially from many of the reforms such as Family

---

[91] R. H. Butterworth, D.Phil. thesis, 254–6.
[92] Gallagher, 'Scottish Catholics and the British Left', 220. [93] Scott, *The RCs*, 97.
[94] J. Keating, 'Catholic Influence in Trade Unions', unpub. paper given at the Plater College Summer School, Aug. 1991. See also ead., 'Roman Catholics, Christian Democracy and the British Labour Movement, 1910–1960', Ph.D. thesis, Manchester, 1992.
[95] *Communism: A Catholic Worker Special* (Manchester, 1950), 8–9.
[96] Walsh, *From Sword to Ploughshare*, 23–32.

Allowances. The Bishop of Leeds accused RAB Butler of sleeping 'with a copy of *Mein Kampf* under his pillow'.[97] True to form, the *Tablet* recommended a Conservative vote in 1945 as closest to Catholic social principles, and later saw hope in a Tory 'property-owning democracy', though the Tories disappointed such hopes when they returned to power in 1951 by continuing with the Welfare State.

The problem was that the post-war changes in nationalization and social policy were becoming a fact of political life, at the same time as reconstruction was literally bulldozing the traditional social basis of the Catholic community. Thus, social Catholics had to decide between accommodation and opposition, leading to a major split in their ranks in the 1950s. By 1952 Bob Walsh was defending an alliance with the Labour party in *Blackfriars* and would soon run as a Labour candidate in Bury. Walsh argued that Labour party policy was not at odds with Catholic thought, and even chimed with *Quadragesimo Anno* which had accepted that certain forms of property must be reserved for the state. Improbably, he even argued that the opportunity was present for Catholics to occupy the role of 'moral advisor' to the Labour movement formerly provided by the Nonconformists.[98] Battle-lines in the CSG were clearly drawn in 1951 when the economist Michael Fogarty published an article entitled 'I like the Welfare State' in the *Christian Democrat*, appealing for an end to attacks on the Welfare State in the name of Catholic principle.[99] Such views were set against those of the editor, Father Paul Crane, who saw the Welfare State as 'embryonic Communism' and warned that contemporary social policies could lead to totalitarianism and 'a Dachau of our own devising'.[100] By the late 1950s, when Crane was eased out of the editorship, the movement was severely divided and, despite Crane's success in sustaining membership, effectively moribund long before the Guild's ultimate demise in 1967.[101] Crane went on to promote his views in his own paper, *Christian Order*. Significantly, the last years of the Guild were run under a very different regime, as the Church authorities stepped in in 1959 after three years of 'uncertainty and dispute' to impose a diocesan framework, with priests appointed by the bishops as 'Diocesan Directors'. Archbishop Grimshaw of Birmingham noted that the Lay Committee 'cannot of course be an autonomous body, answerable to nobody . . . Democracy, I am afraid, is not the Church's constitution.'[102]

This last comment identifies a recurring feature of Catholic political engagement both in Britain and Europe: the strength and weakness that came with the tradition of complete obedience to episcopal authority. By the 1960s the Catholic community in Britain was going through a process of change. In considerable numbers Catholics were now enjoying access to higher education, resulting in a better educated, more questioning and assertive laity. The quintessential lay movement of the 1960s, the Newman Society which drew inspiration from Cardinal Newman as a symbol of a

---

[97] Coman, *Catholics and the Welfare State*, 45.

[98] MacDermott, 'Irish Catholics and the British Labour Movement', 252–3.

[99] *Christian Democrat*, Nov. 1951, pp. 256–9. The riposte was R. Lyle's 'I Dislike the Welfare State' in the Dec. edn., pp. 283–5.   [100] *Christian Democrat* Mar. 1950, p. 49, and Jan. 1951, p. 2.

[101] Coman, *Catholics and the Welfare State*, 80–4.   [102] *Tablet*, 14 Nov. 1959.

more open Catholicism opposed to the spirit of the First Vatican Council, owed little to the social and political movements which have been discussed in this chapter. The English hierarchy may have been unprepared for the coming of the Second Vatican Council, but the evidence of the pressure for change was already evident in the Catholic community.

3. Conclusion

This chapter has traced the rise and fall of a distinctive Catholic political tradition which, although never able to make much impact on national politics, played a major role within the Catholic community and, occasionally, beyond it. Although it drew inspiration from European, American, and even Australian developments it was never just a pale reflection of them. It possessed an indigenous strength which largely derived from the small but committed group of Catholic activists who cropped up in many guises in the overlapping initiatives of these years. The movement may be judged a failure in the sense that by the 1960s Catholic social principles were no longer seen as a model for the remaking of British society, even though, of course, the Catholic faith itself had an enduring religious significance. Similarly, the patterns of organization adopted by lay Catholics in the decades after 1918 were no longer deemed appropriate to the changed society of the 1960s. However, it would be wrong to judge a small movement (representing a minority within a minority) too harshly. The Catholic movements discussed in this chapter played a significant role in educating and empowering ordinary working-class Catholics. Bob Walsh, for instance, noted that ACTU began to decline when a whole generation of its leading figures moved into responsible trade-union posts.

The overall failure of this movement is perhaps not surprising, even if the reasons for it are open to debate. Activists were wont to lament the 'apathy' of the Catholic masses, although the problem was, perhaps, that they were apathetic about political Catholicism in particular rather than about politics or trade unionism in general. Moreover, the attitude of the Catholic hierarchy was never straightforwardly supportive towards these movements, and the tensions between the hierarchy and a more assertive laity certainly intensified in the 1950s. Ultimately, the dream of a distinctive Catholic social and political movement was engulfed in the fundamental changes that overtook British politics and society after 1945. In the 1960s Catholics' political engagement continued to fragment—into Third World development work, into left-wing political radicalism,[103] or into intransigent campaigning on questions such as abortion. In recent years, however, there have been signs of an attempt to relaunch a national political force in the inter-denominational 'Movement for Christian Democracy'.

There are welcome signs that the relative neglect of twentieth-century Catholicism and its associated political and social movements by historians is already being

---

[103] See B. Sharratt, 'English Roman Catholicism in the 1960s', in A. Hastings (ed.), *Bishops and Writers*.

remedied. Indeed, many of the factors that fostered this neglect carry relatively little weight today. The marked Catholic diffidence in analysing the events of the twentieth century (especially Catholicism's relations with Fascism) should decline as the events of the potentially embarrassing 1930s recede. Moreover, while the lack of explicitly Catholic political institutions (such as parties and trade unions) made Catholicism fit uneasily within the mainstream study of British party politics, it is increasingly recognized that religion did not cease to play an important role in British politics with the ending of the nineteenth century. Catholicism, as a religion which maintained its position during the twentieth century and, indeed, grew in numbers, may be discordant with a typical view of British politics which sees religion as a declining force in a secular society. However, the remarkable resilience of Catholicism in the final decade of the century, especially in comparison with the travails of the Church of England, may well force a reappraisal of the reasons for its success.[104]

[104] See e.g. H. Young, 'Suddenly, Catholics are Major Players in National Life', *Guardian*, 27 Apr. 1993.

9

Ireland

DERMOT KEOGH AND FINÍN O'DRISCOLL

1. Historical Background

The role of the Catholic Church in Irish politics has often been misunderstood and misrepresented by novelists and by academics from different disciplines.[1] To many observers of nineteenth- and twentieth-century Ireland, the bishops and the priest took centre stage in the development of Irish politics; the phrase 'Home Rule is Rome Rule' was used extensively in the 1880s to denote clerical power and it continues to be echoed in Northern Ireland today.[2] The fall of Charles Stewart Parnell in 1890 was popularly but mistakenly ascribed to the exclusive machinations of the hierarchy: 'the Bishops and the Party | That tragic story made,' wrote William Butler Yeats in his poem on the death of Parnell.[3] In 1903 Horace Plunkett wrote disparagingly about the state of the country and ascribed much of the blame to the backwardness of the Catholic Church.[4] This view was also echoed in a popular book entitled *The Pope's Green Isle*, published in 1912.[5]

The thesis of a clerically ridden political country was rejected by Mgr. Michael O'Riordan in his work *Catholicity and Progress in Ireland* (1906).[6] This was written in a polemical fashion and very much as a rejoinder to Plunkett. Writing almost half a century later, the novelist and republican activist Peadar O'Donnell argued 'that this is not a cleric-dominated country but suffers more from a yahoo-ridden church'.[7] Although in no sense a historian, this trade-unionist, revolutionary, and novelist may have been closer to a more enduring and more accurate interpretation than many of the more 'informed' scholars.

The historical experience of Irish and continental Catholics differed significantly in the nineteenth century. Unlike the process of Italian unification, Irish constitutionalist nationalists depended for their success partially on the active support of the Church. In the 1820s the Catholic Association demonstrated the capacity of Daniel

---

[1] See e.g. P. Blanshard, *The Irish and Catholic Power* (London, 1954); F. S. L. Lyons, *Culture and Anarchy in Ireland 1890–1939* (Oxford, 1979).

[2] K. Heskin, *Northern Ireland: A Psychological Analysis* (Dublin, 1980).

[3] C. C. O'Brien, *Parnell and his Party, 1880–1890* (Oxford, 1957), 297; also id., with M. McEntee, *A Concise History of Ireland* (New York, 1972), 123–4.

[4] H. Plunkett, *Ireland in the New Century* (London, 1904).

[5] W. P. Ryan, *The Pope's Green Isle* (London, 1912).

[6] M. O'Riordan, *Catholicity and Progress in Ireland* (London, 1906).

[7] P. O'Donnell, 'The Clergy and Me', *Doctrine and Life*, 24 (Oct. 1974), 539–44.

O'Connell to mobilize the Irish populace. He could not have achieved as much as he did without the active support of a number of the bishops and the clergy. With the achievement of Catholic emancipation in 1829, O'Connell's subsequent failure with the Repeal Movement in the 1840s may be attributed partially to a lack of clerical enthusiasm and commitment.[8] Nevertheless, O'Connell succeeded in laying the foundations for a nationalist movement which wedded Catholicism and nationalism. While the relationship between the hierarchy and nationalist leaders in the latter part of the nineteenth century may have been strained and stormy, the fusion of the twin ideologies of Catholicism and nationalism became the motor force which ultimately led to independence. That was achieved with a predominantly lay leadership.

The first—and probably the only attempt—to create an autonomous, clerical-directed political movement came with the formation of the National Association in 1864. Under the direction of Cardinal Paul Cullen—a major reforming force in the nineteenth-century Irish Catholic Church—the National Association sought to act 'not as auxiliary to nationalists, nor as a guide to the people, but as a driver and commander'.[9] Its modest proposals for land reform, educational segregation, and the disestablishment of the Church of Ireland, failed to attract widespread support among the laity. Paradoxically, the National Association failed within a year. The Irish felt much more at one with lay political leaders. The relationship between Catholicism and nationalism was restored in the 1880s under the leadership of the Protestant landlord Charles Stewart Parnell. In return for ensuring the careful resolution of the 'educational question' along denominational lines, the Irish Parliamentary Party was in the privileged position of enjoying for a time the active support of the Irish hierarchy.[10] However, the alliance between church and nation came under severe strain as a consequence of the Parnell divorce crisis. That episcopal–political alliance was never completely restored.

By 1918 a new political force, Sinn Féin, had appeared. The Easter Rising, two years before, had redirected the course of Irish politics and gave a prominence to the physical force nationalist philosophy. The writings of one of the executed leaders, Padraig Pearse, became far more important to that post-First World War generation than the speeches of the Irish Parliamentary Party leader John Redmond, who died in 1918. His successor, John Dillon, witnessed the demise of the party in the general election of that year. The Anglo-Irish War (1919–21) brought to the fore a new generation of political leaders led by Michael Collins, Arthur Griffith, and Éamon de Valera. In that changed political climate, the Church hierarchy had the task of attempting to rebuild consensus with Sinn Féin.[11] Despite the Sinn Féin espousal of

---

[8] See, notably, V. Conzemius, 'The Place of Daniel O'Connell in the Liberal Catholic Movement of the Nineteenth Century', in D. McCartney (ed.), *The World of Daniel O'Connell* (Dublin, 1980); H. Rollet, 'The Influence of O'Connell on French Liberal Catholicism', ibid.

[9] E. R. Norman, *The Catholic Church and Ireland in the Age of Rebellion, 1859–1873* (London, 1965), 135–90.

[10] See, notably, E. Larkin, *The Roman Catholic Church and the Home Rule Movement in Ireland, 1870–1874* (Dublin, 1990).

[11] See, notably, D. Miller, *Church, State and Nation in Ireland, 1898–1921* (Dublin, 1973); E. Larkin,

violence, that task was ultimately achieved. The new generation of Irish leaders were, in the main, strong Catholic nationalists, Éamon de Valera being to the fore.

2. The Formation of an Irish Catholic Social Movement

The rise of Irish nationalism in the latter part of the nineteenth century focused on the land question. Social agitation for tenant rights became a very strong feature of that struggle.[12] However, the role of the urban poor and the Irish working class failed to gain coequal status with the land agitation until the early twentieth century. Clerical involvement in land agitation was quite strong. Paradoxically, this was not the case in the struggle for trade union rights and the defence of the urban poor. When James Larkin and James Connolly, two of the most prominent Irish labour leaders, began to agitate for trade-unionism and labour politics they were met with stiff resistance from a number of prominent clergymen.[13] Connolly was a revolutionary Marxist and Larkin was a strong syndicalist. Neither men exhibited a doctrinaire hostility to Catholicism, but they clashed from time to time with clerical power. Ecclesiastical denunciations of socialism increased in Ireland shortly after the first wave of industrial unrest in Belfast and Dublin between 1906 and 1910. Atheistic socialism and its threat to Irish society were the subject of a series of Lenten Lectures by a Jesuit priest, Fr. Robert Kane, in 1910.[14] Connolly, in replying to Kane in his pamphlet *Labour, Nationality and Religion*, said that he reduced the preacher to 'mere sound and fury, signifying nothing'.[15] Kane represented an extreme strand of Irish social Catholicism. But there were other clerics who did not share his point of view; they supported a more radical approach to the resolution of industrial unrest in the cities. For example, Fr. John Kelleher, defended the labour movement against the employers during the 1913 lockout.[16] He was supported in his views by members of the Capuchin order in particular who worked with the inner-city poor. The Professor of Political Economy at UCD Fr. Tom Finlay SJ, who had already played an active role in the Irish Co-operative Movement, declared in 1913 that it was the duty of the State to provide the necessary means in order to solve the social problem. The Jesuit-run journal *Studies*, first published in 1912, contained numerous articles outlining the need to tackle the Irish social question in accordance with the principles of the social encyclicals. The Jesuit Order's small, but extremely prolific, publishing house—the Irish Messenger Office—published a 'Social Action Series'. By 1918 there were twenty-eight titles each costing one penny, some of which sold up to ten thousand copies. The most prolific writer in this series was a Fr. Lambert McKenna SJ. Born in 1870, he entered the Society of Jesus in 1886 and studied in Dublin, Jersey, and

---

'Church, State and Nation in Modern Ireland', in id. (ed.), *The Historical Dimensions of Irish Catholicism* (New York, 1976).

[12] J. J. Lee, *The Modernisation of Irish Society, 1848–1918* (Dublin, 1973); T. W. Moody, *Davitt and Irish Revolution, 1846–82* (Oxford, 1982). [13] Miller, *Church, State and Nation*, 269–73.

[14] Quoted from J. Connolly, *Labour, Nationality and Religion* (Dublin, 1910), 16; no exact transcript of Kane's Lenten Lectures exists but Connolly's quotations from it are allegedly very accurate.

[15] Ibid. [16] J. Kelleher, 'On Strikes', *Catholic Bulletin*, 1/1 (Dec. 1911), 590.

Louvain. His main area of interest was in the revival of the Irish language and he kept in close contact with the work of Padraig Pearse. After the publication of his work the *Social Teachings of James Connolly* (a work which won the praise of many in the Irish labour movement), McKenna was obliged by his order to concentrate more on his Irish language interests and on his teaching duties at Belvedere College. He published minor articles on socialism and communism in the 1920s, which often showed a detached and critical view which singled him out from many of his clerical peers.[17] McKenna's non-doctrinaire approach helped to build bridges between the Church and labour. He died in Dublin in 1956.[17]

The most advanced discussion on political and social catholicism took place, perhaps surprisingly for some critics of the Catholic Church, in the national seminary at Maynooth. From as early as 1907 a small group of professors and students produced treatises and papers on the social question. The controversial and independent-minded Dr Walter McDonald headed this small group and he was ably assisted by Dr Peter Coffey and Dr William Moran. Coffey, for example, developed a dialogue between Catholicism and socialism in his pamphlet *Between Capitalism and Socialism*. His ideas were more fully developed by Moran in his enquiry *Social Reconstruction in an Irish State*, which was published on the eve of independence. The latter argued that the capitalist system was unworkable. He felt that the only means of achieving a just society was through the creation of a new political order:

We believe that such would become, as a matter of fact, the tradition of a Distributive State once firmly established, especially among a people believing in the Catholic philosophy of life. It was the tradition throughout the greater part of Europe during the Middle Ages, and it is still a strong tradition among the peoples of Ireland.[18]

Moran further argued for the establishment of this new political order:

It is hardly necessary to point out that reform, on such lines as are here suggested, can never be given a fair trial in Ireland until we get our own government . . . It follows that Irish social reformers, and the wage-earners of Ireland in particular, should so educate, organise and discipline their forces, as to be able to make social reconstruction on Catholic lines one of the chief planks in the platform of the first Irish Government.[19]

Such radical sentiments were not shared by the Irish bishops and nor were many Irish nationalist leaders particularly attracted to the task of immediately transforming social structures. The end of British dominance in the Irish Free State [Saorstát Éireann] did not result in a social revolution. It was a question of the social revolution that never was. As Professor Patrick Lynch commented: 'There was little use for idealism and less scope for utopianism in the Irish Free State of 1923.'[20]

[17] See esp. L. McKenna, 'Character and Development of Post-War Socialism', *Studies*, 8 (Sept. 1920) and id., 'The Bolshevik Revolution in Hungary', *Studies*, 10 (Sept. 1922).
[18] W. Moran, 'Social Reconstruction in an Irish State', *Irish Theological Quarterly*, 15 (Apr. 1920), 109.
[19] Ibid. 260.
[20] See P. Lynch, 'The Social Revolution that Never Was', in T. D. Williams (ed.), *The Irish Struggle 1916–1926* (London, 1966), 53.

3. The Kingship of Christ in the New Free State

The 1921 Treaty with Britain secured the right to independent government or dominion status for the Irish Free State. Accepted by the Dáil (Parliament) on 25 October 1922, the Treaty was opposed by Éamon de Valera and a remnant of Sinn Féin. Civil war blighted the first two years of the new state's existence and its legacy had an even more corrosive effect on the Irish body politic. There was a deep division in Irish society and an enduring bitterness between the two sides. That bitterness was in inverse proportion to the small number of wartime casualties; only somewhat over 600 lives had been lost.[21] Éamon de Valera and many of his political associates had been arrested in 1923 and had remained in prison until 1924. The new government had the immense and unenviable task of attempting to administer a country bankrupt at birth. The social question took a secondary place to considerations of law and order in this climate. Reflecting on the post civil-war era in 1936, Professor George O' Brien wrote: 'The anti-treaty party has certainly made the Free State safe for the bourgeoisie.'[22]

The Irish hierarchy had taken the side of the government during the civil war. They had supported William T. Cosgrave in his fight against Éamon de Valera and the anti-Treatyites. The bishops found that that they came to enjoy a position of privilege and influence in post-independent Ireland despite the fact that the British-inspired 1922 constitution was not a particularly Catholic document. However, all the members of the government, with the exception of the Minister for Finance Ernest Blythe, were members of the Catholic Church and the ethos of the new state became distinctively Catholic under the leadership of the President of the Executive Council, William T. Cosgrave. This was reflected in many of the state's new laws and legal initiatives, governing, for instance, censorship, education, and divorce.[23]

The Catholic bishops, therefore, did not feel defensive about the role of religion in the new state. While there was no threat to the social order, the hierarchy sought to initiate a crusade of national moral renewal following the 'lax' ways of post-First World War Europe. Concern over the growth of materialism and the spread of alien influence in the countryside was also a major preoccupation of the clergy and of the hierarchy. Sermons and pastorals regularly returned to those themes and encouraged the shunning of foreign dances and newspapers. For example, the hierarchy had encouraged the formation of the League of Saint Brigid in January 1920 which was organized to give 'Irishwomen an opportunity of unity against the inroad of foreign immodest fashions'.[24] Lenten Pastorals between 1922 and 1926 dealt specifically with the threat posed by the influx of foreign [evil] literature, immodest dress and

---

[21] See, notably, C. Townshend, *Political Violence in Ireland* (Oxford, 1983); J. J. Lee, *Ireland, 1912–1985* (Cambridge, 1989), 56–9. In regard to the reaction of the bishops to the Civil War see D. Keogh, *The Vatican, the Bishops and Irish Politics, 1919–1939* (Cambridge, 1986).

[22] G. O' Brien, *The Four Green Fields* (Dublin, 1936), 100–1. A neglected work that contains many interesting observations on Irish politics and nationalism.

[23] D. Keogh, *The Vatican, the Bishops and Irish Politics*, 123–57, and J. H. Whyte, *Church and State in Modern Ireland* (Dublin, 1980), 24 ff.   [24] *The Irish Catholic Directory* (1921).

deportment and the growth of sexual promiscuity caused chiefly by the ever-growing popularity of the Dance Hall. After a synod of Irish bishops, held in Maynooth in 1927, a joint pastoral outlined the social obligations of the laity:

Between the State then or Society and its members there are reciprocal duties and obligations. Rulers and subjects are bound as parts to promote the good of the whole community—the former by securing preservation of peace, protection of rights and promotion of the general prosperity, the latter by obeying all just laws, by faithfully discharging the equitable duties and bearing the burthens allotted to them.[25]

With the development of a close working relationship between the new political élite and the Church, the hierarchy sought to depoliticize the Irish clergy. Similarly, there was no wish to allow members of the clergy to participate in radical social experimentation. There could, however, be cooperation between the Church and labour provided that it was not taken too far.[26] Therefore, Fr. Peter Coffey, one of the more original minds working on the social question in Ireland, found that his work was repeatedly censored during the 1920s. The Sinn Féin revolutionary, Fr. Michael O'Flanagan, who had been suspended from his ministry in 1918, remained ostracized in the 1920s and prevented from performing his priestly duties.[27] Severe ecclesiastical discipline dissuaded other clerics from encouraging innovation in the area of Church–labour cooperation.

The Irish hierarchy were also suspicious of innovations by lay people. Frank Duff, a member of the Department of Finance, founded the Legion of Mary in 1921. This organization was devoted to prayer and the performance of good works. Spreading rapidly, it recruited many lay members who met in discussion groups and recited the rosary. One of Duff's earliest activities was an attempt to rehabilitate Dublin prostitutes in one of the inner city's most notorious red light districts called Monto. He was assisted in his task by the *Garda Síochána* and the Special Branch (the division of plain clothes police). Despite the immediate popularity of the Legion, recognition from the Archbishop of Dublin, Edward Byrne, was very slow in coming. They had received a modified form of benediction from the Archbishop in 1926, but it was not until 1928 that he said that 'they were being sympathetically examined with a view to formal approval'. The Legion of Mary, a very subdued form of the Catholic Action movements elsewhere in Europe, continued to be treated with suspicion until 1933 when Frank Duff received a 'very special blessing' from Pius XI.[28] Even then episcopal and clerical suspicion was not fully removed.

However, the pre-independence debate on political Catholicism did not suddenly disappear after the civil war. Even the ever-cautious Catholic Truth Society published pamphlets entitled *Catholics and Citizenship* by Bishop Thomas Doherty of Galway. A former seminarian and the Minister for Home Affairs, Kevin O' Higgins, wrote an essay entitled *The Catholic Layman in Public Life*. But while there was a

---

[25] *Irish Ecclesiastical Record*, 30 (Nov. 1927), 532.   [26] Ibid. 535.
[27] D. Carroll, *They have Fooled You Again: Michael O'Flanagan (1876–1942), Priest, Republican and Social Critic* (Dublin, 1993).   [28] L. Ó. Broin, *Frank Duff* (Dublin, 1982), 32–40.

steady flow of such literature it was of a rather cautious kind. Irish bishops were not living in a situation where the state was an enemy. There was no necessity, therefore, to mobilize battalions of political Catholicism in a state where the overwhelming majority of leading politicians of the major parties were bishops *marqués*. Their main objective was to prevent members of the clergy from making ill-judged calls for social experimentation which would upset the equilibrium between the hierarchy and William T. Cosgrave's government.

However, Irish interest in political Catholicism received a significant boost with the publication by Pius XI in 1925 of the encyclical *Quas Primas*, which encouraged the faithful to overcome social and political divisions and unite under the leadership of the Kingship of Christ. The encyclical was published in the *Irish Ecclesiastical Record* in English and the central address in the Maynooth Union in 1926 was delivered by a Jesuit, Fr. Edward Cahill, on the theme of the Kingship of Christ in Ireland.[29] Times had changed. Fifteen years before, the union had been debating the role of socialism in Irish society.[30] Cahill founded the League of the Kingship of Christ or, as it was better known in Irish, An Ríoghacht, on 31 October 1926. Its main objects were:

a) To propagate among Irish Catholics a better knowledge of Catholic social principles.
b) To strive for the effective recognition of these principles in Irish public life.
c) To promote Catholic social action.

An Ríoghacht sought to transcend the political divisions of the country; it maintained that it was 'not associated with any political party, and takes no part in political controversy or activities, except where and in so far as the objects of the League (viz., Catholic social interests) are involved'.[32] An Ríoghacht grew swiftly at first but quickly slowed down after study branches had emerged mainly in Dublin and Belfast. It later spread to Kilkenny and to a number of smaller Irish towns. Initially An Ríoghacht had a very active *Ard-Comhairle* (National Executive), including George Gavan Duffy and Sir Joseph Glynn. An early document, *Notes on the Projected National Programme*, stated that 'A Catholic social programme, such as the League contemplates would be directed towards the gradual building up of a Christian state on the lines of the national tradition but suited to modern circumstances.'[33] The movement argued that a number of areas such as forestry, fishing, the manufacturing industry, and the control of credit and currency were in need of careful and detailed economic planning to bring about the resurrection of the Irish state and the resolution of the social problem. Education was singled out as an area in need of protection

[29] Fr. Edward Cahill, the most important and prolific member of An Ríoghacht, was born in Callow, Co. Limerick, in 1868; he received his secondary education at Mungret College, Co. Limerick and three years of theological training at Maynooth. He entered the Society of Jesus on 8 June 1891 and was ordained six years later. His career in teaching took him first back to his Alma Mater at Mungret but he moved to Milltown Park in Dublin in 1924 as Professor of Church History, Lecturer in Sociology, and later as spiritual director.

[30] E. Cahill, 'Ireland and the Kingship of Christ', *Record of the Maynooth Union* (1925–6).
[31] *An Ríoghacht Constitution*, Cahill Papers, Jesuit Archives, Dublin.   [32] Ibid.
[33] *Notes on the Projected National Programme*, Cahill Papers, Jesuit Archives, Dublin.

against statism.[34] This was difficult to justify, and may account for the group's lack of mass appeal. In a country where education was denominationally controlled there was not the remotest prospect of the State taking over control of anything. Cahill, the main ideologue of the group, belonged to a generation who were formed in the years after the fall of Parnell. He remained throughout his life a strong nationalist and Irish speaker.[35] Cahill was also heavily influenced by right-wing Catholic ideas prevalent in France after the First World War; he devoted himself to the exposure of alleged Jewish-Freemason-Communist conspiracies in Ireland. One of his first published works, *Freemasonry and the Anti-Christian State*, appeared in 1929 and it quickly went into a second edition. The pamphlet was described by an enthusiast as being indispensable to every Catholic who wished to see Catholic principles in public life.[36]

Contrary to the view that An Ríoghacht was politically non-partisan, Cahill argued that the remedy for the social question lay in the reorganization of Irish political life.[37] He urged a strong united Catholic vanguard to counter 'the false principles or fatal exaggerations of Liberalism, Collectivism, Communism, and the ultra-nationalistic and secularist aspects of Fascism'.[38] He identified a combination of factors as causing the weakening of Irish society: emigration, the gradual decline of the *Gaeltacht* (the Irish-speaking region in Ireland), the 'un-Christian' press, and cinema and betting. He concluded:

In Ireland we are confronted with the strange anomaly of a profoundly Catholic nation devoid of most of the features of a Catholic civilization, and suffering from all the material, and very many of the mental defects which usually result from an un-Christian social regime.[39]

Cahill's call to Irish Catholics to establish a new social order did not win mass support.[40] An Ríoghacht never became a national movement like Duff's Legion of Mary. It did, however, exert an influence on a number of Irish intellectuals.

The Holy Ghost priest, Fr. Denis Fahey, was a close confidant of Cahill's and he shared the Jesuit's more extreme ideas.[41] Fahey, however, had been more exposed to the extreme conservative elements within continental Catholicism while studying in France and in Rome. In France he digested the anti-Semitism prevalent in Catholic society at the time of the Dreyfus Affair. He admitted later that he was influenced by

[34] Ibid.
[35] For a more detailed discussion of this period in Irish intellectual history, see esp. T. Garvin, *Nationalist Revolutionaries in Ireland, 1858–1928* (Oxford, 1987).   [36] *Irish Catholic* (Feb. 1929).
[37] E. Cahill, *Ireland's Peril* (Dublin, 1930), 28–9; see also id., *The Irish Catholic Social Movement* (Dublin, 1932); id., *An Alternative to Capitalism* (Dublin, 1936). The full text of this pamphlet later appeared as a series of articles in *Irish Ecclesiastical Record*, 34/9 (Sept. 1929), 34/10 (Oct. 1929), 36/12 (Dec. 1930), 37/2 (Feb. 1931).
[38] Id., 'The Catholic Social Movement', *Irish Ecclesiastical Record*, 36/12 (Dec. 1930), 576.
[39] Id., 'The Social Question in Ireland', *Irish Ecclesiastical Record*, 34/9 (Sept. 1929), 223.
[40] Id., 'The Catholic Social Movement', *Irish Ecclesiastical Record*, 37/2 (Feb. 1931), 123.
[41] Born in 1883 in Kilmore, County Tipperary, he attended the Holy Ghost run Rockwell College between 1895 and 1900. At the turn of the century, Fahey entered the noviciate of the Holy Ghost Congregation in France. Returning to Ireland for study, he made his final vows in 1907. Later, he travelled to Rome to study in the Gregorian and the Angelicum, taking doctorates in theology from both institutions. Ordained in Rome in 1911, Fahey returned to Ireland in 1912 and took up a teaching post at the Holy Ghost-run school Blackrock College as Professor of Moral Theology.

the Holy Ghost Father, Henri L'Floch and the Jesuit Louis Cardinal Billot. Both were leading advocates of the condemned *Action Française* movement.

Initially Fahey avoided any involvement in Catholic groups—though he did promote the work of An Ríoghacht on occasions—and it was not until 1945 that he established his own group, Maria Duce. Fahey's main academic concern was a desire to explain the reasons for the breakdown of moral and spiritual order in contemporary society. A neoscholastic, he argued that 'the Supreme Way' given by God was the 'true order'. Under constant threat from the forces of naturalism and evil, Fahey identified the enemies of this true order as Satan, the Jews, and others. All conspired to form the International Communist Movement of the twentieth century. This final enemy was a carefully orchestrated movement, directed by Jewish financiers and Freemasons. On the need for Catholic political action, Fahey stated:

A truly Catholic social order would be opposed on the one hand to Protestant liberalism and on the other hand to Jewish Marxism. . . . Political thought and political action, therefore, in an ordered state, will respect the jurisdiction and guidance of the Catholic Church, the divinely instituted guardian of the moral order, remembering that what is morally wrong cannot be really politically good. Thus the natural or temporal common good of the State will be always aimed at in the way best calculated to favour the true development of human persons, in and through the Mystical Body of Christ. The Civil Power will then have a purer and higher notion of its proper end, acquired in the full light of Catholic truth, and political action, both in rulers and ruled, will come fully under the influence of supernatural life.[42]

Fahey, who accepted the authenticity of the Protocols of the Elders of Zion long after they had been discounted as a forgery, was proposing the establishment of a confessional state in Ireland with the Catholic Church as the established Church.

The extremism and radical confessionalism of both Cahill and Fahey did not gain the approval of their respective religious superiors. The Irish bishops, moreover, were not remotely interested in seeking to give pastoral direction to such disruptive and divisive ideas. Alive to the danger of encouraging the development of a mass following for clerics of such extreme views, the hierarchy actively discouraged the development of any interest among the diocesan clergy of the country in the ideas of both men. No pastoral need would be served by endorsing the slavish importation of continental Catholic radicalism. Ireland was, *de facto*, a Catholic state where the Church had secured a privileged position during the first decade of its existence. The development of popular political Catholicism, at variance with the governing party, could only have undermined the power and the influence of the bishops.

4. Vocationalism

The publication of *Quadragesimo Anno* in 1931 gave new impetus to the international Catholic social movement and that militancy spread to Ireland at a time when the political future of the Cumann na nGaedheal government seemed uncertain. The following decade witnessed a vigorous growth of clerical and lay interest in various

---

[42] Fahey, *Social Rights of Christ*, 112–36.

Irish adaptations of Catholic Action. Journals such as *Catholic Bulletin*, *Catholic Mind*, and *Irish Monthly* redirected their editorial emphasis and disseminated the ideas of Catholic social teaching. The emergence of new magazines in the first half of the 1930s further reflected the growing importance of that movement; the magazine *Outlook* was founded in 1932, *Up and Doing* in 1934, and *Prosperity* in 1935. *Hibernia* was taken over by the Knights of Columbanus in 1936 with the assistance of Denis Fahey and converted into a mouthpiece for Catholic Action. Neo-corporatist ideas were accepted in Irish universities.

An Ríoghacht, which set about reorganizing its *Ard Comhairle*, saw a growth in the number of its study-circles after 1931. A weekly review of the activities of the organization was established which, it was felt, would 'gradually unfold a national programme of social reconstruction'.[43] The short-lived magazine, *Outlook*, stood above other popular Catholic Action journals of its day. Despite the fact that it lasted for less than a year, it included amongst its contributors a number of the better minds in Ireland at the time: Gabriel Fallon, Alfred O'Rahilly, Francis McManus, and the future president of Ireland Cearbhall Ó Dálaigh. The Professor of Commerce at University College Cork, John Busteed, in 1933 ascribed the origin of Irish economic problems to the failure of Irish statesmen and politicians to recognize the proper implications of papal social teaching.[44]

An Ríoghacht and the contributors to *Outlook* advocated with growing stridency the need for the establishment of 'Agricultural Colonies' in fulfilment of vocationalist ideals. One article in the journal stated: 'The rural surplus population hitherto absorbed by emigration has to be settled on the unoccupied or uncultivated land; and a new social and economic system under which the peasant can find economic independence, security and independence must be gradually built up.'[45] These colonies would be based on a small community principle where each proprietor would have a small farm sufficient to support a family; all other property would be in the control of the local bishop; all members of the colony would be trained in various skills to ensure the successful maintenance of the community; education would be provided by religious orders. The final objective was as follows: 'These co-operative colonies would probably form the nucleus and beginning of a great agricultural co-operative society, which would gradually spread over the country and inaugurate a new social system akin to the mediaeval Christian social organisation.'[46]

As An Ríoghacht worked on the national programme of Agricultural Rural Colonies, its founder and director, Fr. Edward Cahill devoted himself in 1932 to the completion of his major work, *The Framework of a Christian State*. Cahill devoted the first section of the book to an attack on the previous three-hundred years of the Renaissance, the Reformation, and the 'Democratic Revolution' of the Enlightenment. His earlier ideas, which had appeared in pamphlet and article form, resurfaced in this text. Modern society was, in his view, very much a product of the machinations of a

---

[43] Cahill Papers, Jesuit Archives, Dublin.
[44] J. Busteed, 'The World Economic Crisis and "Rerum Novarum" ', *Studies*, 20/7 (July 1931), 23.
[45] *Outlook*, 1/5–8 (30 Jan.–20 Feb. 1932).   [46] Ibid.

Jewish–Freemason–Communist conspiracy bent on the overthrow of the true Christian State found in the Middle Ages. The second section of his book developed the concept of the true Christian State and outlined its essential elements: the family; husband and wife; parents and children; master and servant; the social status of women; the State; justice; charity and patriotism. Cahill held very definite views on the new political order:

That the people may retain the real control of the State, it is essential that the municipal, industrial and professional units be strongly organised, and that the deputies for the governing assembly should at least be the representatives of the organic units, of which the State is made up . . . It is essential, too, that these deputies be well instructed in Christian social principles, and that the people themselves be organised under such systems as now obtain in the countries in which Catholic Action is highly developed.[47]

5. Fianna Fáil and Political Catholicism

Éamon de Valera and his political party Fianna Fáil (founded in 1926) were not slow to harness Catholic social ideas in their political programme. During the 1932 election campaign, Sean T. O'Kelly, the Vice President of the party, stated that 'the Fianna Fáil policy was the policy of Pope Pius XI'.[48] This reflected the strong religious fervour in Ireland during this period. In 1929 the country had celebrated the centenary of Catholic Emancipation and to mark that occasion diplomatic relations were exchanged with the Holy See. The apostolic nuncio, Archbishop Paschal Robinson, arrived in Dublin in January 1930 amid scenes of great fervour. During the run-up to the 1932 election, the governing party Cumann na nGaedheal discovered a plot by a breakaway left-wing section of the Irish Republican Army (IRA) to foment revolution. The President of the Executive Council, William T. Cosgrave, immediately circulated the Irish hierarchy with copies of confidential reports 'proving' the existence of a serious threat to the very survival of the liberal democratic state. The hierarchy responded with alacrity and issued a condemnation of the IRA and other front organizations.[49]

While it is customary for academics to view the division in the 1930s between the Irish Republican Army and the Catholic lobbies as a left–right cleavage, this is to ignore the weight of evidence which ought to place a significant section of the IRA in the camp which supported the reconstruction of Irish society along lines advocated by the papal encyclicals of Pius XI.[50] Sinn Féin leaders, such as Mary MacSwiney, were never converted to Marxism or to the ideas of the Irish left. As late as 1929, the Sinn Féin leadership had petitioned the Pope in loyal terms not to send a papal nuncio to Ireland. They did so as devout Catholics.[51] The shift to the left by certain

[47] E. Cahill, *The Framework of a Christian State* (Dublin, 1932), 626.

[48] *Irish Independent*, 11 Feb. 1932.

[49] D. Keogh, 'De Valera, the Catholic Church and the *Red Scare*, 1931–1932', in J. P. O'Carroll and J. A. Murphy (eds.), *De Valera and his Times* (Cork, 1983).

[50] See id., *Twentieth Century Ireland* (Dublin, 1994), ch. 2.

[51] See id., *Ireland and the Vatican: The Politics and Diplomacy of Church–State Relations 1922–1960* (Cork, 1995), ch. 2.

IRA leaders in the early 1930s, split the 'republican' movement. The brand of republicanism espoused by Mary MacSwiney had little in common with the anticlerical philosophy of leaders of the Second Spanish Republic like Manuel Azaña.

A devout Catholic, de Valera was once held in suspicion by the Holy See who feared a repeat of Spanish anticlericalism in Ireland once de Valera took over. However, in reality, de Valera viewed with great suspicion the extremism of the left-wing faction of the IRA on the one hand and the different extremist Catholic leaders on the other. Éamon de Valera himself was no stranger to Catholic social study, keeping in touch with Cahill. He attended An Ríoghacht meetings on a number of occasions. He had been educated by the Christian Brothers and by the Holy Ghost Fathers. He had a very refined understanding of ecclesiastical politics and he knew how to weigh the importance of the thoughts of individual clerics.

While the Vatican viewed with apprehension the arrival of de Valera in office in 1932, there were many Irish Catholic integralists who hoped for a quick conversion of official policy to one of confessionalism:

The new government which has just come into power should, in the interests of public health and morals, enforce a variety of theatre censorship, and a more rigid film and literature censorship, than the one which exists at present. There can be no proper fostering of Irish culture—not to speak of Catholic culture—until this is done. This is the day of Catholic Action and it is up to the government of a Catholic country to be a Catholic Actionist Government in every sense of the word.[52]

But the enthusiasts were disappointed. Cahill was among their number. Presenting de Valera with a copy of his book in August 1932, the leader of Fianna Fáil replied in Irish: 'I am grateful for the copy of your book, *The Framework of a Christian State*, that you gave to me. It is worth reading and criticizing, and I am sure that often I will return to it for advice and direction in the years that are coming.'[53] That was a reply prompted by the friendship between the two men and by their shared interest in the Irish language rather than by any serious espousal by de Valera of the cocktail of prejudices which passed in Cahill's work for historical analysis. While de Valera was a devout Catholic who remained unattracted by vocationalist radicalism and continental models of Catholic Action, he could not lightly ignore the ideas of Edward Coyne and others who were highly respected members of Irish society. Moreover, vocationalism could not be so lightly dismissed because of its espousal of radical nationalism. Part of the reason for the movement's longevity in Ireland, even after the excesses of fascism, was the manner in which it had identified the alien nature of Irish social structures. Ireland had gained political independence in 1922, but its social structures were rooted in the twin ideologies of liberalism and capitalism. Therefore, in order to bring about a catholic nationalist transformation of Irish society it was necessary to try to eliminate the influences of the Reformation and the Enlightenment so prolifically demonized by Cahill and by his circle.

Éamon de Valera avoided any attempt to reconstruct alternative Irish institutions

<hr>

[52] *Assisi Irish Franciscan Monthly* (May, 1932).
[53] Cahill Papers, Jesuit Archives, Dublin.

in accordance with the philosophy of political Catholicism and Catholic Action. While de Valera had a social philosophy which was heavily influenced by his Catholic upbringing, he was never a convert to the ideas of Cahill. To have sought to implement such a radical restructuring of Irish society would have been opposed root and branch by the civil service. It would also not have pleased Fianna Fáil who had won power in 1932 and had consolidated their hold on government by winning an overall majority in the January 1933 election. In power, de Valera was quickly coverted to the pragmatism of the art of the possible. Moreover, he had inherited a constitutional situation which he regarded as wholly unsatisfactory. It was substantially to that area, and to his portfolio of external affairs, that he turned his attention between 1932 and 1938. But his concern was much more preoccupied with attempting to break the link with Britain than with restructuring Irish society according to the thinking of Fr. Edward Cahill and those who thought like him. As will be seen later, the civil service were the strongest critics of vocationalism. Moreover, the majority of the new cabinet members were not even vaguely interested in the reconstruction of Irish society according to the social teaching of the papal encyclicals. Ultimately Keynes was to prove much more influential than the popes.

The Irish hierarchy felt that they could make their peace with the new government. The bishops, together with Fianna Fáil, continued to oppose any radical manifestations of social Catholicism which would bring Church and State into conflict on economic questions. The social and political profile of the State had been established in 1922 and the bishops had little wish to lend their names to a politically disruptive vocationalist movement. However de Valera, who needed to control the spread of the vocationalist movement, instructed a prominent civil servant, Thomas J. Kiernan, to furnish him with a study of how corporatism could be applied to Ireland. Kiernan worked hard and reported on 29 March 1933 to Sean Moynihan, Secretary to the Department of the President, that 'the scheme could be adopted in Ireland with advantage but the key to its success would be the personnel'. He supposed it was trite to 'say that no scheme can work well unless you have the men to work it but this applies especially to a nationwide organisation such as is involved in the corporative system'.[54] In the accompanying memorandum, Kiernan explained that such organization of the national economy was not fascist. It predated those movements. Kiernan argued that the entire aim of the corporatist system was 'to prevent exploitation, to give an incentive to initiative and to create an organism in which all working citizens find their place in the economic organisation of the nation'. Kiernan idealized the Italian Fascist system and he laid out a blueprint for Ireland. His presentation to de Valera was both radical and rightist. In view of the fact that Fianna Fáil had an absolute majority in the Dáil, even de Valera's intellectual curiosity about corporatism waned. The Kiernan model was never taken up. At no point did either de Valera or his Fianna Fáil government, according to available evidence, ever seriously contemplate changing the Irish political system in favour of either corporatism or Catholic vocationalism. Other domestic and international

[54] Dept. of the Taoiseach, S10183, National Archives, Dublin.

political events intervened to make such a model of society even less attractive to Fianna Fáil.

In 1933 a fascist movement, known popularly as the Blueshirts, appeared in the State. Lasting about two years, it was founded as an association of ex-Free State Army members. Similar in outlook to the Belgian Rexist movement, the Blueshirts perceived themselves as being a nationalist, Catholic, and corporatist organization. Only Christians of Irish parentage were permitted to join. The cross of Saint Patrick was adopted as its insignia. The movement openly espoused a corporatist philosophy, drawing its inspiration from both Mussolini and also from *Quadragesimo Anno*. The first issue of the *Blueshirt*, which appeared on 5 August 1933, carried the following headline in large print: 'THE NATION'S CALL—AN IRISH PRIEST'S VIEWS'. This unidentified Irish priest fully endorsed the objectives of the Blueshirts. He wrote:

I believe, however, that there is at least one group of selfless Irishmen now answering those pertinent questions along the sane, practical and constructive lines. . . . Young men of sterling worth have hearkened to the whispering spirit of a Nation straining to emancipate herself from the incubus of the internecine strife and party bitterness.[55]

The leader of the Blueshirts, General Eoin O'Duffy was an ex-Commissioner of the Garda Síochána (Police Force) who had been sacked by the new De Valera government in late 1932. Under the management of this self-styled Irish *duce*, Cumann na nGaedheal was to merge with the Army Comrades Association (ACA) and the small National Centre Party to form Fine Gael. No stranger to Irish political life, O'Duffy had commanded the Irish Republican Army (IRA) in Monaghan during the War of Independence (1919–21). General Michael Collins, according to Tim Pat Coogan, regarded O'Duffy at one point as his political successor.[56] But O'Duffy had not pursued a political career in the 1920s. He was to serve as Chief of Staff of the army for a brief period. His most enduring contribution to the new state was the role that he played in the establishment of the Garda Síochána. However in August 1933 O'Duffy, who mistakenly felt that he had widespread support inside the Gardai and the army, found himself on the wrong side of the law. His tactic was to engage in an immediate trial of strength with de Valera. O'Duffy decided to hold a mass march of Blueshirts to the cenotaph outside Leinster House to commemorate the deaths of the former Vice President of the Executive Council and Minister for Home Affairs, Kevin O'Higgins (shot by the IRA in 1927) and Collins (killed in a civil war ambush in County Cork in August 1923). The similarity to Mussolini's March on Rome was not lost on the government and rumours circulated of an impending coup attempt. De Valera banned the proposed march and O'Duffy was forced to back down. By 1934 O'Duffy's erratic style of leadership was causing concern among his party colleagues. He had never been elected to the Dáil where a strong supporter of parliamentary democracy, William T. Cosgrave was leader of Fine Gael in Dáil Éireann. Failing to gain a substantial victory for Fine Gael in the local elections of 1934, O'Duffy was pushed to one side by his party on 21 September. The leadership returned to

---

[55] *Blueshirt*, 5 Aug. 1933.
[56] T. P. Coogan, *Michael Collins: A Biography* (London, 1990), 339.

W. T. Cosgrave. Meanwhile, O'Duffy continued in politics. He established the National Corporate Party, but this had almost completely disappeared by 1936.

With the outbreak of the Spanish Civil War, Irish public opinion rallied behind the cause of the Spanish Nationalist forces. This emotional reaction was fuelled by press reports of atrocities perpetrated by the Spanish Republican militias, and descriptions of the civil war as a 'battle between Christianity and communism in which there can be only one victor'.[57] Meanwhile, de Valera and the Fianna Fáil government steered a judicious diplomatic course by signing the Non-Intervention Act and maintaining diplomatic relations with the Madrid government. Resentment against this policy soon manifested itself with the formation of the Irish Christian Front in August 1936. The movement was characterized by its ability to organize mass demonstrations in the main towns and cities around the country. It was led by Patrick Belton, TD (Member of the Irish Dáil), whose political allegiance changed from Fianna Fáil in 1927 to Independent, and to Fine Gael in 1933. He was a fierce critic of de Valera's foreign policy especially in regard to the latter's stance on the Italian invasion of Abyssinia in 1935.[58] Many of the sentiments he raised in parliamentary debates during the Abyssinian crisis were repeated in the summer of 1936.

The primary aim of the Irish Christian Front was to provide medical supplies for the Nationalist forces.[59] The movement was vociferous in its condemnation of the de Valera government for refusing to recognize the Nationalist regime and maintaining diplomatic relations with Madrid. However, the movement's agenda also included the demand for the establishment of a Catholic political order in Ireland. In the beginning this was set out in the vaguest terms. However, Belton subsequently elaborated his policy to cover the areas of political and social organization. In January 1937 Belton announced to the press that:

We believe that the fundamental law or constitution of a Christian society should itself be openly, clearly and unequivocally Christian in letter and in spirit; ... We hold that this Fundamental Law should enshrine the basic Christian principles pertaining to political, social and economic life.[60]

He continued to demand that the rights of the family, the origin and nature and limits of political authority, and the right to private property should all be enshrined in this proposed Fundamental Law.

The Irish Christian Front earned for itself the praise of *Ossevatore Romano* in 1937 and the hierarchy singled out the 'laudable zeal' of the Irish Christian Front for commendation at their annual meeting in Maynooth in October 1936. Cardinal Joseph MacRory admired their efforts and attempted to forge links for them with members of the Spanish hierarchy. However, as the initial reaction to the Spanish Civil War died down after the summer, a more sober tone began to be employed by the newspapers and commentators. With reports of the air raid on Guernica (26 April 1937) and the realization that this civil war was not a clean crusade against communism,

---

[57] *Irish Independent*, 16 Aug. 1936.
[58] See D. Keogh, *Ireland and Europe, 1919–1989* (Cork, 1990), 63–97.
[59] Ibid.   [60] *Irish Independent*, 25 Jan. 1937.

public support for the Irish Christian Front waned. Besides, the public were wary of Belton's stated objectives. The hierarchy's support also began to wane after the summer, with unease being expressed by some members as to the real use of the funds. Furthermore, the hierarchy had never endorsed Belton's demands for a Fundamental Catholic Law. A Special Branch (Irish security police) report on the movement commented that many priests distrusted the main aim of the movement.[61] Meetings were often disrupted by hecklers claiming that the Irish Christian Front was a front organization for O'Duffy and the Blueshirts.[62] By mid-1937 the organization's activities were confined to Belton and his small coterie of followers and its projected aim of establishing a true Christian social order in Ireland had disappeared. It did however have success in sending medical supplies to the Nationalists. O'Duffy also reappeared in the Irish Christian Front. However, he translated his concerns for Spain into an ill-starred attempt to send a brigade to fight for Franco. He stated that this brigade would assist the Nationalists, 'convinced that the cause of Franco is the cause of Christian civilisation'.[63]

Despite O'Duffy's extremism and open association with fascism, a number of prominent clerical and lay academics continued after the departure of the 'green *duce*' to advocate the establishment of a corporate order in Ireland. Fr. Edward Coyne, a confrère of Cahill's in the Jesuits, was among the most influential spokesmen for the ideas of vocationalism. The Professor of History at University College Cork, Dr James Hogan, and the Professor of Classics at University College Dublin also lent respectability to that ideology. Tierney's critique of the democratic system centred on his view of the unworkability of the capitalist system based as it was on the philosophy of liberalism. He saw the 'third way' proposed in Catholic social teaching as the path forward for Irish society.[64]

In an article in *Studies* entitled the 'Reform of Democracy', Tierney argued that the existing democratic system led to over-centralization of power and privilege and the dictatorship of the elected minority. Instead democracy had to return to its origins in the organic state through 'a Corporate Chamber representing not accidental *ad hoc* associations, but organic vocational groups which should have their own functions and duties in society'.[65] But this model of society, as has been seen earlier, had been rejected by de Valera. That did not mean, however, that he was not prepared to pick pieces of that philosophy and graft them on where appropriate to his policy.

Continental-style Catholic Action movements did not meet with much success in Ireland in the mid-1930s. Frank Duff's devotional Legion of Mary grew in strength and influence in the decade. It eschewed politics. But that did not prevent it from continuing to remain under suspicion by the Archbishop of Dublin, Edward Byrne, who continued to withhold recognition of its *Handbook* up to his death in 1940.[66] Even the most diluted form of organized lay Catholic Action was sufficient to put

---

[61] There is a detailed special Branch file on the activities of the Irish Christian Front. See Dept. of Justice, D/34/36, National Archives, Dublin.   [62] Ibid.
[63] E. O'Duffy, *Crusade in Spain* (Dublin, 1938), 11.   [64] *United Irishman*, 6 Jan. 1934.
[65] M. Tierney, 'Ireland and the Reform of Democracy', *Studies*, 23/91 (Sept. 1934), 381.
[66] L. Ó. Broin, *Frank Duff; A Biography* (Dublin, 1982), 43–58.

members of the Irish hierarchy on the defensive. Where, however, there was a mention of communism it was customary for the hierarchy to be less discriminating. The Legion of Mary remained very vigilant on that question. Their branches served as a training ground in Catholic apologetics. The hierarchy were, however, very cautious of the activities of extremist bodies like the anti-communist League of St Patrick in 1934 and a range of other small ginger groups led by militant Catholics.[67]

De Valera, meanwhile, looked with some favour upon other rural-based neo-corporatist developments which in the 1930s did not threaten in any way Fianna Fáil's dominance of the Irish political system. Muintir na Tíre (People of the Land) was founded in 1931 by Fr. John Hayes, a curate at Castleliny in County Tipperary. Influenced by both the work of the Irish Land League in the 1880s and the Belgian *Boerenbond* of the 1890s, Muintir na Tíre focused on the need for self-help schemes in agricultural areas. It also sought to emphasize the need to disseminate Catholic social principles. Stephen Rynne describes how Muintir na Tíre was established in the countryside.[68] Writing in 1938, Fr. Hayes stated that for four years Muintir na Tíre had been:

endeavouring to sow the seeds [of corporate organization] in rural Ireland. It has been endeavouring to prepare minds. Action in the realms of thought precedes action in the realms of fact. It is only by a change of mind we can hope to succeed in changing the realm outside. Rural weeks and Rural week-ends have been the method.[69]

6. Political Catholicism and the 1937 Irish Constitution

The ability of the Catholic social movement to influence the thinking of Éamon de Valera was tested and again found wanting in 1936 and 1937 when the drafting of the new constitution was taking place. The final document was characterized by the strong influence of Catholicism on its contents. This was very much evident in the framing of the preamble articles 40 to 44 on fundamental rights. The preamble read as follows:

In the Name of the Most Holy Trinity, from Whom is all authority and to Whom, as our final end, all actions both of men and states must be referred,

We, the people of Éire,

Humbly acknowledging all our obligations to our Divine Lord, Jesus Christ, who sustained our fathers through centuries of trial,

Gratefully remembering their heroic and unremitting struggle to regain the rightful independence of our Nation,

And seeking to promote the common good, with due observance of Prudence, Justice and Charity, so that the dignity and freedom of the individual may be assured, true social order attained, the unity of our country restored, and concord established with other nations, Do hereby adopt, enact, and give to ourselves this Constitution.

---

[67] In 1934 a group of prominent lay and clerical figures formed the League for Social Justice and Charity. This was a discussion group whose aim was influence Irish governments to adopt papal principles of social reconstruction. There were a number of such groups spread throughout the country.

[68] S. Rynne, *Father John Hayes* (Dublin, 1960), 157.

[69] J. Hayes, 'Vocational Organisation for Farmers and Farm Labourers', *Irish Monthly* (Sept. 1938), 596–611.

Article 41 drew heavily on Catholic social teaching for its concept of the family and the rights of women. Section 2, subsection 1 and 2 reads:

In particular, the State recognises that by her life within the home, woman gives to the State a support without which the common good cannot be achieved. The State shall, therefore, endeavour to ensure that mothers shall not be obliged by economic necessity to engage in labour to the neglect of their duties in the home.

Section 3 of article 41 contained the provision that:

The State pledges itself to guard with special care the institution of Marriage, on which the Family is founded, and to protect it against attack.

No law shall be enacted providing for the grant of a dissolution of marriage.

Article 43 enshrined a contemporary Catholic social teaching view of the rights of private property. Article 44, while guaranteeing freedom of conscience and the free profession and practice of religion, acknowledged 'the special position of the Holy Catholic Apostolic and Roman Church as the guardian of the Faith professed by the great majority of its citizens'. The article on religion went on 'to recognise' the other Churches in Ireland at the date of the coming-into-operation of the constitution. Article 45, concerning the directive principles of social policy, conveyed some of the radicalism of Catholic social thinking. There was very little in the articles cited which might be described as vocationalism or political Catholicism. However, the constitution did incorporate vocationalism in relation to the corporatist composition of the upper House of the Oireachtas (parliament), the Seanad (Senate). But that had much more to do with the consolidation of Fianna Fáil clientelism and the securing of a majority for the governing party in the upper House of the Oireachtas than it had to do with loyalty to the implementation of Catholic corporatist principles.[70]

Despite the international climate of the 1930s and the persistence of the vocationalist lobbies at home, the new Irish constitution remained quite selective in the manner in which it relied upon Catholic social teaching. Catholic rightist groups, in particular, were very disappointed with the final document. Activists like Alfred O'Rahilly, Edward Cahill, and Denis Fahey were radically opposed to the final wording of article 44 which failed—in their view—to establish the Catholic Church as the one, true church. The future archbishop of Dublin, John Charles McQuaid, who had done so much to help de Valera draft the constitution, remained decidedly uneasy about article 44.[71] But he felt that he had to compromise and live with that compromise. However, his confrère in the Holy Ghost Order, Denis Fahey, was not quite so reconciled to that situation. He was to campaign until his death in 1954 for a constitutional amendment to remove the existing article 44 and to have it replaced with a more confessional formula. The section of the article, quoted above, was removed in a referendum in 1972. However, de Valera's constitution of 1937 was perceived to be a very Catholic document by Pius XII.[72]

[70] Keogh, *Twentieth Century Ireland*, ch. 2.
[71] Id., 'The Constitutional Revolution: An Analysis of the Making of the Constitution', *Administration* [Dublin], 35/4 (1988), 4–85.
[72] Id., *The Vatican, the Bishops and Irish Politics 1919–1939* (Cambridge, 1986).

The constitution was passed by referendum on 1 July 1937. Fianna Fáil was returned to power by a very slender majority in a general election held on the same day. On 27 April 1938 the new Seanad met and on 4 May Douglas Hyde was elected, unopposed, first president of Ireland. He entered office on 25 June. That same year, de Valera signed an all-important Anglo-Irish agreement which brought the 'economic war' to an end and returned the ports which the Treaty of 1921 had left in British hands. In a snap election in June 1938 de Valera secured a greater majority on the strength of his having signed that agreement and upon procuring the return of the treaty ports. As world war approached, Fianna Fáil was safely and firmly in power. De Valera was to remain in office until 1948.

Political Catholicism in Ireland in the 1930s had not been very successful. In contrast, Frank Duff's Legion of Mary and Fr. Hayses's Muintir na Tíre exhibited healthy signs of attracting a greater following. As all the political parties in the Oireachtas were at least nominally Catholic, the challenge which faced social Christians in other European countries was not in evidence.

7. Vocationalism's Last Stand

It was precisely because de Valera was in such an unassailable political position in 1938 that he proved to be indulgent on the question of political Catholicism. The Irish vocationalist movement had refused to die. It had made something of a revival in the unpromising international climate of 1938–9. This was partially helped by the urgings of the hierarchy to introduce Catholic broadcasts from Radio Éireann. Originally, such a scheme had been proposed by Dr Frank O'Reilly of the Catholic Truth Society. Members of the hierarchy, accompanied by O'Reilly, had an informal meeting with the Taoiseach (Prime Minister) in 1937 following which an informal committee was set up. It consisted of Sean Moynihan, Thomas J. Kiernan, then Director of Broadcasting, and O'Reilly. A number of schemes were put forward but in October 1939 a meeting of the hierarchy decided to drop the proposal for Catholic broadcasts.[73]

In the mean time, de Valera had agreed on 10 January 1939 to the setting up of a Commission on Vocational Organisation. There had been a series of radio lectures in early 1938 on *Quadragesimo Anno*. This had revived interest in vocationalism. The broadcasts were also a response to the hierarchy's concern about the need for Catholic programmes on the national radio station. It would be a mistake to view this development as indicating a new-found interest by de Valera in the workings of vocationalism. The Taoiseach had a very precise understanding of what he understood vocationalism to mean. It did not reflect the integralist strategies of Cahill or Fahey. Writing to T. J. Kiernan in 1938 when the lecture series was being planned, the secretary of the Department of the Taoiseach, Maurice Moynihan, wrote:

[73] Sean Lemass, Memorandum to Cardinal William Conway, 19 May 1965, Dept. of Foreign Affairs, Irish Embassy to the Holy See, 14/121, National Archives, Dublin.

From what I know generally, however, of the Taoiseach's mind in the matter, I think that he would like to have lectures of a rather practical nature included in the proposed series. He is particularly interested in the actual workings of Vocational Organisation where it has been tried. He has expressed interest from time to time in the Whitley system of Industrial Councils in Great Britain, feeling as he does, that in some respects conditions in that country are more nearly akin to our own than conditions in Continental countries.[74]

It is telling that de Valera felt that Irish social conditions had more in common with Britain than with the Catholic states of the continent.

Soon after the completion of this series of broadcasts a motion—sponsored by Michael Tierney and Frank MacDermot (an Independent)—was passed in the Seanad on 21 July 1938 favouring the setting-up of a Commission on Vocational Organisation. It was decided that the commission should be about twenty-five strong and de Valera sought suggestions for nominations from various sources. The newly appointed Bishop of Galway, Michael Browne, was encouraged to take the chair when both men met in August 1938. The government approved the terms of reference and appointed the members of the Commission at their meeting on 10 January 1939. Browne was in the chair. There were representatives from Labour, Employers, Agriculture, and Church and University groups. Browne proved to be an unfortunate choice as chairman. Highly intelligent and very hard-working, he had a very strong temper and was inclined to show his irritation on occasions.[75] The Commission held its first meeting on 2 March 1939. It worked swiftly and did not allow the outbreak of war in September to interfere in its schedule. Browne had overseen the study of a number of European countries where corporatism had been adopted.

The Commission laboured on through the war years. But as the war progressed, vocationalism diminished in importance and relevance. The horrors of Nazism and Fascism became more apparent. Even neutral Portugal, led by the Catholic dictator Salazar, lost its lustre as did the regime of General Franco. Ireland remained neutral during the war. Éamon de Valera's government found it very difficult to maintain that status and to provide for an island country on the periphery of a convulsed European continent.[76] Fianna Fáil fought a general election in 1943 which did not leave the party with a commanding majority in the Dáil. Risking the strategy of 1933 and 1938 when Éamon de Valera had secured majorities in two snap elections, he went to the country in 1944 and repeated his earlier successes.

The Commission on Vocational Organisation's report was published in August 1944. Lemass, anticipating its publication, laid out his philosophy of economic development to an audience at the Trinity (College) Philosophical Society on 28 October 1943. It was completely at variance with the findings of the commission. Lemass was not alone in his feelings of antipathy towards the report. Senior civil servants were furious about the manner in which the bureaucracy had been treated in

---

[74] See S10812, Dept. of the Taoiseach, National Archives, Dublin.
[75] There is ample evidence of this in the personal papers of Bishop Michael Browne, Galway diocesan archives.   [76] See Keogh, *Ireland and Europe 1919–1989*, ch. 3.

the document. The comments of individual departments were very critical. On 21 February 1945, Lemass told the Seanad:

I have read the report of that commission on more than one occasion and I have been unable to come to any conclusion as to whether the querulous, nagging, propagandist tone of its observations is to be attributed to unfortunate drafting or to a desire to distort the picture. The commission spent a great deal of energy upon its researches, and a very long time in preparing its report, and I think it is unfortunate that the report, when published, should be such a slovenly document.[77]

Bishop Browne was incandescent with anger and he engaged in a testy debate with Lemass which did his cause no good even if he ultimately won the argument. The Jesuit Edward Coyne had been the bishop's main adviser throughout the controversy. He wrote on 11 April 1945 that there was a possibility that the government might be persuaded by Lemass to issue a white paper in an effort systematically to discredit the report.[78] But that did not happen. Some months later, the Minister for Agriculture, Dr Jim Ryan, was chosen to put an end to all controversy on the matter. A little less confrontational and less controversial in style than Lemass, he spoke on 20 November 1945 in the Mansion House, Dublin. In diplomatic language, he let it be known that vocationalism was no longer particularly relevant. There the matter rested. The Commission on Vocational Organisation was buried without trace. That particular manifestation of political Catholicism had run its course. In autumn 1945 there were few illusions left about the virtues of vocationalism, corporatism, or fascism. Italy and Germany were in ruins and Spain and Portugal were no longer role models for any significant Irish social movement.

8. Political Catholicism in Post-War Ireland

The perfunctory dismissal of vocationalism by Éamon de Valera and his cabinet left many of the committed members resentful towards the Fianna Fáil government. The movement which had shown so much promise in the 1930s drew in 1945 upon an ever-diminishing pool of interested followers. Bloodied but unbowed, a loyal group of Fr. Denis Fahey followers established Maria Duce (Under Mary's Leadership) in summer 1945. While this group caused some disruption, it never had more than about forty active members. It was, however, to attract a far larger group to its various study evenings. The inspiration for the establishment of that organization came also, according to its members, from the dissatisfaction of a group of laymen who had corresponded with the press on matters of Catholic interest. But 'repeated rebuffs' made them aware of the need to unite: 'Truth, it seems, is poor propaganda, and the vested interests who direct the policies of these papers are careful that its startling and naked reality should not obtrude itself on the public attention.'[79] There

---

[77] *Seanad Debates*, 29. 1323–4, 21 Feb. 1945.

[78] Edward Coyne to Browne, 11 Apr. 1945, B/8–44, Browne papers, Galway Diocesan Archives, Galway.

[79] Leaflet 'Fiat: Its History and Aims', in Maria Duce (1), Edward Fahey papers, Archives of the Holy Ghost Fathers, Dublin.

was little need for Maria Duce activists to identify those hidden forces; they were the Freemasons, the Jews, and the Communists. The war against the manifold enemies of Catholicism was declared yet again.

In the words of its founders this organization pledged 'to vindicate the Social Rights of Christ the King'. Its purpose was to foster among its members 'a knowledge of and a zeal for Christ's Kingly Rights in every sphere of human activity'. Membership was open to all Catholics of 17 years of age or over. After a three months' probation if judged worthy they would be 'enrolled at one of the ceremonies of consecration that take place at regular intervals'. Maria Duce had an integralist programme for the establishment of social order which, in essence, favoured the establishment of a confessional state:

The Catholic Church is the One True Church and ought to be acknowledged as such by States and nations. The non-Catholics ought always to be treated in accordance with the teaching of the Church and the principles of Christian Charity, so that the rights of all human persons be respected.

The state must recognise the Catholic Church as Divinely appointed to teach man what favours or hinders his supernatural destiny.

The Social Doctrine contained in the Papal Encyclicals ought to be reduced to practice in such wise as to promote the virtuous life of individual members of the mystical Body of Christ organised in families, Vocational Associations and States.

Maria Duce's charter went on to outline the need to organize society along vocational lines in order to 'avoid the pitfalls inherent both in the unbridled individualism favoured by Capitalism and in the excessive State-control sponsored by Communism'.[80]

Maria Duce, dissatisfied with the press, established its own newspaper *Fiat*. It was first produced on a hand duplicating machine and appeared to enjoy some success. Published every six weeks, the paper pursued many of the old themes familiar to readers of Fahey's work. There was an article in issue 10 entitled ' "Anti-Semitism" at Oberammergau'. It reproduced many of the arguments earlier advanced by Fahey:

We may be able to do little to foil the Jewish attempt to use Russia as a means for Bolshevizing Europe, but we must resist all attempts to impose Jewish Naturalism here. We must particularly oppose the Jewish control of money and credit and the powerful Jewish campaign for Naturalism in the Press and the Cinema, all of which are weapons in the 'softening up' process for Bolshevism. . . . If we wish to survive as a Nation and preserve our Catholic civilization, we must, however, combat the undeniable Judeo-Masonic attempt to promote Naturalism in this country, whatever form it may assume.

Fiat also reproduced an article on the alleged Judeo–Masonic control of the United States, of the United Nations, and of other international organizations. An article in *Fiat* (no. 27) listed the 'Jewish Rulers of UNO', the 'Jews on the Atomic Energy Commission', and the 'big three' who comprised the 'secret government of the

---

[80] Maria Duce leaflet, Maria Duce (2), Edward Fahey papers, Archives of the Holy Ghost Fathers, Dublin.

U.S.A.'. *Fiat* also wrote in defence of Senator Joseph McCarthy; 'no political figure in the United States to-day, or possibly even in the whole history of the great Republic, has become the target of so much organized slander and vilification as Senator McCarthy. No bounds are known to the venomous attacks made daily on his person by apologists of subversive and anti-Christian elements.' That 'campaign of hate' had even been in evidence in the editorial (31 March 1953) of Fianna Fáil's *Irish Press*. Closer to home, *Fiat* attacked the Irish Association for Civil Liberties (IACL). In issue 29, it sought to make a Masonic connection between the local association and sister organizations in Paris and in New York. Seán O'Faoláin, the Irish novelist, was the president of the IACL. Other members included Senator Owen Sheehy Skeffington, the painter Louis Le Brocquy, and other prominent Irish academics and public figures. A rival organization, the Irish Theatre and Cinema Patrons' Associ-ation, was supported by Maria Duce which expressed considerable concern over the negative impact on local society of such alien forms of mass culture.

Who joined Maria Duce and what was its relationship to Church authorities? The second question is easier to answer than the first. It proved to be little more than a study group which met on a Sunday to listen to a lecture by Fr. Fahey. Its president was Tom Agar and vice president Thomas Roseingrave. The latter was a major intellectual force inside the organization. Although he believed in the basic philo-sophical tenets of Maria Duce, he tended to exercise a moderating influence over the type of tactics which the movement sought to employ. Roseingrave, who was also involved in Muintir na Tíre, was very close to Fahey, who saw him as one of his brightest lay disciples. But if the contents of *Fiat* are used as an indication of the intellectual calibre and vision of the membership of Maria Duce then it was a move-ment sadly lacking in talent or charisma. It had a core membership in Dublin but did not, however, spread to the countryside in any numbers.

But Maria Duce did enjoy the recognition of John Charles McQuaid. A member of the Holy Ghost order before becoming archbishop in 1940, McQuaid had been a highly intelligent member of a much younger generation of seminarians. There was a mutual respect between Fahey and McQuaid. Moreover, McQuaid was not un-appreciative of the lifelong efforts and dedication of Fahey. Neither was he un-sympathetic to Fahey's Mariology and theology of Christ the King. But he was cautious and the relationship in the post-war period was never particularly close. Nevertheless, McQuaid was prepared initially to give a qualified sanction to the work of Maria Duce. His initial response may have been partly conditioned by his deep concern about the onset of cold war, the growing power of communism, and the dangers of the outbreak of a third world war.

The Archbishop hardly regarded the replacement of Éamon de Valera's Fianna Fáil government in early 1948 with a five-party coalition led by John A. Costello as a disaster. Quite the reverse. He was a close friend of the new Taoiseach who would prove to be much more compliant in his handling of Church–State issues than his predecessor had been. The Inter-Party government of 1948–51 was quite integralist in its thinking. By March 1949 membership forms for Maria Duce also contained the line '*permissu Ordinarii Diocesis Dublinensis*'. But Maria Duce remained a movement obsessed with the ghosts of the inter-war years. It was involved in a number of very embarrassing episodes, such as the picketing of the Theatre Royal during a visit of Danny Kaye whom they alleged had communist connections. Earlier, Maria Duce had attacked Gregory Peck and Orson Wells. Maria Duce also directed much of its activities in 1950 towards the radical reform of the religious article in the constitution, article 44. This involved an organized letter-writing campaign to the Department of the Taoiseach. McQuaid acted on 14 February 1951 against Maria Duce. His secretary, Christopher Mangan, wrote to Tom Agar on 14 February 1951:

I am asked by His Grace the Archbishop to inform you that he has decided to withdraw the *Permissu Ordinarii Diocesis Dublinensis*—from your six-point programme. The Archbishop bids me therefore to request you to refrain from printing this permission on any further literature, which you may have printed.

His Grace would also appreciate it if you will kindly refrain from styling, in your literature, your organisation as a Catholic Action body, since an essential requirement of a body being Catholic Action is that it be approved by the Bishop of the Diocese; this approval has not been given by the Archbishop to your organisation.[81]

In the course of the next few months a clash between Church and State over the Mother and Child Bill (the provision of free post-natal care to mother and child up to the age of 16) brought the government crashing down. Éamon de Valera and Fianna Fáil returned to power with the help of a number of independents. Between 1951 and 1954 when de Valera again lost power to an Inter-Party government, Church and State were at loggerheads over changes in secondary education (1954) and the redrafting of the Mother and Child provisions. On both issues, de Valera and Fianna Fáil proved tough and ultimately defeated episcopal intransigence.

Meanwhile, the fortunes of Maria Duce continued to wane. Its cause temporarily received what they thought was a major advance when Cardinal Alfredo Ottaviani delivered a speech at the Lateran university in Rome on 2 March 1953. This was to mark the occasion of the 14th anniversary of Pius XII's election as pope. Its comments on the relationship between Church and State greatly pleased the leading members of Maria Duce. Fahey sought and obtained permission to translate it into English and publish it as a pamphlet. In a letter to Ottaviani on 6 September 1953, Fahey congratulated him on his 'luminous, timely and courageous lecture on the duties of a Catholic State in regard to religion', and asked for his approval for the translation. Fahey went on to explain that he had been lecturing about the Kingship of Christ for more than twenty years 'so your Eminence's splendid pamphlet is a source of precious encouragement for me and I thank our Blessed Mother for it'. Fahey was convinced that the lecture would 'certainly do an enormous amount of good in Ireland'. The real purpose of Fahey's enthusiasm for Ottavani's speech was that he saw it as a means of reopening the debate regarding the Constitution. The

---

[81] Fr Christopher Mangan to Tom Agar, President of Maria Duce, 14 Feb. 1951, Denis Fahey papers, Archives of the Holy Ghost Fathers, Dublin.

hierarchy, and the Archbishop of Dublin in particular, must have been concerned about the divisiveness of having the article 44 debate raised again. It had been resolved in 1937 not entirely to the satisfaction of McQuaid. But he was prepared to live with the compromise. Moreover, there was neither political support nor widespread enthusiasm among Irish Catholic intellectuals for any reversal to a confessional state model. This was quite evident in the contribution by prominent Irish laymen in the Catholic journals.

For example, a future president of Ireland, Cearbhall Ó Dálaigh (1974–77), lectured in the West of Ireland in March 1953. The content of his speech did not please Roseingrave who wrote to Fahey on 25 April:

I was strongly tempted to tell him what I thought of his Galway speech. Even if we overlooked the defective Art 44, the government are proceeding just now (as they have already done) to introduce legislation in conflict with Catholic Social teaching and against the directive principles so excellently expressed in the constitution. . . . So we must hit back hard. The march of events have each day convinced me more and more that unless the air is cleared, principles clearly defined, without ambiguity which is often today passed off for fact or diplomacy, and a firm stand made, it will be very difficult for us to avoid the experience of the Spain of 1936.[82]

So, if Fahey and his colleagues had hoped to use Ottaviani's speech as the basis for a new campaign, they were again disappointed by the Archbishop. The archdiocesan censor refused permission for the publication of the pamphlet.

There was, therefore, to be no integralist revival in Ireland in the 1950s. Fahey died the following year and Maria Duce quickly diminished in membership. In 1972, following the retirement of John Charles McQuaid, a group of Maria Duce Catholics met at Leopardstown to mourn the departure of the Archbishop. A cadre of the old guard had continued to meet through the 1960s.[83] The works of Fr. Fahey were kept in print by the devout. But Maria Duce remained very much a fringe group. The Legion of Mary and Muintir na Tíre, unlike Maria Duce, continued to play an important part in the Catholic life of the country. But neither could be categorized as fitting into the concept of political Catholicism. Irish Catholics continued—as they had done in previous decades—to find political expression through the major political parties—Fianna Fáil, Fine Gael, and Labour—all of which belonged ideologically to the Christian Democratic bloc in Europe in the 1950s.

9. Conclusion

Éamon de Valera retired as Taoiseach in 1959. In becoming president later that year, he formally retired from political life. Although he was to serve as president for two terms, de Valera did not actively continue to influence the direction of Irish society. But the 1960s, for all the apparent radical change, remained very much part of the era of Éamon de Valera. His successor, Sean Lemass, had always displayed a much keener economic mind than that of his predecessor. Despite being hampered by the

[82] See correspondence files, Denis Fahey Papers, Holy Ghost Archives, Dublin.
[83] S. O'Keefe, 'Maria Duce is Alive and Well and Living in Dublin', *Hibernia*, 9 Aug. 1974.

poor electoral performance of Fianna Fáil in the general election of 1961, his government proved to be the most innovative government since de Valera had taken office in 1932. Lemass quickly put an end to the quest for autarchy. He positioned Ireland in the early 1960s to become a member of the European Economic Community—but failed due to the veto of General Charles de Gaulle against the British in 1963. Nevertheless, Lemass sought to modernize Irish society. A national television service was established and that helped reinforce the impact of the Second Vatican Council which brought new ideas into the Irish Church. In this respect the 1960s certainly marked an important era of change for the Catholic Church. Integralism was not entirely dead. Small fringe parties continued to fulminate against the pluralist philosophy of figures such as the former Fine Gael Taoiseach Garret Fitzgerald (1983–87) which was perceived to pose a challenge to traditional Catholic values. Such parties, however, could not hope to win mass support and most Irish Catholics continued to identify with the major political parties. Catholicism thus remained a central element in Irish politics; but movements of political Catholicism remained on the margins.

Index